VOLUME TWO

STORMY EVOLUTION TO MODERN TIMES

A HISTORY OF YOUNG PEOPLE IN THE WEST

VOLUME TWO
STORMY EVOLUTION
TO MODERN TIMES

A HISTORY OF
YOUNG PEOPLE
IN THE WEST

EDITED BY

Giovanni Levi and
Jean-Claude Schmitt

TRANSLATED BY

Carol Volk

The Belknap Press of
Harvard University Press
Cambridge, Massachusetts
London, England   1997

Originally published as *Storia dei giovani, 2: L'età contemporanea*, © Guis.
Laterza & Figli Spa, Roma-Bari, 1994; and *Histoire des jeunes en occident,
2: L'époque contemporaine*, © Éditions du Seuil, Paris, 1996.

Published with the assistance of the French Ministry of Culture.

Library of Congress Cataloging-in-Publication Data
Storia dei giovani. English
    A history of young people in the West / edited by Giovanni Levi and
Jean-Claude Schmitt ; translated by Camille Naish.
        p.   cm.
    Includes bibliographical references and index.
    Contents: v. 1. Ancient and medieval rites of passage—
v. 2. Stormy evolution to modern times.
    ISBN 0-674-40405-X (v. 1 : cloth : alk. paper).—
    ISBN 0-674-40406-8 (v. 2 : cloth : alk. paper)
    1. Youth—Europe—History. 2. Youth—Italy—History. I. Levi,
Giovanni, 1939–   . II. Schmitt, Jean Claude. III. Title.
HA799.E9S7613   1997
305.23'5'094—dc20   96-34751

CONTENTS

Illustrations follow pages 26 and 250.

CHAPTER 1

IMAGES OF YOUTH
IN THE MODERN PERIOD

Giovanni Romano

For those who expect art historical images to provide unequivocal documentary truth about young people as a segment of society,
paintings and their commentaries offer few reasonable paths for research.
We should neither harbor illusions as to the functional nature of pictorial
representation nor underestimate the risks resulting from unconscious or
involuntary elements in the information provided by individuals (the artists) with whom we have no possibility of communicating. What documents of the plastic arts mainly illustrate is a segment of our intellectual
creativity, from conception to criticism. Secondarily, and without this having been the artist's intention, artworks can also inform us about other
aspects of life in society, but to venture into this territory it is necessary
to verify the mediating influences surrounding the painting, and to resitu-
ate them in ancient régime societies. It happens too often that full documentary value is attributed to a work of art; this practice—which art
historians have warded off with great difficulty—finds fertile ground
among certain historians of other aspects of cultural life. For every discipline addressed, documentary value must be assessed by specialists
equipped with the right instruments; for those who attempt to travel
beyond their discipline, it is valid to ask, as a preventive measure, whether
they have a permit to drive outside their region.

"*Ars utinam mores / animumque effingere / posses, pulchrior in ter-
/ ris nulla tabella foret /* MCCCCLXXXVIII" (Art, if only you could

express the soul and mores, there would be no more beautiful painting on earth): this inscription on the portrait of Giovanna Tornabuoni (fig. 1) by Domenico Ghirlandaio highlights the fifteenth-century painter's frustration, faced with the impossibility of rendering feelings and moral attitudes convincingly. This failure was all the more bitter for Ghirlandaio and the other painters of his generation because, beginning in the 1480s, a general demand for sentiment (especially amorous sentiment) seemed to take hold of Italy's literary public and princely courts, resulting in the rebirth of Petrarchan lyric poetry and in the production of such an exemplary novel as Sannazzaro's *Arcadia*. Young people were the natural victims of this "epidemic," and it was no doubt they who seized upon this easy, sentimental literature. Painting and sculpture, however, were hard pressed to follow in the steps of the written word and hobbled along for some time, resisting the plastic documentation of youth as such (except in a few old-style and rare portraits).

The credit goes to Leonardo da Vinci for having crossed outside the confines of the presumed limitations of the art. In the 1480s he endeavored to represent every mental state—in particular, "amorous" ones. The texts of the period all acknowledge his merit in doing this, and he himself was quite aware of it when he wrote this legend to accompany a portrait, in a definite response to Ghirlandaio's lament: *"Non iscoprire, se libertà tà'è cara, / che'l volto mio è carcere d'amore"* (Do not reveal, if freedom is dear to you / that my face is a prison of love; Forster, III, fol. 10v). The legend serves not only to reinforce the psychological and sentimental intensity of the portrait but also to infuse the image with such seductive power that it becomes something of a magic charm. Hence the popularity of the love portrait during the last decade of the fifteenth and the first years of the sixteenth centuries, sometimes accompanied by allusive symbolism: a chaste ermine in Leonardo da Vinci's portrait of Cecilia Gallerani (fig. 2); a burning candle in the portrait by Lotto in Vienna; a bitter orange in the so-called Ludovisi portrait by Giorgione, in the Palazzo Venezia in Rome (fig. 3).

After a long domination of male portraits, this is one of the rare periods in Italian culture when the two sexes were equally represented in the pictorial limelight, as equal protagonists in the dialogue of love. Portraits of lovers were destined for personal and private enjoyment and were sometimes hung facing one another—when the love stories culminated in marriage, that is; in other cases, the portraits brought out the strain of feelings that were difficult to express, as in the rare drawing by Michelangelo (fig. 7) representing Andrea Quarantesi. Many portraits of women were linked not to a particular love story, but rather to their courtesan status (fig. 6), their expertise in "mental states" being due to their personal, amorous, and literary knowledge.

This impressive surge in the appearance of young victims of love, a nearly unique instance in the history of European art, was clearly not due to the artists alone. It was the discovery and promotion of an undeniable human faculty that paved the way for a social group heretofore relegated to the shadows—and soon to retreat into them, once traditional society realized the destructive power inherent in the domination of sentiment over the rules of propriety in communal life. As the century progressed, portraits of youth gradually melded into a category no longer determined by age but by caste (fig. 9 and 10). Even family portraits passed from images of free and sentimental intermingling (fig. 8) to an irreproachable cataloging of heirs and nubile maidens, either to matrimonial ends (fig. 11) or as an external measure of the prestige of the family; in the portrait by Lavinia Fontana now at the National Gallery of Bologna (fig. 12), Senator Ulisse Gozzadini exhibited not only his daughters but also the two sons-in-law he had acquired.

Caravaggio was thirty years old when he painted three canvases that were to illustrate the life of Saint Matthew on the walls and altar of the Contarelli Chapel in San Luigi dei Francesi (1600–1602). Though he was no longer a newcomer having to prove himself, the works nonetheless inspired considerable hostility. Texts of the period tell us that the elderly Federico Zuccari decided to verify the cause of all the commotion in person. His pontificating and somewhat perfidious verdict was that there was no reason for scandal, since the presumptuous Lombard had merely copied a painting by Giorgione on view in Venice (which was probably an invention on his part, intended to defend his reputation as a painter and professor who had seen it all in the course of extensive travel).

For Caravaggio, the large canvases in San Luigi dei Francesi were a way to be definitively recognized as a "mature" painter, a recognition that was delayed longer that it should have been due to the fact that his style (of life and of painting) could not be reduced to the customary rules. Old Zuccari's verdict, in the face of these masterpieces, was a final attempt to prevent this radical alternative to traditional painting and the traditional conception of the painter's profession from taking hold in Rome, but his testimony got away from him, and Caravaggio could thereafter consider that he, and painters younger than himself, had won the match. Things would take an unexpected turn, however, and two suits brought by Caravaggio's competitor Giovanni Baglione, as early as 1603 and 1606, show us that the Caravaggian front was undermined from within by destructive rivalries, and that someone like Baglione (who was the same age as Caravaggio, but with a less controversial résumé) could concentrate the adversaries' attacks.

I believe it would be useful to systematically study this dramatic shift from one generation of painters to another, according particular attention to the behavior of the younger one, to see whether the witnesses of the period were indeed telling the truth about the lives of those painters whom we consider to be "followers" of Caravaggio (at least beginning in 1606). From what we already know, it seems that we can loosely distinguish a social group defined by common origins, lives, and professions (it was with a professional goal in mind that all these artists converged on Rome, which was still a cultural capital and a major art market). Rarely of Roman origin, and thus unable to count on family connections, these artists grouped together by geographic origin and according to the necessities of their mutual poverty. The luckiest succeeded in becoming integrated into the "family" of a cardinal, but even they were in fairly unstable situations, which naturally affected their moral and sentimental life, as well as their religious practice. It seems they married late and preferred to live in small groups, camping out together in furnished rooms until some professional upset brought about a recomposition of the cluster that had formed to face

common difficulties. A separate group was forged by the Protestant painters from the northern countries, who created a gay, youthful society among
themselves (the Bentveughels).

The course of Caravaggio's life was representative in this respect, with
its episodes of poverty, exploitation, suffering, despair, and provocation;
dozens of similar life patterns could be cited, each favored by chance to a
varying degree. On this group of artists, the legal, judicial, and ecclesiastical sources (in particular, the parish registers) are as rich in information
as artistic witnesses are poor: for many of these artists it is impossible to
find a single identifiable work in the art historical archives. This shows us
how unreliable figurative proofs are concerning facts that are not the
primary subjects of the works. Caravaggio's paintings (fig. 13, for example) are invaluable testimonies to the art market and the tastes of Roman
collectors during the first decades of the seventeenth century, and to the
manner in which a new type of altar painting was being defined. Most
often, paintings of the period were executed according to a certain type
of commercial, stylistic, or prestige-related strategy, but they tell us nothing about the daily lives of their creators, unless we wish to hazard the
slippery slope of projection, compensation, and sublimation.

It is no doubt too easy, in the case of Artemisia Gentileschi, to draw
a connection between a certain thematic consistency (Judith slitting Holo-
pherne's throat) and the trauma revealed by her famous suit against
Agostino Tassi, who had raped her, but we cannot, ipso facto, transfer this
type of reading to the paintings of male heroes. Young triumphant Davids
(fig. 14) abound in the paintings of the Caravaggians, but so do sacrifices
of Isaac, in which two generations enter into dangerous conflict: how
should this statistical observation be interpreted? Caravaggio's personal
case could perhaps be resolved by a heavy-handed manipulation of the few
available indications of his homosexual experiences, but before entering
into gossip, it would be better to have clear ideas about how these practices
were viewed at the time in artistic circles, and about their presumed
frequency in the type of life common to all the young Caravaggian painters. Whatever the case, the question seems to end with Caravaggio himself:
after him, the determinant reasons for iconographic choices were, on the

one hand, a desire to compete with the master and thus to fight the same battles, and, on the other hand, the collectors' preference for certain themes that had become canonic in portraiture. Paintings were purchased for the quality of their technique, the difficulty or currentness of the subject, or even for their *succès de scandale*. Some years later (but still not long after Caravaggio), Aurelio Zaneletti, a collector and friend of Guerchin, could commission two paintings to hang side by side, one representing Joseph rejecting the wife of Putiphar, the other, Amnon chasing Tamar (fig. 20) after having seduced her (the two canvasses are now in Washington). The virtue of man versus the readiness of woman? I personally would not be so sure about the virtue of Joseph and the guilt of Tamar. But the two paintings did offer excellent occasions to represent nudes in attractive poses; they are pieces of pictorial bravura more than reflections of the artist's emotions. Concerns inherent to painting thus win out over personal concerns, and the latter emerge, if they emerge at all, so mediated as to be unidentifiable in any serious way. Historical criticism should not be a kind of divination; the critic should not bring to the work the kind of attention the analyst brings to his patient's dream. For one thing the analyst works with a mass of information that is theoretically infinite (as are the number of sessions), and, if all goes well, with the active collaboration of the patient; we, on the other hand, are working with a corpus of painted "signs" limited by the destruction of time and the whims of collectors, and we cannot, furthermore, have any direct relationship with the "dreamer."

It is conceivable to take as one's subject of research the great popularity in the seventeenth century of biblical and evangelical themes depicting youth (in particular those paintings inspired by Caravaggio or, more generally, those that are "modern"), but I fail to see what the youth of the time would have had to do with the endless series of Tobiases with Angels (fig. 21), Intoxications of Noahs, Cains and Abels, Lots and His Daughters, Rebeccas at the Well, Jacobs and Esaus, Josephs and His Brothers, Davids and Sauls, Repudiations of Agars, Tamars Recognized (and later chased), Samsons and the Ray of Honeys, Returns of the Prodigal Sons, Jesuses and the Temple Doctors, and so on. If there is still a small area to which research can be applied, I would tend to think that it should be in other types of paintings, of which the initial if not the primary intention was to illustrate certain stages of youth. Thus we could compare different treatments of the Education of the Virgin, seeking indications of the seventeenth-century feminine ideal; or consider the many paintings in which con artists and fortune-tellers (fig. 15 and 17) are on the lookout for naive young men on street corners (familiar scenes in the daily lives of our painters); or identify a kind of early elegy to bohemian life in the refined paintings of Valentin (fig. 16), with their young people playing cards, drinking, making music, and living it up in large empty rooms or beneath the coolness of Roman carriageways. No doubt it is possible to see a desire at work here to represent the lives of contemporary young Romans, even if this intention fell within the then imperious rules of fashionable collecting.

If I had to find an indubitable testimony to the Caravaggian era, I would seek it in the two portraits of young people, conceived as a pair, painted in Rome by Cecco del Caravaggio (alias Francesco Boneri) and now in Madrid (for one of these, see fig. 18). They are portraits of fiancés of popular origin; the two individuals are surrounded by objects and animals that are joyous allusions to eroticism (a comparison with Flemish captioned engravings, those signed with the monogram HSD for example, leave no doubt about this). If the reality of a moment in the life of young people emerges directly here, it is because these paintings were conceived with such a goal in mind. Unfortunately, these documentary paintings are almost unique: it was rare for fiancés not belonging to the upper classes to be able to afford a double portrait; moreover, the obvious lasciviousness of certain of the symbolic objects represented meant that such works were reserved for the family circle. We are forced to deduce that these types of paintings fell victim, over time, to a kind of slaughter. I believe, nonetheless, that Ribera's *Girl with a Tambourine* and *Drinker* (both in private collections), or the extraordinary portrait of the fiancée of Massimo Stanzione (fig. 19), now in San Francisco, were part of this trend inaugurated by Cecco del Caravaggio.

The cultural revolution brought about by Caravaggio would leave traces for at least two centuries, propagated through both direct and indirect channels. So long as this popularity lasted, images of young people were easy to find; no longer solely status symbols for those who commissioned them, the repertory of these portraits provides frequent encounters with adolescents and youth in the work of Ceresa (fig. 22), Ghislandi, Ceruti (fig. 23), and others, especially in the painting of northern Italy. For a seductive illustration of the history of Italian youth, one could isolate certain characters who often reappeared in the paintings of Ceruti, such as the young street porters captured sympathetically by the artist during a moment of rest. These are fine examples of what was called at the time "genre painting," but the depictions never surpass the particularity of the individual represented, never grasp a manner of being or reflect a sentiment of belonging to the social category portrayed.

From southern Italy come other slices of life, in the paintings by Traversi, who proves more discerning in his documentary impulse. His school and salon scenes are now famous (the pinnacle being his *Marriage Contract*, at the Barbarini Palace in Rome), but the information they provide on eighteenth-century youth reaches us through the realm of the unsaid: these are young people of good society—not the common boys dear to Ceruti—who are prisoners of rules of behavior that are not their own, rules that give them freedom, or the illusion of it, only at the moment of marriage, when it is too late to experience youth's natural difference. From this point of view, Traversi's *Marriage Contract* has something of the steady hallucinatory quality of a nightmare, bringing to mind a seventeenth-century painting with a similar theme but a more carefree tone, Giovanni San Giovanni's *Wedding Night* (Florence, Uffizi Gallery). The canvas was created for a collector of easy tastes, Don Lorenzo de Medici (and I have said how heavily the tastes of collectors weighed), but it is so rare to glimpse a basic scene in the life of young people, far from the prurience of pornography, that this painting is worth recalling.

"The world is the reverse of what it should be, since the young man, who follows no other rule of judgment than nature, and is thus a highly competent judge, is always taking the true for the false and the false for the true." (Leopardi, *Zibaldone*, August 2, 1821). The difficulty of relations among the new generations, who were brought up on the enthusiasm of the first wave of romanticism, and the frustrating experience of the world of the Restoration, which refused any functional role to youth, were summarized by Leopardi as follows: "Youthful passion, the most natural, universal thing in the world, a matter of great importance, used to be taken into consideration by statesmen. But this living, weighty matter is no longer accounted for by politicians and governors, who consider it nonexistent" (August 1, 1820). For Enlightenment thinkers, and subsequently for the romantics, it was in nature that original purity and unsullied virtue resided. This belief had the effect of reemphasizing this stage of life, which seemed the least subject to the compromises of civilization and its artifices, to such an extent that I believe one could calculate the percentage increase in the number of portraits of young people between the end of the eighteenth century and the first thirty years of the nineteenth (with prominent examples even in Italy—think of Batoni, for instance). The subjects varied (a fiery portrait of a young warrior, a thoughtful young man amid antique ruins or surrounded by the spectacle of nature), but the artist's attention was constantly drawn to the psychology of the personage: *"Des Menschen Gegenwart, sein Gesicht, seine Physiognomie der beste Text zu allem ist"* (The best starting text is the image of man, his face, his physionomy; J. K. Lavater, *Physiognomische Fragmente*, vol. 2 [Winterthur, 1784], p. 76).

From among this repertory, a particular subgenre that even better characterizes the ways of the young generations (their exalted illusions, according to Leopardi) may be distinguished. I am thinking here of paintings representing several youths of the same age, symbolic souvenirs of their friendship during a season of life that will never return: the *Freundschaftbild*, "portraits of friendship," of the young German painters in Rome in about 1810 to 1820. Friendship was an instrument of cohesion and solidarity against the aggression of the surrounding world (that of older people), and often even within the family. The double portrait of Joséphine de Lorraine and her sister Charlotte (fig. 24) by Lorenzo Pecheux (1779) is utterly explicit in this regard: in it we see the two sisters sacrificing to the altar of friendship in defiance of Cupid (the inscription on the pedestal reads "FRATERNAE AMICITIAE SACRUM"). But even without such a caption and without the existence of a direct relationship between the persons represented, this underlying theme can also be found in the world of Matteini, De Boni (fig. 25), Bossi, Tominz (fig. 27), and others. More complex and more interesting still is the case of the large drawing (fig. 26) by Tomaso Minardi (Faenza, Municipal Gallery), depicting the painter, his master Giuseppe Zauli, and his friend Michele Sangiorgi as captivated witnesses to the dialogue between Socrates and Alcibiades: here the young generation confronts acknowledged masters of another age. It would be interesting to consider whether this is a direct illustration of certain ideas expressed, again by Leopardi, regarding friendship: "If we put aside the exalted illusions, which markedly favor friendship among the young, there is no doubt, especially today when grand and beautiful illusions no longer exist, that friendship is easier between an old man and a young man than among young people" (September 17, 1821). Leopardi had in mind his own relationship with Pietro Giordani (as we can clearly see from a note dated January 20, 1821), but I believe that, as a whole, this first romantic generation demonstrated a continuous and difficult fluctuation between awareness of its otherness and of its own strengths (that of a group bound by solidarity) and the search for moral guides who could be recognized without conflict as ideal father-master figures. A systematic study of this particular type of portrait would facilitate our approach to this other theme, which is typical of the condition of youth.

CHAPTER 2

THE MILITARY EXPERIENCE

Sabina Loriga

War wears the face of youth. According to Gabriele d'Annunzio, it was to "sacred youth" that "the priest of Mars" turned when he said: "Go, take up your gear, obey, you are the seed of a new world." Many other poets and artists have celebrated the warrior virtues of "our boys" or the "proletarian heroism of twenty-year-olds."[1] Youth was also evoked by all who recalled the pointless sacrifice on the battlefield of so many "fresh smiling faces"; as Ezra Pound wrote in 1920:

> There died a myriad
> And of the best, among them
> For an old bitch gone in teeth
> For a botched civilization.[2]

On many propaganda posters at the beginning of the twentieth century, the military finger was pointed at the young man, reminding him of his duty toward his country.[3] The same theme also inspired earlier hymns and chants: "The new Jacobins wanted to take our youth and lead them to slaughter," says a Tuscan tune of 1849; "I don't want to die so young," confirms a song in memory of Salvatore Misdea, who, in the spring of 1884, locked himself in a room of the Pizzofalcone barracks in Naples and began shooting randomly in a moment of madness, killing five comrades and wounding seven others.[4]

What these images of youth often celebrate is an initiation: military service sanctions the boy's entry into the adult world. The young drummers depicted by Marie-Joseph Chénier and Edmondo De Amicis propagate the image of the child performing his military duty as if he were already a man. In all these literary and artistic evocations, the military institution is like an existential boundary, ensuring the economic, affective, and sexual emancipation of the young man. The in-depth history of this representation of the profession of arms has yet to be written. Nonetheless, thanks to various studies on the institution of the army, it is now possible to analyze the way in which the image of a rite of passage toward adulthood developed and slowly became fixed. In the pages that follow, I shall confine myself to offering some exploratory thoughts on the various ways in which millions of soldiers, volunteers or not, were confronted with the reality of war for more than three hundred years, from the seventeenth to the early twentieth century.

In the seventeenth century, "the century of the soldier," more than 10 million men served in the various armies of Europe.[5] Despite strong drives toward pacifism, the two centuries that followed were barely more "civil": between 1618 and 1763, France spent sixty-three years at war, the United Provinces of the Netherlands sixty-two, Spain eighty-two, England barely forty-five, and Austria ninety-two.[6] These wars of "professionals" were soon followed, from 1792 to 1815, by "revolutionary wars," then by the long series of "wars of nations," from the Crimean War of 1855 to the outbreak of the First World War.[7]

Even independent of periods of conflict, one of the characteristics common to the history of Europe has been the constant increase in military forces. In the eighteenth century, the armies of France and Russia had on the order of 300,000 men, Austria 200,000, Prussia 150,000, Sweden and Great Britain 100,000, Spain and Piedmont 50,000.[8] For the most part these troops were volunteers, but some had been forced into uniform. The first country to experiment with the obligatory levying of forces was Sweden, where, in 1544, the Riksdag instituted an annual census of men and the right to call to arms one man out of five in case of necessity. One century later, the dire need for war labor forced Spain and England to establish national armies and led War Minister Louvois to draw 25,000 Frenchmen by lots for the defense of a fortress. The presence of military men in society, already highly in evidence, became more widespread when soldiers recruited by force began undergoing intensive training even during peacetime. In Piedmont, recruits from provincial regiments created by Vittorio Amedeo II immediately following Spain's War of Succession had to participate in semi-annual training periods and perform certain tasks such as surveying borders or maintaining public order. And in Prussia, the *Kantonsystem* introduced in 1732 by Frederik William I, the "Sergeant King," compelled all male subjects to perform military training two to three months a year, beginning at the age of ten.[9]

Thus obligatory levying lent a more national character to the armies, and brought military professionals together with civilians who also had normal lives (houses, jobs, and so on). The principle according to which all able-bodied male citizens had the right and duty to defend their country would be definitively established with the French Revolution. Faced with the foreign threat, on September 5, 1798, the Directoire enacted the Jourdan-Delbrel law, declaring that at the age of twenty, all citizens would be enrolled together ("conscripted") on the recruitment lists for the next five years. Universal conscription, which following the example of the Napoleonic armies would be adopted by all the countries of Europe (Great Britain excluded), had the effect of increasing the numbers: in France alone, the revolutionary and Napoleonic wars called to arms nearly 4 million young men.[10]

After 1815 European governments sought to reduce the sizes of their armies. Austria abandoned obligatory conscription; Holland and Belgium (beginning in 1830) decided to resort to it for exceptional cases only (when volunteers were lacking); France and Piedmont preferred a lottery system, which enabled them to recruit less than 20 percent of able-bodied twenty-years-olds, and offered those who had drawn a "bad number" the possibility of paying a replacement. After a period of hesitation, however, the system of obligatory conscription would be readopted and perfected in all countries (with the exception of Great Britain).[11] Under William I, Prussia reestablished seven-year obligatory active duty (three years of activity, four years in the reserves), and in the years 1872 and 1873, France and

Italy established obligatory and individual military service, abolishing the system of paid replacements while reducing the duration (from five years to three), thereby considerably increasing the percentage of conscripts (which in France, in 1889, went from 50 percent to 73 percent of recruits).[12] In the years that followed, obligatory military service was adopted in Turkey and Japan and in many countries in eastern and northern Europe, from Montenegro, Romania, Serbia, and Bulgaria to Sweden, Norway, and Belgium.[13] As Francesco De Sanctis observed before the Italian parliament in 1878: "War . . . has taken . . . on such power and dimensions that the new duties imposed in the future on all European peoples will bring about a real social transformation. Whatever we may think of these transformations, all powers will be forced to find the solution to this major problem: how, in case of war, to place the whole of the nation under arms."[14]

With universal and obligatory conscription, mass armies again occupied the foreground; railroads enabled the transportation and resupplying of enormous numbers of men in uniform (Tables 1 and 2). In 1870, the race for military power was led by the North German Confederation, which succeeded in uniting 1,200,000 men (twice the size of the Grand Army that Napoleon led into Russia), and in 1914 by the German Empire, which had 3,400,000 men.[15] The concern with increasing the numbers of troops ended up fueling the demographic debate: the supply of men and the birth rate become elements for evaluating military power. Thus, in 1867, Alfred Legoyt wrote in the *Journal des économistes,* the official organ of liberal economists, that infant and general mortality were still too high in France, and he insisted on the obligation of "preserving a large number of precious beings for the country, which will add to its strength, its greatness and security down the road." According to the head of the Bureau of Statistics, between 1800 and 1850, the French population increased by barely 31 percent (from 27,300,000 to 35,800,000 inhabitants), while England grew by 47 percent (from 15,200,000 to 22,500,000) and Germany 45 percent (from 24,700,000 to 35,700,000):[16] "France and Austria rank last . . . but whatever the cause of these sizeable differences, we should consider them seriously, as within an easily calculable period of time, the current order of the European states in terms of size and power

Table 1 Military personnel (in thousands)

Year	France	Germany	Italy	Great Britain	Austria	Belgium	The Netherlands	Denmark	Sweden/Norway
1850	439	131	41	201	434	35	30	26	68
1860	608	201	183	347	306	40	39	25	68
1870	452	319	155	257	252	40	39	39	58
1880	544	430	167	248	273	46	41	6	65
1890	596	505	257	278	332	45	42	18	65
1900	621	624	262	487	308	51	31	11	73
1910	652	673	252	372	315	48	28	15	35
1920	1,457	114	1,350	596	29	156	14	16	72

Source: P. Flora, ed., State, Economy, and Society in Western Europe 1815–1975, vol. 1, The Growth of Mass Democracies and Welfare State (London, 1983), pp. 245–253. The numbers relative to Germany in 1850, 1860, and 1870 are only for Prussia. Those for Italy in 1850 and 1860 are only for the Kingdom of Sardinia.

Table 2 Percent of military men in the male population ages 20–40

Year	France	Germany	Italy	Great Britain	Austria	Belgium	The Netherlands	Denmark	Sweden/ Norway
1850	6.5	4.7	5.3	4.3	14.5	4.3	5.4	10.3	7.2
1860	9.0	6.6	2.3	7.2	9.7	4.7	6.5	8.7	7.1
1870	6.5	7.7	3.3	5.0	7.3	4.5	6.3	12.9	6.0
1880	8.1	5.7	3.3	4.4	7.2	4.9	6.1	1.8	6.4
1890	8.6	6.1	5.1	4.4	8.2	4.3	5.7	5.3	6.4
1900	8.8	6.3	5.3	6.6	6.9	4.2	3.6	2.8	6.4
1910	9.0	5.8	4.7	4.5	6.7	3.5	2.8	3.4	—
1920	22.6	1.1	22.9	7.4	2.5	10.8	1.2	3.0	—

Source: P. Flora, ed., State, Economy, and Society in Western Europe 1815–1975, vol. 1, The Growth of Mass Democracies and Welfare State (London, 1983), pp. 245–253. The numbers relative to Germany in 1850, 1860, and 1870 are only for Prussia. Those for Italy in 1850 and 1860 are only for the Kingdom of Sardinia.

will be profoundly altered by the simple inequality . . . in their population growth rates."[17]

The army has not always turned specifically to youth, nor, a fortiori, has it been populated exclusively by young men. Certainly under the ancien régime the majority of soldiers were men in the prime of life, young mercenaries who had decided to leave home following conflicts with their families or communities that were often material in nature (a bad share of the inheritance for the youngest son, for example), but they were not the only category of soldier, as we shall see. There were also men of riper age, sometimes old men, and, conversely, there were young children. Among the troops sent by Spain into Flanders in the early seventeenth century, many soldiers were in their thirties and some older (in the Walloon and Spanish companies, some soldiers were even in their seventies). A century later, in France, 16.6 percent of recruits were over forty and 11.8 percent under twenty-one, while in Piedmont, 8.4 percent were under eighteen and 10 percent over thirty. Analogous percentages can be found on the other side of the Atlantic, in the English colony of Massachusetts, where, during the Seven Years War, 24.7 percent of recruits were under the age of nineteen and 18.4 percent were over thirty.[18]

For a long time the age of a soldier was hardly considered important: anyone could enlist; what counted for recruiters was one's physique. As we read under the heading "age" in Panckouke's *Encyclopédie méthodique,* "Among the unpoliced nations, the start of military service is not determined by age but by strength."[19] The question of age came up starting in the second half of the seventeenth century, and it became a topic of discussion all over Europe during the century that followed, for two main reasons: the high rate of mortality in the garrisons and discipline problems among the troops. In both cases, the problem elements were not so much the older soldiers as the very young ones, the sixteen- or seventeen-year-old kids. They were dying in too great a number, not only on the battlefield, but also during peacetime, racked with a putrid sickness called hospital fever or with "prison fever," due to the foul air of the barracks, which favored the spread of exanthematous typhous (transmitted by fleas),

dysenteries of bacillary origin, smallpox, and other illnesses that "impreg-
nated the clothing, linen and equipment with poisonous vapors."[20] As the
military inspectors observed, those most often struck down by illness were
not the older soldiers, who seemed capable "of bearing the burden," but
the youngest.[21] The second problem was discipline: not only did the
younger soldiers turn out to be more vulnerable physically, but they also
took a long time to learn "to serve as one should" and were sometimes a
hindrance on the battlefield.[22] Thus certain officers demanded older recruits, and the Marquis de Sade could write:

> If only people would see that the main goal is not to have very young
> soldiers but to have good ones; and that by following the current preju-
> dice, it is perfectly impossible for this so useful class of citizens to ever
> attain perfection, with recruits taken in so young, without our knowing
> if they have what it takes to be admitted, and without understanding that
> it is impossible to possess the necessary virtues so long as young aspirants
> are not given the possibility of acquiring them through a long and perfect
> education.[23]

This military debate was occurring in the context of a larger debate
on the age of adulthood. Just as the legal age giving one the right to make
a will, swear an oath, or take religious vows was gradually being increased,[24] so there was a growing consensus to regulate the age of soldiers
and subject voluntary enrollment to paternal consent: if a minor enlisted
against the will of his parents, the latter had the right to demand that the
contract be declared void.[25] Thus the age limit for enlisting kept increasing:
in France, it was sixteen in 1681, seventeen in 1763, eighteen in 1793, and
twenty in 1798.[26] This tendency would reverse itself only at the start of
the twentieth century, when adolescents began to be recruited again.[27]

Furthermore, despite this progressive increase in official age limits,
armies continued to take in very young boys: in 1870 when the war with
Prussia broke out, France had 5,000 child troops.[28] Recruiters didn't always
respect the rules, and to live in the garrison it was not necessary to have
formally enrolled in the army: there were plenty of women, children, and
old men in the barracks. Though the presence of civilians living within
the army is difficult to quantify, certain pictorial evidence has been left to

us by Jacques Callot and Pieter de Hooch for the seventeenth century, by Antoine Watteau and Thomas Rowlandson for the eighteenth, and by Horace Vernet, the painter of Napoleon and Charles X. We also know that in 1567 the Duke of Alva was in charge of 8,646 foot soldiers and 965 horsemen, but that he had a total of 16,000 mouths to feed, and that six years later, in 1572, 3,000 Spanish foot soldiers were accompanied by 2,000 civilians, mostly servants, women, and children. Two centuries later the French army numbered 30,200 soldiers and 12,000 civilians. As the commander of Les Invalides recognized, "there are generally many married soldiers in all our companies . . . and we absolutely cannot do without [women] to wash and mend the soldiers' linen." Until the end of the nineteenth century, it was normal for women to participate in the lives of soldiers as washerwomen, menders, venders of food and drink, and prostitutes.[29] Some came alone, of their own initiative (sometimes disguised as men), but many were merely following their husbands and brought their children with them—who were thus prepared from childhood for the profession of arms. In a drama by Sébastien Mercier, *Le déserteur*, the hero, Durimel, has spent his childhood "in almost all the places where the spectacle of war was played out."[30]

Certain officers considered this cohabitation of the sexes an obstacle to discipline. A French statute of 1686 revealed that married soldiers were less effective than the others in battle, because "the needs of their wives and children prevented them from applying themselves as they should, from serving well."[31] Yet the presence of women and children was useful for the cohesion of the army. While single soldiers were rootless, capable of deserting over a trifle, the married soldiers were relatively stable: they deserted less frequently and were less homesick. One Monsieur Garrigues de Froment wrote in 1755: "It's an unfounded bias in France and elsewhere that married soldiers or fathers head into the firing lines and expose themselves less courageously than do others. Centuries of experience tells us . . . that they fight with the same courage, are less quarrelsome and debauched and infinitely more attached to their bodies and to their homelands than the unmarried soldiers."[32] The presence of children also had its advantages from a professional perspective. In the second half of the eighteenth century, the idea spread that it was fitting to give a military education to orphans, foundlings, and especially to the children of soldiers, in the hope that this would inculcate an inclination for military life.[33] In the 1780s, the populationist Moheau related his dream of turning these children into perfect soldiers: "Engaged in advance by the nourishment that will have been provided them since birth, will the children of the most handsome men of the nation not preserve the beauty of the species? Born under a tent or in a barrack, having worn strips of uniforms as their first garments, will they not soon be infused with a military spirit?"[34]

During the Revolution, the armies continued to take in very young boys. Joseph Bara, the heroic drummer immortalized by Marie-Joseph Chénier in *Le chant du départ*, died in an ambush at the age of fourteen, while the Terror saw the invention of the "battalions of hope," children of the troops who would inspire Stendhal's admiration in the *The Life of Henry Brulard*:

> I burned to be part of those battalions I saw parading past. I see today
> that it was an excellent institution, the only one that would be capable of
> uprooting the priesthood in France. Instead of playing at the chapel, the
> children's imagination turns to war and grows accustomed to danger.
> Then, when their country calls them at the age of twenty, they know the
> routine, and instead of trembling before the unknown, they recall the
> games of their childhood.[35]

From 1805 to 1807, French high school and university students, divided into companies, were issued uniforms and began devoting four hours a week to military preparation; in 1811, the Guard regiment of orphans was created, a special body of adolescents between fifteen and eighteen years old. The idea of forming a "generation of citizen warriors," to use Ugo Foscolo's term,[36] was very popular throughout the century, and in 1880 the first "school battalions" were created in Paris: two years later, more than 20,000 armed students marched in the July 14 military revue.[37] Although of short duration, the experiment with student battalions, provided for in the Jules Ferry law,[38] marked an important step: while expressing the hope for the militarization of all youth, it acknowledged the need to separate adolescents from conscripts. Several years later, children would be expelled from armies all over Europe in favor of separate premilitary preparation: adolescents would be trained for physical strength and soldierly discipline, but outside of the barracks. The best institution to conduct such training, it was decided, would be school, as an Italian deputy highlighted in 1890 in a speech in favor of physical military exercises:

> The citizen-soldier is not trained in the barracks but in school; for only those who in school and at home have learned the passion for freedom, the holy love of country, and that for it, one must vanquish or die on the battlefield, can be citizen-soldiers. The young men who will enter the army at the age of twenty, having received military training in adolescence, having had target practice in their gymnasiums, will arrive beneath the flags as already-formed soldiers, and, more important, should circumstances require, they will be able to constitute . . . a contingent of 800,000 courageous boys, even though they are not yet incorporated into the army.[39]

During these same years, the armies also began excluding women. In 1840, France already had forbidden soldiers' wives from serving as vendors, or *vivandières;* fourteen years later, only nurses would be authorized to follow the troops in Crimea. In England, in the 1860s, the Law on Contagious Diseases put women who lived in the garrisons in the category of prostitutes, whose presence, it was determined, was not only useless but dangerous. The other European countries in turn enacted the same separation of Mars and Venus. Only in faraway regions—on the American frontier, in India, in North Africa—was it still possible to find women following the troops.[40]

With obligatory military service, introduced for the first time in France in 1798, the call to arms became a set event in the life of men between the ages of twenty and twenty-five. Whether bitterly or mockingly, songs began to speak of military service as a profound injustice inflicted on the young and on youth. But war was not the only thing at issue: the song *Bonapart l'ha mandà a dire* (Bonaparte sent him to say), which spread throughout northern Italy, spoke of the sadness of leaving one's family and of brutally severing the most important affective ties.

It is no doubt for this reason that the departure of conscripts was often solemnly celebrated: in Brittany, parents accompanied their sons to the edge of the village, where they asked them to cut off their hair and place it in a coffin. According to the prefect of Finistère in 1807, in certain localities this farewell ceremony took on religious overtones as well: "The way in which most good people part with their children who have been called to defend their country is touching and worth noting. They lead them a certain distance away. There they kiss them, bidding them an eternal farewell; then, after parting ways, they return home reciting prayers, some the *De Profundis.*"[41]

Under the ancien régime, many volunteers left their homes because they felt that their social bonds were threatened. As recruiters were well aware—since they sought "to get involved with the families and become acquainted with all the affairs of the village"—the decision to enlist was often the unpleasant legacy of a quarrel: "You have to go to all the festivals, propose nothing the first two or three days, and wait for money to start running out: that's when the peasants are ready to enlist. With a little cunning and care, you can also take advantage of quarrels. There are always fights on these occasions, and rather than dealing with the law, the young people prefer to enlist."[42]

With the Jourdan-Delbrel law, leaving for the army ceased to be a solitary act, instead becoming a collective event that reinforced the feeling among youth of belonging to a specific age group. The prefect of Landes wrote in 1799: "Calling up an entire class turns this class into a coalition whose members are ready to help each other out and protect each other. It touches all the families and interests them in the same cause. Hence the protection afforded deserters, who are offered many places of refuge."[43] However, this solidarity among conscripts easily turned into social resentment. As was well known by the thousands of young people who, year after year, protested against the "revolutionary lotteries," the injustice the army inflicted on youths was not equally distributed: discrimination began with the drawing of numbers and characterized military life as a whole. Isser Woloch brought to light how few sons of the middle classes were called to arms during the Napoleonic wars: between 1808 and 1813, only

7 percent of candidates for judicial functions were incorporated (versus a national mean of 19 percent), while 42 percent were rejected for medical reasons, 30 percent freed from the obligation of serving by the lottery, 15 percent able to pay a replacement, and 6 percent sent back home for family or other reasons.[44] What shocked contemporaries the most was the number of those discharged, and of "dodgers." Five "Dijon republicans" could legitimately ask: "Why is it that the blood [of the poor] flows abundantly while that of the rich is spared? Why, despite all the laws, do these young gentlemen find the means to clog offices and hospitals, to hold quills or lancets while their comrades are shooting rifles?"[45]

Another scandalous subject was the recourse of the rich to replacements, available for the equivalent of ten years' pay for an agricultural worker—a considerable sum. It was in the hope of saving up such a sum that boys from the region of Maine, while still children, began putting aside "the tiny profits they made gathering wild fruits, flowers, and mushrooms."[46] The injustice of the replacement was sorely felt, and certain military men, including Lazare Carnot, spoke of the "shameful commerce in human life," of the "market of men" and the "youth trade."[47]

Faced with the injustice of the military authorities, many young people felt justified in using any means possible to escape conscription. A hasty marriage was often the solution; the subprefect of the Lario district (Côme) deplored this practice:

> The most handsome, best-built boys are lucky enough to be pleasing to women, and thus have the possibility of finding one to marry them, thereby sparing them from conscription. This constitutes a kind of elimination process from the four lists of young valid men, which end up being reduced to those with poor builds, weak constitutions or defects, who are certainly incapable of providing real service and of having that impressive and dignified bearing so necessary for a soldier.[48]

These hasty marriages were often unhappy, because the "young ill-fated boys" did not have the maturity necessary to become heads of families. In other cases, with the complicity of their parents, young men contracted "fictive" marriages with older women, who were often later abandoned in exchange for a subsidy—but not always: in 1810, for example, in the village of Vinteuil, a certain Pierre Labbé, who had contracted marriage with a women in her seventies, fell into "a dark reverie," lost his appetite, and ended up committing suicide.[49]

To escape conscription, other young people had recourse to illness, which they simulated or actually inflicted on themselves. The prefect of Seine-Inférieure recounted how conscripts had all their teeth pulled out, chewed incense to provoke cavities, or gashed their arms or legs, making the wounds incurable by applying arsenic-based substances to them. The list of these illnesses was varied: the only difference, an Italian doctor would later write, was that the peasant boys were more apt to resort to "deafness, enuresis, or wounds, which require great resistance to physical pain," while city boys preferred to resort to "weakening treatments, palpitations, convulsions, or vision problems."[50]

To those who wished neither to marry nor to fall ill, there remained the possibility of dodging. Between 1792 and 1814, hundreds of thousands of deserters and absentees "were hiding out quietly in the homes of their family or friends." The boundary between compassion and protection was unclear, and the help of the community was often reinforced by the indolence "of the civil, and perhaps also military, authorities who were not doing their duties."[51] The work of Isser Woloch established that in France, under Napoleon, the mechanism of obligatory conscription functioned on the whole rather well, at least until 1811, but that it inspired numerous protests.[52] In 1799, the prefect of Nièvre wrote to the minister of the interior:

> These youths who cultivate the earth find, in the vast forest surrounding them, asylums that are impenetrable to the police who are ordered to look for them; those who float wood take refuge, thanks to the trains, in cities situated all along the Yonne river; and those who work in the forges and furnaces are the main supports to ordinarily indigent families. For them, fear of abandoning their families to poverty compels them to hide wherever they can when it comes to the draft.[53]

To break the complicity of civilians, Napoleon clamped down on dodging, ordering thorough searches of villages or sending mobile col-

umns, which had to be provided with food and lodging, to the homes of
deserters and absentees. This method of persuasion, which had already
been tested in the seventeenth century, was adopted by various countries
of nineteenth-century Europe. The measures could be particularly severe
in Italy, where dodgers constituted a reservoir of workers for organized
crime.[54] In 1863, the year of Italy's first national levy, the reports of the
Ministry of War calculating the number of dodgers relative to the total
number of conscripts gave a national average of 11.8 percent; but if one
subtracts the exempt, the rejected, the postponed, and so on, the dodgers
represented a quarter of the total.[55] The provinces where conscription was
least welcome were those that had never experienced it before, such as the
Marches, Umbria, and especially those in the south, where certain cities
had an official rate of insubordination approaching 50 percent.[56] A French
Zouave, the Viscount Oscar de Poli de Saint-Troquet (son of a military
man who had been stoned to death in Orleans in 1848 while attempting to
repress a popular revolt) recounted that many young people preferred to
leave their village rather than join the service; that they armed themselves
and took refuge in the woods.[57] During the summer of 1863, after having
combed through 154 municipalities in Sicily to get ahold of "anyone we
might meet in the countryside with the age of a dodger and the face of an
assassin," General Giuseppe Govone proceeded to arrest 4,550 dodgers
and 1,350 wrongdoers.[58] Thanks to such police operations, the number of
dodgers would show a major decrease in the years that followed: in 1864
it fell to 5.8 percent (13,476 of 232,154 recruits); in 1865, to 4.8 percent
(10,708 of 223,548 recruits); and after 1866 it stabilized at about 4 percent,
increasing only slightly in the 1880s.[59]

In the sixteenth and seventeenth centuries, young men entered the
workforce before performing their military service. Unfortunately, the
information at our disposal as to the professional composition of the
armies is still fragmentary and uncertain, and a comparison between different countries is not possible. But the available data show that many

soldiers already had a profession.[60] In his study of Massachusetts in the eighteenth century, Fred Anderson was able to establish that

> the soldiers of Massachusetts Bay were generally young men, younger than the age at which men in their province usually married . . . Nearly three-quarters of all soldiers were under 30 years old. The overwhelming majority of them had been following a manual occupation of some sort before joining the army, typically a job related to agriculture. These men either worked for themselves and were called "farmers," "yeomen," and "husbandmen," or they worked for someone else as "laborers." The last formed the largest single occupational group in the army, over a third of the men whose occupations are known. Farmers, yeomen, and husbandmen formed a smaller but still substantial group, just over one-fifth of the soldiers. "Husbandmen"—an appellation that implied the ownership of at least some part of one's farm—predominated among them. With the exception of eighty-one sailors and mariners, the rest of the soldiers with manual occupations—two out of five men—were artisans of some sort. Soldiers had been following fifty-seven different trades before enlistment, among which woodworking was the most common, followed by leather-, metal-, and cloth-based crafts. Fewer than two in every hundred soldiers—just 42 of the 2,175 with known occupations—had nonmanual occupations. Seven of them, all officers, called themselves "gentlemen"; most of the rest had been pursuing such modest commercial callings as victualler, tobacconist, and trader.[61]

Moreover, children were not excluded from work in ancien régime society: we know that boys helped work the fields starting at the age of seven or eight, and that an apprenticeship with an artisan or as a domestic began at about the age of fourteen.[62] The adolescent population was also fairly mobile: in general this mobility was limited to brief stays within the same region, but apprentices sometimes traveled hundreds of miles to find a job.[63] Some even left their country: more than half of the 5,000 English immigrants who crossed the ocean in 1635 to head for the New World were between sixteen and twenty-three years old, and even ten- or eleven-year-olds went off alone, with neither family nor employer. But working did not necessarily imply independence, as Keith Thomas reminds us:

1. Domenico Ghirlandaio, *Giovanna Tornabuoni*, 1488. Lugano, Collection Thyssen-Bornemisza. The inscription, to the right, deplores the impossibility of expressing the sentiments and moral attitude of the person represented.

2. Leonardo da Vinci, *Cecilia Gallerani*. Kraków, National Museum (Czartoryski Collection). An ermine, symbol of chastity, in the arms of Ludovico il Moro's young beloved.

3. Giorgione, *Double portrait*. Rome, Palazzo Venezia. Amorous melancholy is revealed by the bitter orange the young man holds in his left hand.

4. Raphaël, *Agnolo Doni.*
Florence, Pitti Museum (photo:
Fratelli Alinari). This painting
accompanies the portrait of his
wife, Maddalena Strozzi (below),
and was executed shortly after
their marriage (1504).

5. Raphaël, *Maddalena Strozzi.*
Florence, Pitti Museum (photo:
Fratelli Alinari). Like the painting representing her husband
(above), this is an example of
the new, nonrhetorical type
of portrait of the early
Renaissance.

6. Giulio Romano, *Young Woman*. Lisbonne, Calouste Gulbenkian Foundation. The subject of this portrait was very likely a courtesan.

7. Michelangelo, *Andrea Quarantesi*. London, British Museum.
Andrea Quaratesi (1512–1585) was a friend, correspondent, and perhaps even an amateur pupil of Michelangelo's.

8. Lorenzo Lotto, *The Family of Giovanni della Volta* (1547). London, National Gallery. An example of a family portrait that still shows a free and natural relationship between parents and children.

9. Federico Barocco, *Young Woman*. Copenhagen, Royal Museum of Fine Arts. A portrait intended to highlight the social status of the person represented, not her youth.

10. Agnolo Bronzino, *Ludovico Capponi*. New York, Frick Collection. Another painting emphasizing social status.

11. Anonymous (Lombard painter), *The Family of Alphonse III Gonzaga, Count of Novellara*, 1581. Rome, Colonna Gallery (photo: Fratelli Alinari). The number of children, ensuring the continuation of the family line, plays an important role in the family portrait.

12. Lavinia Fontana, *The Family of Ulisse Gozzadini*, 1585. Bologna, National Gallery (photo: Gabinetto fotocr. Fico, Bologna). Senator Gozzadini presents his daughters and their respective spouses.

13. Caravaggio, *Maddalena pentita*. Rome, Doria Pamphili Gallery. "He has painted a seated young woman . . . and, by adding a pot of ointment, a necklace and other jewels, he has made her into a Magdalen" (G. P. Bellori, 1672).

14. Caravaggio, *David with Goliath's Head*. Rome, Borghese Gallery (photo: Fratelli Alinari/Giraudon). Goliath's head is a self-portrait of Caravaggio.

15. Caravaggio, *The Cheaters*. Fort Worth (Texas), Kimbell Art Museum. An early example of scenes of the lives of young people, which are a recurrent theme in Caravaggio's work.

16. Valentin de Boulogne, *The Fortune-teller*. Toledo (Texas), the Toledo Museum of Art.

17. Georges de La Tour, *The Fortune-teller*. New York, The Metropolitan Museum of Art (Rogers Fund, 1960).

18. Cecco del Caravaggio (Francesco Boneri), *Fiancée with a Dove*. Madrid, Prado Museum. This painting forms a pair with a male portrait (now in the Royal Palace of Madrid) depicting a rabbit, another animal that symbolizes erotic activity.

19. Massimo Stanzione, *Portrait of the Fiancée*. San Francisco, The Fine Arts Museum (on permanent loan from the Hispanic Society of America). The chicken with its bound feet clearly alludes to the conjugal bond.

20. Guercino, *Amnon Chasing Tamar*, 1649. Washington, D.C., National Gallery of Art. This tableau forms a pair with a *Joseph and the Wife of Potiphar* (also in the National Gallery), both painted for the collector Aurelio Zaneletti, a friend of Guercino.

21. Bernardo Cavallino, *Tobias's Departure*. Rome, National Gallery of Antique Art (photo: Fratelli Alinari/Giraudon). The theme of Tobias's adventuresome youth was especially popular in the naturalistic painting of the seventeenth century.

22. Carlo Ceresa, *Young Boy*. Milan, Municipal Museum of Castello. The prevailing realism of the Lombard painting tradition assured an ample supply of portraits of youth.

23. Giacomo Ceruti, *Fillette*. Bergamo, Carrara Academy. Ceruti was one of the most prolific creators of portraits of youth in seventeenth-century Lombardy, and he was also interested in depicting working youths.

24. Lorenzo Pecheux, *Joséphine of Lorraine and Her Sister Charlotte Sacrificing on the Altar of Friendship*, 1779 (preparatory drawing). Turin, private collection. Love, vexed by the choice of the two sisters, breaks his bow.

25. Vincenzo Giaconi, based on the painting by Martino De Boni, *Martino De Boni and His Friend Antonio Canova*. Venice, Correr Museum, Drawing and Engraving Room (Vol. Cocogna 504). "Believe me, when you get to know him, he's a very moral and very pleasant man" (Canova to Giannantonio Selva, June 11, 1796).

26. Tommaso Minardi, *Socrates in Dialogue with Alcibiades*, 1807. Faenza, Municipal Gallery. Tommaso Minardi and his friend Michele Sangiorgi appear in the middle ground on the right; in the center is Giuseppe Zauli, Minardi's master.

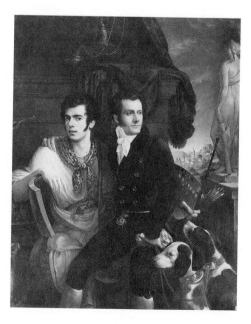

27. Giuseppe Tominz, *Portrait of the Artist with His Brother Francesco*. Gorizia, Provincial Museum. In early nineteenth-century paintings, brotherly solidarity was represented in the same manner as friendship.

The graduated scales of the wage assessments show that the young were not to be paid an adult wage until they were sixteen, eighteen, twenty, twenty-one, or, very commonly, twenty-four. That was the earliest age at which the statute of artificers, following the custom of London, envisaged the emancipation of urban apprentices. In husbandry apprenticeship was to last to twenty-one or twenty-four . . . Many guilds had restrictions to delay achievement of independence even after apprenticeship had ended. By law a trained craftsman could usually be prevented from practising on his own until he was thirty.[64]

Thus, before entering the army, many soldiers had already worked for several years and spent long periods far from home. It is likely that the decision to enlist was often related to dissatisfaction with this situation of semi-independence and the gap between responsibilities at work and weak influence within the family. It seems this was the case for Martin Guerre, in fact, a fairly well-off twenty-three-year-old peasant who was married, with an infant child, when he decided to leave his village of Artigat and enlist in the troops of Philippe II, "out of fear of his father's strictness."[65]

Even in the nineteenth century, in many cases recruits had some work experience: before their service, they had participated in the family's agricultural or manufacturing endeavors, served as domestics, or worked in factories. As emphasized by Jules Maurin, the number of conscripts still in school was very low in France: at the end of the nineteenth century, they represented only a small percentage of those called up from Lozère and Hérault, for example.[66] In 1868, the official number of working children between the ages of eight and sixteen was 99,500; in 1896, 9.8 percent of the working population was under nineteen years of age.[67] Despite the law of 1881 that made primary education obligatory, many poor families continued to send their young children to work. In the first decades of the twentieth century in England, the workforce at cotton factories and mines was made up mostly of children and adolescents working under the direct control of their parents; in the 1880s Charles Booth noted that nearly 80 percent of the migrants to London were between the ages of fifteen and twenty-five,[68] and in 1909 only 6 percent of parents were in a position to give their children a secondary education.[69] The problem of child labor was so extensive it began to be perceived as a "social scourge."[70]

It was so viewed because, among other things, it risked weakening the race and undermining a nation's military power. In Italy, the medical boards noted "the lack of health and robustness in our youth": in 1856, Professor Temistocle Carminati noted that out of 316,047 conscripts, 73,866 were declared inadequate (28,997 for shortness, 6,428 for thoracic inadequacy, 38,441 for deformities or infirmities).[71] Seven years later, the military doctor Federico Cortese, author of a work entitled "Illnesses and Defects That Limit Conscription in the Kingdom of Italy," insisted on the physical degradation of youth in both the north and the south:

> The harm done to the physical capacities of youth, who are given tasks that exceed their resistance, is not only to be regretted in the Neapolitan provinces of Benevento, Abruzzi, and Calabria, where the effects can be seen in emaciated, sallow faces, extreme shortness, and precocious aging, but it is also common in many mountainous regions of northern Italy itself . . . Here too, prepubescent children are used to carry loads on their heads or shoulders, over steep paths. In the small province of Massa Carrara they carry marble, in Sicily sulfur, not to mention the work in the fields, the difference being that the workday in the sulfur mines is limited to six hours, while farm work is indefinite. This habit of employing children, resulting from a lack of machines, instruments, and animals capable of sparing human force, explains the frequency of physical defects that will later render the individuals unsuited for military life, such as height problems, scoliosis, curvature of limbs, goiters, hernias, varicose veins, heart troubles, and particularly deformations of the foot, which are fairly widespread in Sicily.[72]

Plunged directly from childhood into the working world, many youths donned military uniforms without ever having attended school. François Furet and Jacques Ozouf showed that in the second half of the nineteenth century the army played an important role in the literacy of the male population. In France, the idea of using service in the armed forces to instruct "young illiterate citizens" dated from the Revolution, when the Convention envisaged teaching reading, writing, and arithmetic aboard the ships of the Republic; but the project was realized only later, at the initiative of certain superior officers, members of the Society for the Improvement of Elementary Education. In 1816 the first regiment schools were founded, and fifteen years later a rule obliged illiterate soldiers to attend at least one hour of classes a day in reading, writing, and arithmetic. Benjamin Appert, one of the pioneers of popular literacy in France, considered these courses to have had an enormous influence: according to the numbers of the Ministry of War, between 1844 and 1849 more than 1,150,000 recruits learned to read in this manner.[73] These regiment schools would also play an important role in Italy, especially during the last two decades of the nineteenth century: in 1880, approximately 90 percent of recruits were taught to read during their military service, with the rate stabilizing at 75 percent in the years that followed.[74] In 1901 the general rate of illiteracy was still 48 percent, but it was only 18.1 percent among soldiers returning home.[75]

The educational role of the army was not limited to literacy training. Reflections on discipline, which began to appear in the eighteenth century, emphasized its "national" function. In 1891 a commander in France named Lyautey published a noted article in which he described the officer as a teacher of military arts, hygiene, and economy. His paternalistic concept of military commanders, influenced by the social Catholicism of Albert de Mun, would be picked up ten years later by Minister of War Louis André, who wrote: "The regiment is more than just a big family: it's a school. The schoolmaster carries over into the officer, who is the nation's teacher."[76] But certain officers denounced "the paradox of well-intentioned individuals" ready to sacrifice military training to the civic, moral, and physical education of the citizen. Nonetheless, in 1903 and 1904 more than 1,200,000 French soldiers had to listen to lectures on alcoholism, tuberculosis, honesty, patriotism, and colonization, organized by the National Society of Popular Conferences. In Italy, many saw the army as a great motor for national unification; a staff officer, Nicola Marselli, spoke of it as "a great pot in which all elements will melt into a united Italy,"[77] while deputy Andrea Borella considered that since "the political atmosphere of southern Italy is not very healthy . . . a levy of 150,000 young men would extract a great deal of this sickly influence and teach them the order and discipline of the North."[78]

In addition, the army often had an indirect educational function, especially in countries where recruitment was national and nonregional in nature, which favored cultural exchanges.[79] Borella and Marselli highlight, for example, the meeting of dialects occasioned by military service. Assigned to garrisons far from their homes, young Italians learned new expressions and created others that later passed from military jargon into everyday language. The barracks did not abolish dialects but, as Tullio de Mauro has noted, favored "a popular, unified linguistic level that was rich in regionalisms."[80]

Once children, women, and foreigners were banned and age limits for service were set, the garrison became a place of separation: separation from the family and from other youths (among young people, a new, provisional, group now formed, that of the "class"). It was also a separation from the opposite sex, as an Italian song from the early nineteenth century ironically noted:

> Look, Napoleon, what you're doing:
> You take all the best boys
> And leave the girls stewing.
> Napoleon, be fair, start a draft for girls,
> Drop the plain ones and take the beauties.[81]

In the second half of the nineteenth century and the first decade of the twentieth, military service no doubt represented an experience of separation but had not yet taken on the value of an all-around initiation. Here, there is a need for more detailed research into the troops' perception of the army, but it seems probable that for young people who had already held jobs and in some cases lived far from their parents, the call to arms was not a passage from family dependence to independence. Conversely, the service was often considered an emancipation for students, who rarely contributed to the family economy and left home fairly late (in France, Germany, and the other countries of the Continent, it was common to be a day student; as for young Englishmen, though their secondary education took place at boarding school, they nonetheless spent long periods of time with their family).[82] For students, donning the military uniform was a fundamental preparation. Eric Leed demonstrated how, far from the paternal home, far from teachers and schoolmates, the student from the West Country or the South Coast suddenly found himself living elbow to elbow with the miner from Durham or the metal worker from Yorkshire.[83] In the course of this communal experience, in which family and school roles were temporarily put aside, the young man had to confront his future: new prospects for work and relations with the opposite sex lay in store.

It is therefore not surprising that the image of military service as a rite of passage was especially strong in schools, as an element of nationalist ideology. German textbooks, which were constantly recalling 1813, the year of the great insurrection against Napoleon, and French schoolbooks, with their bellicose rhetoric exacerbated by the defeat of 1871 and the loss of Alsace-Lorraine, saw schoolchildren as "future soldiers": "You see, my child, it will be up to you to heal the wounds [of the nation]," read the caption to an illustration by Cham.[84] History lessons sought to transform "classes into privileged cells of a new temple, erected in the service of national worship."[85] The message was repeated in gym class, which became obligatory in almost all the countries of Europe: "For youths . . . accustomed over time to the use of weapons, their bodies more vigorous," the military man was also an example to imitate on a physical level.[86] In the last decades of the century, the theme of a national "renaissance" through the new generations was stressed not only in secondary or university teaching but also in the activities of numerous student organizations. In England, where Guy Fawkes night (commemorating the failed attack on Parliament in 1606) and other traditional rites of youth were becoming demonstrations of patriotism,[87] certain students wanted to form armed groups within the schools. Edmond Warre, for example, revitalized the Volunteers, a militia within Oxford that had been active at the time of Napoleon. This bellicose attitude was shared by many French, German, and Italian students, who could be found in the front ranks of nationalist demonstrations and who, come 1914 and the First World War, would volunteer in large numbers.[88]

For many of these groups, the army would constitute a social and affective separation between adolescence and adult life, a dividing line between school and work, between the family into which one is born and the family one creates. It may also have been a place of sexual probation. As George L. Moss has demonstrated, taking up arms was considered a virile mission.[89] Already Methodism and Pietism had sought to promote an ideal of virility (according to John Wesley, only real men could have a spiritual life), but until the end of the nineteenth century, the theme was rare in military thought. In the eighteenth century, in the superiors' evaluations of their soldiers, we find numerous commentaries on their physical strength, their soldierly bearing, sometimes their "civil" manners, but never an allusion to their virility. In 1786 Gaetano Filangieri (a publicist and legal expert influenced by Rousseau) lamented the harmful consequences of firearms on the human race:

> When the idea of war was that of a struggle in which men had to participate as human beings and not as machines . . . , when the arms employed demanded rather than excluded skill and power . . . , then, just as the robustness and vigor . . . of individuals played the largest part in the outcome of wars, so physical perfection of the body became the primary instrument for the security or ambition of peoples . . . But now . . . that the real soldiers, the real warriors, are the rifles and cannons . . . now that the soldier dies without knowing who killed him, flees, chases, attacks beings he neither sees nor touches . . . now, I say, war has changed its aspect, and legislators have lavished on perfecting arms the care formerly devoted to perfecting men.[90]

It was during the Napoleonic wars that consideration of physical force began to give way to that of "male vigor." In the aftermath of the defeat at Iéna (in 1806), Friedrich Ludwig Jahn, the inventor of the *Turnen*, a political-military exercise that was to lead to "the resurrection of the German nation," proposed giving youth a style of life imbued with virility; the same project was propounded by Ernst Moritz, the prophet of German nationalism, who exclaimed after the battle of Leipzig (1813): "I witnessed a bloody encounter between real men."[91] Several decades later, a certain Victor de Laprade, an ardent defender of physical education, reminded mothers that "if your child grows up without being a man, if he walks effeminately toward his virile duty . . . your tenderness has ill formed his soul: if he does not know how to die, you did not know how to create."[92] And the Swiss Rodolfo Obermann, a professor of physical education, stated that it was necessary to "physically predispose youth to true virility, rather than to this hermaphroditism that retains only the external form of the man."[93]

For the young man, the first test of this virile power was the review board's medical examination, and there existed in central and northern Italy the dictate that "he who is not fit for the king is not fit for the queen either . . ." But while attributing great importance to physical exercise, many nationalist groups considered that the basis for "a virile and austere education" lay elsewhere: what counted was neither brute strength nor even courage but "a model of morality and good habits."[94] Virility was a character trait, the opposite of the boredom with life referred to in England as "Byronism," in Germany as "Wertherism," and in Italy as "Leopardism."[95] In his *De l'éducation militaire*, Paul Déroulède assigned military education the mission of "transforming youth into a legion of brave Frenchmen, and [of] arming them from childhood with that assemblage of male feelings and virile habits that make for a true soldier."[96] In 1878 Francesco De Sanctis reminded the Italian Parliament that "it was not enough to decree on paper that there be a military resembling that of Prussia in order to have one like Prussia's. To be a man is a prerequisite for being a soldier, and a man is not formed in three years, nor in four nor in seven; he is formed by a virile education from the start."[97]

This obsession with virility that dominated ministerial circulars, recruit training manuals, and many other official texts could also be found in the literature of the period. In *500 millions de la Bégum*, published in 1879, Jules Verne said of his hero, Marcel Bruckmann, age twelve, that "the misfortunes of France had left their mark on him in the form of a virile maturity."[98] In the twentieth century, virility found an illustrious representative in Ernst Wurche, the hero of one of the most popular works of postwar Germany *Der Wanderer ʒwischen Beiden Welten,* by Walter Flex, and in the English poet Rupert Brooke, a "young Apollo with blond hair who dreamed of the moment of combat, splendidly little prepared for the miseries of life." A new warlike stereotype (which we find in Ernst Junger, describing the battlefield in sexual terms) encouraged young men to repress thoughts of women: already physically ousted from the garrison, women also had to be banned from the soldier's mind. As Ludwig Tugel later wrote in his novel, *Die Freundschaft:* "A soldier with a wife, no, no . . . it's impossible; when one must give oneself in battle, body and soul, one cannot be bound to a woman."[99]

In the last quarter of the nineteenth century, when monuments to the dead began appearing all over Europe, this virility was also expressed through death.[100] In 1877, at the inauguration of a monument dedicated to past students of the high school of Lyons who had died for France, Victor de Laprade expressed to the current generation his wish that "one day . . . your names may be inscribed here, by the hands of our children."[101] On the other side of the Channel, Sir Garnet Wolseley said he envied the death of the young soldiers, and he was not afraid to exclaim: "Had I sons, I would be proud for them to die on the battlefield."[102] In a country such as England, where the mortality rate was falling regularly (from 22 per 1,000 in 1870 to 13 per 1,000 in 1910) and where death was thus increasingly associated with old age (the average life expectancy went from forty in 1850 to fifty-two in 1910),[103] young people themselves exalted in the sacrifice of their very existence. "To die young, pure, ardent," sang Horace A. Vachell in *The Hill:* "To die swiftly, in perfect health; to die saving others from death, or worse—disgrace—to die scaling heights; to die and carry with you into fuller, ampler life beyond, untainted hopes and aspirations, unembittered memories, all the freshness and gladness of May—is not that cause for joy rather than sorrow?"[104]

According to David Cannadine, this unlikely vision of heroic death on the battlefield was to crumble in 1914. Marshal Alfred von Schlieffen had predicted victory in forty days, but month after month, year after year, the list of the dead reached horrifying proportions.[105] On the battlefield of Ypres, Verdun, the Somme, Caporetto, more than 8 million young men would lose their lives: "barely" 114,000 Americans, 500,000 Italians, 700,000 Englishmen (as well as another 300,000 subjects of the British Empire), close to 2,000,000 Germans, and as many Russians. But relative to population, the heaviest toll was taken by France, with 1,300,000 dead, or 16 percent of recruits, and 2,000,000 wounded, half of whom would receive disability pensions for the rest of their lives.[106] The rhetoric of virile death was superseded by the less romantic rhetoric of the unknown soldier, and the European elite began bemoaning its "lost generation."[107]

The association between war and youthful "virility" thus ripened slowly through the nineteenth century, spreading and strengthening only in the first decades of the twentieth. In the armies of the ancien régime, soldiers were mostly young men in peak physical form, but older and sometimes even old men were also enlisted, and the garrisons were often full of women and children. It was only at the end of the eighteenth century that the military institution began its transformation into a homogenous milieu (both with respect to the sex and the age of the soldiers), when military service went from being a profession to a duty assigned to all men between the ages of twenty and twenty-five. With the law of obligatory universal conscription, adopted in France at the initiative of General Jourdan and later throughout most of Europe, the function of the soldier became a part of the life cycle: the life of the male population was thenceforth divided in two (before and after the review board, the drawing of numbers, the call to arms), and within the population of male youths, a more restricted age group formed, that of one's class of conscripts.[108]

Yet this fundamental reform in army recruitment, which contributed to defining the boundaries of youth, did not have a uniform impact, and even by the second half of the nineteenth century, not all youths had the same vision of military service. One of the main elements influencing these differences was one's relationship to one's family. For those who had been part of the working world since childhood and had already left home as adolescents, the army was just a new step in personal emancipation, whereas for the young men in school (rarely contributing to the economic life of the family and leaving the family relatively late), it was a fundamental initiation, a step between the family of birth and that formed by marriage, between economic dependence and the choice of a profession. On the threshold of the twentieth century, then, it was mainly among the more educated classes that the call to arms began to be seen as having an existential and ritual significance, and it was among these classes that, in certain cases, the battlefield came to be considered a sexual trial, sanctioning the passage to virility.

"DOING YOUTH"
IN THE VILLAGE

Daniel Fabre

At what point did the young people of the ancien régime and the nineteenth century—who were not always set apart by a distinguishing institution—abruptly assert themselves as an organized body within each local society?[1] At what point did they come into the foreground, were they called on to demonstrate, within acceptable limits, the entire range of their ways? What common, regularly occurring event offers us the best vantage point from which to observe this age group, as modern and contemporary societies define it, in the still largely dominant villages but also in most sections of the city? No doubt about it: it is the local festival, the *fête majeure.*

Every year, on a fixed day, this festival assembles the largest gathering of people from an area—residents, relatives, and those who have moved away. It doesn't involve extraordinary rituals, it doesn't last several weeks like certain carnivals; unlike large processions, it doesn't transform the entire area, but within the festival, each authority—religious and civil— each level of belonging—to the village, the province, and the nation—has its symbols. On this occasion the sexes maintain distinct roles; most of all, it is understood that this is where "youth will be youth." A formal or implicit delegation of authority gives the young people the duty and the right to act publicly, to produce a festival for everyone while making the singularity of their own status known.

Though this practice is widespread, it is not easily understood; that the festival is the temporary kingdom of youth is known but not always expressed. Indeed, each year everyone acts as if youth has to reconquer what was in fact conceded to it from the start. A look at the map showing the names of such festivals held in France at the end of the nineteenth century confirms this tension.[2] In large regions, a dominant institution seems to superimpose itself. When it is a *patronale*, a *ducasse* (dedication), a *kermesse* (church mass), a *beneisson* (benediction), or a *voto* (votive mass), the festival is under the auspices of the parish and its tutelary saint; the Breton *pardon*, the Provençal *roumavagi*, the Basque *romeria* orient the celebration toward the penitential pilgrimage. Thus it must be acknowledged that the term *fête locale*, local festival, which grew increasingly widespread in Languedoc under the Third Republic, was a move away from this long-standing religious control and an attempt to secularize the event. Yet occasionally other terms neutrally evoke the large crowds—*assemblées* and *apports*—or the merrymaking, laughter, and dancing—*riotées*,

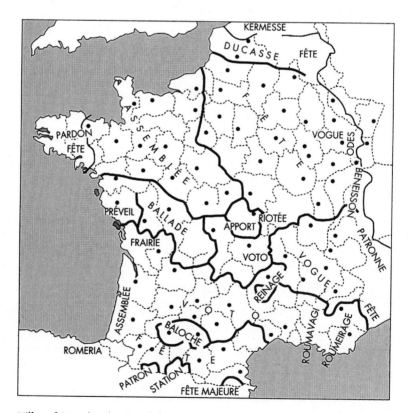

Village fairs—distribution of the most common names

ballades, and *baloches*—better suited to youthful escapades. Two names even suggest that a compromise occurred: the Angoumois *frairie* refers naturally to a brotherhood, a charitable society, but it also evokes a fraternity that only the festival can bring about; as for the *reinage* of Velay, it refers to the custom of the late Middle Ages whereby the election of a king or a queen established a separate order, most often a youthful and festive one, which the local church took great care to control by conferring the title on whoever offered the church the most candle wax, and by hosting the ceremony under its vaults.[3]

While it is true that this duality of patronage reveals two entirely contradictory manners of festival giving, it also points to their necessary connection. And thus the *fête majeure,* the ordinariness of which normally casts it into the shadows, is quite revealing of the complexity of the roles devolving to youths, who are not relegated to the margins as during carnaval. Rather, they are placed at the center of a small society that, while revealing its internal differences, attempts to merge into a single whole for the occasion. This contradiction is also present in the way in which time is treated during this festival—which is, of course, an echo chamber for every passing novelty, the stage on which the latest styles are tested and adopted: new ways of singing, dancing, dressing, tastes in music and food are avidly absorbed by the young in order to distinguish themselves from their elders—a fact already deplored in 1547 by Noël de Fail with regard to his village gathering in upper Brittany.[4] But it is also a strong repository of memory: manners and customs scattered over the course of history are mixed up, clumped together, or superimposed, one upon the other. Not that the tradition is purely cumulative; on the contrary, it is a form of expression that is continuously expanded, its language reinvented, its compromises renewed—and this is accomplished by the constant vigilance of its main actors, the young people who *form the link.* Thus it is possible, based on the quasi-contemporary observation of a village of the Languedocian Montagne Noire in the 1960s, to regressively establish the recurrent features of what we can properly call "Youth," while highlighting the changes that have marked the history of village youth over two centuries.

UNDER THE GREENERY

The Municipal Council composed of nearly every family head, has for many years voted to include in its budget a subsidy of 100,000 old francs for "the festival." It is the only official act relating to the event, and the money serves, just barely, as remuneration for "the music." Until 1940, the population level—only 200 inhabitants in winter in 1935—was such that the festival could be autonomously financed: the commune gave nothing; the collections of young people and the free services offered by innkeepers were enough to pay the musicians. This had been the custom in the Montagne Noire at least since the mid-seventeenth century. In the 1960s came a period of transition; the municipal subsidy did not eliminate the young people's levy on the cafés for gifts in kind, and the accumulated contributions safeguarded collective control. The festival was not yet an anonymous product, purchased from an entertainment company, but still emanated from the local people. The mayor consulted the youth in the choice of an orchestra; the least expensive was always booked for the three days of the dance. Neither the quality of the music nor the value of the entertainment was judged; the main thing was that the musicians be known for their spirit, their gift for "creating ambiance." Whether they came from the plains or the city, they had to inspire that instant familiarity that, even until the 1930s, greeted the local players of *bodega* (bagpipe) and *graile* (oboe).

The date for the festival has never been open to question: it is that of the parish patron, Saint Louis, August 25, in actuality the last Sunday of the month. Three weeks prior, a small fair held in a communal meadow dotted with old trees serves as a prelude. Across the road from the site of this fair are the church and the cemetery. The twenty or so cows and the several dozen sheep presented on this day are of interest only to the people who have come on foot from the *cós*, the farms dispersed around the area. Children and young people hover instead around the traveling merchants and shows. They stock up on candies, masks, false noses, and, most especially, on firecrackers of every variety. When night falls, the village has already tipped into a new time zone. The races, masks, and sounds, often furtive and broken, often left only to the kids, foreshadow the events to come. But after August 9, something changes in the air, the festival is on everyone's mind, on everyone's lips; a kind of seasonal fever takes over the local youth.

From then on, in the evenings after dinner, the young people get together to "make the ball," to build with their own hands the site of the dance, the future ephemeral heart of the region. There is in fact no ready-made location, no party hall, no central square in this mountain village scattered along the road and dispersed into hamlets; every year, it all has to be rebuilt. This construction is marked in each of its stages by some uncertainty, hesitation, a vague menace. The regularity of the custom—which in fact is never broken and which can likely be traced to the mid-eighteenth century, when the shacks of woodcutters and shepherds formed this parish around the church and its royal Saint Louis—is always accompanied by doubt and hesitation. The first question arises quickly: where will the dance take place? In principle the site moves every year, from one café to the next. No one questions the fact that the café owner "rakes it in" during the festival, for he must, in exchange, provide the majority of the meals for the musicians and for the most involved core of youths. But this business arrangement is never explicitly stated; the youths must plead their case. "This year, I'm not doing it, I lost too much two years ago," the café owner "whose turn it is" brutally announces; then the endless discussions begin. We know the inevitable outcome, since only a death during the year can dispense a café proprietor from this rewarding obligation. Nonetheless, until the very last burst of music, the youth festival will seem at risk of cancellation or a sudden halt imposed either by the adult authorities—the café owner, the mayor, who can also be threatening—or by the vagaries of the weather, which, at the end of summer, is rife with fog and storms.

This sword of Damocles is not without its effect on the behavior of the young people during the three weeks of preparation. They act with urgency, but most important, they make a point of demonstrating their discipline and hierarchy, offering constant guarantees of their seriousness. The leaders emerge automatically: they are the oldest bachelors, who are, in fact, "of the class"—conscripts awaiting military service. None is over twenty and almost all have been through school. Around them are grouped the "vacationers" whose parents rent or own houses in the village; they are not, at this time, considered secondary residents, as family attachments connect them to the area, and their integration with the local youth goes without saying. Next come the guests, relatives, or friends who are welcomed into each house during this prefestival period. The shared work quickly merges these three circles into one, which also shares the rudiments of a common language. Indeed, while some of the local young men are comfortable with the area's mother dialect—the *langue d'oc*—the high schoolers know its basics, and the outsiders quickly learn it. For all boys at this age, the language of men at work and in the cafés becomes a slang of recognition whose idiomatic expressions and interjections, from the age of fourteen on, begin to punctuate conversation in the heat of joint activity. But from the center to the periphery of this circle of youth, the possibility for initiative decreases, especially since the manual dexterity and skills required for the delicate construction operation—a real structure has to be mounted after all—belong to those from the region.

The heaviest materials are gathered by the whole group: logs and beams from the year before, stored in a hangar; heavy truck tarps loaned by the wood conveyors; the town's fire ladder, which is removed from the shed where it resides next to the hearse; whole fir trees; and cartfuls of boxwood and conifer branches levied from the national forest or, most often, from the forest of the chateau with the permission of the master—a final echo of vassal-like submissiveness on the part of youth.[5] The adults keep a discreet eye out, murmur words of advice, and pitch in only at the last minute, taking pleasure in watching the young people struggle against their clumsiness, grumbling about their lack of ability. These recriminations always mount in the fever of the final days, and this is part of the game; more than a banal stigmatizing of inexperience, they affirm the division of the festival work at a point when, out of necessity, the adults are happy to step in.

Though the location of the dance migrates every year from one café terrace to the next, its shape and appearance are strictly determined by tradition. Right from the start, one practical reason seems to prevail in arranging the space: the orchestra has to be seen and heard. A platform is built, using a tarp for a roof. The large dance floor is protected in the same way, its edges defined by a ring of tall posts, while a circle of boards nailed from one to the next forms rustic benches. The preparation of the actual dance floor does not occur until the last day; it requires several loads of sand, which are tamped down by passing the hand roller over and over them, and a top layer of sawdust, generously furnished by the carpenter. His apprentice, in fact, is one of the youths. All that remains is to illuminate the scene, no longer with Chinese lanterns, as the old people did, but with electric bulbs whose flashing colors highlight the shadows and shapes of the floor. Lights notwithstanding, however, this floor would be nothing but a boring skeleton if it weren't covered with greenery, which boys and girls mesh together for days in advance. The entrance to the dance floor, opposite the orchestra platform, is framed by two fir trees, as tall and full as possible, while the edges of the platform are softened by moss and by braided boxwood trimming. All the surfaces are covered with branches of fir, spruce, and larch, woven so tightly that no open space, no tiny hole remains. Garlands of boxwood are strung on either side of the street leading to this symbolic forest transplanted from the countryside, this thick den of greenery on top of which the girls scatter red and white paper flowers at the last moment. Even before the music strikes the ear, the scent of the different wood resins wafts from the dance floor. The woodsy covering is enough to establish another world, a kingdom of music, dance, and chivalry. In the village itself, for boys and girls to approach each other would be unthinkable; even between fiancés a public kiss would be unseemly. But this forest authorizes them a hundredfold. What gives it this quality? Its place on the calendar of rituals that punctuate the green side of the year.[6]

Everything really begins here on the Monday after Easter, which families celebrate by eating an omelette. Youths between the ages of fourteen and twenty—between their diplomas and military service, as the previous generation would say—head into the woods together, to the thick grass—always green beneath the snow—that carpets the banks of the flowing rivers. There, after sharing the assorted meats they have brought, the girls whip the eggs and the boys make a fire that is always too big, even for the large pan. This forest meal, followed by some timid conversation—the youngest are there for the first time—is a prelude to the long meadow season. The *"ramades"* and *"juncades"* of old, by which, on the eve of May 1, the boys honored and judged the girls by strewing flowers, branches or thorns before their doors, are nothing but a distant, faded memory for these young people, but "going to the meadow" remains a well-estab-lished custom. Everyone leads the cows there together often enough for penchants to be confessed amid an array of games in which every stage—drawing lots, making up teams, chasing one another, or conversing—forms a language of which desire, often unsure of itself and of its object, is the sole subject. As the leafy forest grows thick, a small island in the heart of the undulating prairies, the boys never fail to engrave on the flanks of the beeches and ash trees, with the tip of the knives they are never without, the hearts and initials that more openly reveal their prefer- ences. Most will await the festival to know if their feelings are reciprocated. And the very next day another season will begin, that of long autumn walks, the coed group reconstituted for berry and nut gathering journeys along paths that are rediscovered each year for the occasion. The dance, then, is the only moment when the tide of amorous expression is reversed, which is why so much energy goes into setting up an intensely green parcel of nature in the midst of the village, full of moss, boxwood, firs, and other conifers; in this *locus amoenus,* love must find its gestures and words.[7]

Thus the nights of preparation, when the air is filled with the pounding of hammers, the grating of saws, the shouting of orders, the squabbling and laughter of boys turned workers for the occasion, are already part of the festival. The age group begins to define itself. From the most distant hamlet or isolated farm, on foot or by bicycle, every youth hastens to arrive. Under the pretext of "working on the dance," the girls can stay out late, and in fact no mother would risk keeping her daughter away from the group entrusted with such a serious mission; a *tustet,* a small charivari outside her door, would be her just reward.[8] Fully partaking in the festival is indeed a higher calling for all the young people of the area, one that first and foremost implies lending a hand in the patient construction of the ritual site. In so doing, are they not collectively experiencing the sometimes peaceful, sometimes turbulent confrontation between youths and adults, who differentiate themselves from one another while cooperating in a paradoxical relationship of conflicted solidarity? By the last night, the "ballroom" is completed, a surprisingly harmonious and fragrant palace has taken shape; the elders come to see it, judge it "pretty," and congratulate the youths. At this point begins a time of condensed and varied events, the three intense days and nights of the festival.

WELL-TEMPERED COURTLINESS

Things are only really ready at the very last minute and even then, on Saturday afternoon, the floor still has to be finished off, some branches reattached, some defective bulbs replaced, so that one may be seen "working on the dance"; the youngest also want to put their stamp on the collective project while everyone can see them. Though the dance begins officially on Saturday night, a large family meal precedes it, and the relatives and young guests who form circles around each table give the festivities a test run. The "good houses" can be spotted from this point on: they are those overflowing with "youth," especially girls, those where each and every cousin has been called in. This is in fact the only occasion, along with weddings, when distant and slightly forgotten branches of the family are called upon, taking on new value as soon as their daughters reach dancing age. Strained and sometimes forgotten ties are rewoven. How many cousins have been unearthed through the mere power of the festival! Added to relatives are school friends, girls who are often little known to the village boys and who therefore bear the charm of "foreigners"—which is what they are called. Not that they are any freer than the local girls; the mothers watch over them as over their own daughters. Faced with this sudden influx, the houses are in an upset. The bedrooms are packed, unused rooms are occupied, boys are sent to sleep in the barns. In the village, four or five *ostals*[9] are bursting with this festivity—to their great pride and joy—the twenty others contenting themselves with the usual table companions.

At ten that night, after a "supper" with plenty to drink at the café, the musicians "strike up" the dance, which the mayor opens, his wife on his arm. The program never changes: a series of *paso-dobles* and strongly trumpeted marches, a few slow dances, popular songs for the young (including in the 1960s the very first electric guitars), then a series of old dances, mostly *javas* and waltzes, with violins and accordions. Toward midnight, for the cotillon, the orchestra picks up the rhythm, intersperses refrains of bawdy songs, and delivers a potpourri of whimsical dances— some performed crouching, back to back, with a change of partners at each strike of the band leader's broom. Paper streamers and confetti shoot clouds of color through the chaotic swirl, and the climax is reached when the male dancers take their partners by the waist and lift them as high as they can, the white corollas of their underskirts opening as the orchestra kicks up the refrain. No age group monopolizes the dancing; the young are of course the most eager, since the best must excel at all the steps, including the waltz, but the elders make it a point of honor to keep up, except with the brand-new American dances. In the early 1960s, all references to the local tradition have disappeared. No *branle*, no rondo, no bourrée; barely a carnival tune slips in. Yet these nights of dancing remain havens for the musical memories of all generations. From the Viennese waltz to the latest rock and roll, they incorporate an astonishing variety of styles, with one common feature: all are couple dances, a fact that barely subsides during the finale, when couples merge into fleeting chains, hand in hand, or hands on shoulders.

There is nonetheless a dimension to these dances that only the young fully enjoy. An orchestra implies a singer, and since, in those days, all the popular songs were French, a trendy repertoire developed from festival to festival. After the disappearance, in the 1940s, of the fair singer who was also a song peddler, before transistors and turntables became commonplace, the dance was the "medium" that ensured the uniform updating of musical tastes, launching the hits of the day. The songs one learned at festivals in nearby villages were requested and enthusiastically recognized the day of one's own festival; the young dancers hummed them, joining in on the chorus. It was the girls who were mainly concerned with picking up the popular songs, whether at dances or on the radio. They sang them on summer nights, when the small local youth group danced in the road to the sound of their own voices. The words were essential, for, despite their shorter and shorter life spans, these one-summer ditties sketched out for each "wave" of youth a complete view and perfect map of eros. Based on very simple melodies, year after year these novelty verses offered a complete catalogue of the situations of love. Like rich traditional songs, they provided words to designate and recognize intimate experiences which could only be expressed in song.[10]

On the first night, the feared—yet long-awaited—moment has finally come to put this knowledge of love to the test, for more than a site where couples meet and form,[11] the dance floor is where everyone exposes him or herself to the dangers of flirtation. Until the 1950s, a girl could not refuse an invitation to dance without setting off insults and scuffles. But it shouldn't be deduced that only boys could assert their preferences. Rather, a kind of preliminary negotiation averted friction and scandal and spared egos: every girl had her unwritten "dance card," and every boy knew which few girls he could and should ask to dance. Thus invitations piled up without a peep, since a marriageable girl "danced all the dances" and, most important, was never left on the side of the floor, open to the request of a stranger. This system diminished the effects of the great choreographic revolution of the nineteenth century, which broke up large collective dances into twosomes.[12] At those large dances, only fleeting glances and encounters allowed the fledgling couple to map out its own space, but when the duo became the rule, the fact that one was obliged to have an uninterrupted exchange reestablished the preeminence of the community of young villagers. By 1960, the cutoff was complete; even at the local festival, no collective order governed the dances, everyone had to rely on his own appeal, history, and courtly know-how, at risk of the humiliation of remaining without the anticipated partner. And only the "broom dance," in which one changes partners at random, leaves a glimmer of hope of communicating with the girl who has evaded offers all evening long.

If the dance, in its visible plenitude, no longer embodies the ideal village community, this community remains quite present on the benches all along the sides of the dance floor, where the largest space is reserved for those who are not there to dance but to watch. The palace of greenery is, in fact, fully illuminated, no corner remains in shadow; the dance in the dark suddenly commanded by the orchestra is never more than a brief intermission, a play at transgressing the rule. Visual and acoustic aggression—the "nightclub" style that would transform village dances in the 1970s—has not yet diverted these watchful eyes, ever on the alert and glued to the dance floor. Dance partners accepted, refused, or repeated are noted and evaluated; certain flirtations are considered to have matrimonial futures, judgments are pronounced on good or indecent behavior, reputations are made and destroyed. The *branles* of old, of which the rondo, single or multiple, was the perfect form, demanded everyone's participation, though the young demonstrated the energy characteristic of their age; now, however, the dance is constantly divided, the young dancing in shifting couples beneath the gaze of a motionless circle, a chattering chorus of old women, the source of all rumors, vectors of continuity and control, the multiple voice of social order.

On the first day the festival ends fairly early, shortly after two in the morning, for the big day is to come; indeed, on Sunday the highly varied rituals overlap and intertwine, requiring with particular intensity the intermediary position and mediating action of youth as a group.

BONDING SUNDAY

Early the next morning, by about eight o'clock, every house is on its feet: in preparing for mass, the real festival costume is donned. Nothing reminiscent of the old local dress—only the horse traders with their smocks and the haymakers with their caps still wear the apparel of yesteryear—but a few indications are enough to situate each individual in his or her age group. From the age of fourteen on, the boys dress like men: dark suits, white shirts with starched collars, ties, polished black shoes. The differences lie in the details: lighter fabrics, a tighter cut to the trousers, a knot in the tie that is more or less voluminous, according to the fashion that year, distinguish the young. As for the girls, they are more easily detected, as a section of the feminine color palette is reserved for them exclusively. On the death of her husband, a widow covers her hair and wears black for the rest of her life; young married women are more freely colorful; and adolescent girls wear mostly white. Thus on the Sunday morning of the festival, the girls put on new dresses—pants would be indecent in church, and suits are reserved for the women—the light-colored backgrounds of which are just barely dotted with lively splashes of small flowers or red fruits. The fashion for starched, white, overlapping petticoats, for small heels that lengthen the leg, transform them into large flowers with inverted corollas. Most prefer to go bareheaded.

The entire commune is at the nine o'clock mass: people from the village and from the hamlets and farms have climbed the hill to the church, a building entirely covered in gray slate. Though it votes Socialist, the area is quite religiously observant, but on this day the attendance in the white and pink gladioli-covered nave is exceptional. The men, packed together in the rear, form a black, compact mass; the young people, who arrive early, have access to the gallery, which overlooks the nave, above the entrance portal. The children occupy the middle ground. And way up against the balustrade, at the foot of the altar, are the clustered rows of women, heads covered with kerchiefs or scarves that indicate their age groups depending on whether they are black, white, or colored. The female singers, young and old combined, take their places in the first side chapel, along with the orchestra musicians, whom the youth have "loaned" to the church for the morning. The brasses, clarinet, electric organ, and "American jazz" guitar have come to accompany the hymns. From the profane to the sacred, the musicians in their gala attire circulate comfortably. This convergence is exceptional in every way: except for Christmas night, when he may welcome the players of old pastoral instruments, the priest makes do with the harmonium and the female chorus, but the festival authorizes, even dictates, the strangest combinations, for it is an act of social communion as much as a religious celebration.

"L'ite missa est" does not bring an end to the strict division of the sexes. After mass, women and girls push open the gates of the nearby cemetery, where they visit the dead, "tidy the tombs," and lay flowers on them; in other mountain villages, the day's mass is specifically dedicated "to the souls," who are not forgotten in the votive jubilation. In the meantime, the men, the first to leave the church, have already walked around it to conduct another memorial ceremony, forming a circle around the village monument to its war dead, a simple column at the center of a gravel square, roped off by a heavy chain. As soon as everyone is quiet, the mayor begins in a booming voice by reading the list of soldiers killed; their names are inscribed on two marble plaques, one for each World War. A veteran carrying the flag responds in echo: "Died for France." The orchestra drummer punctuates each name with a roll on his snare drum, and at the end of the litany his trumpet-playing comrade strikes up the call of the dead. The men are all there, clustered together, stiff and reflective, hands behind their backs. It's not a kind of reflex patriotism that causes them to freeze up like this, in front of the monument and flag, but true emotion at hearing the given and family names they still bear, awakening family traditions and shared memories with each of them. This is also the moment when the title "conscript," with which the eldest still flatter the young men of the festival, takes on its fullest meaning. This male population, alive and dead, is always "classified" vis-à-vis war, or at least vis-à-vis the position of soldier or combattant, an important status that has formed the link between the village and the nation ever since the French Revolution.[13] When the series of names comes to a close, the mayor and the eldest veteran strew flowers at the foot of the column. Soon the youth brighten up again.

Boys and girls amble down the road together along poplar-lined meadows and find themselves on the leafy dance floor, where the orchestra strikes up a few measures of accordion "aperitif" dances, with which everyone shakes off the weight of the somber morning. Then the "table tour" begins. Atop a cart pulled by a tractor or on the open-topped bed of a van, its wheels hidden under an interlacing of greenery and flowers, are perched the musicians, a few young ringleaders, and three or four girls. This miniature ball hits the road, escorted by a turbulent train, making its way from house to house. They arrive as one family is sitting down to a meal; the host invites the youths inside. In the wicker basket presented to him, he deposits a small monetary offering, proposing drinks for the boys while the girls swiftly pin small paper flowers on lapels and blouses. The musicians remain on the threshold and decline the invitation: the tour is long and at each stop they must play the tunes requested of them. Such are the terms of the deal: money and sweet wine for a wealth of music. The range of melodies is poor but meaningful: an old song on which everyone, even the elders, can join in, and here and there the national anthem or the *Internationale*, depending on the political tendencies of the most active family heads. Marked by these stops, with each host endeavoring to retain the visitors as long as possible, the road ahead stretches on. At about four in the afternoon, when the tour reaches the *còs*, the small distant farms, snatches of music float in the air, reaching the village intermittently, designating its outer limits. Yet the melody is increasingly halting, hesitant; true, the musicians have not betrayed their principle, they have drunk nothing in the homes, but bottles have nonetheless magically emerged from sacks, full of the irresistible drink of the festivals of lower Languedoc, the *carthagène*, an unfermented wine muted with alcohol, intoxicating in its sweetness. It is not unheard of for the troop of almsmen to return drunk, or for the outraged girls to abandon them midway. Every year vows are taken to remain sober, yet no one pays attention: the obligation to drink is always strong, and youth clings to its "table tour" as an inviolable right, a custom whose form it perpetuates, whose limits it guarantees. By inviting all the households to share the cost of the festival, it ensures collective participation yet also establishes itself as more of a predatory than a productive age group. Whatever is collected goes for the music, banquets, and drinks; that it be spent immediately is the only rule. Moreover, the youths are free to circulate among social classes—another quality of their special status—from the poor to the rich, from "royalists" to "communists," from landowners to sharecroppers, thereby giving concrete form to communal accord; youth alone, during the festival, possesses such power.

The group passes throughout the area, from table to table, hence the tour's name. It visits all houses except those in mourning that year, which keep their shutters closed, alone and silent; approaching these homes, the

noisy cortege grows quiet. But everywhere else, it barges in, interrupting
the gatherings of relatives and young friends. The big Sunday meal is a
delicate web of contradictions, an intentional assemblage of ever-updated
contrasts. On the one hand, "tradition," backed by the homemakers, determines the menu with unchanging precision. As an appetizer, the assorted
cured meats—*charcuterie*—are abundant, making, in fact, their last appearance of the year: after the summer, the fair, and the festival, the pork chest
will be empty. A lamb will also be killed and served roasted, along with
the obligatory farmyard poultry. Since on this crest of the Montagne Noire
garden vegetation comes in late, this is the day when the beans and peas
are first tasted. A sugary pale-yellow custard, accompanied by cookies,
brings the repast to a sweet close. From the remains of the pig to the baby
vegetables and the just-weaned spring lamb, this meal is on the cusp of the
main food calendars. Furthermore, it realizes an ideal, with the abundant
and fine fruits of the vine as signs of a perfect self-sufficiency. The indigenous nature of the local festival is thus affirmed by the home-grown
components of this exceptional meal. Yet it is also considered good form
to serve the first grapes of the plain, which instantly projects us into a
different arena, a world familiar to boys and girls from the eighteenth
century until the 1930s, who assembled into *cólas,* work teams, and descended to harvest and gather grapes in the low country,[14] returning with
wine and fruit for the festival. Today people simply buy them in Carcas-
sonne or Narbonne, but this foreign element has assumed its own solid
place on the Saint Louis menu. This coexistence of the local and the
foreign that runs throughout the festival (consider the music and dance) is
reflected at mealtime, thanks to the increasing mobility of the adolescent
girls. Since the 1920s, many have chosen to attend several years of "extra
courses," or at least "homemaking school," after earning their grade school
certificates. They return with new culinary knowledge that, though never
overturning the core of the menu, quickly becomes integrated into its
surroundings. Thus egg-mimosas are introduced as appetizers, madeleines
and pound cakes as dessert. In the 1970s, these girls would encourage the
adoption of the first frozen products, which are not used as replacements

for anything and never modify the predictable succession of meats; the Malagasy shrimp and frozen Italian cakes, however, add strong notes of exoticism. Thus the large festival meal, which "has always" united the temporal rhythms of local production, now includes marked references to two distinct worlds: one close, the other distant, one domestic, the other foreign. Fertile contradictions to which the young girls have given discreet but powerful impetus.

Over the course of this Sunday, ambling from one place to the next—house, church, cemetery, monument—by way of the village's roads and paths, the festival reveals its foundations better than ever. It is not the flat reflection of a social world, nor its illusory transfiguration; rather, at every moment, it points up differences and works to overcome them. A mosaic of rituals is what makes the "community" of the village exist; it is never more than will and representation.[15] On this day-long stage, youth is the intermediary; a transitive age par excellence, it is the perpetual bonding agent. While allowing each house to demonstrate its unique qualities, youth's table tour gathers them into a whole. It is present at religious and civic ceremonies, where "its" musicians are indispensable actors in the solemn rituals. Moreover, at each of these sites, youth administers the encounter of the here and the elsewhere, of the old and the new. Boys and girls, each in their own way and in their own spaces, become tireless messengers of a *frairie*, of a "fraternity" that brings honor to the region. During the preliminary stage of constructing the dance floor, they reassured everyone of their capacity to complete a collective project; on this Sunday, it is the collective itself that they are invited to bring into play, to show off for all to see. The rituals are both the means and the ends of this task. Yet the young people's experience is not limited to this successful exhibition of social harmony. We saw the extent to which it was necessary to oversee the dance in order that any possible deviation would be contained. We have seen the risk that uncontrolled intoxication poses to the table tour. It is also accepted that "youth will have its way" under conditions of disorder, violence, and excess, and this excess is part of the religious festival as well—its dark side.

BOYS' NIGHT

Beginning on Saturday, but mostly on Sunday, in two cafés not far from the dance floor, another party is brewing. This one is considered more dangerous. In waves, between the series of dances, the young men come to drink beer and pastis—stronger alcohol remaining the prerogative of the barflies—and it is here, during these short breaks, that violence can erupt.

Custom has it that during the festival period the village declare its openness to visitors. The week prior to the fête, the youths have a small poster printed up locally, which they plaster all along the mountain roads. Sometimes a banner overhanging the two entrances to the village proclaims "Welcome" in big letters. Every successful festival must confirm the village's capacity to receive guests at this moment when it gathers and bonds. But in reality there are two kinds of guests. Those connected to one of the homes through a family tie or school friendship are essentially adopted; they are part of the local youth even if they are still designated by their place of origin: Paul from Mazamet, Monique from Cuxac. This network fuels the dances and love affairs and, later on, the marriages, since it is considered more desirable to marry a distant cousin than one's immediate neighbor. It is within these networks of family and friends—which extend out to the two sides of the mountain, cities included—that lasting bonds are formed.[16] Those who show up at the festival in gangs have a very different relationship with the village. These boys barge onto the dance floor, in tight formation, just to inspect the proceedings. They're not there to dance, they have no chance of inviting a local girl to the floor, but they have to be seen together and recognized before they settle in at one of the cafés. In the face of their attitude of defiance, instantly the local boys unite. Shoving and fighting matches pit the local group against the others from nearby villages. They are well acquainted with each other, they encounter one another regularly throughout the calendar of mountain festivals, but there is always a little bone of contention that revolves around some point of honor. An ambiguous remark about a local girl is enough reason for the insults to fly, and these are soon addressed to the entire population, to the village as an entity. This friction is predictable and therefore, most often, prevented. Sometimes, after a volley of abuse and a few blows, the adult men at the café, mostly woodsmen and miners, intervene. But generally the café proprietress, by her mere presence and, when necessary, her lively rejoinders, tempers the belligerent parties. She knows the boys' parents and she lets them know it; they're not really foreigners. She reigns supreme over other circles of men, whom she welcomes on other occasions—for hunting or veterans' banquets—the only woman, maternal and respected, at these male assemblies. The boys' arrogance doesn't impress her.

Other incursions, rarer and more worrisome, occur with the arrival of gangs of youths from the nearby towns and cities, gangs who no longer identify with a specific place, whose reason for being is specifically to be free of any belonging or genealogical continuity. They are there one summer, gone the next. The village fears them because they instantly break the accepted order, which assigns a place, a time, forms, and limits to any challenge. Everyone curses these battles, which instantly destroy the structure of their delicate rituals and trigger a violence that is necessarily absolute: even a vendetta is impossible to carry out against these destructive strangers, since they'll never be found again. Their raids unify the men of the commune, their guests, and their allies, but real force must also be called in. Once the police are required, which is actually quite rare, the local youths consider their festival to have gotten away from them.[17]

The looming threat, the verbal game of aggression, the after-the-fact stories are indispensable stimuli; they add spice to the festival, give the impression of running at least imaginary dangers, put everyone to the test of fear, exalt courage. Their threatened presence at the margins, and their repetition, maintain a reassuring sense of community. Violence, a force of dissolution when it truly intrudes from the outside, is an element of solidarity when it is mimed and mastered. But unusual explorations also germinate in the café at night, where the festival, through its main participants, seems to rebel against its own proclaimed values. Turning its back on unanimity, it broadens its cleavages, explores its dark side, gives the impression of undoing its own world. Far from strangers and foreigners, it cultivates an interior "estrangement,"[18] to the point of scandal.

This "divorce" is in the works while the first series of dances is still in full swing. Several young village boys, whether poor dancers or uncomfortable once the orchestra shifts to modern music, tired of being rejected, retire to the café, to the reassuring company of their elders. The older men, who made a fleeting appearance early in the dance, are gathered there in the large dining room, or around tables that are placed outside if the weather is nice. Together they drink more than usual, but it's a beautiful evening, and they talk until the end of the dance. The truth is their intoxication results less from alcohol than from words: hunting stories, of course, since Saint Louis is the opening of the season, dirty jokes, arm wrestling, and stories about the strong men of the past. As the night progresses, the attention focuses on a few figures: the inveterate drunkard who is more intoxicated than usual on this occasion but still gabby, the hardened bachelor who defends his jolly reputation better than ever, the village idiot, who gets carried away every year by the atmosphere of the party in which he plays a staring role. A circle forms around the group, a flood of questions pours in about "getting lucky," love interests, marriage plans—everyone wants to hear the anecdotes they've heard a thousand times. On this occasion a farcical spectacle takes place, played out between the clever and the simple amid a concert of insane laughter. The dialect or the deliberately burlesque mixture of French and the *langue d'oc* is unleashed at these impromptu encounters, where a few familiar marginal characters shine. In many ways, these men of all ages are enacting the reverse of the erotic display being performed on the dance floor. In the leafy loggia a certain seriousness causes most of the young dancers to stiffen somewhat—as seen in the tenseness of the boy who seeks an invitation in a glance, in the feigned indifference of the girls who are waiting. The amorous approach is a difficult art, and everyone must apply him or herself to going through the rigorously coded but well-known steps. At the café, on the other hand, these poses are mocked, the underside of courtliness is bared, and the comic gallery of failed Don Juans, which several men present embody, is on view. From the hapless innocent who will never wise up, to the inveterate skirt chaser, by way of the complacent cuckold, each one is ridiculous in his own way, reminding this closed chorus of men of the cunning of women and the transgressions of love.

While the boys' energy was occupied in hatching encounters with girls, here, outside the dance arena, night separates them—as though maleness had to forge itself separately, comfort itself, in the tavern. This goes on throughout the festival, as when the civilized "table tour" veers off in favor of the drinkers in the end, sending the girls fleeing when they aren't unceremoniously seized and thrown in the washhouse or the trough following much running, shouting, and splashing. The same thing happens during the meal on Sunday evening, which brings together the musicians and the local boys in the café's back room: obscenity rages, a far cry from the official pomp; as soon as the food reaches the table it elicits lewd comments; at dessert the youngest, who is blindfolded and made to fold and unfold napkins, finds himself before what resembles an exposed female sex organ, or else mimicking masturbation without realizing it. This behavior, which is kept fairly secret, paves the way for the wildness of Sunday night, in which only the boys of the village participate. This is when the other side of their ritual is revealed.

At about two in the morning, a strange impatience comes over the young men. They are finding the dance too long, they press the musicians to finish up, to turn out the lights. When the last guests are gone and the girls accompanied home, the night is suddenly darker and the silence absolute. The village changes hands; youth is in charge. Near the stream, at the bottom of the road that rises toward the church, they begin piling up everything that they find lying about outside. Soon a cart is next to a barrel planted with a bush, flowerpots, benches, a bicycle, gutters and drain pipes, wash tubs . . . The pile grows by the hour; the most incongruous objects are jumbled into a formless mass. To top it off, the youths risk hoisting heavy tools—a plow, for instance—into the air, up to a treetop. And then, the ultimate refinement, they switch shutters among houses: green for red, wood for metal—a silent commotion of materials and colors. The henhouses, which are placed on top of the pigpens, are carefully emptied of their eggs, and sometimes of a hen. Rabbits and ducks

are situated higher on the hierarchy of possible thefts—taking one always
has a punitive connotation; an especially difficult customer is chosen for
such treatment. In addition, on this night, a few *ostals* are given a noisier
surprise. With a running start, the boys slam the shutters, or else rhythmi-
cally pound the door using a large rock or a heavy block manipulated by
a long string. Covering the chimney with a bag, tightly plugging a drain
pipe with a rag, which then spews dishwater into the middle of the street,
lighting a sulphur-dipped wick and dropping it in the cat flap, delicately
coating a doorknob with manure—these are all part of the repertoire of
youthful farces.

These pranks are not limited to the night of the festival, but as they
are the exclusive prerogative of youth, they are concentrated, expanded,
and intensified on this evening. Only the long nights of Christmas, the
return of the conscripts and, sometimes, Bastille Day stimulate as much
symbolic aggression, which, at the very least, confirms youth's exclusive
command of the night.[19] Beneath their unbridled and improvised appearance, these practical jokes are full of meaning. First of all, they generally
establish youth's relationship to the world awaiting it. What, broadly
speaking, are the boys doing on this night? They are constructing chaos,
a spectacular albeit circumscribed chaos, mixing up objects, changing their
places—what was below is above and vice versa—and, especially, subvert-
ing the rules of ownership. Their pleasure derives from this disorder. One
need only witness the exclamations of chagrin the next morning, the
vituperation and disputes among adults faced with the confused heap—
their main concern being to separate one person's possessions from another—to measure the efficacity of this confounding gesture, this dismiss-
ing of spatial divisions and of the ordinary arrangement of objects that
attest to the power of each home. Everything is mixed up, doors are
pounded, fences broken, and barriers trampled. As for the theft, it is
entirely ritualistic, which is to say codified in its forms, its objects, and its
victims, to the point of defining a customary illegality. Like the pursuit
and the matrimonial ransom which, like it or not, accompanies every
marriage, it is a tolerated tithe. Furthermore, the young men's appropria-
tions are provisional; they apply only to immediately consumable goods,

which prohibits any personal or collective hoarding and usually elicits the goodwill of the victims. The story of the woman who unknowingly roasted a hen for a youth who had stolen it from her the day before is told as a fable; it illustrates the deep convergence, the assumption of a pre-established harmony between what is stolen and what is given. Such, in any case, is the higher principle invoked when voices are raised against the ruckus, for there is always a debate on the disorder, its limits, and its effects.[20] At this point, other dimensions of these rituals are revealed; I will discuss two of them.

The first appears when one looks closely at the choice of victims for the most serious thefts, the loudest rackets, and repeated bullying. These victims are never chosen at random. When the youths shake the door of the young widow, who dresses in black and acts devout but is known to receive the old bachelor on the sly, when they spatter rotten eggs on the spruced-up shutters of the local Emma Bovary's complacent husband, when they terrorize a group of old women, suspected of witchcraft, by whispering the name of the devil under their doors—*Grifou, Grifou!*—when they invent special tricks to torment a misanthrope, the boys are launching clandestine rumors in the night that pass through the grapevine by day. They are therefore the agents of strict social control, voices of order, persnickety defenders of common values. And their actions trigger a raucous reaction. Indeed, while the women singled out for amusing satires or cruel pursuits generally remain quiet and nurse their shame, others let their anger fly. The curmudgeon who is sent leaping from his bed by a *tustet* has a role to play in the theatrical give and take of the farce. Without his cries, his effusiveness, his chasing, there would be no more game, youth would have no partner. Yet one must know where to stop. So long as the annoyance doesn't turn to persecution, so long as the annoyed party is happy simply to brandish his rifle or even randomly shoot a few rounds in a spirit of jest, the community is within the bounds of the tolerable. Beyond that, the consensus unravels and, without turning into a violent event or a criminal affair—which is rare—a paradox in all respects unthinkable emerges: this youthful disorder against the collective order becomes the latter's supreme weapon.[21] For far from reestablishing law and bringing peace, it deepens quarrels and hardens enmities. Moreover, it scorns the value attached, increasingly in the country since the eighteenth century, to private property and private life, the recognized sphere of which spreads, encloses, and defends itself. During these nocturnal expeditions—which leave more and more traces in judicial archives—youth clashes with the progressive but irreversible passage toward an individualistic society.[22] That the festival night now incorporates most of these customs confirms, it seems, their growing limitation. Punitive harassment cannot, like the rowdiness of yesteryear, be spread throughout a season. It no longer sparks a long conflict-filled drama. Instead, it takes place within this brief time span, which is exceptional in every way and outside of which it hardly exists. On the other hand, it gains in expressivity by being included in the local holiday, the finger-pointing disorder contrasting with the conciliatory ceremonies as the night contrasts with the day.

The weakening of the boys' punitive activity has nonetheless not erased a second dimension of these rituals. As we have seen, the nocturnal wanderings, the shouting, the overturning and dislocating of things from their usual positions mark the transition of youths, who are on the threshold of the village society into which they will "settle down," while designating them as revealers of hidden and hushed-up scandals. But if we analyze them in detail, these behaviors in and of themselves form an experience that the society recognizes and designates by the mysteriously tautological idiom *"faire la jeunesse"*—"doing youth"—which applies only to boys. What is meant by this? Essentially, it is the dangerous exploration of the margins, of the boundaries that separate the distinct polarities that serve to conceptualize the world: what is untame and what is civilized, the masculine and the feminine, the living and the dead. Often as a group, but sometimes alone, youths scour these limits and return with a knowledge that transforms and matures them.[23] Let us consider, by way of example, this last division—between the living and the dead—a division that is very present in this Montagne Noire village. We have seen the extent to which the dead are associated with the daytime ceremony, but their presence is even more in demand at night. To scare the old women, for instance, the youths not only hoot the name of the devil through the cat flap, but they also invoke the dead and play ghost, spreading terror.[24] For this they even go so far as to try out death themselves, to the great displeasure of the adults, who are concerned that this exploration, which they recognize as necessary, may be without return. Yet isn't that the risk one runs by imbibing unlimited quantities of alcohol? How many, come the wee hours of the night, roll dead drunk into the ditches, a way of "doing youth" to the limit? The experience is common and accepted, except when it becomes too explicit.[25] In the course of such a night of insane intoxication, one of their own having fallen into a deep drunken sleep, the youths pretended to bury him, smack in the center of the village, erecting a cenotaph topped with a cross and a funerary inscription bearing the name and birthdate of their dearly departed, fallen on the bottle-strewn field of honor. Since they are always up the earliest, the old women are the ones to first assemble around the macabre simulacrum; with the gestures and wails of mourners, they curse these youths who dare mimic death to such a degree they would attract destiny's anger.

A rich play of echoes unifies the successive acts of this nocturnal drama. The café charade, which highlighted the failings of the erotic and matrimonial relationship, is transformed into corrective action through the farcical tricks the youth play on the offenders. But while acting as the age-old weapon of the community, youth's behavior—chaotic, insulting, dirty, and rough—sets it apart and can bring on censorship. The boundary is quickly crossed from the licit "boys will be boys" to unacceptable "hooliganism." The increasing possibility that various levels of public authority will be brought in—within the village and, especially, beyond it—presents a possibility of recourse for the victims, who can easily turn the audacious youths into fair game for the police.[26] The first act in this deliberate marginalization is, as we have seen, the separation of the girls from the boys. Even if some of them seem to participate, increasingly, in the boys' expeditions, the girls drop out of their own accord come the heart of the night, with its scatological core of obscenity, its moment of true violence, its ultimate step toward the dead. There is every reason to believe that, for the boys, this unbreachable gap marks the territory where their masculine identity is formed and confirmed. From this perspective, the festival's sequence concentrates and reverses, temporally, the normal biographical chronology. Indeed, here, each sex constructs itself separately, through its differences, without forgetting *the other*, of course, but maintaining the distance that feeds expectation and its rituals. When the time comes, courting will be a test, an attempt to enter into the common language at the heart of which boys and girls try to make the wealth of their prior experience bear fruit.[27] At the festival, the courtly approach comes first and occupies the foreground. A unique moment in the green season of the year, the dance floor in the midst of the village is the main stage, the climax of the drama. And suddenly, come night, the boys desert the floor they so patiently constructed and seem to be regressing toward their near past, emphasizing their differences in the form of aggression, a past incarnated in the village by the "simpletons," "wild boys," and "crazies" stuck in a state from which they have been unable to return.[28] This turnabout no doubt increases the dramatic intensity of the festival, as do the obstacles or reversals that are part of all great rites of passages, marriage in particular.[29] But this moment of controlled dissolution must ultimately end in the triumph of a renewed order, as embodied in the final rituals.

On the morning after this night of insanity, Monday, the village gathers, but in individual homes. The leftovers of the prior day's feast are consumed. Certain guests are already leaving to get back to work. The schedule of dances continues, but the dancers are almost all village people and their youngest guests. As if to be excused for their nocturnal escapades, the youths let the adults have their way: the old dances abound, the violin and the accordion dominate.

And then, at about five in the evening, in the oblique light of an already autumnal late afternoon, the festival makes its last stand and reweaves more tightly than ever what the eruption of darkness almost undid. The farandole attracts the youths for the last time. Hand in hand, boys and girls slip into the long chain, which snakes through the streets, alleys, and courtyards, slides between the café tables, noisily reverberates on the planks of the *ostals*. No fancy footwork here, as found in certain provincial farandoles that were reviewed and refined by masters of military dance after 1830.[30] One need only run along with the chain, marking the step with a slight hop onto the standing leg, the other leg hovering a moment in the air before setting down in turn. The movement is difficult when the pace accelerates, but the youths demonstrate an ease undiminished by the hard work of the festival. The essence of the dance lies in its speed and the unexpected meanderings of the leader, as he devises tricky places to go. Traveling from inside to out, from the private to the public, from the official to the common, the dancing line, accompanied by two musicians—on the clarinet and the snare drum—unifies the communal territory with a lively final outpouring of bodily forces. But this profligate expenditure of energy remains subject to the rhythm of the music and the step, the alternation of couples. The farandole casts the village into harmonious disorder while reconnecting with the foundations of what has been tradition since time immemorial; the only living dance in an archaic repertoire, it provokes a long shudder of collective emotion as each participant feels the immediate sensation of entering into a moving social whole, spreading into the remotest cracks in space and the unfathomable depths of time.

Once the last dance is over, when the music has died down, a few youths try to prolong the festival at all cost, kicking up a rumpus late into the night, as if to ward off the lassitude and melancholy that is creeping over them. In a series of ever more mellow evenings during the following week, the construction is completely dismantled; the "dance hall" leaves no traces. Then the vacationers leave, followed shortly thereafter by the middle school students. After the potato harvest, the labors of autumn, and the chopping of firewood, the village is ready to burrow into winter.[31]

What traces will remain for the future historian who wishes to know what occurred during these three days? Very few: an entry in the communal budget, the remnants of a poster perhaps, a brief announcement in the local paper, and, in the event of a serious incident, a newspaper account. All partial snapshots that reveal very little of the complexity of this youth-filled event. In this sense the case I have chosen to describe is exemplary, as it highlights the multiplicity of behaviors that the local festival combines. In it, youth emerges as the guardian of rituals of communal cohesion and as the main actor in its burlesque and violent dissolution. But this youthful violence is both a weapon of social control and a necessary experience in the process of transformation into a complete adult and villager. The festival period, full of sudden turnabouts, alternations, and simultaneities, scenes, concentrates these contradictory tendencies; better than any other moment, it exposes their necessary relationships.

Of course, given the confluence of factors in the early 1960s, the elements of this festival are inscribed in their own time. A comparative history of these elements—clothing and cooking, dance and music—that denote the festive metamorphosis would be welcome. We have seen the extent to which youth, since early modern times at least, has been the age of crazes and the agent of change. The groups of seasonal migrants, the young maids of bourgeois homes, the soldiers, and the middle school students have all, throughout the centuries, been magnets for the unknown, promoters of novelties, and the festival has been the time and place when new fashions have appeared par excellence. In addition, one cannot help but be struck by the force of what the village people themselves call "custom." The youths are its enthusiastic servants, for it situates them on an ongoing time line and within a society they will perpetuate. There is no doubt that the "cultivated" differences between boys and girls, and their mutual courtly conversion, are, in our three centuries of records, the source of the constant inventiveness that assures the festival's efficacy. Herein lies the profound originality of village youth. They do not have at their disposal the spectrum of outlets for young people that the cities immediately offer—or, rather, these outlets are not separate. There are no student, artisanal, or worker ways of "doing youth." The network of religious or political organizations would, in most country towns, have only a late and limited success. Despite sometimes perceptible differences in wealth and status in the village, when it comes time for the festival, there is only one "youth." This doesn't imply an immobile self-sufficiency: the Reformation, the nineteenth-century Catholic renaissance, the Republic's introduction into the village, and the militant nation have all played their roles and lent their references and languages to the festival without overturning its framework.

And yet the rupture exists, first as a general axiom—"youth must pass"—always more strongly affirmed for women, because very early on the men were snatched up by a history that, acting from the outside, changed their lives and instituted the necessary breaks. The more or less forced recruitment of the military and, most of all, universal conscription have filled this place. Even today this departure, while it inaugurates a period in which masculinity is supposed to mature, evokes the memory of earlier departures toward the battlefields and horrors of war. In May 1914, on a muddy road in Westerwald, the great photographer August Sander captured "in passing" the image of "Three peasants on their way to a dance": the rustic cane in one hand, the black hats on their heads, they make their way, stiff in their party clothes—finery on loan for the ordeal of the dance and, no doubt, the joyous chaos of the night.[32] We cannot fail to see the shadow of the massacre hovering over them, which will definitively tear them from their place, leaving only the trace of a name—a massacre that, still today for most European villagers, marks a fissure in time and reveals the tragic clause, the blood tax, the contract uniting the modern state and its youth.

CHAPTER 4

WORKER YOUTH: FROM THE WORKSHOP TO THE FACTORY

Michelle Perrot

Youth—"a word," according to Pierre Bourdieu. *Worker:* the adjective only complicates matters. For the idea of the nineteenth-century "worker youth" is difficult to grasp, so much so that one sometimes wonders if it really existed, if the very notion has any meaning. Nonetheless, adolescence and youth are concepts that were solidifying at the time, the former from the biological and moral perspective defined by Jean-Jacques Rousseau, who devoted book four of *Emile* to this puberty-driven crisis of sexual identity, "that critical moment" that must be prolonged the better to be checked. "We are born, so to speak, in two stages: the first to exist, the other to live; once for the species and once for the sex . . . Just as the roaring of the sea far precedes the tempest, this stormy evolution is announced by the murmur of budding passions: a muffled agitation warns of the approaching danger."[1] Associated with universities, with students, with democratic or national struggles, the concept of youth was taking on a more intellectual and political meaning, as brought to light by the works of Jean-Claude Caron with respect to France. Yet these two foundations—sex, studies—were lacking when it came to workers. Or rather, sex was not lacking but was fantasized as a form of worker savagery, thereby escaping the curiosity that lit upon the sex lives of middle schoolers, which became, over the course of the eighteenth century, "a public problem," according to Michel Foucault.[2]

As for the high schools and universities, bastions of bourgeois youth, workers never had access to them, relegated as they were to the preceding stage of primary education. "Worker youth" would come into its own more fully in the nineteenth century, as the contours of working-class childhood became more firmly defined, taking a clear form and mobilizing public health specialists, pedagogues, and philanthropists into battle.[3] "At least save the children," cried Montalembert. They held the key to the future, the key to the race, to industry, to the nation. *The Eight-Year-Old Worker*, by Jules Simon, caused a scandal.[4] But not the fourteen-year-old adolescent worker, for whom labor was the expected horizon. Unlike young bourgeois, young workers did not benefit from a period of latency and formation that allowed for individual social development and eventually for autonomous expression. Their precocious start in the working world absorbed their energies without giving them the rights of adults. As apprentices they had no legal status, despite persistent efforts on the part of craft and trade guilds to establish it. The "apprenticeship crisis" refers to this disorganized age group, which was apparently better handled by traditional than by industrial society. The latter recognized only individuals, or at the most, families.

More than ever, the family was the decision-making authority so far as youth was concerned. It had its own logic, which was not necessarily that of its members, a holistic more than an individualistic approach, favoring the whole over its parts. This logic applied notably to women and young people, and was a logic that the then-forming working class adopted. Its identity was founded neither on gender nor on age; on the contrary, it meant to subsume these. The working family—and class—needed its young, but it demanded of them work, obedience, and, ultimately, silence. They expressed themselves little, and when they did, their voices were repressed.

DEPICTIONS

Hence for the historian there is a problem of sources. The direct and mediated expressions of worker youth are submerged in conventional and stereotyped discourse, which neither studies nor even workers' autobiographies (to be questioned like all childhood stories) can escape. This youth was represented rather than described, and the depictions bear the mark of the social, sexual, and political anxiety that youth inspired. The nine-teenth century became afraid of its youth, and particularly of its worker youth, whose wandering, libertine behavior and rebellious spirit it feared. Three symbolic figures stand out: the apprentice, the "Apache," the young female garment worker.

The equivalent of the bourgeois middle schooler, the apprentice was represented as a rebellious adolescent who ditched his boss to run about the streets of the big city, blending into its sounds, absorbing its frustration, taking advantage of its resources, living on the fringe of legality, picking pockets, making hasty getaways, ever ready for riotous assemblies, dem-onstrations, fighting, or barricades. "The apprentice becomes a street ur-chin in Paris, he becomes the naughty boy of our big cities. He tries smoking, drinking, swearing," writes Ducpétiaux.[5] This gone to seed Gavroche-like character was the impetus for riots and disorder. The *Ga-zette des tribunaux*, "a poetic anthology of poverty and crime" (Eugène Buret, 1840),[6] contributed a great deal, with its criminal write-ups, to the glorification of the young vagabond, the ultimate romantic creation. Here is Béasse—age thirteen—before his judges:

Judge: You should sleep at home.

Béasse: Do I have a home?

Judge: You live as a perpetual vagabond?

Béasse: I work to earn my living.

Judge: What is your station in life?

Béasse: My station? First of all, I have at least thirty-six of them; second I don't work for anyone. I've been my own boss for a while now. I have my day jobs and my night jobs. By day, for instance, I hand out leaflets free to everyone that passes; I run after the coaches to carry packages when they pull up; I parade around the avenue de Neuilly; at night, I have the theaters; I open the coach doors, I sell reentry passes; I'm very busy.

Judge: You'd be better off with a position in a good house doing an appren-ticeship.

Béasse: Yeah, a good house, an apprenticeship, that's boring. And then, those gentlemen, always complaining and no freedom.

Judge: Your father doesn't need you?

Béasse: I don't have a father anymore.

Judge: And your mother?

Béasse: Nope, no parents, no friends, free and independent.

Upon hearing his sentence, two years in a reformatory, Béasse "makes an ugly face, then, recovering his good humor, remarks: 'Two years is only twenty-four months, after all. Let's go.'"[7] This text is part of a long series in which literary images and survey data are inextricably intertwined. Commented on repeatedly at the time, it was resurrected by Michel Foucault, who, in the final pages of *Discipline and Punish,* turns Béasse into one of the symbols of "popular illegality," evading the punishments then being established. Béasse, the archetype of the street kid on the edge of childhood, rejects the servitude of family and work. A counterexample is Jesus the carpenter, the "good apprentice" of patronage societies, who is the opposite in every way. He loves his parents, including his adoptive father, his workshop, his noble profession: working with wood, from which he carves his cross.

Béasse is an adolescent and a loner. The "Apache," however, a term used at the beginning of the twentieth century, is a young man, eighteen to twenty years old, who lives in the city with a group. He is a young worker from the urban, mainly Parisian peripheries; his gang or group is named for his neighborhood, and he is in conflict with his family. He rejects salaried work and his parents' proletarian situation, as well as being "down and out." Factories and poverty are his nightmare; he has unfulfilled desires for consumption. He likes to wander, to stroll the large boulevards; an outsider, hailing from the suburbs, he wants to be in the heart of the city. He is well dressed in a silk scarf and a cap and, most important, well shod. An airy elegance causes him to be labeled effeminate by the workers from the city's outskirts. He is always ready to hop into an automobile, a car being the supreme ambition. The Apache dreams of outings, friends, and love. He likes dancing and girls. In Apache gangs, the status of women is ambiguous, both free—they'll gladly switch men if they are no longer satisfied—and subjugated. The men fight for the women, the women sell themselves for the men—who act partly as pimps. Money counts, but not money alone. Attraction plays a large part in the formation of couples. The Apache is sentimental, a dandy who knows the ropes, has a sense of honor, and a taste for distinction. He doesn't resign himself to anything. He wants to be someone, see his name in the papers. An instinctual anarchist, he considers theft to be fair restitution and practices "individual recovery" on the bourgeois, or "suckers," who fall into his hands. Spending time in the prison of Fresnes, the great Parisian penitentiary that was inaugurated in 1898, is practically a rite of initiation. Criminologists scrutinized the graffiti on the walls, which the Apaches decorated with pierced hearts inscribed with the names of their lovers and with vengeful "Kill the Pigs" slogans.

The Apache's very name developed out of a news item and the press that featured him. He was born in 1902 with the trial of Manda versus Lecca over a bloody battle for a girl, Casque d'or. "This trial is a trial of Apaches," an obscure court clerk reportedly exclaimed during the interrogation of a young "terror." In any case, youth related to this Indian image, peddled by their childhood books, and Apache gangs flourished. The press seized on their exploits. By grouping a wide variety of misdeeds attributed to youths on the front page and under a single heading, "Paris Apache," newspapers such as *Le Journal* and especially *Le Matin*—Parisian dailies with circulations of over one million—built up the Apache myth and condensed for the social imagination an emblem of collective fear, which worked its way into the security-seeking mentality then at its inception. The alleged resurgence of juvenile delinquency is a central theme in critiques targeting the "crisis in punishment," attributed to lax public opinion and overindulgent judges. The Apaches were used as an argument by those who were against abolishing the death penalty, an idea proposed by radicals and socialists in the great 1908 Chamber of Deputies debate. It was claimed that the Apaches, a term by then synonymous with hooligans or ruffians, understood only physical force, that corporal punishment put them in line and humiliated them. Doctor Lejeune asked the question, Must Apaches be whipped? and responded in the affirmative. That young people related to this identity is another matter that signals the beginning of a group consciousness. We will return to this. But it is important to emphasize the role of the media—in this case the press, which was in its golden age—in the creation of public perceptions.[8]

Young working girls were considered first and foremost as bodies, a combination of sweetness and debauchery. The "little garment worker" kindled the sensual daydreams of students and old men alike. Romanticism idealized the discreet and obedient *grisette*—the young gray-clad milliner—the ideal companion for the student, whose house she would keep in exchange for a more delicate love life than she would find elsewhere. This at least is how the golden legend of the Latin Quarter had it, which probably overestimated the students' attentiveness.[9] A monument to the *grisette*, erected during the Third Republic near Montholon Square, would perpetuate this nostalgic vision for a time. The vulgar materialism of the Second Empire spoke only of the semi-prostitute *lorettes*—women of easy virtue. The garment workshops, with their interminable late nights—like any site where women are among themselves—excited many an imagination: What do they do, what do they say, these girls whose sewing machines heat their wombs? (according to the doctors). Toward the end of the century, these workers were alleged to consume drugs, which allowed them "to hold up"; the morphine users experienced an artificial paradise.[10] Artificial flower makers and feather dressers suggested the caress of rustling finery; embroiderers and lacemakers, the softness of underclothes. Upon contact with water and linen, washerwomen and ironers—favorite impressionist subjects—kindled desire. In the streets, milliners and shop girls, happy, elegant "errand girls," were followed. What a boon this free circulation of such attractive working-class girls was for chasing and flirting in a stilted society! And what luck for the poet to meet a girl who was poor and pure—Martha, in the case of Rainer Maria Rilke—in search of the ineffable, wishing to go dancing on the town, "always," as she would say, "with the premonition that it would be for something far greater than the ball."[11] Eroticized or sublimated, the image of the young working girl was shot through with every fantasy—exaggerated fantasies, subsuming women's bodies—and fragmented into a thousand pieces, unable to be grasped. But she remained anchored to sex, while the image of her companion, the young working man, evolving toward a more definite delinquency, called for more firm intervention. Youth as a whole must be saved.

SOURCES

These three depictions underlie the sources at our disposal. While the novel of apprenticeship was developing, and in particular the bourgeois novel focusing on sentimental education, literature, though teeming with poor children, paid little heed to young workers.[12] Those in Zola's novels are hot-blooded; they make love and strike like vigorous young animals, as seen by Mouquette and Jeanlin in *Germinal* (1885). Studies have more to say, due to the concern aroused by the alarming observations connected with conscription. From the Restoration on, the statistics compiled by examination boards show high rates of exemption for shortness, bone deformation, rickets, scrofula (in fact tuberculosis), eye problems, and so on. Generally, they highlight the poor physical state of twenty-year-olds. Public health specialists, such as Villermé and Ducpétiaux, or anti-industrialists, such as Villeneuve-Bargement, noting the dark spots formed by the industrial districts in a first anthropological mapping, attempted to establish a connection between factory work and the degradation of the body. The work of Jean-Paul Aron and Emmanuel Le Roy Ladurie have greatly nuanced this picture, without invalidating it entirely,[13] while William Coleman and especially Colin Heywood have argued against it.[14] They do not believe it possible to claim a clear correlation between industry and physical deficiency or mortality, but rather to note overall ill health. The bodies and souls of young workers became special objects of investigation. They were the target of the first parliamentary studies in England, the *Blue Papers*—a prime source for Marx in book I of *Das Capital*—and of French studies: the major investigation by Louis-René Villermé, published in 1840,[15] was predicated on the need to spare working class *children* in order to save the race. The 1845 work by eminent philanthropist and Belgian statesman Edouard Ducpétiaux, *De la condition physique et morale des jeunes ouvriers et des moyens de l'améliorer* [On the Physical and Moral

Condition of Young Workers and on Ways of Improving It],[16] takes stock of the question. A wealth of information and an important bibliographic source, it indicates the intensity of the research effort into the situation of youth, which was commensurate with the anxiety it engendered. But it also shows the perplexity of investigators, who were conscious of being unable to truly pin down their subject. "We will often be obliged to combine in our information young workers with adult workers: the confusion of sexes and ages in the workshops must bring about a corresponding confusion in customs," wrote Ducpétiaux (vol. 1, p. 199). In reality, researchers were mainly concerned with protecting working youth and setting limits on their exploitation, which was on the rise rather than on the decline. The hesitation as to the boundaries, or the absence of such, is a good illustration of the difficulty of conceptualizing this age of life called youth, much less the working segment within it.

As for workers' autobiographies, they number a few dozen in France, many more in England or Germany.[17] Stories of apprenticeships have a significant place among them, varying according to religious cultures and moral and political traditions. The attention granted religion or private life was always considerable in England, as well as in Germany, where the childhood story is often a dramatic description of poverty. French stories are more political, closed to intimate concerns—not to mention sexuality—and rather optimistic. Thus for Norbert Truquin, the memory of his rootless and abused childhood was accompanied by the happy memory of freedom.[18] Very strongly marked by the traditions of citizenship and the worker movement, these French stories were most often voluntarist and selective testimonies that sought to be exemplary and meaningful. Hence their relative equanimity. Rather than describing daily life, they sought to relate a process of integration, whether into work, the city, or the worker movement. From *Mémoires d'un compagnon* by Agricol Perdiguier (1855), to *Fils du peuple* (1937) by Maurice Thorez, the collective was granted more importance than the individual, concern for others more than concern for oneself. Childhood was more developed than the later period of youth, because it furnished material for family portraits. Youth was mainly perceived as an initiation to work and a coming into awareness. The social aspects of youth, and especially sexuality, are not mentioned. Modesty reigns, the body is nonexistent.

Finally, stories by women are very rare and were late to appear. They dwell more on private mishaps or the expression of personal dreams, as we see in the writings of Jeanne Bouvier. We are still miles away from the marvelous autobiographical "novel" by Lise Vanderwielen, *Lise du Plat Pays* (1983), which finally gave the *I* full rights to express itself (but in the third person!).

On the whole, the male stories obeyed the convictions of the adult age in which they were written: youth should be a time of apprenticeship, and its success consists in realizing this. In other words, they speak of discipline far more than of revolt, or if revolt is mentioned, it is collective revolt. An exception to this is found in the anarchist autobiographies, which are rare and were written considerably later, and which valorize youth as an age of resistance and refusal, in the manner of Rimbaud or Kropotkin. René Michaud's *J'avais vingt ans* (I Was Twenty Years Old, 1967) is a good example of this. An adolescent from the Cité Jeanne d'Arc, a migrant haven in Paris (thirteenth arrondissement) at the turn of the century, he learned the trade of shoemaking at countless "shops": "It was not yet the era of security, of rootedness," he writes. "To many youths of my time, the notion of seniority was appalling. For us, the old-timers were a pack of fainthearted mediocrities: the boss's groveling dogs."[19] Michaud is representative of the Belle Epoque libertarian culture that Georges Naval (*Travaux*, 1945) or, more indirectly, Céline (*Journey to the End of the Night*, 1932), expounded on. The very title of Michaud's book is significant: age is waved like a banner. The age of twenty may not be the most beautiful time of life, but it is an irreplaceable moment, to be lived intensely. An awareness of youth is expressed here that is a prelude, an accompaniment to its seizing of autonomy. But Michaud's story no doubt bears witness as much to the moment it was written as to the Belle Epoque itself.

Thus depictions structure reality as much as they express it, and it would be pointless to contrast one with the other. They say something "true" about youth while amplifying and distorting it. This constant problem for the historian, who is dependent on the words of the past, is exacerbated when it comes to marginal or marginalized groups—the poor, women, and youth—who are imagined, often with fear and trembling, more than they are really understood.

With these words of warning in mind—which are not just pro forma—let us attempt to move on.

THE BOUNDARIES OF WORKER YOUTH

The fluidity of working-class youth, the absence of well-defined boundaries with respect to childhood, and later to adulthood, poses a major difficulty. On top of the customary boundaries, more precise but necessarily changeable legal definitions were superimposed. Nonetheless, they map out a territory that was increasingly distinct from childhood.

To begin with, the First Communion, despite a de-Christianization that varied according to the region and milieux, and an equally variable worker indifference, remained a quasi-universal rite of passage, the persistence of which, even in areas that were fairly nonreligious, has been emphasized by Pierre Pierrard.[20] It was a matter of propriety and respectability to which mothers were particularly attentive.[21] Twelve was the most common age for boys; it was closer to eleven for girls. The First Communion generally marked a farewell to the Church, at least for the boys: "Before, we went to vespers with the women; after, we went to the tavern with the men."[22] According to a priest in Pas-de-Calais, "for many children, the First Communion is the emancipation proclamation, the beginning of young manhood."[23] The cutoff was far less clean for the girls, for whom, in the second half of the nineteenth century, the white dress of the communicant foreshadowed that of the bride. Lise Vanderwielen remembers how moved she was to "see myself all in white in the mirror."[24]

The First Communion coincided increasingly with the start of an apprenticeship; this was why many parents sought to make it as early as possible. In the first half of the century, many children were already working, but in the second half, with the help of schooling, "placement" occurred after the First Communion. The First Communion garments— an investment whose longevity was limited by the growth of the adolescent—helped make a good impression on the workshop master or at the hiring office when the applicant was presented there by his mother (mothers often accompanied their sons to this appointment). At the age of eleven, and the day after her Communion, for which she had spent a year preparing at a religious boarding school, Jeanne Bouvier began work at a Lyons silk mill. In the Cevennes, girls automatically replaced their mothers at the factory after this ceremony.[25]

At the end of the century, the grade school certificate was added to or substituted for the First Communion, because 1882 legal provisions had made it obligatory.[26] Cheating became increasingly difficult, especially after the work laws of 1874 and 1892, and given the visits by work inspectors, who had become a genuine "corps."[27] In 1876, 26 percent of adolescents between twelve and fifteen had the certificate, 72 percent had it in 1888, and 80 percent had it in 1891—not that we can presume to know their true level of education. In fact, the law of 1892 set the legal working age at thirteen in order to coordinate academic requirements and factory structures. The certificate thereby became for young workers what the high school degree was to their middle-class counterparts: "the obstacle and the standard."[28] Their childhood ended at thirteen. Thus the Ferry laws succeeded in removing childhood from the industrial sphere, at least so far as major industry was concerned, which was the only area truly inspected. In 1876 the under-twelve category constituted 6.5 percent of those inspected; in 1888, only 1.1 percent.[29]

Did the young worker then enter full-fledged adulthood? Absolutely not. He required protection and oversight. In terms of protection, according to the law of 1841 it was illegal to make those under the age of sixteen work on Sundays or more than twelve hours a day. The law of 1892 forbid those under the age of eighteen from working at night or descending to the bottom of mines, and limited the workday of those under sixteen to ten hours. After sixteen, adult rules applied. A young worker category was thereby created—from twelve to sixteen, or from thirteen to eighteen—that corresponded to adolescence, the biological perception of which was becoming more refined. Indeed, these measures were taken in the name of "unfinished growth," of lesser resistance to fatigue.

As for oversight, it varied according to the customs and laws. Great Britain emancipated its young workers earlier, if we are to believe Ducpétiaux. At the age of fourteen, families ceased treating them as children: "they no longer receive corporal punishment" and are allowed to keep a portion of their salaries. "Often they pay for their room, board and clothing themselves. They arrange their own work commitments without an intermediary, and become free agents, in the full sense of the word."[30] In France, an authoritarian country, the break came later, with the family and the state demonstrating a same distrust of youth. In principle, according to a study in 1840, a young worker could "contract" at the age of fifteen "with the consent of those on whom he depends."[31] In reality parents were reticent, particularly opposing the departure of the young, who were invited, even forced, to turn in their proceeds. The story of the youth record book illustrates this resistance.

The law of 1841 stipulated that, until the age of sixteen, this record book be entrusted to the father, and that afterward it be transferred to the adolescent, in what was the beginning of relative economic independence. This fact was regretted by the author of a monograph, *Les ouvriers des deux mondes* (school of Le Play), regarding the weavers of Sainte-Marieaux-Mines (Vosges): "Generally, the child of sixteen, armed with his own book, treats his parents as equals, and is welcome at their table only in exchange for a boarding fee, the price of which he lowers as much as possible in order to devote more money to his pleasures." The author recommends delaying until eighteen the transfer of the personal record book: "In Paris, in the big cities, in the factories, we would have fewer deserters of rural life."[32] His wishes would be granted by the Republic, which was highly respectful of the father's prerogatives.

The record book, which was eliminated for adults in 1890, was perpetuated for minors and even rendered obligatory until the age of eighteen. Generally, the Third Republic tended to raise the legal age in all areas. In 1906, it was raised to eighteen in penal matters, with the result that young prostitutes who wanted their freedom were forced to remain in the correctional houses of the Good Shepherd; this led to incidents and revolts.

As for families, they used the record book as a means of exerting pressure, as Jean-Baptiste Dumay recounts. An apprentice at Creusot at the time, and in conflict with the management, Dumay had a hard time obtaining his family's permission to leave. "Since I was still a minor, according to the laws in effect at the time, I needed the consent of my parents for the mayor to stamp my work book, which was a kind of domestic passport without which a worker couldn't hit the road . . . They hesitated several days but ended up yielding after an altercation I had with them over a romantic affair, which came about on top of my differences with the Creusot management."[33] This was in 1860 and he was eighteen years old.

A period of relative freedom then began for Dumay, or in any case one of great mobility, a situation we find in other biographies as well, at least in those of men. For girls, it could be the opposite; everything depended on the presence and vigilance of the family and its moral code. In any case, two age brackets formed. The first, from twelve or thirteen to sixteen or eighteen, corresponded to adolescence; the second to "youth" in the strict sense. The first was constrained and controlled; the second more open, if not happier. The latter was considered a dangerous period by moralists, who feared nothing so much as the circulation of the working-class young.

As for the end of youth, it was an even more fluid and essentially more personal matter, depending for each individual on the age of marriage— the point of no return. The rituals of the past persisted, such as the acceptance of the aspirant into the ranks of the *compagnonnage,* or trade guild, which Agricol Perdiguier, its champion, wanted to see restored. He himself experienced this moment as a sacred initiation, humbly progressing through the stages of a hierarchy to which the elders held the key. "It seemed to me that I was still too awkward to obtain such high favor . . . I was timid, too lacking in confidence, and I needed the elders to embolden me so I could rise in the hierarchy of the guild." At nineteen, he was accepted as a member and endowed with the badges of the first rung: a cane, blue and white ribbons, and "a very sweet, very flattering, difficult-to-carry new name": Avignonais-the-Virtuous.[34] Three years later, he was initiated to the third order and became a "dignitary": "I wore the blue scarf in place of the white and, in addition, an extra spike in my bouquet." He nonetheless wrangled with an "old man" who reproached him for his youth "and who couldn't understand how a very young man could have greater authority than he."[35] He won out, however, and undertook to reform his society. When he returned to his hometown, in Morières, near Avignon, after four and a half years of touring, he was a full member at age twenty-two years and nine months. "I am returning to the village, planning never to leave it again, never to travel, to settle down, get married, live, and die there."[36] Youth is over, in due and proper form.

But such rites of passage grew increasingly rare as the guilds fell into decay and became obsolete, their hierarchical structures and age scale no longer accepted by the young workers. Conversely, youths could not escape conscription and an appearance before the examinations board, instituted in 1818.[37] Young men who turned twenty that year were assembled at the main gathering center of their canton for the random drawing of their numbers. The examination board then examined them as a function of this number, in ascending order, to verify whether they were "good for service" or not, and it continued its examinations until a contingent of a predetermined size was attained. Thus, a high number was "a good number." Until 1889, when military service became obligatory for everyone (with disputed exemptions), the wealthy could buy their way out. Most young workers aspired to be exempted by the examination board, since military service was long (seven years at the start of the nineteenth century!) and unpopular. But they also feared being seen naked, being judged short, deformed, or in ill health. This close physical examination was difficult and a certain dishonor progressively became attached to an exemption, which could dissuade girls from marrying a man.

Conscription tended to unify an age group—one was from "class X"—and to create a feeling of belonging, the start of a generational awareness. Increasingly it was accompanied by banquets, on the model of those of musical societies,[38] with eating, drinking, and singing of patriotic or uplifting songs. Tipsy, the merry conscripts roamed the countryside, brandishing their flags and metal badges, singing, making noise, often ending their boyhood in a brothel; less frequently, they brought the "girls of the class" along. Van Gennep and Michel Bozon have described this rite of passage, which replaced the youth festivals then fallen by the wayside, notably during the second half of the nineteenth century.[39] Yet the general public was less than appreciative of these manifestations, which were synonymous with disorder and obscenity, the public nature of which was condemned by Victorian society. "Incidents" often occurred—signs of a marginalization of youth, which had lost its status, its traditional role as festival organizer, and the right to its own merrymaking.

In any case, for young men military service was a final stage, the passage out of youth. Aside from school, the army was the main disciplinary institution, the only outlet for "difficult youths." Young delinquents were in fact pushed to enlist; at the end of the century, Félix Voisin, a philanthropist and penitentiary administrator, even created a fund to provide for this. This is why military service inspired so much animosity and a great deal of absenteeism (more than 124,000 absentees between 1889 and 1914)—"a sure sign of the awareness youth is beginning to have of itself," writes Yolande Cohen[40]—as well as a vague antimilitarism of which young anarchists became the representatives and propagandists early in the century, supported by direct-action trade unionism. This rather exceptional form of youth awareness as such was not specifically worker based. The war would sweep through it, striking its terrible blows.

For girls, there was no rite of passage as clear-cut, nor as widespread, as conscription, but there were local initiatives. Just as the young peasants of Minot (Burgundy) spent their fifteenth winter with the seamstress,[41] there existed, here and there, *fêtes de la Rosière*, festivals at which a maiden was awarded a wreath of roses by her village for her virtuous conduct, and later "beauty queen" festivals, celebrating pretty and virtuous young girls. There was nothing specifically for working girls or which marked the end of their youth. We do have one example, however, of a revived ritual: the festival of the Catherinettes, for unmarried woman of age twenty-five and over, the evolution and ambiguities of which have been analyzed by Catherine Monjaret.[42] Descended from the ancien régime and the festival for unmarried girls, in the second half of the nineteenth century the festival of the Catherinettes became the festival of young working girls in the Parisian couture industry. A lively celebration during the Belle Epoque, it became even more so during the 1920s and 1930s, when dressmakers' assistants left their workshops to take to the street, under the disapproving eye of right-minded observers. Connected to the celebration of one's twenty-fifth birthday, it was not a rite of passage properly speaking but rather a warning bell, a way of warding off celibacy. It had a strong sexual connotation, and its often caustic nature signaled that, in any case, youth was over.

The end of youth meant settling down, getting married, forming a new couple; this is the only way to leave one's family, to become emotionally and economically independent. It was a moment that working class families delayed as long as possible, judging by the relatively advanced ages of brides and bridegrooms, a slight drop in age during the nineteenth century notwithstanding (from 28.7 years of age in 1821–1825 to 25.2 years in 1901–1905 for men, and from 26.1 to 24.1 years for women).[43]

Ultimately, between an abbreviated childhood—despite increased schooling—and a late marriage, working class youth was long.

THE PRESENCE OF THE FAMILY

In the nineteenth century, the family was, as we know,[44] the primary regulating authority of a society atomized in principle and hostile to any form of intermediary organization. "Between the State and individuals, there should be only the void," said the revolutionary Amar. At the meeting point between the public and the private, the two "spheres" that also governed sexual roles, lay the family.

The working-class world partook of this order. The family, its basic structure, governed marriages, reproduction, apprenticeships, plans for the future, imposing its global designs on the individual wishes of its members, particularly its young and female members. For the working-class family was patriarchal; its obedience to the father was reinforced by the Civil Code, which considered this authority legitimate. Proudhon, the theoretician of anarchy who inspired French trade unionism, was also the most enthusiastic partisan of the patriarchal family. Here as elsewhere, the father represented organizing rationality. Agricol Perdiguier dreamed of being a farmer; since his two elder brothers preferred to work the land, he was forced to return to his father's workshop. His father decided he would be a cabinetmaker: "He was the master, I obeyed."

If the law supported the working-class family, economic evolutions reinforced it, contrary to an apocalyptic vision of industrialization, one that has been considerably nuanced by historiography since the 1960s. In particular, historiography has emphasized the major role of proto-industrialization, the rural and village mobilization of energies within the domestic system, which also brought about the transformation of peasants into workers. The family was the base for the start of industrial work, for which home weaving was the model. Supervised by the father, the wife and children worked, each at his own task and in his own place, around the heavy loom. Depending on the number of children, there might be several looms; rural industry encouraged fecundity.[45] While home weaving succumbed to mechanization early on in Great Britain, the same was not true in France, a land of slower and more gentle industrialization; it continued until the midnineteenth century, and even beyond, as we see in the Cambrésis of Grandma Santerre, whose life story was compiled by Serge Grafteaux.[46]

Artisanal industry, which we mustn't forget remained the primary setting for workers in the nineteenth century, firmly maintained the family dimension, clinging to the workshop, the home workshop especially, as an anchor. The ribbon manufacturers of Saint-Etienne, an example of worker autonomy noted by Kropotkine,[47] have used electricity to maintain themselves to our day, while becoming female-dominated.[48] In this family workshop, where dwelling and workplace are combined, birth rank determines the children's futures, the main goal being to pursue the profession. Whether boy or girl—here it's all the same—the eldest will be placed "at the helm," while the younger ones may pursue their education. If the eldest, turned "company president," is a girl, she is likely to remain single. "I was forced into it," one of these former workshop directors told the historian who was interviewing her sixty years later, confessing a lack of vocation she would never have dared mention at the time, so strongly did family discipline govern lives, with its focus on the structure of the trade.

The inheritance that working-class families passed down was the trade, or at the very least the job, the only thing that could be transmitted. The Revolution having abolished corporative privileges (with the Allarde decree), various methods were employed. In the case of trades that were connected to a region, for instance, a "technological inbreeding"[49] occurred that was highly attuned to technological changes. The ribbon manufacturers of Saint-Etienne are but one example; the complete list would be long: the wool shearers of Sedan, the glove makers of Grenoble, the cabinetmakers of Faubourg Saint-Antoine (Paris), the cutlers of Thiers, the porcelain manufacturers of Nevers, and so on. In these cases, the family exercised total control, both over the jobs and the skills. In most cases, however, families and jobs were more dissociated. In the case of manufacturing, workers sought at least to regulate apprenticeships, in number and in quality, preferentially recruiting their own children, to whom they taught the "knacks" and trade secrets. But for this they needed the complicity of the employers. In Marseilles, the tanners succeeded in reinforcing the hereditary nature of the trade, with 9 percent of tanners being tanners' sons in 1820 and 45 percent by the midnineteenth century.[50] In Berry, the industrialists gave preference to the sons of workers. In the porcelain industry, where the training period was considered to be five years long, apprentices used their work breaks to good end. During these "special moments, they tried their hand in turn, followed out of the corners of their eyes by fellow workers."[51] The assistant decorators were carefully selected by the workers themselves, but they were "all sons of workers."[52] In the blast furnaces, the children were first servants, then, at about the age of twelve, hodmen for the refiners. For a long time they were without fixed jobs and without any certainty of getting one, but no one contested the hierarchy and the preference shown to family members for advancement in the field.[53] The situation was the same in glassworks, where Eugène Saulnier was a glassmaker like his father,[54] in construction, where Martin Nadaud was a mason boy alongside his father, and in the stone quarries. In Montataire, "the father puts his young sons to work. The eldest son teaches the trade to his younger brother, the uncle to the nephew, and so on. Stone cutting is thus learned, so to speak, in the home."[55] The employers gladly accepted these practices, which spared them having to subsidize expensive apprenticeships. At the same time, they became increasingly fussy about the modes of production, which they intended to control. Conflicts grew over "worker demands." Under the Restoration, frequent coalitions opposed workers and paper manufacturers, seeking to break the monopoly on hiring. In the Lyons area between 1890 and 1914, the question of the limitation of the number of apprentices was at the heart of many strikes, which generally failed.[56] To overcome worker resistance and break the old alliance between families and trades, employers introduced new machines, and thereby a new organization of work, one that was simplified and more transparent, and which dispelled the "secrets." This was what happened in glassworks, the final bastion of these practices and theater of such battles. Ultimately, the glassworkers lost, after which, the trade having lost its privileges and appeal, parents began discouraging their children from entering it. To replace them, industrialists appealed to public assistance children, who were thus doubly "bastards"—their nickname—and doubly exploited.[57] Without family protection, conditions could take a turn for the worse for young workers. In Nancy, a young mechanical turner, the son of a gardener with no family connection to the workers of the forge, was "beaten for the slightest mistake."[58]

Short of a profession, families attempted at least to obtain work, "a job," for their offspring, getting them into the factory where they worked. In the Normandy textile industry, in Yvetot, for example, "all the weavers are sons or nephews of weavers."[59] A high degree of stability was found, with workers remaining with the same establishment almost from birth until death. Worse were the monoindustrial factory-cities such as Baccarat or Le Creusot, which organized recruitment themselves, taking over the training of their workers, who were reduced to a dependent state that was often internalized. The factory was the workers' sole horizon; getting their children in became an obsession. It was the fixation of Jean-Baptiste Dumay's stepfather, who was completely integrated into the paternalism of the Schneider family and wouldn't rest until he got Jean-Baptiste hired at Creusot and even married him in the region, putting constant pressure on him to return. The same was true in tobacco manufacturing, where the industry's state-authorized status favored protected networks; here, the cigar makers prepared the way for their daughters, a rather exceptional case of an inherited profession and career for women.

Industry favored the family tradition in other cases, as when it sought to reproduce a workforce that was difficult to establish and preserve, not so much because it required exceptional qualifications, but because of the discipline involved. This was true of mining: rather than a trade—the mineworker was no more than a strong laborer—it constituted a way of life that was dangerous, difficult, and deadly, and ultimately had little to recommend it. The myth of the "beauty of the miner's life" was entirely manufactured through epics and propaganda, reaching its climax during the Liberation, with the national need for energy.[60] Instead, historians have shown how difficult it was to establish a stable work pool, which was acquired notably through a policy of family housing and employment,[61] presenting advantages for the laborers during periods of unemployment, but becoming unacceptable with the evolution of customs and the improvement in living standards. As soon as the historical moment loosened its constraints, young people fled. In 1911 in Carmaux (Gard), thirty miners had to be hired for every one that stayed. Increasingly, mining seemed a last resort, and youth rebelled against an authoritarian professional and family structure in which the miner-father reigned over his constellation, his subordinates and children. The situation was especially delicate for the haulers, young men aged eighteen to twenty-one (the law of 1892 having forbidden the descent into the mines before this age), whose lack of status posed many problems.[62]

Thus, in all cases, when it came to relations between workers and employers, the family was strategically placed. At the center of the conflict were the youths, both protected and directed, supported and commanded by the ambivalent reality of the family. Working within a series of constraints, the family attempted to optimize its resources (as economists would say), making many of the decisions for their children, such as their training, their type of work, their job and its location, the use of their salary, the formation and splitting off of new couples, which, as we shall see, it attempted to delay as long as possible. Fecund by necessity more than by choice, the family even began to control births. Thus the lives of youths, and their very existence, depended on it in no small measure.

Several series of factors arose, however, that upset the functioning of the working-class family, causing it to have to adjust, stretch, and even dissolve. The first was industrialization itself, which, after having used the family to its own ends, could dispense with it when it began to impede worker productivity. Contributing to this tendency were economic crises, notably the great depression at the end of the century, marked by the deindustrialization of the countryside and the disappearance of the village factory. Ultimately, what industry sought were fully independent workers. But this growing individualization of the salaried employee was often in keeping with the aspirations of young workers.

Migrations, even if they occurred within an extended family framework, established a distance that lent itself to emancipation for youth. Jeanne Bouvier moved from Dauphiné to Paris with her mother in the early twentieth century, but soon lost sight of her mother and gradually integrated into the capital. The large cities, Paris in particular, were zones of emancipation for youth. The most enterprising knew this and dreamed only of getting "up there." Leaving, traveling, meant escaping, enlarging one's horizons, making the world one's own, taking a risk, win or lose. How many young workers like Rimbaud may have existed? Tales of apprenticeships are always stories of travel.

But first, one had to work.

WORKING

The relationship to work was no doubt what most distinguished a working-class childhood from a working-class youth in the nineteenth century. The former was increasingly protected from the working world; the second was devoted to it. The under-twelve age group disappeared from the mines and factories,[63] and its presence was reduced even in family workshops, mainly due to school attendance and many families' growing belief in the value of education. Not so for adolescents. After the age of thirteen, with the restrictions already mentioned, work was the norm. After the age of eighteen, one was an adult in terms of responsibilities but not in terms of rights. Thus the workshop, the factory and the construction site became youth-filled settings. "Factory outings," a great postcard subject of the early twentieth century, showed groups of men and women—from the glassworks, textile, or metallurgical factories—who were very young indeed.

The difference between childhood and adolescence also resided in the nature of the bonds of dependency. While for children, the introduction to work always occurred through, within, or with the family, as young children accompanied their parents or elder siblings, things became more complicated and varied with adolescents.

In craft industries, the paternal workshop tried to hold on to youths, for better or for worse. Work inspectors complained of not being able to penetrate these closed worlds where, with the power of father and master being combined in one person, anything went. Workdays were endless, health rules unheard of, and punishments harsh. The idea that a good lesson was taught with physical force, an idea that was being fought in public schools, persisted among the working class. Fathers didn't notice that their sons had grown up. Jean Allemane could not abide the fact that his father, a typographer, had slapped him when he was sixteen; he cited this moment as the start of his revolt against authority and of his socialist "conversion."[64]

Nevertheless, most youths did not have such work opportunities available to them and had to find jobs elsewhere. Among the most qualified, the old idea persisted—inherited from the Middle Ages and codified by the trade guilds—that mobility allowed one to improve one's knowledge and know-how, but it was believed that such travel was best pursued later on. Colin Heywood, who conducted statistical polling in eight industrial cities of various sizes in the midnineteenth century, noted that the percentage of adolescents between the ages of fifteen and nineteen living with their parents was always higher than 74 percent for boys and 92 percent for girls, casting a new light on the image of the vagabond adolescent.[65] Of course living with one's parents didn't mean working with them, but at the very least it implied a limited range of movement. True mobility began later on. Families kept their adolescents in their midst.

In any case, a unanimous feeling abounded that the apprenticeship system was "in crisis." For the modern period, Peter Laslett has identified a vast system of placement for children and adolescents, mainly in domestic work, which he called "life cycle service." This system, broadly spread throughout all of Western Europe, was both technical and social, corresponding to the idea that a certain distance was required from one's family to learn not only a trade but also to learn of life. However, the often harsh conditions of apprentices were made even more difficult by puritanism and its hatred of sexuality. Keeping adolescents away from home was the equivalent, according to André Burgière, of "avoidance behavior," including avoidance of incest, which was increasingly condemned (on this point, a great deal of research would be desirable). Hence a suspicious, highly rigid attitude developed toward apprentices, who were seen as figures of temptation, "the slaves of Europe," as one German autobiography termed it.[66]

In the nineteenth century the apprenticeship system persisted, but reduced in volume, breadth, and means. The sexual division of tasks was reinforced. Domestic placements, in the city at least (in the country, farmhands were just as numerous as female servants), were mainly for girls and increasingly rare for boys: the lift attendant of Balbec was a relic, while the "Françoises" grew increasingly numerous.[67] For the boys, what counted was acquiring a trade, learning from a master, a father substitute, and from qualified colleagues. The role of the extended family—mostly uncles, cousins, and elders—or of neighbors was key in the choice of a workshop. At thirteen, Eugène Varlin set off from the Marne to Paris to learn the craft of bookbinding from his uncle on the rue des Prouvaires. Jean-Baptiste Dumay began work for Cail, a reputable mechanical factory in the Grenelle area of Paris, thanks to workers from Creusot.

In principle, employment in a workshop should have been accompanied by a contract stipulating the rights of the two parties. This is what Ducpétiaux advocated, furnishing a model and calling for oversight by charitable societies.[68] Yet there was no obligation to have a written contract; nothing called for one, not even the law of 1851, which was optional and merely reiterated the principles of fair apprenticeship.[69] Of the 19,000 apprentices counted in Paris in 1845, 10,000 received room and board, but only one-fifth had a written contract. Worse still, at the end of the century, according to the census of 1898, of the 602,000 adolescents under the age of eighteen working in industry and commerce, 540,000 worked without a contract. The contract, it seems, had fallen into disuse. It was replaced by a simple verbal commitment, which was easily broken, whether by the master, who could fire his employee from one day to the next according to his needs and moods, or by the apprentices, who were quick to flee. The Conciliation Board spent its time on these questions: between 1868 and 1872, in Paris, 75 percent of the cases the board considered concerned the breaking of *verbal* apprenticeship contracts.[70] This was because, as everyone observed, the working and living conditions were deplorable. The apprentices were poorly fed and even more poorly housed—under stairs, in storage areas, in the workshop itself. According to an autobiographical account by Gilland, "all these little wretches slept at the foot of the workbenches, each on a camp bed that was unfolded at night and had to be put away in the morning."[71] Work inspectors were constantly protesting against the total absence of hygiene in the "bedding" of the apprentice bakers and pastry chefs, or of the young *ovalistes* of Lyons. (An *ovaliste* was a mill worker who, with the aid of an "oval," a twisting machine, transformed the raw silk from a cocoon into silk thread. Ed. note.) The awareness of tuberculosis made people sensitive to the lack of clean living conditions. In addition, the use of physical force, a paternal privilege, was tolerated on the part of the master. The jeweler who employed little Guillaume in the story told by Gilland developed a scale of punishment: "He struck his children with a rattan walking stick, which he bought expressly for this purpose, and which he replaced several times a year. After the blows, there was the dry bread, the brown bread for one day, one week, sometimes a month."[72] Hence the occasional revolts undertaken individually—in 1841 the young Pottier was condemned to twenty years of forced labor for having assassinated his master, a wood sculptor in Paris, who had beaten him with his tools and had caused the death of one of his fellow workers[73]—or collectively, such as the one related by Gilland, a "conspiracy" aborted by the "tyrant." As the age of apprentices increased—they were more and more often adolescents—corporal punishment diminished; but the blows and angry throwing of tools replaced it.

Even in less extreme situations, the apprentice was the "scapegoat" of the workshop, good for everything and for nothing, harassed by all, a servant to everyone including the boss's wife, who made him do house-work and run errands. The apprentice cleaned the instruments, the stables, the workshop, swept, put things away; as a messenger boy, he carried packages and chests and made deliveries, dragging heavy loads in the handcarts that in the nineteenth century were still an essential means of transporting merchandise.[74] The "chassis pullers" crisscrossed the streets of the capital, taking advantage of the opportunity to dawdle or run around. They could be found in large numbers, charged with loitering, at the Petite Roquette, which became a prison for minors in 1836. They were fewer in number, however, than the boys "with no trades," who were more vulnerable still. Being an apprentice meant one had passed a certain selection process after all, which presupposed an attentive family and a minimum of education.[75]

More troubling still was the fact that, most of the time, these "child laborers" learned nothing. Their employers neglected them, while the ever harried workers grew impatient with their clumsiness, chiding them and preferring them to be complacent "good boys" than curious workers. Or they would be told to perform the same task, the same action, over and over, always creating the same thing, the same piece of the final product. Apprentices provided nearly free or very cheap labor, and in this respect, the situation was even worse in the provinces, where work was more limited. In Savoy, for example, in 1879, the unpaid apprenticeship generally lasted two or three years, "and one might even wait four or five years if one received room and board at the employer's home."[76]

Those most motivated to learn snatched snippets of knowledge here and there, took advantage of breaks if they could find willing elders to instruct them, or "looked over their companions' shoulders," as Jules

Simon noted, who, like all philanthropists, deplored this system. Or else, if they could, they changed companies—this "turnover," to use the 1930s expression, being to this day a substitute for apprenticeship. This is how Eugène Varlin learned his trade as a bookbinder, and Jean Allemane that of typographer. Varlin was thirteen when his uncle brought him up from the provinces to Paris (in 1852) and first set him up elsewhere before taking him into his own shop. The uncle was demanding and harsh, and Eugène left him a year later; at fifteen, he began to earn a living. His work book gives us an idea of his itinerary: from 1855 to 1858 he had five different employers, always in the sixth arrondissement, the main publishing district. Rejected for military service in 1859, he "made the rounds" for another five years until 1864, when he became a foreman at Despierres, rue de l'Echelle, from which he was soon banned for organizing. He set up his own business at about the age of twenty-six. "My specialty is *couvreur* [leather cutter] for lightweight bindings; but I can do whatever is needed," he says. A skillful artisan, he earned a good living, up to eight francs a day.[77]

Jean Allemane followed a slightly different path, remaining four years (1855–1859), from age twelve to sixteen, no doubt bound by contract, at a large printer (Dupont) and only later beginning an intensive journey through professional and factory life before settling down. Fifty years later, René Michaud attempted to acquire a familiarity with the various aspects of the shoe industry, which was divided into separate operations; he went from one shop to the next, determined to master a trade. "We were the last nomads of industrial work, and the number of companies I passed through one by one, my 'turnover,' would qualify me in the eyes of some wise psycho-sociologist as a pathologically unstable individual . . . But since there was no regulation of apprenticeships, you had to use your initiative."[78]

These snatches of information shed light on the "apprenticeship crisis," both industrial and disciplinary. Technological changes broke down the trades, notably in Paris, a city of traditional craftsmanship. "The specialty has taken over everything," says a report of 1877.

In most industries, secondary workshops have been created where only one object or even a fraction of an object is produced all year long. And it is mainly in the small workshops that the apprentices are found in large numbers, because these are the only places where they can be the source of profit for the employer, who oversees the work himself. Yet it is hardly by making the same object over and over that they can become true, good workers. Can a cabinetmaker be trained in these Parisian workshops that fabricate only sewing tables or night tables of a certain model, and even these with the help of machine tools? Can the apprentice become a chairmaker when his only work has consisted of assembling the various parts of a chair which, due to the necessities of transportation, arrives disassembled from the provinces or abroad?

And the report concludes: "Apprenticeship is falling into decay." The remedy? A network of professional schools supported by the state, for "the parents are too poor to pay tuition sufficient to cover even the teaching costs.[79] The worker movement came to the same conclusion, developing, after numerous exhibitions and congresses, a true "educational theory."[80] What it mainly demanded was "integral teaching," sacrificing neither general culture, which made the citizen, nor professional knowledge, which made a good, complete worker—an education that never dissociated theory from practice. "The adolescent tries out a technique the same day he studies its theory; he honors the labor of the worker, of his hands, at its true value," said Ernest Roche at the congress in Marseilles (1879).[81] These wishes would remain in vain, however; French technical and professional education was and continued to be a failure. This was due to the lack of knowledge of industry on the part of the educational system—unlike those of Great Britain and especially of Germany—and its indifference toward, even its disdain for workers, which young people took as discrimination.[82]

Hence the apprentices' "spirit of mutiny," their insubordination, their tendency to "bolt," their insolence. Here is an excerpt from the register of a job placement agency in 1874: an apprentice "after two days with his employer, left in a rather rude manner, under the influence of his aunt. He returned to the secretary's office, saying that he had left because his parents had been unable to come to an agreement with the employer on the terms.

The secretary sent him to a company named Hendrickk, where he presented himself in such an inappropriate fashion and made such exorbitant demands that Mrs. Hendrickk thanked him for his visit."[83] "You can't expect anything from apprentices," stated *La République Française* (August 18, 1884). "They have no real knowledge, but instead, they're familiar with every street in Paris and even those in the suburbs." This perpetual lament reflected a real situation, which Alain Cottereau pinpointed: the refusal of an increasing number of apprentices to accept their plight, a situation aided by the Parisian employment market. Older and educated (in 1860, 87 percent of Parisian workers knew how to read and write), the "apprentices" of the late nineteenth century showed signs of an impatient awareness.

AT THE FACTORY

By virtue of protective legislation, children disappeared slowly but surely from the depths of the mines and the gates of the factory, which thus became the young workers' territory. According to the 1897 census, large industry employed 223,385 boys between the ages of twelve and eighteen and 210,182 girls of the same age, almost the same number. But a growing sexual segregation separated jobs and work areas: textiles were mainly an affair for girls and women, for example; boys didn't stay in the industry past adolescence, unless they went on to careers as supervisors or in specialized tasks.

In all these workplaces—mines, construction sites, factories—hiring was done through the family, which often functioned as a team; the young worker served as an auxiliary to his parents or an elder sibling, and was so integrated into the family workforce that his salary was merged with theirs. When working for people other than his family, he was remunerated by the head of his team. His relationship with the employer was thus always mediated; in the employer's eyes, he didn't exist. Young workers often got jobs in factories because they "weren't good in school," or because they were bored. Many witnesses of the day—Dumay, Saulnier, and Navel, for example—speak of this boredom with school. "I was sick of wearing out the seat of my pants on the school bench and was anxious to follow in the footsteps of my oldest brother," says Eugène Saulnier. "The certificate, for me, didn't represent much. My father decided, perhaps with some regret: 'You'll make a good glassworker.'"[84] The formalities were simple: "A two-minute meeting between father and the director, and it was all settled." It's true that in this instance we are talking about a village factory. In the large companies, getting a job was more complicated. Some recruited directly from the schools. At Creusot, hiring was done in groups of six, ten, or twelve, according to the need: "The schoolmaster started with the oldest class and said to the students: 'So many apprentices are needed at the forges, so many at the assembly or at the boiler works. Who wants to go?' And they all raised their hands so long as they were at least twelve years old, without any advice from their parents, without any taste for the work available, but prompted by a single motivation: the pleasure of leaving school," recounts Dumay,[85] who at the age of thirteen, in 1854, got started at the assembly workshop in just this way. Generally, the young factory workers were less educated than the apprentices at urban workshops.

Right from the start, the factory youth were inserted into the production process, where they served as cogs in the wheel. More than apprentices, they were referred to as "aids," "auxiliaries," or by the name of the operation they performed; they were spinning mill fasteners, hosiery brushers, menders, sheet feeders at a printing press, blast furnace hodmen, haulers in the mines, glassworking boys, and so on. Sometimes they performed temporary, repetitive functions with no future; sometimes they climbed the rungs of a profession. An example of the former was found at Creusot, where apprentices always made the same parts: "the turners were divided up about thirty to a group, and each one was specialized in some particular bolts or nuts, always about the same, for six months, a year, two years or even longer, and they developed an extraordinary dexterity through the routine. A young apprentice earning one franc daily managed to produce up to two hundred bolts a day"—which would have cost ten francs to buy from a manufacturer. The apprentice learned nothing, but he brought in money for the factory and for his family, which was often pleased to have it. One needed energy to break out of this trap, as Dumay did, at the age of eighteen, when he decided to go to Paris.

Mines and glassworks belonged to the second category. In rare detail, Eugène Saulnier recounts how he learned the knacks of the trade and rose through the glassworking hierarchy. Hired as a substitute for a boy missing from a "team" (composed of three blowers and their three young helpers), he was next a secondary furnace worker, a driver, and finally a first degree blower, for there is always a gradation. At seventeen, he had "a trade to his name," which he prefered to that of farmhand. He earned more and felt respected. He took pleasure in climbing through the ranks: "When I settle into my place, the others have already worked for me," he said. His ascension was fairly rapid, a fact he owed to an old worker, called Father Pilon, who taught him well; but he recognized that such a climb often happened "by luck" or according to the decisions of the elders, who were very influential. The trade was as much a pyramid of power as of knowledge, and this was even truer of work in the mines or construction. Young workers were therefore dependent on a multitude of individuals, and age played a large part.

The elders were not always accommodating. "The [experienced] worker, lord and master, had to be served," says Saulnier.[86] Caught up themselves in the urgency of the task to be completed or the hunger for payment by the piece, the older workers were often crass and brutal. Dumay, a laborer at Cail (Paris, Grenelle) at nineteen, had to cart around thick, cold sheet metal, which he delivered to the tracer, "who chuckled when he saw us blowing on our fingers." Fifteen days later, he began work in a forge to replace an absent puddler boy (the very rapid rotation allowed for rapid hiring). There he spent a night that left him with bitter memories. Clumsy, he was abused by the puddler, "a thirty- or thirty-five-year-old man built like Hercules, who spoke of giving me a thrashing," called him "awkward, lazy and good-for-nothing," and ended up throwing his tongs in Dumay's face, which fortunately he evaded. "The forge workers always spoke to their assistants like that,"[87] says Dumay, sadly, who decided to leave this job as well.

These "on the job" apprenticeships were not necessarily difficult. It was a matter of learning simple and repetitive tasks: "opening and closing, opening and closing" the glass mold, "nothing more, nothing less." "Glued to my stool," flush to the ground, "I had no time to contemplate what was going on around me," says Eugène Saulnier, who mainly remembered how tired he felt. When he dozed, his blower kicked him in the shins. The days were endless: after the age of sixteen, there was no limit on them; the pace of the adults reined without restriction. The weeks were endless, too: provisions were even made so that on Sundays the youths could clean the machines and straighten the workshops. Saulnier considered himself lucky to have Sunday afternoons, "Fat Sundays," free. Breaks were shortened by tasks of drudgery—the workers demanded that everything be ready for them when they returned—or sometimes by training exercises. Hence the requests made to spare their energy: the young metal workers of Lille requested to no longer be required to go to school during dinner time; the margin stops working for Parisian printers asked not to be required to wash tools during mealtime and the right to five minutes of recreation "to break bread," for they were officially forbidden to eat while working and "they [found] the afternoons long."[88] Meals were gobbled down fast, the contents of the barely reheated mess tin quickly swallowed. The overheated adults drank a lot, and the youths were introduced to alcohol early on, which gave them a feeling of manliness.

Often exhausted, less accustomed to the pace of the machines, taking risks to finish more quickly with their maintenance work, distracted by their desire to communicate with their peers, the young workers were susceptible to accidents. According to the prefect of northern France, eighty-one workers were wounded in one month in 1853, fifty-seven of them under the age of twenty. Mutilated hands, chopped off fingers, broken or wounded limbs were daily occurrences, when the damage wasn't more serious: garments were caught or bodies were snatched up by the fearsome hooks of machines operating out in the open without protective barriers, especially during the first half of the century, when factories were quite careless in this regard.

It is not surprising, then, that the military examination board rejected so many young workers. The situation did improve somewhat in the second half of the nineteenth century, for reasons that were both general (global improvement in the standard of living) and specific: the removal of children from the workplace, better conditions of hygiene and safety. The work inspectors, who were extremely vigilant on the first point, became concerned with the latter after 1900, though their attention was not specifically geared toward young people.[89]

Was the factory harsher for youth than the workshop? This is debatable. Norbert Truquin preferred the Picardy spinning mills—where at about the age of thirteen he began as an attacher of broken threads—to being subject to the whim of his former employers. "In manufacturing, the workshops are heated, sufficiently aerated and well lit; order and cleanliness reign; the setting is social . . . the time passes merrily," he said of the days (about 1845) when factories went essentially uninspected.[90] It is likely that the general reinforcement of industrial standards weighed especially on the young people, who were caught between tense employers and nervous workers. The factory became a prison they despised, a situation that fed the libertarian psychology of the early twentieth century.

Were there revolts? The factory lent itself to collective action more than the workshop. The unhappy workshop apprentice was too isolated; his only options were making trouble or running away. Young factory workers, who were greater in number, formed groups that could assert themselves. To consider this a social movement in the sense of Alain Touraine's sociology of interaction would be an exaggeration. It was more a matter of protesting, especially through strikes. These protests were manifested in two ways.[91] First by participation in the conflicts of the whole. Young people were present in general worker movements, eager to demonstrate. Between 1871 and 1890, 16 percent of demonstrators arrested were fifteen to nineteen years old, and 6 percent of the leaders tallied belonged to this age group. Profiles of young "leaders" abound, outspoken youths with rebellious tongues and, sometimes, engaging charisma. This was the case of Félix Cottel, a young union activist from Troyes, where the brushers moved into action to get him rehired. This was also the case of Etienne Rondeau, seventeen, a laminator who was an excellent worker

and leader from Vierzon. "I'm not a slave," he said, prodding his comrades.[92] In the most homogenous industries, where they were well integrated, the young people sometimes sparked unrest. This was true especially in the egalitarian textile industry, where they were well represented.
In Troyes, it was the brushers, workers aged fourteen to sixteen—"the
children"—who prompted most of the hosiery workers' conflicts. In the
spinning mills, the fasteners, greatly affected by the accelerated pace of
production and the corresponding cut in the labor force, were highly
active. In Alsace, between 1850 and 1870, they supplied more than 22
percent of the strikers, bringing the women along with them.[93] Throughout
France, they were responsible for more than half of the strikes between
1870 and 1890, and they had strong persuasive powers. In Vienne (Rhône)
in 1890, the attachers, adolescents aged twelve to sixteen, persuaded the
women—trimmers and weavers—to demonstrate in what would be the
first "May Day," when they lashed out against the city's manufacturers.

In the mines, the situation of the draggers or haulers was more delicate,
and their role as inciters depended on family structure. In the mines
bordering the Massif Central, they often acted as instigators: this was the
case in 1846 in the Loire and in 1878 in the Allier, for example. In the
hierarchical north—of France and more broadly of Europe—where profession and family were constructed around the father, the "miner king"
in the prime of life, the haulers were in a subordinate position. They were
reduced to silence not only within the family but also within the unions,
which always placed restrictive clauses on their votes; in Seraing, for
example, one had to be twenty-one to vote in an assembly.[94] The young
workers' fairly frequent strikes were not taken into account much by their
elders, who considered them as having no voice within the union chapter,
and that their time had not yet come. Most often, the young workers
accepted this, kept quiet, and repeated the cycle, raised as they had been
to worship the cult of the father, the male hero of their black hell, their
role model. But during times of crisis or tension, this segregation could
lead to generational conflicts that translated into flight or confrontation,
including with the union, for one day's youths were the next day's young
adults.

The same was true of all hierarchically structured industries, where youths were considered as auxiliaries whose unrest disturbed the order of things. This was the case in the printing business, where the sheet receivers and sheet feeders were considered fairly insignificant, and in the glassworks, where strikes by the "kids" or even by the "big boys" were always treated with scorn. Family pressure was then added to that of the employer to bring an end to conflicts, which were considered simply to be anomalies. We should note, nonetheless, that this industry showed an inclination toward youthful organizing; in Aniche in 1893 the glassworkers called a "congress of kids" and for a while, a newspaper, *Le cri des jeunes* [The Cry of Youth], was published for eighteen- to twenty-year-olds.[95]

The fact that young workers in a large factory like Creusot would make demands was considered unacceptable or, worse, childish. Jean-Baptiste Dumay related how, in 1858, following a reduction in their meager salary, he convinced his comrades to "take collective action against the foreman, who was at the time a petty tyrant of the worst kind . . . and who was literally horrified to see us approach him like that, thirty claimants together. He said he didn't want to receive a delegation, but that each of us should tell him his personal desire individually." Dumay advanced first; the others fled; Dumay was fired, which was fine by him since he wanted a change of pace.[96] Many youth strikes reflected this feeling of being fed up and the desire for something else. But at the time, the possibilities for autonomous action were extremely limited.

LIVING IN THE CITY

Which is why, as soon as they could, at around eighteen, or even at sixteen, young people sought to get away, turning to their advantage the positive image of travel as an educational tool, a legacy of the *"tour de France,"* of which Agricol Perdiguier, in the midcentury, gave a nostalgic autobiographical account. The narration of his tour occupies two-thirds of his *Mémoires d'un compagnon.* Perdiguier made his voyage, mainly through the French Midi, between 1824 and 1828, from the ages of nineteen to twenty-three. He derived from it a tale of initiation, the circularity of which— from Morières to Morières, his village in the Comtat Venaissin—suggests the polishing of the apprentice, now transformed into a "complete trade guilder." He tells of his introduction to work, the foundation of his identity, in this case in the greatest of the woodworking trades, that of cabinetmaker—the trade that Rousseau wished to give to *Emile*—whose materials, skill, and instruments are lovingly detailed. Later he was introduced to guild practices and, finally, to France, whose customs, landscapes, and cities—centers of civilization—he discovered. It is a defense of the "journey by foot" and of its educational virtues for working-class youth, a tribute to organized mobility. The tour de France was an introduction both to work and to civic life. On a primary level, his story is also a kind of lively reportage, full of charm, stuffed with concrete information about the work lives and leisure time of his fellow young guild members, a monument and a document.

The young metalworker Dumay did his tour from 1860 to 1861, when he was nineteen and twenty, without guild support but constantly taking advantage of a large family network, all of whom worked in the trade, and fellow Creusot workers, whose qualifications made them leaders in the large metallurgical factories.[97] Dumay left Paris regretfully—"I liked the capital"—but he wasn't learning anything there anymore. With his friend Thomas he headed south, by way of Auxerre, Dijon, Pommard, Epinac, Lyons, the Rhône Valley, Nîmes, Uzès, and finally Marseilles, working for large companies or in modest workshops on a weekly basis, sleeping in furnished rooms, at the homes of often kindly landladies, or in barns. He almost never traveled alone, changing companions and combining mail coach, railroads, and walking, all the way from Lyons to Marseilles. "What a fine time, what a pleasure to recall, what joy along the way with my little bundle at the end of a stick!" singing and joking. Hired in La Ciotat by the Imperial Stagecoach he remained there fourteen months, retained by "a mutual love, the memory of which is still sweet today, forty years later." But then he drew a bad number for military service, which quashed any amorous plans, obliging him to seven years of service (from 1861 to 1868), his account of which is quite exceptional within working-class autobiographical literature.[98] During all this time, he never lost contact with his family, who were still drawing him to Le Creusot. When his service was over, it was there that he returned to work and to marry a local girl, on November 21, 1868, at the age of twenty-seven. This carefree, rebellious young man—who, unlike Perdiguier, incited several strikes along the way—became a militant republican and socialist.

Eugène Saulnier, the young glassworker, also dreamed of leaving the glassworks of his adolescence to learn more about the trade: "The little odds and ends I had learned to make with my blowpipe left me hungry." His older brother, Armand, a glassworker in Dordogne, bragged of his prowess and his salary. "He worked like the old guys, with every inch of his body, and was happy he had left us." Eugène decided to leave too. He was sixteen years old. "So this is it, Eugène," everyone said to him, "you're going on your 'tour'?" His mother balked at first, but resigned herself to it: "It was written into the destiny of glassmakers. Until we master it, the profession makes our souls nomads." And then, said Eugène, "it was time for me to sow my wild oats."[99] He joined his brothers, began working in the glassworks, shared a room, and discovered a different social atmosphere; the proximity to Bordeaux made people more confrontational than in the country: the "kids" would go on strike, tired of not being considered true apprentices. Saulnier was more stationary than Dumay: two years (1908–1910) in Dordogne, two years (1910–1912) in Choisy, near Paris, until his class was called up. "I wasn't interested in being rejected. It would have been a scandal in Plessis. They would have wondered about me; it wouldn't have seemed serious."[100] Decidedly, times were changing. Drafted in 1912, he was caught up in the Great War and returned to his hometown only in 1919, at the age of twenty-seven, to marry Alsine, his "betrothed" for twelve years.

These three examples show us the many functions of these voyages: initiations into a trade, into social interaction, into love and to politics. They were the young workers' real "university"—an essential period of breaking away, of discovery, personal choice, encounters, and integration into the city, at a time when cities were playing a major role.

More effervescent—Paris, especially, was beloved by the nineteenth-century proletariat—cities offered countless possibilities, a huge expansion of one's horizons. Young people were hungry for leisure activities. They appreciated all forms of theater, which Perdiguier adored, the café concert and the cinema, whose success they created. More concerned with their bodies than the older generation, they frequented the shower-baths; every week, Saulnier went to the hot baths with his friends. They also swam and went boating in warm weather. As for *sports* (a recent term), they enjoyed kick boxing and wrestling more than fencing, which was practiced by the better heeled (Norbert Truquin for example). At the beginning of the twentieth century, the taste for boxing soared, commensurate with the hopes to which it gave rise.[101] Styles changed, but a growing taste for competition and physical exercise was in evidence. In addition, youths gathered in their rooms and barracks, at cafés and bistros, to play billiards and cards, to talk, or simply to drink together. In the early twentieth century, the habit of outings in the country, on bicycles and in gangs, caught on.[102]

Gangs were, traditionally, centers of intense youthful sociability. They formed around places of origin, neighborhoods, or trades—on this point, the guild members were skittishly particular, a trait that was attenuated over time. The Creusot youths were ticklish on "points of honor" and fought in the kick boxing *salles* or dance halls, unable to bear the occasional mockery of their provincial ways: "We could never have resigned ourselves to hearing the masons of Creuse called insulting names," said Martin Nadaud. Conflicts that were settled by duels (of which there was a revival in the nineteenth century) in intellectual circles or among the leisure classes were resolved with bare fists, and collectively, in the working class. Between gangs, blows were counted. There was a working-class violence in which a taste for physical exploit—a release for the body, constrained by the gestures of work—combined with a desire for prowess. Dances were both places for meeting the opposite sex and sites for scuffles over girls, who were fought for like territories to be conquered. "You cannot imagine today how much value was placed on strength at the time," said Nadaud.[103]

More value than was placed on politics, which, on an everyday basis, remained an adult affair, especially since age limits excluded youths from voting, often even within the unions. Young workers—most often in groups—demonstrated more than they joined associations. They were passionate at the barricades, which legend nonetheless associates with them too systematically. It took an important event for them to mobilize, and they were often hesitant. Norbert Truquin was an interested young spectator in Paris in February 1848, but the Revolution didn't interrupt the course of his ordinary life. In June, however, he supported the insurgents from the National Workshops, who were put down by the Mobile Guard, which recruited from among unemployed youth. The studies of Charles Tilly and Pierre Caspard allow for solid sociological comparisons: the average age of insurgents brought before the tribunals was thirty-four; that of the Mobile Guardsmen was twenty-one and a half, with one-half of them aged seventeen to twenty. There was no difference professionally between the two groups; they belonged to the same category. However, while 63 percent of the Mobile Guardsmen were born in the provinces and were new to Paris, the reverse was true for the insurgents. Age, in short, counted less than one's degree of professional, local, and political integration.[104]

The roads to political participation were varied. Many autobiographies insist on the transmission of a family republican tradition issued from the Revolution, mention the role of an elder—often a brother—or other encounters, and above all emphasize the importance of friendships with fellow workers, readings, or café discussions. Martin Nadaud speaks of the Café Momus in Paris, whose manager was an old soldier from the imperial guard (the role of officers on half pay was considerable in the oral tradition): "The revolutionary air we breathed at Café Momus kept us from losing the hope of one day seeing the realization of our dream, the advent of the Republic."[105] Secret societies, such as the Provençal "barracks," whose underground influence has been demonstrated by Maurice Agulhon,[106] seduced young people. Informal socializing, which predominated in the first half of the century, suited them better than formal, more hierarchical organizations. By considering young people to be minors and subordinates most of the time, unions and political parties hardly favored their integration (see Yolande Cohen).[107] Hence, at the start of this century, their attraction to the more welcoming libertarians. The flair of "tragic bandits" (for example, the Bonnot gang, whose desperate resistance to a police assault in 1912 fascinated poor children),[108] even the insolence of the Apaches, seduced them.

But at age twenty, politics entered into competition with love.

WHERE THE GIRLS ARE:
THE YOUTH OF FEMALE WORKERS

Childhood is more of a neutral term. Youth is thought of in the masculine sense. Philanthropists and researchers have nonetheless been sensitive to the presence of girls in workshops and even more so in factories, generally deploring it, particularly from a moral point of view. Prostitution—the "fifth quarter" of the day of young working girls in Reims (see Villermé) always hovered around the factory doors. Emphasis was placed on protecting them, separating them, or even removing them, much more than on giving them an identity and training. Thus legislation (the laws of 1874 and 1892) created the category of "minor girls" (age eighteen to twenty-one), who were cast on the side of adolescents: "They are forbidden to. . . ," plain and simple. The relations between the sexes was nonetheless essential. How was "gender" constructed among working class girls?

In the family, first of all. There was little segregation during early childhood: boys and girls played the same games, performed the same tasks. Little girls participated as much as their brothers in protoindustrial or manufacturing operations, mixed together in a nod to childhood dexterity, performing tasks that would later be considered the "strong suit" of women. The differences began with formal apprenticeships, which, whether educational or industrial, largely excluded girls. School was considered secondary for them. The state had little input; the Guizot law (1833) forgot them. The Church, however, replaced the state. Poor girls were entrusted to nuns or charitable ladies. In these little schools, they received training in prayer, morality, sewing, and a rudimentary education; usually at about eleven, they prepared for Communion. The gap in literacy between girls and boys varied according to the region, but remained steady.[109] The Ferry-type school, whatever its political objectives may have been, almost brought about equality, differentiating little between the sexes. Segregation was then imposed through the family, and first of all by way of the mother.

The mother, key to the transmission of roles, of memory, of daily gestures, initiated girls into everything in principle, though the ways in which industrial society may have altered these age-old practices, like the production of the trousseau—that "long history between mother and daughter"—have not fully been measured.[110] In domestic industry, the mother taught her daughters how the work was done, as in the hosiery industry of Troyes or the haberdashery of Saint-Etienne, where girls had no choice about replacing their mothers. This training received no recognition; people spoke of the "innate qualities" of the girls, who were born with "a needle between their fairy-like fingers."

For these reasons, no particular qualifications were recognized in them. This also released mothers from having to place their daughters in apprenticeships, or if they did, they were pseudo-apprenticeships, pretexts for shameless exploitation.[111] The study of the Paris Chamber of Commerce, which in 1870 to 1872 counted among apprentices 8,904 girls versus 18,127 boys, clearly denounced this abuse. In some instances, employers acquired cheap labor through long-term contracts; metal burnishers or diamond cutters were compelled to stay with the same masters for low wages from the age of eleven to nineteen, even though the trade could be learned in two or three years. In some instances they were systematically used as domestics: "in the textile industry, the apprenticeship mistresses seem . . . to ignore the existence of article 8 of the law of 1851. They seem instead to take on apprentices for housework or work of any nature."[112] In other cases, the term *apprentice* was a cover for lesser-paid productive work, learned in a few months or even a few days: this was true of the *ovalistes,* or reelers, of silk in Lyons, whose harsh fate had remained unchanged since the eighteenth century.[113] In 1877, their day began at seven in the morning and ended at about nine or ten at night, with only three half-hour breaks. "Few of these apprentices knew how to read and write; they worked in poorly kept workshops with insufficient air circulation and where the health laws were not observed."[114] The food was mediocre; the sleeping conditions as well. As a result these young girls were in a disturbingly "sickly state," prey to consumption, tuberculosis. The conditions for apprentice girls were worse than those for boys, and this was aggravated by the fact that they could neither revolt nor flee. There was no female "turnover." The girls were riveted to their positions by everyone's will, and first of all by that of their fathers.

Possibilities for a few opened up, nonetheless, within the design and fashion world and its associated trades. Garment workers—artificial flower makers, feather workers, milliners, embroiderers, and so on—acquired on-the-job skills that were highly in demand, the basis for a better salary and a certain prestige. Jeanne Bouvier recounted her journey through the couture workshops of Paris, describing the channels by which she managed to break through.[115] But what was normal or praiseworthy for a boy was suspicious for a young girl, who had no business having ambition and ordinarily had to pay for it with solitude or a bad reputation. The caustic Catherinettes festival takes on full meaning here.

Ultimately, girls were not meant to have professions but only to work provisionally, while awaiting marriage and the chance to manage their own household, the nineteenth-century working-class ideal. Hence the limited job market. The two main sectors were domestic work and clothing and textiles. The former, which was increasingly female-dominated, grew in keeping with urban development. For young girls, notably migrants, it was an almost obligatory phase that many families considered a quasi apprenticeship. One was "placed" at the age of thirteen or fourteen, through relatives, a priest, or a notable family, first in the area, then farther and farther away, urban wages being higher. Thus, for girls, the ancien régime tradition of the "life cycle servant" was preserved. In reality, it concerned the peasant class as much or more than the working class, which was increasingly reticent about the personal service implied by domestic work. A young worker, new to the city, might seek out and marry a serious young maid whose savings would allow him to eradicate his debts. However, his own daughter would not necessarily work as a domestic. By the second generation, workers' daughters preferred the factory.[116]

The other pool of work for young girls was in the textile and garment industry, which employed nearly three-quarters of the female workforce, and no doubt an even high percentage of young working-class girls—who could nonetheless also be found in the pit heads of mines, sorting coal (photographers loved their kerchiefs and their little blackened faces), in the confectioneries, in paper mills, in chemical and canning factories, and so on . . . anywhere the raw materials were soft, the tools simple, the operations divided up and repetitive. But most young girls piled into the textile factories where, from the age of twelve to twenty-five, they constituted the bulk of the labor, with young boys as assistants and men as bosses. The latter were domineering and harassing, often granting themselves "droit du seigneur" as a hiring bonus. In Amiens, where the menders were the object of "complacent exchanges" among clerks, foremen, and sons of manufacturers, the mayor in 1821 posted a decree forbidding "spinners, male or female, from choosing their assistants of the opposite sex."[117] Given the relationships in age and power, the young working girls were easy prey for wandering hands and lewd demands. And they could hardly complain, caught as they were between everyone else's desires, unaided by the obliging attitude of families who had long been indifferent to this sexual domination. Hence the abundant rumors, rather than facts and studies. Initially silent, the worker movement increasingly denounced these abuses, and at the end of the nineteenth century the "lubricity" of the foremen was one of the great themes of the textile-producing North's working-class newspapers. The question of the droit du seigneur was at the heart of the large strike of Limoges porcelain makers in 1905, aimed at the director, a lover of "young flesh." Marie-Victoire Louis conducted an inquiry of great breadth into this poorly known area,[118] highlighting the extent to which the subjugation of women—and of girls, whom she didn't distinguish much, as they were hard to detect—occurred through the domination of their bodies.

As for the moralists, they paid little attention to this sexual exploitation, denouncing instead the dangers of promiscuity and debauchery among workers themselves. For some, a vision of factories as large brothels became an obsession. The solution: total segregation, even complete confinement. Three models were possible. First, there was the old tradition of workrooms run by charitable ladies and nuns. In Paris, in 1879, 3,760 girls between the ages of twelve and twenty-one hemmed tea towels and handkerchiefs twelve hours a day for church congregations.[119] In the provinces, the role of nuns or "semi-nuns," such as the Béates, was far greater still; in 1853, 1,100 of them taught lacemaking to young girls of the upper Loire, then hired them, a situation satisfactory to all, so it seems. Second, there were the orphanages or institutions for girls who had been placed in correctional facilities by the courts or by their families, sometimes called "repenters" (often ex-prostitutes), who were supervised by religious institutions that emphasized atonement by way of severe discipline and nonstop work without profit. The competition was stiff for the "free" working girls, who on many occasions protested against these convent-workshops, notably in the Loire, where several such workshops were torched in 1848.

Finally, the third model was that of the factory-boardinghouse, created by Boston industrialists in Lowell, Massachusetts, in about 1830 for the daughters of Massachusetts farmers.[120] These young girls came to work in the factories between the ages of seventeen and twenty-four, received high salaries, built dowries for themselves, and then married easily. Furthermore, Lowell offered a complete system that aimed to control every aspect of the young girls' lives—work, leisure, prayer, all distractions—with a clear concern for morality. The organization fascinated observers; the Saint-Simonian Michel Chevalier described it at length in his *Lettres sur l'Amérique du Nord* [Letters on North America], not without reservations as to "Anglo-American prudery" and "the hint of sadness and boredom" that emanated from this industrial hive. Ducpétiaux, on the contrary, related the idyllic spectacle of "five thousand of these young girls, all dressed in white and carrying silk green parasols," welcoming the visiting President Jackson in procession. He marveled at "the healthy glow and contentment of the working girls in these factories."[121] The system was imported to the Lyons area in 1836, first to Jujurieux (Ain), then little by little throughout the southeast in the Rhône area and the Cévennes. It was estimated that about 100,000 young girls were incorporated into these establishments at their peak. Their parents, peasants for the most part, signed a three-and-a-half-year contract with the employer and had to pay a penalty of 50 centimes a day (the rate in 1880) if the contract was broken. The factories housed workers in packed dormitories, fed them (when they didn't bring their own provisions to economize), and provided supervision.

The technical training was assured by secular forewomen; the material and moral know-how, by nuns, who founded special orders to this end. The young girls never left the gates of the factory, which had its own chapel. Work was performed beneath the crucifix; it was punctuated by prayers and canticles (at some point young workers would attempt to mix in other couplets). Hygiene was worse than mediocre, and corporal punishment persisted, as in religious boarding schools. This contributed to the increasingly heated controversies over these establishments. Praised on the one hand by a diverse group that included the publicist Louis Reybaud, the partisans of the school of Le Play and the liberal Paul Leroy-Beaulieu,[122] they were criticized, on the other hand, by radical republicans, who denounced the dominant role of the Church. After 1892 the work inspectors, the republic's "light infantrymen," began to fight against these factories.[123] Frequent strikes occurred, more and more frequently supported from the outside, revealing to the public the archaism of a system that nonetheless subsisted until the 1930s in somewhat secularized form, due to its popularity among rural families. "Blessed is the farmer with daughters," was the saying in Le Bugey; "thanks to them, he can pay his debts and buy land." Ultimately what was striking was the disciplinary and moral aspect of the girls' work, the place of the body, the hatred of sexuality, the strength of the controls placed on them. What distinguished them, clearly, from their brothers, was their absence of freedom.

As much as and more than their male counterparts, the young girls were excluded from public life. There was no question of their joining a union, which was difficult enough for their mothers to do. Strikes were equally out of the question. They nonetheless did lead a certain number of them, which were even more visible than those of the boys, due to their concentration, notably in the silk industry in the southeast of France. The *ovaliste* strike of Lyons (1869) was conducted by very young girls, including many Italians, whom the employers quite simply fired. They camped out on the streets, next to their trunks. Their leader, Philomène Rosalie Rozan, who roved the streets of the city brandishing a cane like a sword, was for a moment courted by the First International; there was some talk of sending her as a delegate to the workers' congress in Bâle, which would have been a major first, as the congresses, sites of public speaking and appearances par excellence, were all male. But nothing of the sort occurred.[124] Another leader was Luci Baud, who left a rare autobiographical testimony regarding the conditions of silk workers and the strike in Vizille (1905). Representatives of a young labor force, the strike leaders were themselves mostly very young women; between 1871 and 1890, 42 percent of them were fifteen to twenty-four years old (according to police records). Their own working youth colored their modes of action: they formed groups, danced farandoles, brandished flags, were accompanied by their young assistants, and sang—most often the *Marseillaise,* but sometimes, in the meetings, sentimental couplets. Which is why many claimed not to take these workers' "child's play" seriously and treated them with bemused indulgence or, if need be, a sententious moralism. When it came to young girls, their morality was always suspect, their virtue cast in doubt. Added to which was the reprobation of families who feared the breaking of contracts. All this made it difficult to persevere and succeed in these youthful strikes, which most often dissolved without results. It is probable, nonetheless—as more contemporary evidence suggests—that the strikes left their mark on these gray lives, with their taste for boldness, their whiff of pleasure, their festive air.

We find the same moral coloration in all the forms of work envisaged for girls: there were always lessons in housekeeping, which some—Emile Cheysson, for example, an eminent statistician and disciple of Le Play— saw as a means to improve domestic service, as if it were still the only professional future imaginable for working-class girls. Other areas were nonetheless forming among the service sectors, which even before 1914 were becoming female-oriented. Typists, post office workers, teachers, nurses, midwives—all these positions presented new potential identities. Working-class families eagerly pursued these routes: in Saint-Etienne the professional schools had more candidates than they could accommodate, often the daughters of haberdashers, and families criticized the excessively large place given over to manual labor. For workers' daughters, to become a teacher was still an unattainable, and repressed, dream, as shown by the compositions written in 1877 for grade school certificates in two Parisian districts: "I would have liked to be a teacher, but my parents were opposed," or "but I have to work," or "my father doesn't want me to."[125] Over time, these allegedly unattainable ambitions would begin to become reality.

In short, the young girls of the working class were laden with every handicap, social and sexual. It was particularly difficult for them to transform their destination into a destiny. Migration, with all its risks, was one of the few escapes possible. The working class did not lend itself to the emancipation of girls; its collective identity rested on a rigorous separation of sexual roles, on masculine symbolism, on the power of the father. The period between the two world wars would glorify the young hero, the figure of the conquering communist, for instance. Young girls would remain their shadowy companions.

LOVE

"At nineteen we think less about political struggles than about pleasures, which we often gave to one another," writes Jean-Baptiste Dumay. "I had some amorous adventures in the region, as did all the boys of my age, adventures that have no place in this story."[126] That is all we learn. Of the sentimental and sexual education of young working-class boys and girls, we know almost nothing. Fantasized about by observers, this area was passed over in silence by autobiographers, who, especially in France, considered that what was private should remain hidden.

Increasingly separated, boys and girls lived primarily among themselves, within the boundaries of their sex. They had camaraderies and friendships, which were more visible among young boys, who could be seen at work, in town, in the cafés, in the neighborhood, in fights, in demonstrations of all sorts, but they were hidden among girls, who were more solitary, though we mustn't underestimate female complicity and solidarity, so often invisible to us. Of homosexuality, whether male or female, we know even less, except for what we may glean from a prudish allusion by Agricol Perdiguier (who presented himself personally as a model of chastity), giving us to imagine its existence among young apprentice cabinetmakers.

Encounters between boys and girls were hardly facilitated by this segregation, notably in town, where the makings of the contemporary "solitary crowd" were already in place.[127] Late marriages, however, left a long period of sexual freedom, which was all the more problematic as contraception existed in only rudimentary form—the "be careful" of coitus interruptus, which presupposes self-control and concern for the other. Not everyone was as scrupulous as Agricol Perdiguier, who wrote, "I couldn't give myself to fallen women, whom I didn't love, and I didn't wish to betray young Sophie, my sweet, tender friend, and propel her into misery, dishonor, as the price of her love. To seduce a young girl with fine promises, with endless professions of affection, to make her a mother and then abandon her, to cast trouble and despair into her family, to break her heart, kill her, murder her, was not in my principles, in my nature. I loved, I burned, I suffered, I was tortured, shaken, pulled in opposite directions by my passions and my conscience." But, he continued, "I didn't want to get attached, I didn't want to settle down outside my region."[128] How many others may have experienced these agonies of the young migrant?

Most young men had too little money to frequent brothels, which did, however, have a working-class clientele.[129] Martin Nadaud, who would marry in his village in 1839 at the age of twenty-four, and who related his engagement and marriage at great length, hinted at the fact that in Paris, his companions did have recourse to them. Other sexual exchanges could be brief or limited. No doubt young workers had not forgotten "love country-style,"[130] facilitated by barns and thickets. The urban setting complicated the gestures of love, causing anxiety over being caught or stigmatizing such liaisons as shameful libertinage. In Sedan, "illicit relations between young people of both sexes are unfortunately rather common. It would no doubt suffice, to put an end to them, or at least to diminish their frequency, to extend to libertinage the means employed against drunkenness," writes Ducpétiaux, who was horrified by the licentiousness of young English workers: "There are cabarets with rooms where boys and girls go up two by two; generally sexual relations begin at fourteen or fifteen years old."[131]

Renting a room in someone's house, an ordinary practice for the trade guild members on their tour de France (the mother-innkeeper took care of their lodgings) and for their traveling peers, often meant courting the wife or the daughter of the establishment—Dumay was very interested in the pretty faces of his landladies—and sometimes sharing her bed. For this reason, boarding was despised by moralists.

To live in a furnished room, a more expensive solution, allowed for more freedom. Eugène Varlin, a binder, ingenious in all matters, had created a new kind of cooperative; he shared a dwelling with six friends and a woman who looked after their laundry and their sexual needs, sharing her bed with each one in turn.[132] No doubt he considered himself to be in the avant-garde of free love! Young working girls also adopted the furnished room solution. Jeanne Bouvier expressed her joy at finally having her own room, on the sixth floor, in Paris.[133] Gervaise's room, in Zola's *L'Assomoir*, was the symbol of a new life.[134] Furnishing it oneself was an additional sign of freedom. But living alone was always risky for girls. Any sexual relations, whether regular or temporary, bordered on prostitution in the eyes of the world. The police chased after those deemed "clandestine," forcing them to become "registered" professionals, who were easier to control: an exemplary case of the handling of "popular illegalisms."[135]

As soon as they could, young people left home, despite the resistance of their families, who were thereby deprived of their salaries. All testimonies gathered by the parliamentary study of 1872 confirm this. In the factories of Lavoulte (Gard), "many, as soon as they are earning money, leave home and move into a boarding house the way a single bachelor would." In the textile industry of Picardy (the region of Amiens), it was common to find boys and even girls, ages sixteen and seventeen, who "set up house" and stopped contributing to the family income,[136] though they remained single. This became the norm for both sexes. At La Croix-Rousse, in 1851, which was studied by Yves Lequin, marriage was unusual before the age of twenty; between twenty and twenty-four, almost no young men had taken wives and the vast majority of girls were single; this was also the case for almost half of the men aged twenty-five to twenty-nine.[137]

There remained, however, the "unknown cohabitation." No doubt it should not be overestimated; we cannot entirely trust the data collected by the Saint-François Régis Society, which was necessarily selective, as it was dedicated to regularizing illegitimate unions.[138] The practice was nevertheless quite widespread, it seems. In Saint-Cuentin, it was recorded, "many, and they are perhaps the least depraved, live together publicly, as if they were married." Marriage, in fact, often came later; the illegitimate birth rate was only twenty-five percent.[139] This is confirmed by many observers and in the well-informed study by Michel Frey.[140] In Paris, the working-class arrondissements were those with the highest rates of cohabitation, which may have accounted for as many as 472 per 1,000 residents, and included more than a quarter of all couples.

Should we view this well-documented popularity of cohabitation as a form of a "popular civilization" (Louis Chevalier), or as an expression of romantic love and youthful liberation (Edward Shorter)?[141] Probably neither. Michel Frey shows that, on the one hand, it was not a specifically working-class practice but more broadly one of the lower middle and even middle classes; and that, on the other hand, cohabitation was often a stopgap measure while awaiting marriage, which remained the normal and desirable situation, especially in the working-class world: "Concubinage is a time of frequentation that leads to marriage."[142] This was particularly true in the minds of women, who were always in a position of inferiority on the matrimonial marketplace, running the risk of finding themselves alone with one or several children. The inequality of relations between the sexes, further reinforced by the tightening of village regulations and by clauses of the Civil Code forbidding paternity suits, which had been common under the ancien régime,[143] meant that sexual freedom was mainly freedom for men.

Many were the girls seduced and abandoned, the unwed mothers left to care for the fruit of illegitimate loves. And while domestics formed the largest contingent in the Paris maternity hospital, many young working girls, abandoned by their boyfriends, were also found there. For example, there is the story of Ernestine Pallet, brought before the court for having strangled her baby after being abandoned by the child's father. An illegitimate child herself, who had been aided by a vigilant aunt, Ernestine had been placed in an apprenticeship with a metal polisher from the age of twelve to sixteen. At sixteen she met a twenty-two-year-old worker, Eugène Legault, a tough guy and a drinker, with whom she nevertheless fell in love. Despite violent rebukes from her aunt, she moved into a furnished apartment with him in Belleville. A year later, she was pregnant; she gave birth to a son whom she nursed herself. She wanted to marry, but Eugène refused, stole her savings, and left. Hence the infanticide, for which extenuating circumstances were granted; in 1881 she was condemned to five years in prison.[144] The legal chronicle abounds with incidents of this type. As for popular morality, it condemned neither cohabitation nor unwed mothers, whose own mothers often helped out as best they could, even aided, at times, by the family of the boy-seducer, especially when he hadn't yet performed his military service. There existed a certain reprobation, especially on the part of women, for the father who didn't fulfill his duties. The mother of Amédée, a young worker at the turn of the century, forced her son to marry the girl he had gotten pregnant, despite his keen resistance.[145] Nonetheless, over the course of the century the illegitimate birth rate continually dropped, and that of regularized situations grew. Sometimes parents were opposed to such legitimizations, as to the couple itself, for economic or social reasons. Working-class families, even in their destitution, had their own matrimonial strategies. Many marriages were pragmatic.

Love relationships also ended in violence. The young women of the working classes were the main victims of crimes of passion committed by partners who couldn't tolerate their free behavior and their desire for pleasure.[146] Young working women began playing the games of love, the great adventure of modern times—and they took their companions along with them.

Thus both constraint and freedom were present for working-class youths in the nineteenth century. The discipline of work grew more oppressive and more standardized, but various crises, ruptures, migrations, and the like brought some autonomy, mostly for young men. Young male workers tended to take actions to liberate themselves, to individualize. Further, in the early twentieth century the emergence of a libertarian youth became worrisome, as did agitation against military service, the increased visibility of youth gangs, the growth in juvenile delinquency, and the revolts in houses of correction. Already some timid solutions were brewing that would later develop into political and youth movements.[147]

The problem of childhood was believed to be resolved; that of youth was beginning. The twentieth century would address it as a special issue, an area for intervention. In the nineteenth century, we did not find our working-class youth. But we did at least encounter boys and girls attempting to snatch from work and life a time that might indeed be called "youth."

CHAPTER 5

YOUNG PEOPLE IN SCHOOL: MIDDLE AND HIGH SCHOOL STUDENTS IN FRANCE AND EUROPE

Jean-Claude Caron

School, in all its forms, has long been a part of the social and cultural landscapes of European societies. What institution could be more strongly associated with the notion of youth? This association results from a long evolution, which in Europe, at different times but within a similar overall chronology, would turn school into a state affair, to borrow the title of a recent publication[1]—a state on the rise, emerging as a rival to the Church for progressive control of various academic standards. Our examination of school here, however, will not be focused on drawing up an inventory of this educational institution nor of its administrators or teachers, but on sketching a portrait of those for whom it was intended: youth. The statistical weight of these young people in the nineteenth century, though declining, remained quite significant: the under-nineteen category represented approximately 42.5 percent of the French population in 1780, 35.5 percent in 1881.

To deal with the entirety of the question of young people in school would not be possible within the framework of this essay. I have therefore chosen to consider an age group that corresponds to the years of secondary education: from the end of primary school, which was already quite widespread even before becoming obligatory, to the start of higher education or professional life. It is an age that fluctuates and is difficult to pinpoint: Furetière, in his famous dictionary published in 1690, defines the term *adolescent* as "the young man from fourteen to twenty or twenty-five years old."[2] Slightly less than two centuries later, Pierre Larousse's *Grand* *dictionnaire universel du XIX*ᵉ siècle maintained the same age range and added that, during these years, "hygiene and education must prepare and, in a sense, provide the foundation for the physical and moral health of the man." Whereas the main responsibility of primary schooling lay in teaching the rudiments necessary for life in society, secondary education, occasionally completed by higher education, was additionally charged with giving a moral education to the future adult. In France, as well as throughout Europe, the century from the 1780s to the 1880s was key in the establishment of this secondary schooling: from the Enlightenment's plans for reform and the legislative work of the Revolution to the beginnings of democratization in access to middle and high school, lay a century of struggle and halting exploration into both the definition and the creation of what would progressively become a place of autonomous academic standards and would assert itself as the meeting place of the rising classes.

This study also limits itself to those who followed a curriculum that was more academic than professional: the student rather than the apprentice. It should be understood that we are dealing here with the history of a minority—those who continued in school beyond primary education. It should be understood as well that this minority dwindled as it approached the top of the university pyramid, and that within this minority existed another minority that would very slowly win the right to education: women. We are dealing with a privileged youth, a cultured elite whose uniqueness stands out all the more in a Europe that was still not entirely literate, a social group whose unity was based as much on frequenting the same places and acquiring the same knowledge as on common social origins. These are some of the characteristics of the young people in question—whether middle or high schoolers—in the study of whom one final problem arises: that of sources.

These young people rarely expressed themselves in writing, unless we consider their schoolwork to be a source—which it is, but due to its highly standardized nature, it tells us more about the functioning and ideology of the schools. In fact, with few exceptions, the available sources are often indirect: the headmaster and the rector, the father and the tutor, the policeman and the judge, the journalist and the novelist, all expressed their views of this segment of youth, with its Latin classes and recreation breaks—especially as, in the romantic period, the rising middle classes discovered and affirmed the value of youth, and their faith in education and training. But ultimately few traces of direct expression remain from these youths about themselves. What remains are memoires and other reminiscences, which often accord an important place to the years of knowledge gathering: whether violently critical (as they sometimes are), laudatory, or nostalgic (as is often the case), these wonderful texts present a vision of the present, or even of the future, as much if not more than an objective snapshot of an often mythicized past. Needless to say, their contents are necessarily the fruit of a selection process, a product of time and the distortions of memory.

PEDAGOGICAL REBIRTH

The end of the eighteenth century was marked by a pedagogical rebirth in which, along with the definition of new practices, were simultaneously affirmed the idea of the all-powerfulness of education in shaping man (Helvetius: "Man is really only the product of his education") and the awareness of youth as a social asset, as the object and subject of the political renewal for which many were calling at the time. Jean-Jacques Rousseau and his *Emile ou de l'education* (1762) naturally come to mind. The ancien régime was marked by the pedagogy developed in the Jesuit and Protestant schools; the personal relationship between master and student, the ideal of Erasmian humanism, had given way to a relationship between a master and his class that was not without innovation, as evidenced by the practice of theater among the Jesuits. Until the suppression of their order in 1773 by Pope Clement XIV, the Jesuits had a major influence on secondary teaching throughout Europe—in the West and even more so in the East. In Poland, Austria, and Hungary, disciples of Ignace de Loyola were in abundance, in competition with only a few other orders and with the Protestant colleges.[3] In seventeenth-century Europe, approximately 150,000 students attended more than 500 Jesuit middle schools.[4] Within this system the humanities were unquestionably dominant, the sciences and mathematics remaining affairs for specialists or enthusiasts—who were increasingly numerous in the eighteenth century. Instruction in Latin and ancient history trained generations of rhetoreticians, who often had better knowledge of the Roman Republic than of the Bourbon reign. Louis-Sébastien Mercier, a good observer and a fine writer, scoffed at the paradox of this system, which was also in use in the public middle schools: "An absolute monarch pays teachers to solemnly explain every eloquent declamation ever made against the power of kings."[5]

The spoken or declaimed word took precedence at the time over the written word, and gave birth to pieces of bravura imitated from the art of the ancients; debates, ceremonies, and awards furnished a framework for this oratorical jousting. These speeches bring to mind the law student conferences of the nineteenth century, but there, speaking was practiced in the role of prosecutor or defense counselor, with a professional goal in mind. The preeminence of the "disputatio" lost steam, however, over the course of the nineteenth century: aided by the invention and widespread distribution of the metal pen, writing won out in the form of the dissertation, the crowning achievement in a student's education. As for the goal of learning under the ancien régime, it was generally agreed that it aimed to produce educated as opposed to trained graduates: not that one didn't learn something, but the goal of education was not to furnish a diploma or a profession; instead the accent was placed on the formation of gentlemen, prototypes for a hierarchical society *(société d'ordres)* based on Christian thought. Ultimately the goal was socialization, and not social mobility, a phenomenon that would be out of place in a hierarchically structured society. The case of Valentin Jamerey-Duval is, by its rarity, evidence of this: a simple shepherd who finished his education in an incomplete and sporadic fashion, he was noticed by some men of the court of the duke of Lorraine and became the librarian of the Emperor François and an experienced numismatist. Jamerey-Duval was the perfect—but, again, rare—example of a common man formed by his education. This "wild child," who had run loose in the days of Louis XIV, died in Vienna at the court of the Empress Marie-Thérèse.[6]

The seventeenth century Counter Reformation had already produced its share of treatises on education, with Madame de Maintenon and Fénelon its best-known representatives. The "white, tender and soft" soul of the child was volleyed back and forth (Sacchini, 1625). But John Locke (a pure product of the Westminster School and of Oxford), in his *Some Thoughts Concerning Education* (1693), a work intended for gentlemen's sons, had attempted to consider the whole of the child and the adolescent, his physical and moral needs, his upbringing and his education, including his physical education and apprenticeship in a trade. Locke and Rousseau would bring out the birth of the body and the physical being of children, who would no longer be seen as mere copies of adults, as they had been awkwardly represented by painters for centuries, nor as little men, already touched by original sin and who had to be saved by hook or by crook, but as naturally good creatures. From the infant to the young man, the Malthusian eighteenth century reinvented the ages of life, marked by education and training, allowing the enlightened man to be created in stages. The goal, as Louis Trénard has emphasized, was no longer immortality, but happiness.[7]

THE BIRTH OF NATIONAL EDUCATION: YOUTH AT STAKE

We know the great role played in the French Revolution by the generation educated during the Enlightenment in schools run by religious orders: Robespierre was born in 1758, Danton in 1759, Desmoulins in 1760, Saint-Just in 1767. Between Locke and *Emile* lay the years of the Enlightenment, and the new belief that the transformation of society occurred—preferably—through the education of the enlightened citizen, the prototype necessary for a society of freedom (Voltaire) or of equality (Rousseau), based on thought that was deist, even atheist for some (Diderot, Helvetius, d'Holbach). At the center of this Rousseauist education, which was bookless (Nature served that function) apart from *Robinson Crusoe*, was the awakening to sensibility, to observation, to autodidacticism, to the rejection of apparent constraint ("There is no subjugation as perfect as that which maintains the appearance of freedom") and of punishment, to the preferred virtue of the humanities. We know Rousseau's disdain for the education of women: it is a position that would lastingly influence the nineteenth century, less with respect to primary education than to secondary and higher education. There was a point in common, nonetheless, between Locke and Rousseau: the belief in the personal relationship between the master (tutor) and the student. This belief was being affirmed at the very moment when the practice of such teaching, still preponderant among the nobility, was being rejected by the bourgeoisie, which was filling middle school classes with its offspring, and when parliamentarians and philosophers were defining the basis for national education. La Chalotais, in his remarkable *Essai d'éducation nationale ou plan d'études pour la jeunesse* (Essay on National Education, or Plan of Study for Youth) (1763), compiled a harsh critique of the religious schools' control over teaching and the curricula of middle schools; Rolland d'Erceville (1768), Lamoignon (1783), the authors of the *Encyclopedie* (notably d'Alembert), and Filangieri in Italy (1785) expressed the same desire for reform.

In this approach, one thing was clear: with the projected nationalization of the educational system, youth became an important political and social issue. Roger Ducos stated this before the Convention in 1792, when he called for the creation of "a new generation through uniform education." State leaders, whether favorable or not to the Revolution, understood that with the birth of public opinion, the younger generations had to be controlled. In Spain, Manuel José Quintana, poet of the resistance to the French occupiers and apostle of education as a source of public good and individual happiness, summarized the educational stakes in one sentence: "He who teaches rules." In France, Guizot, spokesman for the liberal bourgeoisie, echoed him in 1832: "The most unshakable basis for social order is the education of youth." In Italy, a state in the making, Cavour closely followed anything that concerned education. He was a fine example of those seeking to develop a liberal, nonconstricting education that would serve the state and aid in the formation of a national sentiment without questioning social inequalities. A reader of Rousseau, a traveler who had studied the French, English, and Swiss educational systems, Cavour wished to reconcile *"forte ordinamento dell'istruzione sociale, e larghissima libertà dell'insegnamento privato, non ufficiale"* (the strong organization of social

instruction and the broadest freedom of private, nonofficial teaching).[8]
What better means for social control than school, which therefore fairly
rapidly became an object of great concern and even a place of obligatory
attendance in many states (such as Prussia and most German states, the
Scandinavian states, Piedmont, Scotland, England, Hungary, and so on),
well before the France of Jules Ferry, though the laws were not necessarily
enforced.

The French Revolution would influence Europe via its educational
plans, which, though largely unimplemented, would often serve as the basis
for national educational systems. Of these projects (by Mirabeau, Tal-
leyrand, Condorcet, Daunou, Le Pelletier de Saint-Fargeau, and the like),
we should note in particular the affirmation of the right and obligation to
receive an education (1793), the plans to create establishments that accepted students without distinction, and for a pedagogy in which the
collective would take precedence over the individual. The nineteenth century would attempt to realize this fusion between a Rousseauist ideal and
the new faith in the virtues of instruction. Chateaubriand was an example
of this transition. He received his early education from private tutors, but
later attended the middle school of Dol, where he learned mathematics,
drawing, weaponry and the English language (his father intended for him
to enter the royal marines), as well as Greek and Latin, under pressure
from his mother.[9] Little by little, the tutor, the symbol of private or
individual education, would be eliminated, subsisting only in the wealthiest
classes or in the countries that resisted the "movement," such as the Russia
of Nicholas I. Thus, aside from a brief stint at a gymnasium in Moscow,
the young noble Pyotr Kropotkin, future theoretician of anarchy, received
his entire education from three tutors—first a Frenchman, then a Russian
and a German—before entering the corps of pages.[10] Such practices were
in the minority, socially and geographically. In a Europe to be reimagined
and reconstructed in search of new values after the crumbling of a society
based on the search for salvation, in a Europe seeking to define the rules
for new social relationships, the role of school in forming a bond among
men emerged. It was a quasi-religious conviction that we find expressed
by the nineteenth century's most influential pedagogue, Johann Heinrich

Pestalozzi (1746–1827): "There is for our part of the world, which is crumbling morally, spiritually and politically, no salvation possible if not by education, if not by the formation of humankind, if not by the formation of man."[11]

This disciple of Rousseau, one of the eighteen foreigners to be honored with the title of French citizen by the Convention of 1792, made distinctions, in man, between growth *(Wachstum)*, formation *(Bildung)* and education *(Erziehung)*. Throwing into question the concepts of classes, curricula, and schedules, he aimed for the development of knowledge (the head), of know-how (the hand), and of knowing how to be (the heart), his objective being the construction of the autonomous personality. Could one have imagined that at the moment when Pestalozzi was developing this method, which was adopted and adapted in the primary school systems of a certain number of countries (Switzerland and the German and Italian states), these same countries and others would be putting systems of secondary education into place based on principles that were diametrically opposed? That middle schools *(collèges)* or high schools *(lycées)* in France or in Italy, *Realschulen* or *Gymnasien* in Prussia, *institutos* in Spain, and grammar or public schools in England would be defining highly rigid schedules and programs? That any pedagogical innovation or attempt at innovation was meeting with the triple resistance of teachers, administrators, and families? That the development of an autonomous personality was not an objective to be attained but a scourge to combat, even if it meant breaking those who refused to fit the mold? Ernest Lavisse, a middle schooler in Laon, then a high schooler in Paris under the Second Empire and the future "pope of official history," would have harsh words for this teaching: "We lived outside of nature as we did outside of history."[12] Pedagogy, for its part, was not taught to middle school teachers before the creation in 1883 of a chair at the Sorbonne, entrusted to Georges Marion; and it was only at the turn of the century that Ferdinand Buisson and Emile Durkheim would make their marks in the educational sciences.

With this in mind, Marie-Madeleine Compère resituated the history of the middle and high school within the long-term quest for identity (from about 1750 to about 1830), and refused to see 1789 as the moment of genesis for secondary education.[13] It is fitting here to recall the brief but interesting experiment with central schools (from 1795 to 1805). Created at the initiative of Lakanal, Fourcroy, and Daunou, such schools' innovation lay in basing teaching more around the exact sciences, antechambers to the polytechnic schools, and in eliminating the system whereby the group of a particular year's students took all the same classes: instead each student belonged to a section (12 to 14 years old, 14 to 16 years old, and 16 to 18 years old) and established his own program from among the subjects offered. The experiment was brief and occasionally successful but encountered resistance, though hardly more than that encountered by the Napoleonic high schools that were based on principles that were diametrically opposed. These, described as actual barracks where students marched to the sound of the drum, as opposed to the clerical-sounding bell of the ancien régime, nonetheless educated a generation of intellectuals that would blossom in the nineteenth century. Among them was Jules Michelet, born in 1798, whose childhood years were spent in a difficult familial and political context: he received a very weak primary education, then attended a boarding school—though not without tears and resistance—where he learned the rudiments of Latin before entering Charlemagne High School. The social and cultural disparity he experienced there, the persecution of some of his classmates, and the disdain of some of his professors, did not prevent him from asserting himself and devoting his life to teaching.

SCHOOL VERSUS THE FAMILY

In a work published in 1869, *Nos fils*, Michelet expresses his belief in the republican school well before Ferry, contrasting humanism (Rabelais especially) with medieval teaching, the pedagogues of the Enlightenment (not without criticism of Rousseau) with the religious orders. He shows how pedagogues such as Pestalozzi, Fellenberg, and Fröbel attempted to reconcile moral concerns, religious teaching, and quality education, and most of all sought to replace home education—a tradition Michelet does not reject, though he warns against the risk of smothering the child. Continuing Pestalozzi's line of thought, he arrives at an organic compari-

son between the individual blood mother and the collective educational
mother: "The true mother, school, is emerging, which will instruct and
nourish every child." Of this nourishing school, Michelet expects civic
propaganda, social advancement, and moral unity. Let us recall that these
words were published in 1869, and are at the root of the flowering of works
adopting these same ideas after the defeat of 1870. In this secular version
of the educational mission, middle and high schools were the keys to the
system: while Michelet strongly condemned the educational methods and
systems he experienced as a student, he was a staunch defender of classical
teaching, of the Greco-Latin humanities. He established this position in a
speech he gave at the awards ceremony of the Sainte-Barbe middle school
in 1825. Latin translation and composition and philosophical dissertation
were the exercises to be favored in order to educate enlightened citizens.
These trained and educated classes were the ones that would enable progress to occur; they were the classes whom Michelet again encountered in
his audience at the Collège de France (from 1838 to 1851).

Thus the nineteenth century saw the confirmation and triumph of a
school system that took over all of education at the various stages of
childhood and adolescence, under the sometimes intrusive, sometimes distant eye of the family. Balzac, a boarder at the Oratoriens middle school
in Vendôme from 1807 to 1813, was far from overwhelmed with family
visits. The pain of being far from home and the break with one's family
involved for students attending boarding schools, which remained preponderant until the end the century, provoked rebellious reactions (as in the
cases of Flaubert, Vallès, and Maxime du Camp, defeated insurgents for
whom the end of middle school represented real deliverance) or desire for
flight (as was the case for Lavisse, who went to bed every night with his
face turned toward home, or for Jules Isaac, a boarder at Lakanal filled
with a "contained but mad desire to get a thousand miles away").[14] Are we
dealing here with highly sensitive personalities, unrepresentative of the
general population? Perhaps we should instead emphasize the contrast that
may have existed between the middle-class family value system, geared
from early childhood toward individualism, including in the area of discipline, and the form of collective discipline that boarding school could

represent. Victor de Laprade denounced the "homicidal education" (*Education homicide*, 1867) dispensed by these middle or high schools, which were compared to convents, army barracks, or prisons. Since Michel Foucault, we are more familiar with the process of internment which, simultaneous with the asylum, the prison, or the workshop for working youth, influenced the establishment of a network of middle schools, beginning in the seventeenth century, that were less closed than convents, but very far from the humanist principles of education, just as the Napoleonic high schools would turn out to be far from Rousseauist principles. Yet this was the model that would win out, often over the family. Even in 1856, Lacordaire, director of the middle school of Sorèze, spoke out againt "the annoying shadow of the home"[15] and recommended entrusting to teachers the education of children from the age of seven onward.

Let us be careful, nonetheless, to avoid anachronism by opposing school and the family too strongly. Already, under the ancien régime, the teaching dispensed by the Jesuit middle schools sought to compensate for the insufficiencies of family education in the areas of morality and religion. In the nineteenth century, this desire to substitute institutional for family education, within the broader context of the secularization of society, was clearly expressed, whatever its origin and goal (note the many socialist currents—Saint-Simon, Fourier, Proudhon, and the like—that were interested in education), but was only beginning to be implemented. As Philippe Ariès has pointed out, this process would be completed only in the second half of the twentieth century, and it continues to develop with the growing areas of education entrusted to middle and high schools (road safety; respect for the environment; prevention of nicotine, drug, and alcohol addiction; sex education; the fight against racism; and so on).

THE "ALL-POWERFUL DOMINION OF SOCIAL CLASS"

School became dominant in the nineteenth century by linking its fate to the secularization of society: this was true of primary education, where, after a long battle between church and state, the Ferry-Goblet laws (1880 to 1886) completed a process begun during the Restoration. In 1880, we can consider that all boys and girls received an education, even if their attendance was somewhat dependent on the season and their inclusion in a particular socioprofessional category. The same was true in the many countries where schools had long been declared free and obligatory, in theory if not in fact (beginning in the eighteenth century in Prussia, and in the Scandinavian countries). The same could not be said for secondary education, however, that "all-powerful dominion of social class," as Lucien Febvre defined it. At a time (the end of the eighteenth century to the end of the nineteenth) when higher education was reserved for a limited elite of enthusiasts (scientific or literary) or for future professionals (doctors, jurists), secondary education was the laboratory in which future generations of notables were formed. These elites were more lettered than enterprising on leaving secondary school. And elitism went hand in hand with intellectualism: thus the love of beauty was cultivated, based on the same Greco-Latin sources as in the middle schools of the ancien régime, the "un-utilitarian ideal" being pursued with consistency.[16] All attempts to create a "special" or "modern" education, in which the part of Latin would be reduced or even eliminated (Vatimesnil, Guizot, Salvandy, Fortoul, Duruy), met with keen resistance, or, when they succeeded, were subject to mockery. Thus when a commercial class was created at Saint-Barbe, a large private Parisian institution, its students were referred to derisively as "the No Latins" (or as the "grocers' class").[17]

While writing gradually became the mark of knowledge, it nonetheless continued to reproduce the rhetoric of the humanities, and there was no reluctance, during festivals (Saint Charlemagne's Day, for example), to filling the halls and hearts with well-composed discourse. The power of the word was intact among instructors: lecture halls dominated the middle and high schools of all countries, despite occasional denouncements of this one-way abuse of the verb. As Michelet said: "What is torturous about classes in the current system of teaching is the passivity, the inertia, the silence to which the child is condemned. Always receiving without ever giving! It's the opposite of life!"[18] A pedagogue (he composed chronological and synchronic tables, a *Précis d'histoire moderne*), teacher (in high school, university, then at the Collège de France), and tutor (to the son of the duchess of Bourbon then to the daughter of Louis-Philippe), Michelet was also a man of the spoken word, a recognized orator, though vocally somewhat weak.

This appropriation by the teacher of the spoken word in secondary education was even more prevalent in higher education, where the professor remained remote, perched in his chair, dispensing knowledge that was rarely contested and all the more appreciated when the form was up to par with the content. Among the men of golden words figured Cousin, Villmain, and Guizot at the Sorbonne during the Restoration; Michelet, Quinet, and Michiewicz at the Collège de France during the July Monarchy.

STUDIOUS YOUTH, BOURGEOIS YOUTH: GROUP PORTRAIT

Who were these middle and high schoolers? First of all, they were a minority, as revealed by their limited ranks during the entire period under consideration. The numbers cited often vary and are subject to caution, so broad was the range of establishments that could be connected to secondary education. The number of middle schoolers in France in 1650 was estimated at about 65,000 (for a population of approximately 18 million inhabitants) of which more than 40,000 were with the Jesuits. The educational and pedagogical dominance of the Jesuits over the period of education that was not yet referred to as secondary was incontestable until their expulsion from the kingdom in 1762–63. Equally important was the educational role of the Oratorians, at the middle school of Juilly in particular, which at the end of the eighteenth century was attended by Hérault de Séchelles, Louis de Bonald, and Adrien Duport: a digest of the Revolution to come. In 1789, approximately 70,000 middle schoolers (among 25 million inhabitants) were counted in France, versus only 50,000 middle and high school students in 1806 (how many may have been in private establishments, where students were difficult to account for?) and as many in 1820, excluding small seminaries. The number doubled in 1850, then grew again under the Second Empire, reaching approximately 165,000 students at the advent of the Third Republic, including those in seminaries. The figure would stagnate until the end of the century, with approximately

180,000 students in 1895, for a population of 38 million inhabitants.[19] This evolution allows us to grasp the respective importance of the socioeconomic situation and of political events. Economic growth went hand in hand with increased school attendance when it came to secondary schools, though the repercussions of war and revolution cannot be overlooked. It was under the July Monarchy and the Second Empire that attendance grew the most rapidly. But this overall growth conceals strong regional inequalities: 1 child out of 24 attended secondary school in the Seine-Inférieure region under the July Monarchy, versus 1 out of 144 in the Côtes-du-Nord. Germany was hardly more advanced than France at the time of its unification, when it counted approximately 170,000 students in secondary school. But close to 100,000 of those students attended a gymansium, the equivalent of the French *lycée*, or high school, which during the same period numbered only about 40,000 students. The tally in the budding state of Italy was less bright: approximately 50,000 students were in secondary school, half of whom were in the equivalent of the *lycée*. Austria had approximately 80,000 students, of which 60,000 were in that country's 250 gymnasiums. Spain went from 16,000 students in institutes and middle schools in 1858 to 25,000 in about 1878, the 50,000 mark being passed only in 1918.[20] In Russia, the reform of 1828 officially introduced an educational hierarchy: parish schools for the lower classes, district schools for the middle classes, gymnasiums for the upper classes and the aristocracy. The upper classes represented more than 75 percent of the students in gymnasiums in 1833 and still more than 50 percent at the end of the nineteenth century; during the same period, the sons of the urban middle classes in attendance rose from 17 to 31 percent. The gymnasiums of the empire, although practically free, took in only 15,000 students in 1836 and 30,000 in 1863, for an estimated population of 65 million, of which only about 5 million were literate. Attending high school presupposed a complete primary education and a financial ease on the part of the family such that it could both pay for studies and forgo income from the child's labor.[21]

The work of Dominique Julia, Roger Chartier, Wilhem Frijhoff, and Marie-Madeleine Compère shows that, under the ancien régime, the percentage of sons of nobility in secondary schools remained rather weak, though largely superior to its percentage in the distribution of social categories in France: the percentage of sons of the clerical milieux, legal or medical professions, merchants and traders, well-to-do artisans, and, in the most rural regions, heavy laborers remained preponderant. As for the contribution of the lower classes—small artisans or merchants, lower-rank officers, farmers—it remained slight and was strongly subject to the vicissitudes of the time: the price of wheat and the rate of school attendance fluctuated in relation to one another. In this respect, the eighteenth century was marked by a clear regression of middle school students: between the end of the seventeenth century and the Revolution, the number of students went from 1,200 to 250 in Lyons (La Trinité); from 1,200 to 120 in Nantes; from 1,400 to 200 in Bordeaux.[22] For the poorest, the only solution was still the small seminary, followed by a possible ecclesiastical career, but many, such as the young Venetian Giovanni Giacomo Casanova, never reached ordination.

Behind these raw numbers lies a social reality: dropping out, repeating classes, the length of one's educational stay all depended largely on socioeconomic and sociocultural status, but also on the number of children per family or on the distance from home of the educational establishment. There was talk of the social reproduction of the elite, "as if the educational system of the French upper classes had been established before the Revolution."[23] Indeed, the Revolution and the nineteenth century would barely change the status quo, aside from the declining influence of the nobility. To the notables of France, with its bourgeois economic and cultural triumph, corresponded establishments for the sons of notables; it should be noted that even within the middle schools and high schools lay great disparities in educational content and social recruitment, two closely connected factors. Thus, we find 15 percent sons of nobles and 4 percent sons of merchant artisans in Belley, a middle school run by Jesuits, versus 8 percent and 7 percent, respectively, in Grenoble from 1786 to 1791.[24] The 1865 study organized by Victor Duruy gives a very precise image of the social origins of French middle and high schoolers during the Second Empire. It is an image that is not surprising so far as the respective presence of socioprofessional categories goes: less than 2 percent laborers; a little less than 3 percent salaried workers; the world of lower-class urbanites (artisans, merchants) totaled approximately 30 percent, added to which were a little more than 5 percent large merchants and industrialists; land-owners figured at more than 17 percent alone; legal or medical profession-als, approximately 11 percent; the world of civil servants (teaching, the army, various bureaucrats), nearly 20 percent. But the distribution was not the same in the middle schools as in the high schools, which were more elitist. Thus we find nearly 2.5 percent sons of laborers in the middle schools versus less than 1.5 percent in the high schools and 9.65 percent sons of small merchants in middle schools versus 4.06 percent in high schools, whereas the legal professions represented less than 5 percent in middle schools versus more than 8 percent of the high schools.[25] One of the finest literary portraits of a middle schooler issued from the lower middle class is that of Charles Bovary, Emma's husband: son of a former assistant surgeon medical officer with little aptitude for business, raised by his father in a manly and anticlerical spirit and by his mother with the opposite values, he received a rudimentary education from the village priest while roving meadows and sunken roads, then attended the middle school of Rouen, and, following a bohemian interlude, was accepted with-out honors as a health officer—in other words, as a doctor for the poor.

Special, or modern, teaching was more open than classical education: at the high school of Rennes, children from the lower classes (artisans, shopkeepers, small bureaucrats, peasants, domestics) represented two-thirds of the students in the special sections; in the classical sections, the same percentage of children came from privileged backgrounds (land-owners, investors, industrialists, professionals, upper-level functionaries).[26] These are only socioprofessional statistics, unmatched with other data, such as absenteeism, years in school, and so on. But all in all, there was a distinct winnowing between middle school and high school, though less than existed between primary and secondary school: in 1821, out of ap-proximately 6 million children eligible for school (boys and girls), nearly 2 million attended a primary school and only 50,000 a middle or high school, representing only 2.5 percent of the primary school pupils and less than 1 percent of the age group, girls being even more disfavored.

Secondary education, elitist by vocation since its inception, remained so until at least 1914. Guizot said it quite well: if primary school was destined for "all the State's subjects . . . as much in the interest of the State as in that of the individuals," secondary school was intended only "for the men who are destined to have leisure and ease, or who undertake a liberal profession of a higher order, such as commerce, letters, etc."[27] This quasi-official position would hardly evolve until the end of the century: the Third Republic would address the problem of primary education first, followed by that of secondary education for women (the Camille Sée law of 1880). There were few education grants from the state or from municipalities, and their distribution was not always based on pure merit. But without a grant, Daniel, in Daudet's semiautobiographical *Petit Chose* could not have aspired to attend the middle school of Lyons, where his humble clothing provoked the jeers of his classmates and scorn of his teachers.

ELITISM AND SOCIAL FEAR

From the ancien régime to the end of the nineteenth century, many were the journalists and politicians who expressed their fear of seeing the popular classes gain access to secondary education and then demand a social position corresponding neither to their competencies nor to their "interests": what Richelieu and Colbert, but also Voltaire and Rousseau, asserted before the Revolution (too much education among the popular classes threatened the social and economic equilibrium of the society), others (Balzac, Stendhal, Reybaud) reaffirmed in the nineteenth century, fearing the social consequences—amounting to insurrection or revolution—of a surfeit of lettered individuals condemned to inactivity. The rector of Aix-en-Provence spoke harshly of the "mass of deserters of the plough or the paternal stall."[28] And Danton proved them right, in retrospect, when he described his life's course: "I was raised among great lords. When my studies were finished, I had nothing . . . The Revolution [of 1789] came; I and all those like me threw ourselves into it. The Ancien Régime forced us into it by providing us with a good upbringing without opening any outlet for our talents."[29] Fifty years later, Balzac developed a surprisingly similar analysis: "Youth will burst like the boiler of a steam engine. Youth has no outlet in France, it gathers an avalanche of unrecognized capacities, and legitimate and restless ambitions; it marries little, and families don't know what to do with their children. What noise will shake these masses I don't know; but they will dash headlong into the current state of affairs and overturn it."[30] Whether openly stated or silently felt, this fear of a "replay" of 1789 was no doubt one of the main reasons for the limited increase in secondary school attendance in the nineteenth century, a time marked by revolutions that were increasingly social in nature. Louis-Philippe could well enroll his sons at Louis-le-Grand or Henri IV: the bourgeois-king had no need to fear that his offspring would frequeñt the wrong crowd, even if, following the events of 1830, and 1848, the upper classes did begin to withdraw from public schools, a fact that was accentuated by the Falloux law of 1850 instituting freedom of choice in secondary education between public, secular school and religous establishments.

The situation was basically comparable in the other countries of Europe, but with variations: everywhere freedom of choice in education was the watchword, whether in long-constituted states, such as Great Britain, or in developing states, such as Italy and Germany. The freedom to choose one's form of education was accompanied by its corrolary: the refusal to enlarge access to secondary schooling through state intervention. For Germany, the very structure of the country allowed great freedom in teaching, on both the administrative and religious levels, each region conserving its own forms of schooling while integrating the Reich. In Italy, the struggle between clericals and liberals reached its peak, between a Church whose power was crumbling and a rising state, both on the territorial and legislative levels. Scotland had, without question, one of most liberal systems in Europe, where religious schools coexisted with a public school that quickly turned secular to leave each student master of his own religious convictions. But everywhere, secondary teaching emerged as an elitist refuge, the extreme case being England and its prestigious public schools: in 1861, these nine elitist institutions (Eton, Westminster, Winchester, Merchant Taylor's, Harrow, Charterhouse, Saint Paul's, Rugby, Shrewsbury) were attended by slightly more than 2,700 students issued from the highest levels of society; for the others, there remained the grammar schools. The power of the Anglican Church was affirmed by these private and richly endowed schools. Attempts at reform would lead to the Public Schools Act of 1868, which founded schools based on the principle of public financing, but with tuition—and was therefore not a matter of deep social reform at all.[31] It should be noted, nonetheless, that England, like Germany, would greatly develop its network of technical and professional schools intended for middle-class children, with Marlborough, Cheltenham, Wellington College, and the royal institution of Liverpool.

Increasingly, the aristocracy and the upper middle classes fell back on private education. Following the outbreak of successive revolutions, Carlists, Orleanists, Bonapartists, and antirepublicans of every stripe, often associated with the Catholic hierarchy, abandoned public middle and high schools. At the same time, the number of student grants increased. Thus, through a system of compensation, there was a start at democratization that benefited the new classes evoked by Gambetta, an evolution that was more qualitative than quantitative. Furthermore, it was not in the public but in the private schools that one found students from underprivileged backgrounds. The Church had always recruited the most gifted individuals from popular milieus—village artisans, farmers, and so on—giving them an education oriented, ultimately, toward the priesthood. This tradition was maintained in the nineteenth century in the small seminaries, which took in many farmers' sons, who often had no intention of assuming orders. Comparing the social origins of students at the Catholic middle school of Marcq-en-Baroeul, the communal middle school of Tourcoing, and the small seminary in Cambrai, Robert Gildea shows that the three establishments were attended, respectively, by 22.5, 6.5, and 2.1 percent sons of landowners or investors, versus 1.3, 5.4, and 21.1 percent sons of artisans.[32] One remarkable point is that more than 30 percent farmers' sons were found in small seminaries, versus 10 percent in the middle schools. The private secular boarding schools also recruited from the popular sectors: in the one attended by the young Frédéric Mistral, son of a wealthy farmer, the director scoured the countryside seeking minds to form, occasionally exacting payment in the form of work or food.

The middle and high school, the boarding school and the institute also produced students who were little or poorly educated, and whose lack of knowledge was mercilessly revealed by the baccalaureat exam. Far from a formality, the exam gauged the quality of the education a student had received, or the relationship between the assumed level of the students and their true level. It is of course appropriate to consider with a grain of salt the many testimonies of examiners who, already at that time, regretted the candidates' lack of culture, their incapacity to write in proper French, or Latin, the drop in standards, and so on. The statistics nonetheless remain: a success rate of approximately 50 to 55 percent on the *baccalauréat ès lettres* was considered normal. Jules Vallès received his precious diploma only on the third try and probably thanks to the recommendation of a friend, the son of an influencial teacher. Vallès's case, which was atypical because of his committment to radical politics, was less so as regards his difficult search for a social position. The dedication of his *Le bachelier* [The High School Graduate], "to all those who, fed on Greek and Latin, died of hunger," sometimes seems like an exaggeration particular to its author; at best, these words, which nonetheless express the essential problem of the high schoolers' future, have been associated with the difficult period when Vallès lived. It is important not to forget, however, that throughout the nineteenth century, only a small minority of high schoolers continued their studies at a university or professional school. For the others, if they were not already the well-placed sons of investors, merchants, traders, or land-owners, social integration became an all-consuming goal. Recommendations played a key role for those who wished to enter into administration, the ministry, or business, or to become a "paper scribbler." The functionary, or the salaried man, was the most common product of secondary education. Social backsliding, as opposed to social ambition, was one of the great themes developed by politicians and writers of the nineteenth century, the abundant insurrections and revolutions of which were presented as the result of so many disappointed middle class youths, trading their pens for rifles. This blunt assessment, which did not correspond to the reality, is evidence of the fundamental stake secondary education represented, and tended to limit the numbers: neither legal restrictions, nor quotas to limit access to middle and high schools were instated, but a clearly affirmed political will did exist to obstruct the way for children of the lower classes.

MIDDLE SCHOOL, OR THE CONFINEMENT OF THE MIND AND BODY

The size of educational establishments varied a great deal, from fewer than 50 students in small provincial establishments (9 in Sablé in 1842!), to more than 1,000 in well-known high schools such as Louis-le-Grand. Size also varied in the English public schools, between Eton and its 800 students and Saint Paul and its limit of 153, in memory of the 153 fish caught by the apostles during their miraculous fishing expedition. In 1864 the numbers of students in the various French high schools ranged from 79 to 1,867, those in middle schools from 21 to 940. In addition to varying in size, the establishments also varied in the level of their studies: many small boarding schools dispensed only the rudiments of Latin and French, a kind of advanced elementary teaching. The small-town middle schools produced good students, but they fell a peg when they arrived at the big city middle schools: Hippolyte Fortoul, future minister of public education, had this experience when he moved from Digne to Lyons. As for the teachers, their heterogeneity is discretely noted in inspection reports: for every Renan, Sarcey, or Michelet, how many teachers, whether religious or secular, were untrained, incompetent, or—perhaps worse—had no notion of what an adolescent was? The annual inspection report of 1877 estimated at 37 percent the number of top-notch teachers; 43 percent, mediocre; 20 percent (one out of five), incompetent.[33]

In every establishment, there were two categories of students: the boarding students, whose growth reached its peak during the Second Empire (approximately two-thirds of the students, versus one-third before 1789) and the day students, who in the last third of the nineteenth century became the majority again. This great shift had a large cultural component, and also a material one: day student status was much less expensive (about 300 F in 1864) than boarding at a high school (739 F) or middle school (649 F). The day student was often poorly regarded by the administration; he was less easily watched and could bring in forbidden books and newspapers, relate political events, or serve as a messenger for the boarding students. We know, too, how important boarding was in the English public schools, where it was considered to have essential educational value, in addition to being an important source of revenue.

The settings for middle and high schools corresponded little to the pedagogical ideals defined at the turn of the century. Even the large high schools often had decrepit buildings, dormitories with little heat or air, narrow, bare courtyards; gray was the dominant color of the walls. Victor Duruy, then inspector general, visited the high school of Poitiers, which he found "almost shameful with its black walls, its hospital- and prison-like atmosphere." The conclusion of this future minister: "A mother must hestitate a long time before coming to knock on our door."[34] The 1867 inspection of the seventy-seven public high schools found only thirteen in satisfactory condition and twenty-two in a state of great decay. For the few newer exceptions, like Lakanal in Sceaux or Michelet in Vanves, endowed with real parks that lent themselves to physical exercise or sports competitions, how many middle or high schools were stashed in sites not designed for teaching! The religious schools, often housed in former monastery or convent buildings surrounded by gardens, appeared better off. Belley, the middle school run by the Jesuits that educated the sons of important families of Piedmont and Lombardy, was noted for its vast gardens, its alleys of fruit trees, its squares of flowers and vegetables. The buildings were large, clean, and airy. In Sorèze could be found a large park, springs, fresh air, and trees, 200 of which Lacordaire, the director of the middle school from 1854 to 1860, ordered cut down in the interest of achieving more order and light. This was also the advantage of the English public schools, with their large parks covered with dense green lawns.

Sanitary conditions in the schools were worse than mediocre. The rules for students nonetheless aimed to be persuasive, even at the end of the ancien régime: "If a child allows himself to go unclean, every means possible shall be used to correct him, even punishment if necessary."[35] This was wishful thinking: the cold water in the simple common washbasins—when they existed—hardly inspired cleanliness. At the middle school of

Vendôme, at the end of the Empire, one former student recalled: "we wash our faces" in pails of cold water, one after the next, then are combed and powdered by women; the use of baths, monthly in the best of cases, suggests a relationship to cleanliness marked more by the practices of the ancien régime than by the thoughts of the public health specialists. The sisters at Saint-Winoc middle school in Bergues symbolically inspected ears and necks every morning.[36] The lavatories were often repulsive, non-existant paper sometimes being replaced by hankerchiefs. On the whole, these areas were rarely cleaned, and the overcrowded classrooms, with little ventilation, especially in winter when heat was rare, gave off stubborn odors: "A kind of student humus, constantly mixed with the mud we brought in from the courtyards, formed a dunghill of an unbearable stench."[37]

In the majority of cases, the miasma seemed clearly to overpower the flowers. Nonetheless, the epidemics that still affected France in the nineteenth century, notably cholera, generally spared the academic populations in these establishments. There were chilblains and chapped skin, but few fractures or serious illnesses. The food, though vilified by the students, seems at least to have been satisfactory in quantity in most cases: complaints were raised mostly against the excess of preserved foods or the monotony of the meals.

If a student was a boarder, his entire day was scheduled. At Louis-le-Grand in 1769, at the middle school of Niort in 1806, or at the middle school of Tulle studied by Alain Corbin for the year 1864,[38] one woke at 5:00 A.M. in summer, 5:30 A.M. in winter, and went to bed at about 9:30 P.M. at the latest. It was farmer's or laborer's schedule, at a time when economic and social life still revolved in large part around the sun. These were prisoners' hours as well, comparable to those of a central penitentiary such as Fontevrault: the circumstances of the confined boarding student and the detainee intersected. But these were also humanists' hours, if we recall that Rabelais's Gargantua woke at 4:00 and went to bed at 8:00 in winter and 9:00 in summer. During these fifteen to sixteen hours of activity, there were only five class hours, on average, and more than six hours of study; altogether, eleven hours spent in a seated position and, theoretically, silent. Michelet had cause to speak of "assemblies of little paralyzed creatures, legless cripples, little old scribes."[39] These hours often seemed to their followers like a foretaste of the military regimen, especially for the generation that, like Alfred de Vigny, grew up under the First Empire: "Our tutors resembled heralds, our classrooms barracks, our recreation army drills and our exams military revues."[40] We know, too, how important high school uniforms were. Initiated during the Empire, they were eliminated under the Restoration in public establishments, the first step in the demilitarization of schools. They survived, nonetheless, in private establishments such as Sorèze, where the brown jackets were marked by different colors depending on one's grade (green, yellow, blue, red, from the youngest to the oldest), enabling the establishment of a visual hierarchy among the students.

Class sizes were highly variable, but in the large high schools in the nineteenth century, it was not unusual to find contingents of 60, 80, even 100 students in a rhetoric class. In Strasbourg in 1848, the rhetoric class at Jules Ferry had 51 students. Though it is hard to generalize, middle and high schoolers often had a bad time in this cloistered existence, broken only by a few rare walks, always along the same paths, six weeks of summer vacation during the July Monarchy, and a few short vacations, which boarders whose families were too poor or too far away to bring them home spent at the establishment. There was very little or no physical exercise, either: Amoros's pioneering work didn't affect schools directly, and throughout the nineteenth century attempts to create school gym programs were blocked by the mentality of the time and by the school administrations. One exceptional case was the middle school of Sorèze, which Armand Barbès began to attend in 1824: in addition to classes taught by reputed pedagogues, various sports and horseback riding were available.[41] Optional in the imperial high schools beginning in 1854, obligatory at all levels of schooling (grade school, middle school, high school, *école normale*) in 1869, exercise was made obligatory in 1880, in a country still marked by the defeat of 1870. The parallel with the teaching of history is indicative of the desire to instill a spirit of nationalism and of revenge in the hearts of the country's future elite.

We know how advanced the English were with regard to physical education, with middle schoolers devoting themselves to becoming accomplished sportsmen. In England the manly virtues of sports were cultived, and one sport even bears the name of a famous public school, Rugby. It was there that Thomas Arnold developed the ideal of the "muscular Christian." In France in 1869, Michelet called for seaside vacations, botanical and geological walks, and a exercise regime worthy of the name, like that practiced by the Greeks, the spirit of which had been revived by the German Friedrich Ludwig Han, "der Turnvater" (the father of gymnastics). But it wasn't until the end of the century that the activities of the Ligue française de l'enseignement [French League of Teaching] or the Comité pour la propogation des exercices physiques dans l'éducation [Committee for the Propogation of Physical Exercise in Education], and personalities like Pierre de Coubertin, Jules Simon, Philippe Daryl, and even the students themselves, turned sport into a component of education. This was the case at Condorcet, where the high school students created the Racing Club of France in 1882, and at Saint-Louis, whose students created the Stade Français sports club in 1883.

REGIMES CHANGE, THE HUMANITIES REMAIN

As for the subjects taught, we know that the humanities and letters were preeminent, a tradition inherited from the *ratio studiorum* of the Jesuits. Throughout Europe, there was no exception to the rule: the English public and grammar schools, the German, Austrian, and Italian gymnasiums, all cultivated this Greco-Roman heritage, producing a European culture—posession of which indicated one's belonging to a particular social class—and sometimes even a vernacular language. In Spain the various courses of study, which varied as a function of political change, never really affected the primacy of the *humanidades*:[42] but as in France in the 1840s, an ideological combat was clearly taking shape around the teaching of Latin, the language of the Church. In France, La Chalotais, as early as 1763, Diderot, d'Alembert, and many others demonstrated the uselessness of Latin for the majority of the middle school students. Meanwhile, after the innovative but aborted experiment with central schools (1795 to 1805), where scientific subjects had made a major debut, there was a return practically to the middle school curricula of the ancien régime. The study of history was making halting progress: in 1818, Royer-Collard declared it mandatory in royal middle schools, but not until Duruy was contemporary history introduced in philosophy sections (1867); after the defeat of 1870, however, the subject was taught in all grades. Philosophy, a subject central to the debate between clericals and liberals, long taught in Latin, only really gained a foothold under the July Monarchy, and it was once again lowered to the rank of "logic" by Fortoul before being reestablished by Duruy. Despite the slow introduction of living languages (optional in 1829, obligatory in 1838), mathematics (in 1826, taught in one's third to last year), and scientific subjects (physics was taught in philosophy sections in 1826) into the curricula, Latin, French, and, to a lesser degree, Greek remained the basis of every gentleman's education.

No one truly succeeded in questioning this state of affairs, as is reflected in the baccalaureat numbers: in 1830, 34 *bacheliers ès sciences* were granted, versus 2,816 *bacheliers ès lettres*. Among the challenges the count of Haussonville confronted at the 1827 baccalaureat exam were a Latin translation (verses of Virgil's *Georgics*) and a mathematics exercise (a multiplication problem).[43] The attempt at "bifurcation" envisioned by H. Fortoul, minister of public education in 1852 (a literary section and a scientific section beginning five years before graduation) would be eliminated by Duruy in 1863. The special classes of Vatimesnil (1829) or of Salvandy (1847), the advanced primary education created by Guizot in 1833, and the special secondary teaching established by Duruy in 1863 to 1865 would be regarded with a certain disdain in the upper echelons of the university. Vallès, whose angry dedication to *Le Bachelier* I have quoted, became an ardent proponent of a teaching method based on spelling, drawing, mechanics, physics, and chemistry.[44] But not until 1891 was a modern section created in secondary establishments, while 1902 saw the creation of sections leading to clearly differentiated baccalaureats: A (Latin-Greek), B (Latin-languages), C (Latin-sciences), and D (sciences-languages).

Throughout the nineteenth century, academic schedules reflected this weight of the humanities, a holdover from the teaching of the ancien régime. In 1843 the typical middle school student ingurgitated ten hours a week of Latin, Greek, and French, and three hours of writing, versus one hour of mathemathics; in rhetoric sections, he would have only eight hours of humanities, but still only one hour of arithmetic and geometry. He rounded off the week with an hour or two of religion, music, history, and living languages, with drawing receiving greater favor, at three hours weekly.[45] Edgar Quinet, Jules Simon, and Frédéric Bastiat could denounce as they pleased the content of this teaching; Jules Vallès could show how ridiculous the stereotypical exercises were, which consisted in rifling through the Latin dictionaries to versify as best one could; Maxime du Camp could mock the "arrogant pedants who know nothing and are incapable, after leaving school, of explaining a single verse of Virgil"; Victor Hugo could declaim: "Greek merchants! Latin merchants! Prigs! Dogs! Philistines! Pedants! I hate you, pedagogues!"—all to no avail. The cult of the ancients, occasionally threatened due to their paganism, continued to resurface periodically, including under the Republic, which often drew its references from it.

The picture was different in Germany. Although lower in status than the gymnasiums, which alone awarded the *Abitur* that allowed access to the university, the *Realschulen,* the first of which was created in Berlin in 1747 by the pastor Hecker, recruited a fairly broad range of students from within the lower middle and middle classes and played an important role in the training of qualified artisans or technicians. Also inferior to the gymnasiums, the *Burgerschulen* were attended by those who could not or did not want to follow a long course of classical training. This similar categorization of knowledge corresponding to a hierarchical categorization of the educational population was established between the end of the eighteenth century and the beginning of the nineteenth. In Italy, Cavour also argued and legislated for the development of a technical education that would turn out producers and not doctorates and rhetoreticians. In England, the public and grammar schools based their programs on the study of Greek and Latin, disdaining mathematics, the sciences, and philosophy, (national) history and geography being slightly better covered. But there existed many professional schools that trained artisans, even engineers, in all trades.

THE CROWN AND THE RULER

Among the pedagogical practices in use or being developed in the eighteenth and nineteenth centuries, two ancestral means of marking the behavior of students and distinguishing the individual from the collective are consistently found: punishment and reward. The latter was inherent to the pedagogy of the Jesuits, who used it to encourage a spirit of emulation: the nomination of "emperors" with silver buttonhole crosses, tables of honor, prizes in the form of books, the distribution of palm branches, laurels and crowns, in the best antique tradition, all existed under the ancien régime and was preserved after the Revolution, including in public institutions. During the Restoration, the decoration of the lily was added. In the nineteenth century, the distribution of gilt-edged books, sometimes bound in leather, but more often with hard red covers bearing the stamp of the school, furnished a pretext for the great annual ceremonies that the republic would perpetuate and expand, until their (temporary) disappearance in May 1968.

Alphonse Daudet tells the story of the end-of-the-year celebration in a small middle school in the Cévennes under the Second Empire. On the day of the ceremony, a tent was erected in the courtyard, sheets were hung from the walls, the trees were covered in flags, a platform was set up with dark red velvet armchairs, ready for the authorites.[46] At the end of every school year, Lamartine loaded the family carriage with crowns of laurels and all sorts of prizes. Thiers, a grant recipient strong in translation, did the same at the middle school of Marseilles: his departure for the law school in Aix elicited emotional regrets from his professors. In 1822 Auguste Blanqui, eleventh-year student at collège Charlemagne and future socialist revolutionary, received first prize in history and honorable mention in Latin verse, Latin translation, and Greek translation. A student at the high school of Lyons from 1819 to 1825, Jules Favre racked up the awards, compensating for a lack of social status with his academic success: his father, a wholesale woolen fabric merchant, had gone bankrupt in 1815. At the end of the July Monarchy, the young Jules Ferry also won book prizes at the collège Saint-Dié, including first prize in religious instruction,[47] and continued on a roll at the collège royal de Strasbourg, brilliantly obtaining his baccalaureat at the age of sixteen.

Finally, for an elite student, the supreme reward was participation in the general competition (created in 1747, eliminated during the Revolution, reestablished in 1809), to defend one's high school colors and receive prizes or honorable mentions that would increase the reknown and visibility of the establishment. Many of the nineteenth century's political, literary, medical, and legal personalities would distinguish themselves in this competition. That year's turmoil notwithstanding, a particularly eloquent list of award winners was compiled in 1848 in the rhetoric section: Edmond About took first prize in French dissertation, Hippolyte Taine second prize, Francisque Sarcey the first honorable mention, and François Hugo, son of Victor, the second. A scandal occurred in 1856 at the Academy of Toulouse, when Gambetta, a student at the high school of Cahors, publicly refused second prize in French dissertation, alleging that the first prize had been accorded out of favoritism for the son of the prefect of Lot.[48]

At the opposite end of the spectrum from prizes, but their complement within the educational system, lay punishment. Corporal punishment, in use throughout Europe until the eighteenth century, fell into disuse at the end of the ancien régime—except in England and Russia—and was officially abolished in France in 1803. But switches were common in English public schools and in the Russian gymnasiums, thus in two different political systems. Nonetheless, it has been said that, while "in England repressive measures were part of the educational system, in Russia, they substituted for one." Testimonies concur regarding the violence of the Russian high school administrations, and even more so those of military academies, despite their contingent of young nobles, where the whip was used to the extreme limit of the tolerance of pain, sometimes with a doctor's intervention to determine whether the punishment should be halted or continued. There was violence as well in the small Russian seminaries, attended by the poorest of the secondary school students, where switches were commonplace and the punished had to kneel on sharp boards, or, standing, carry a heavy rock with extended arms.[49] In France the idea of punishment was discussed as early as 1769, as shown in the regulations of Louis-le-Grand middle school: the supervisors should use no humiliating or offensive methods and "will refrain from mistreating or striking the students for any reason whatsoever."[50] But the use of the whip, the strap, the ruler, or a wide blade of wood or thick leather, the *ultima ratio patrum,* by the "corrector," was still feared by middle school students of the nineteenth century. Little by little, these punishments, which began to offend the middle classes, were replaced by prohibitions (notably against parental visits), deprivation (of food until 1809, of outings, of recreation, or even of part of one's vacation), or more symbolic punishments (wearing a sackcloth frock, the equivalent of the dunce cap in primary school; sitting at a penitence table for meals, or on a "lazy bench"; standing in the corner with, in the clerical version, one's arms extended as on a cross). Among the most common punishments were "prison" and extra work.

Prison and detention were eliminated only in 1863. Their sometimes large-scale use (at Louis-le-Grand, over 1,900 prison days were "dispensed" to more than 1,100 students during the 1836–37 school year)[51] tended to attenuate the efficacy of the punishment, sanctions probably being perceived as a mark of glory for whoever received them. But certain high schools set up real cells—there were thirteen at Louis-le-Grand, two at Henri IV—with metal bars on the windows and a wicket on the doors through which to survey the "detainees." At the middle school of Vendôme, the students called a cell placed under the staircase "the alcove," and within the dormitories there were also minuscule sorts of cells, known as "wooden breeches." In Rollin, there were cages outfitted with tables that fit around the student's waist, rendering the prisoner unable "to touch any part of his lower body."[52] If the prison regimen in schools was not generally all that harsh, the deprivation of freedom could continue for extended periods in cases where the condemned refused to make amends; thus Lamartine, a boarding student in Lyons, caught after an escapade with two of his friends, served one whole month in prison, his release being obtained only by his mother.

Punishment could also take the form of extra written work; copying exercises could range from a few lines to a dissertation, by way of Latin verbs, and they were perhaps even more feared than the cells, as they deprived victims of recreation or outings, meant more work during study hall or at night, and lacked the prestige of prison. They were the preferred weapon of supervisors, even more than of teachers. Their victims retained a lasting memory and bitter resentment of the exercises, from Victor Hugo, a student at the collège Napoleon under the First Empire, with "its black oak benches, dormitories long and gloomy, / Its paper-pushing schoolmasters whose only desire / Is to consume all your playtime with voracious exercises," to Paul Verlaine, a student at the modest boarding school of Landry during the Second Empire, who, not knowing the preterit of the verb *legere*, was condemned to copy it ten times, with its translation, in the cell. Let us finish this rapid anthology by recalling Jules Vallès's dedication at the start of *L'Enfant*, "to all those who are dying of boredom in school or are driven to tears by their families, who, as children, were tyrannized by their teachers or thrashed by their parents." The Vallésian vision of middle school as "moldy, sweating boredom and stinking of ink," associated, significantly, with his vision of the family, cannot, of course, serve as a yardstick for an "average" understanding of the middle school atmosphere: Vallès, son of a supervisor turned teacher, had twice as many reasons to hate both the school and those who worked there. He too was transformed into a "copying beast of burden."

It is, in any case, appropriate to question this overly uniform vision of the middle or high school as a barracks. Coming on the heels of the centralized school experiment, the strict application of high school regulations sometimes provoked violent reactions on the part of young middle-class students who were used to more freedom and more consideration. Faced with this loss of power and this feeling of diminished dignity, high schoolers reacted by revolting. These revolts were sometimes political in nature—many high schoolers would speak or act in favor of Napoleon in 1814–15—but they were also a rejection of social equalizing. Many incidents erupted—in Lyons, Marseilles, and notably in Toulouse, the "pink city," where the headmaster of the high school, founded in 1806, was quickly overwhelmed by the carousing, brawling, apple throwing, and obscene graffiti. The students left the premises, went to shows or cabarets, pillaged, attacked those who attempted to stand in their way; the replacement of the headmaster by a strong, energetic abbot enabled order to be restored.[53] Such incidents were rather common during the Restoration. At the royal middle school of Marseilles, the nomination of Abbé Denans as headmaster in 1821 provoked students to gradually slip outside the acceptable norms of discipline, staying out all night, building shanties in the courtyard, bringing in firecrackers, books, newspapers, and caricatures deemed obscene, and staging a masked ball during the carnival of 1823, ragging professors and study masters; but there were also antireligious talk and graffiti, fights between Carbonari and royalists, and a general questioning of the administration's authority. This progressive establishment of a counterauthority, with the issuing of a "Middle School Constitution" on the part of the liberal clan, occurred over the course of more than two years, and ultimately brought about a strong response: the dissolving of boarding schools.[54]

Here, in this perception of the behavior of youth that continued throughout the nineteenth century, we are at the intersection of the social and the political: the enforcement of regulations that defined the students' relationship to authority was constantly provoking violent protest. Protest also resulted from the negation of any culture of opposition. No group activity was tolerated in French middle and high schools (the little circles of high schoolers reported by Alain Besançon in Russia didn't exist), nor any form of expression. Activities like those of George Canning, a student at Eton at the end of the eighteenth century who ran a political-literary review, *Microcosm*, and published an article condemning the subjugation of Greece, were no doubt rare in England, but they would have been impossible in France. We are familiar with the later case of Marcel Proust, participating with classmates at Condorcet high school on the editing of the purely literary *Revue lilas*.

RELIGIOUS BEHAVIOR

It is difficult to accurately evaluate the religious behavior of students in the middle and high schools. Those who studied in establishments run by religious orders were obviously forced into practices during the school year that were left to the discretion of the families in public schools, notably attending Mass, going to confession, or taking part in Easter Communion. Students at the middle schools run by the "good fathers" practiced morning prayer and participated as a group in the celebration of the establishment's patron saint and in the processions that were part of national or local religious festivals. Nonetheless, incidents provoked by antireligious behavior existed prior to the Revolution. Marie-Madeleine Compère cites the testimony of an Oratorian, Joseph Villier, who in 1789 demanded the elimination of any compulsion in matters of religion: "I so often witnessed the repugnance of schoolboys at going to Mass, their irreverent comments and grumblings, the distaste they bore and which unfortunately stayed with them long after they left school."[55] But how can we know the reality of the situation when the religious behavior of the students became apparent only in moments of crisis? This was the case at the royal middle school of Marseille already mentioned, where, in the years 1821 to 1823, only a very small number of students frequented the sacraments, the others "bragging loudly of the horrible sacrilege they committed once a year at Easter." Masses were interrupted by murmurs and jeers. Students wrote "terrible blasphemies in the chapel where they had gone to confess." At the Ash Wednesday procession of 1823, "an entire division had the audacity to make fun of the people who attended, to burst out laughing and imitate the religious chants in burlesque fashion."[56] Elsewhere, witnesses reported that middle schoolers would "spit out God's bread" and use the hosts for sealing letters.[57]

Although these are extreme cases, ones that were connected to a situation and a time of unspoken struggle between clerical royalists and liberal anticlericals, this behavior was nonetheless a reflection of the de-Christianization that perceptibly affected middle-class youth in the nineteenth century. Many attempts were made to reconquer lost ground—

brutal and inefficient attempts during the Restoration, more skillful ones under the July Monarchy and the Second Empire. The actions of a man like Lacordaire, a confessor of high school and university students, provide an excellent illustration of the liberal Catholics' attempts to reach out toward youth. Within the broad category of youth, middle school, high school, and university students—France's future notables (Lamennais gave the title *Avenir* [Future] to the newspaper he launched with Lacordaire and Montalembert in 1830)—constituted a special target. As early as the late 1820s, but especially under the July Monarchy, Catholic and Protestant conferences and societies sprang up, seeking to regroup the school youth. Such movements were scattered, few in number in terms of followers, but highly voluntarist and enterprising.[58] While the *pascalisants* (Catholics who receive Holy Communion on Easter Sunday, the minimum recommended by the Church to demonstrate one's Catholic faith) became rarer in the 1830s (at Louis-le-Grand in 1832 they represent only 25 out of 489 boarding students), their number subsequently increased, but was this a good indication of a true rebirth of Christianization? We have the somewhat rare testimony of a boarder at the high school of Bastia, a republican to boot, who in 1878 harshly condemned his father for not having "attended Easter": "If you were young, it would be one thing, but you are at a critical age, an age when one mustn't distance oneself from one's God . . . What a pleasure it would have been for me to receive Holy Communion with you the Friday after Easter!"[59]

Yet in the long run, the general movement seemed to tend in the direction of a very Voltairian deism, even a more or less admitted atheism, while at times respecting the exterior forms of religious practice. Lacordaire encountered this fairly widespread incredulity at the high school of Dijon during the Empire, and lost faith the day after his first Communion. D'Alton-Shée, a middle schooler at Henri IV in 1822, spoke of the visits of preachers from Lent to Easter, including Lamennais, the abbot of Janson, and the prince-abbot of Rohan. The results were mixed: "Despite all these efforts toward a single goal, religious belief was rare among us and hardly ever went beyond the first Communion."[60] Sometimes these efforts even backfired: Barbès claims to have lost all religious sentiment upon contact with his middle school chaplain. Under the Third Republic, nonetheless, high school and university students would play an important role within the French Catholic Youth Association, created in 1886, and in Marc Sangnier's Sillon association, founded in 1894: it was a time of alliance between religious committment and the struggle for the defense of denominational schools. Among the reformed churches, the activities of the Young Men's Christian Association beginning in the 1840s and 1850s—first in London, then throughout all of Europe—are well known.

YOUTHFUL VIOLENCE

The violence of middle or high school life was part of the quasi-mythic vision of these establishments, a vision kept alive in novels (see Robert Musil's *Young Törless*) and in films (from Jean Vigo's *Zéro de conduite* to Lindsay Anderson's *If*). Any attempt at classifying such violent episodes turns out to be difficult, for they were rarely simple: the initial incident, often connected to an internal discipline problem, frequently led to political and religious repercussions. In France, the two Restorations, the 1820s, when the *ultras* (the ultraroyalists) were in power, and the periods following July 1830 and February 1848 were marked by such phenomena. Godefroy Cavaignac, a student at Sainte-Barbe in 1815 at the time of Napoleon I's landing, directed the school's republican camp against the royalists in bloody battles. This was not an isolated case: in many provincial high schools (in Nice with Auguste Blanqui, in Avignon, Bordeaux, Lyons, Douai, Strasbourg, and so on), the older high school students proved to be among the most determined to combat the Restoration and to support a Bonapartism with strong patriotic hues. In 1819 Louis-le-Grand was on the verge of combatting forced religious practice, but the revolt soon spread throughout France and notably in the west. In the 1820s the middle schools of Brittany (Nantes, Rennes, Vannes, Pontivy) encountered a climate of revolt that was difficult to contain, short of expulsions. Other middle schools were affected in France, notably in Caen, Périgueux, and Toulouse.

At the same time, the law faculties of Paris and Rennes and the medical school of Montpellier were also becoming agitated: the high schools produced liberals who, once they become university students, amplified the struggle against the Ultra reaction, which reached its climax after the assassination of the duke of Berry in February 1820. That same year saw the death of Nicolas Lallemand, a law student, killed during June demonstrations for the maintenance of the electoral law in effect. Liberal youths, a product of secondary education, took to the streets and proved to be the most determined adversaries of a regime that could break them only through repressive ordinances, the suspension of professors, and the expulsion of high school and university students. Of twenty-five headmasters named by Monseigneur Frayssinous, minister of ecclesiastical affairs and public education, twenty were priests; when the revolution of July 1830 broke out, sixty of the eighty philosophy professors working in high schools were also priests. The creation of mixed middle schools in 1822 that accepted both ordinary students and candidates for the priesthood, as in the small seminaries, would prove a failure. At the royal middle school of Marseilles, the years under the headmastership of Abbé Denans (1821 to 1823) were marked by both antireligious attitudes on the part of the students and political confrontations between liberals—accused of having formed a Carbonari-type internal association—and royalists; the former overflowed with red ribbons, the latter with fleurs de lys. Until 1830, few years passed without one or more high school revolts in the name of freedom of choice in education. Lamennais, then one of the most extremist Catholic writers, inveighed in the *Drapeau blanc* against the "ungodly, depraved, revolutionary race" educated by the university. This was a recurrent theme in the royalist press, which emphasized the deep split that existed within the generation born toward the end of the Empire. A generation without history, without roots, without a past: the generation of the years 1789 to 1815 was known only in a roundabout way, and thus mythicized. Alfred de Musset wonderfully described this "ardent, pale, nervous generation" of children, "conceived between two battles, educated in middle schools to the roll of drums," and raised from the cradle reading the *Bulletin de la Grande Armée*. When the defeat came, this generation was at a loss; when this vanquished generation, which had yet to live, spoke of glory, ambition, and hope, it was told: "Become a priest."[61]

The frequency of these revolts diminished sharply under the July Monarchy: prominent French families and their heirs identified easily with this regime of economic and political liberalism. In February 1848, jubilation again reigned in the high schools, notably in Avignon and Marseilles. In Paris the students at Louis-le-Grand, rebaptized Descartes, initially took a stand for the republic: they participated in the March high school demonstration and published a daily newspaper, *Le Progrès*. But as early as April some worried about the turn of events, fearful of the consequences of social disorder, about which they were naively frank: "We're already grown and we consider that with all this political agitation, our parents could lose their fortunes and leave us in difficult straits."[62] This fear was exacerbated by the workers' insurrection of June 1848—at which high schoolers fired at the forces of order—and turned to relief at the announcement of the taking of the Pantheon. The few incidents of 1849 and 1850 (at the high schools of Paris, Moulins, Besançon, Le Puy, Toulouse) would be put down by force. Under the Second Empire, politics would be excluded from the curriculum in secondary as well as higher education.

Except during periods of political unrest, the imposition of discipline was incontestably the foremost generator of individual conflicts and of the rarer but more violent collective ones. The importance of the collective, a reflection of the generational and social solidarity that existed among the students, explains both the energy of these revolts and their brevity. Violence occurred in both directions, between teachers and those they taught, between study masters and pupils, and, naturally, among pupils. It often reflected the importance of the social gap that could divide the various segments of the schools. The teacher, whom Lautréamont termed the "pariah of civilization," was disdained at times for his social origins or for his incompetence. In Blois, Augustin Thiery's classroom was graced by a former policeman, an illustrator in charge of Greek, and a grocer who taught rhetoric during his off hours; in Bourg-en-Bresse, Edgar Quinet studied with a fiddler-mathematician and, in Charolles, with an old dragoon capitain who reviewed cavalry regulations with his students. It is true that there was a shortage of teachers at the time. Balzac, Flaubert,

Michelet, Vallès, and many others sketched often cruel portraits of some of them, torturers when they were strong, but victims at the slightest sign of defeat. The case of Vallès and his father illustrates this feeling of disdain, which, while not universal, was fairly widespread, as Paul Gerbod showed in his study of secondary school educators. Unlike the elite graduates of the Ecole normale supérieure and those who had passed their *aggrégation,* who were automatically directed toward teaching posts at the large Parisian institutions and more rarely in the provinces, most teachers could only hope for esteem commensurate with their knowledge and, to an even larger extent, their income.

This provoked particular forms of violence—a covert violence, except in extreme cases. Under the ancien régime, student revolts against school regents were fairly frequent: sticks, stones, swords, bull's pizzles were sometimes used in French educational institutions. In the seventeenth century, several university edicts served as reminders of the prohibition against students carrying arms; an edict of 1763 recommended that the principals and regents watch that "no one give in, in the said schools, to invectives, quarrels, heated debates, blows, so that . . . under no pretense should any firearms, bait, rifles, or fireworks be fired."[63] In England, the public schools were also sometimes the sites of violent rebellions: that of 1779 in Rugby was put down only through the intervention of the armed forces; the last of these revolts occurred at Eton in 1832.[64] In France, under the Empire, the young Lamartine, a boarder at a private institution in Lyons, witnessed a vicious battle, a real fist fight, between an eleven-year-old student who refused to kneel and ask forgiveness for a mistake and a teacher responsible for discipline: the former tore off the wig of the latter who, with the help of servants and cooks, succeeded in throwing the young rebel out on the street.[65] Lamartine would lead the student revenge during a "recreation" period: eyes blindfolded and a sabre in hand, a student had to try to cut the neck of a goose hanging from a string; in cahoots with a classmate, Lamartine used his voice to guide the blindfolded student toward the teacher in question, who thus received, by what seemed simple clumsiness, the sabre stroke intended for the goose. Nevertheless, among the Jesuits in Belley the future poet found a liberal and convivial spirit: there he was among people of his own world.

Students were also victims of the school administration's violence: a violence that cannot really be compared with that of the students, due to the differences in the perpetrators' status, but which sometimes led to real riots. This was the case at the middle school of Eu in 1788, in response to the brutality of the vice principal. A more measured but determined revolt occurred in response to a written punishment assigned by the censor of the lycée Corneille in Rouen: the young Gustave Flaubert took up his pen to ask the headmaster for justice and affirmed the class's solidarity with the pupils threatened with expulsion.[66] In Bourges in 1840, the armed forces had to be sent in. Worse still, at Louis-le-Grand in 1883, the expulsion of a pupil provoked a mutiny, with the breaking of glass, the sacking of a dormitory, and the throwing of various objects; the headmaster and his assistants were overrun. Only the arrival of the police brought an end to the riot, which resulted in the banning of twelve students from all French high schools (an extremely rare case) and the expulsion of ninety-three others from the establishment (sixteen would be readmitted as day students and four readmitted after severe reprimands).[67] The study masters who had far less power and lower social status than the administrators, were often the victims of these power struggles. Alphonse Daudet had such an experience at the middle school of Cévennes to which he had been appointed and where he was confronted with rural students whom he depicts as real brutes: "Vulgar, insolent, conceited, speaking a coarse local slang which I couldn't understand at all. They almost all had that ugliness particular to mutating children, with big hands red from chilblains, voices like young cocks with colds, dumb looks in their eyes, and on top of that they smelled like the school . . . They hated me right away, without knowing me. I was the enemy for them, the supervisor; and from the day I took my seat, it was war between us, a relentless war without truce at every moment." The pathos of the situation, coupled with the cruel description of the insitutions' denizens, illustrates this perception of the supervisor as an outlet for students' excess aggression. This situation is found, in varying degrees, in many other descriptions. Yet Pasteur, a tutor at the Barbet boarding school in 1842, had no such troubles with his students, who were, it is true, at a different age and of a different social background, and who knew that the investment in education was a necessity for them.

Middle school was also the scene of the revenge of the physically strong over the mentally strong; the recreation periods, the revenge over the classroom. The games themselves were sometimes sources of violence: in the northern town of Bergues, the game of *la garuche*—in which one strikes one's adversary with a tightly knotted towel that becomes like a whip—was as violent as a warrior game.[68] Initiation periods also existed, with trials for the newcomer who was not yet part of the group. What was commonly called *bizutage,* or ragging, seems to have originated as a set of practices for student resistance against the administration. Through a perversion of their purpose, the administrators authorized and even encouraged these rites of integration, which, in losing their protest value became violent rituals, justified as part of the necessary acquisition of communal values.

This phenomenon existed in most of the European countries. In the public schools of England, this trial period was marked by the imposition of a certain amount of forced labor or persecution ("fagging") of the youngest at the service of older students. In Russia, we have reports that violence occurred in the gymnasiums and military schools between old and new students, a violence tending toward the perverse and demanding absolute submission.[69] In France, the situation varied according to the type of institution. Forms of ragging (a practice officially banned in 1928) existed in military-type schools, such as Saint-Cyr, starting in 1843; at the polytechnical school, with its period of "absorption," during which the new pupil was subject to the whims of his elders'; and in the large professional schools. These humiliating practices, justified by the idea that the bonds of an elite community were formed by the ordeal, did not at the time have the sexual nature they since took on, when certain competitive institutions of higher education turned coed. They sometimes took on more "benign" forms, as at the Ecole normale where the *"gnouf"* (newcomer) had to tolerate the practical jokes organized by his elders before becoming a "conscript" (a first-year student).

In the middle and high schools, the ragging followed tacit rules set out by the student leader or leaders to test the physical and psychological resistance of the new arrival. In 1779 Napoleon Bonaparte, a poor fragile young foreigner arriving from his native Corsica at the military school of Brienne, was subjected to the hazing and humiliation of his comrades before earning their respect. In 1781, as a new student at the school of Rennes, Chateaubriand was forced to do battle with his classmates: they fought Breton-style or faced off with "swords"—metal compasses attached to the end of canes—pitting rural against city dwellers, semi-Breton speakers against pure French speakers; some 150 years later, at the high school of Quimper, the young Pierre-Jakez Hélias, an incorrigible Breton speaker, still railed against the young bourgeois from the city with their precious language. During the Empire, Alfred de Vigny was ostracized by his classmates for belonging to the nobility. And what can we say about Alexandre Dumas, whose reception at middle school—an improved school, in fact—run by abbé Grégoire in Villers-Cotterêts, was an extremely damp one? If we are to believe the famous novelist—but beware his fertile imagination—his future classmates welcomed him "with a dew that fell like a downpour" on his head: "every student, on a barrel, was posing in the position and in the action of the urinating statue in Brussels. The waters were flowing upon my arrival."[70] A lovely image which, if not authentic, is at least symbolic of the baptismal act that served as a prelude to entering the community. Dumas further notes that, having made the mistake of denouncing this act and its perpetrators, he was forced to face one of them in battle: this parody of God's judgment was favorable.

Michelet, for his part, arrived at Charlemagne high school fragile in appearance and coming from a modest background, two facts that predisposed him to become the butt of clannish violence from his classmates. "From that moment on, I was their toy. They didn't beat me . . . But before and after class, they surrounded me like a curiosity. Those in the back pushed the others, and I had trouble getting away from this hostile crowd, which questioned me only to laugh at my answers, no matter what they were. I was right in the middle of them, like an owl at midday, all startled." This report is astonishingly similar to one by Lacordaire, concerning the high school of Dijon: "From the first day, my classmates took me to be a kind of toy or a victim. I couldn't take a step without their brutality finding the secret to get to me. For several weeks, I was forcibly deprived of all food except for my soup and bread."[71] The absence of resistance on the part of the victims, proof of their submission, gradually led to the cessation of the torments: integration into the group was considered complete. No complaint, no outside intervention, such were the preconditions for this acceptance. As for Jules Vallès, he escaped his difficult situation as son of a teacher, one of his father's students to boot, by publicly receiving punishments presented as unjustified, and also by earning the physical respect of his comrades.

Fights also occurred among students of different establishments, particularly between public and private schools. In 1872 in Charleville, the middle school students and those of Rossat (a private institution attended by Rimbaud) clashed violently, fighting with clubs and forcing the principal of the middle school to accompany his students on walks to avoid scuffles.[72] This clannish violence could prompt the creation of enemy gangs. In the spring of 1879 in Bastia, following a violent dispute in class between two pupils, two groups of six or seven high students wanted to fight "with pistols, revolvers, knives." The combat was forestalled only by the intervention of adults alerted to the matter.[73] Finally, violence occurred between the middle school youths and those of the outer districts, as in Bergues, where each of the two camps was fully aware of the gap in social status dividing them.[74] But this middle and high school violence must be placed in context. Such violence also existed in the world of higher education: in the seminaries, if we are to believe Stendhal's description in *Le Rouge et le Noir* (the threatened Julien Sorel, nicknamed Martin Luther by his fellow students, arms himself with a metal compass); in the world of trade guild members or workers (one need only read Martin Nadaud's account of the bloody Sunday confrontations between construction workers of different guilds); and sometimes between workers and university students, belying the classical assertion that a generational solidarity transcended social distinctions.

SENTIMENTAL AND SEXUAL EDUCATION

The sentimental and sexual behavior of these young bourgeois males is rarely mentioned. But all accounts insist on the emotional pain of the separation from one's family, a prelude to entering the school community, notably in the case of boarding students. The young Törless described by Robert Musil is the archetype of such suffering youth. The tears and shouting, the momentary prostration of the youngest, expressed the emotional breech. Many would seek replacements for the family's affection, and these could take several forms. Sometimes animals were raised: if the school administration was liberal enough, it might be mice or birds—sparrows, magpies, and the like. At the Oratorian middle school in Vendôme, more than 1,000 pigeons were thus reared "to soften our lives, deprived of all communication with the outside and cut off from the caresses of our families," reports Louis Lambert in the novel by Honoré de Balzac.[75] In the case of a more restrictive regime, silk worms, june bugs, stag beetles, and all kinds of insects could be hidden in the dorm.

Sometimes this need for affection was transferred onto a "maternal" teacher. But the ideal substitute was a classmate. Whether of the same age or older, he could become both a confidant, an ear to listen to what the father or mother could not or did not want to hear, and the initiator who would replace family education in the area of sexuality. The depiction of middle school as the site of a sometimes brutal sexual awakening has become commonplace in novels and memoirs: this initiation always occurred through a fellow classmate who was older or more precocious, and it was not without pain on occasion. Elias Canetti, a student in a high school in Vienna, recounts how, informed by a classmate about the way children come into the world ("the man flings himself on the woman like a cock on a hen"), revolted against this revelation; a discussion with his mother confirmed his rejection of this animalistic vision of conception.[76] In *Le Lieutenant-colonel de Maumort*, Roger Martin du Gard treated with an analyst's eye the various stages of sexual revelation for his hero, who attended middle school and then high school in the years 1880 to 1890. A constant theme in this thorough and largely autobiographical analysis is the absence of any female presence in the social relations of the adolescents, an absence that was more or less compensated for by a sublimation of the woman, who was cast into the realm of fantasies. In an almost exclusively male world—in theory, no woman had the right to enter the secondary establishments—the only way for students to have encounters with females—or to brag of having done so—was to spend the night away. Often the imagination got the better of reality. At most one followed a young girl in the street, from a distance, as Michelet and his friend Poinsot did; sometimes one confessed one's (platonic) feelings to the housemaster's wife, with whom one fell hopelessly in love, as did, once again, Michelet: "Unable to express my exaltation through physical channels, I wrote verses, the first I ever composed."[77] In 1823, at the royal middle school of Marseilles, the inspectors were horrified to see washerwomen circulating freely in the dormitories; they hurriedly erected partitions. The students sometimes bragged of their good fortune: At Charlemagne high school, certain of them claimed to visit brothels. These assertions were in contrast with the silence of others, and were worn as a badge of superiority, of distinction, a rejection of conformity. Törless's schoolmates allowed themselves familiarities in word and deed with the farm women of the area surrounding their luxury boarding school, and they frequented a prostitute, a young, gradually fallen peasant girl. But all in all, the sexuality of the middle and high schoolers was mainly verbal, words that stayed within the enclosed world of a small circle. Anything that suggested emotions or sexuality was seen as suspicious by an administration and teaching corps who pretended to have only minds to tend.

More generally, the body was considered suspect—a heritage of medieval eduational thought, like the segregation of the sexes—as evidenced by the minimal hygiene, the near absence of physical exercise, and the surveillance even in "prison" of the solitary sexual behavior of the students. Regarding masturbation, the nineteenth-century educational community remained largely governed by the work by Dr. Tissot, *Onanisme*, published in 1760 and repeatedly reissued. There was discreet but definite surveillance of the "moral purity" of the students, some of whom were suspected of acting as spies for the administration. Among the Jesuits, groups of three students were preferred to groups of two for walks or recreation. At the other end of the social ladder, Antoine Sylvère, known as "Toinou," a student in the modern secondary school run by priests, described the masturbation practiced in class by some of his comrades: "Preciously harvested in a wax or steel nib tin, the product circulated to authenticate the unquestionable productivity of the producer."[78] Classically, the lavatories lent themselves to similar practices, but with the students in twos.

As for problems of homosexuality or sexual violence, they are difficult to determine: the schools and families maintained absolute silence on these matters. At best, mention is made of suspicious books, bawdy songs, expressions considered scandalous, or obscene caricatures, but this was rare, so as not to blemish the reputation of the establishment. In 1807 at the brand-new high school of Toulouse, whose headmaster was overwhelmed, there were drawings "on the wall of the common rooms of the natural parts" of the French teacher. The dormitories were in the hands of students; during one late-night inspection, the headmaster discovered two boarders in the same bed, for which they received a simple verbal reprimand. At the royal middle school of Amiens, in 1835, the directors ordered a student from the older class to stop frequenting a comrade in the younger section, although there was no assertion of a "special friendship" in this interdiction. But the affair degenerated into a rebellion: the students put up barricades with benches and tables and retreated into the study hall, whose door the headmaster had to have broken down; the students then lit a fire and bombarded the headmaster with dictionaries and pieces of wood: only the joint intervention of the police force and the parents enabled calm to be restored.[79]

The violence of this student reaction can be interpreted as an illustration of the extremely tense situations existing in certain establishments. The creation of affective networks, of special relationships and protective behavior, was not necessarily or solely an indication of budding homosexuality, but equally of a lack of affective family relations, which had been brutally severed in the formidably sealed-off boarding schools, and compensated for by a transfer of affection toward a particular comrade. Such situations were acknowledged and forbidden by the rules of the Louis-le-Grand middle school beginning in 1769: "Liaisons that are too particular between pupils often give rise to scandals, slander, defiance toward masters, dissipation, and wasting time. Pupils will take care to avoid them, and the masters are expressly charged with attentively watching out for this."[80] The text remains allusive, of course, but is evidence, *a contrario*, of a clear perception of the affective needs of boys who had been cut off from the world.

Balzac speaks of the "doer," the name given at the Vendôme middle school to the one who placed himself at the service of one of his classmates for all material aspects of daily life. Louis Lambert, the eponymous hero of Balzac's novel and a stand-in for the author, formed a special relationship with the narrator, a relationship characterized by Balzac as follows: "Like two lovers, we got in the habit of thinking together, of sharing our day dreams."[81] Arthur Schnitzler, for his part, recounts how in the Vienna of the 1870s, several of his comrades at the academic middle school felt a passion for one of their own, who was "kind and gifted, pretty like a girl," thereby provoking rivalries: "That there might be a homosexual resonance in the emotions aroused by these passions, neither I nor the interested parties realized at the time; . . . did we even have the slightest idea of the existence of such things?"[82]

Fictional sources—the use of which remains problematic—are more prolix, as seen in the novels by Roger Martin du Gard. In *Les Thibault*, Jacques, the son of a respectable bourgeois family and a student at a Catholic institution, exchanges platonic words of love with a Protestant student he meets at the high school: the "gray notebook" used for this correspondence is seized, triggering the father's anger, the flight of the two adolescents, and Jacques' dispatch to a penitentiary camp. In *Le Lieutenant-colonel de Maumort*, the hero evolves in a Jesuit-run establishment; the students of the older classes all favor a student in the younger class, chosen for his childlike, prepubescent, "somewhat girlish" look—which brings us back to Schnitzler. But "aside from very rare exceptions, these sentiments remained absolutely platonic." This was not the case of Maumort and his friend—but was it a matter, in this instance, of homosexuality, or of a transfer of sexual impulses onto a male partner? Martin du Gard describes at great length the nights in the dormitories where the older students were housed: through a slit in the curtains, we see exhibitionism and obscene gestures, masturbation performed solo or sometimes jointly in the same bed. Subtly, Martin du Gard suggests that the wards' lack of reaction was less out of ignorance of what was occurring than out of a kind of resignation, or even a refusal to intervene in order to preserve the reputation of the establishment and the families. In Robert Musil, we find a briefer but clearer allusion to and description of the relationships among boarders: Törless is fascinated by "the little-girl beauty, still devoid of any sexuality" that emanated from the body of a comrade. But the simple practice of compensatory homosexuality is surpassed in the novel: instead, a totalitarian and sadistic violence is exercised on a scapegoat who becomes the victim of budding tyrants—in whom we see the makings of Nazis—and the object of an increasingly strong, sexually twisted oppression. Death wishes and perverse libidinal impulses are closely intertwined.

What can we conclude from these necessarily scattered bits of information? Alain Corbin has described the existence of groups of male bachelors who had recourse to the prostitution of *filles de noce;* salaried workers and university students formed various "sexual ghettos," to use the expression Jean-Louis Flandrin applied to the age of adolescence.[83] One could extend this notion to high school students who, at an age when working boys of their generation lived in a co-ed world, were confined to their single-sex universe. Apprenticeship traveled from top to bottom, from the "big" boys or the "initiated" toward the small or the ignorant. But the apprenticeship was partial, subterranean, a simultaneous expression of desire and repression. Thus sexuality remained mostly in the realm of fantasy: no information was provided; neither the family nor the teachers lent an ear. Everything was gleaned and digested without being analyzed. Rumor was the source of information. To the precocious intiation to knowledge, to the forced and frenzied absorption of the humanities, corresponded the inhumanity—at least that was how it was experienced—of this sexual segregation. This was bourgeois education: an early intellectual awakening combined with a delay in the awakening of the senses. Hence the recourse to these amorous practices among adolescent males—which it would be inaccurate, generally, to call homosexuality—and, later on, in the course of higher education, the recourse to the prostitute or the young working girl.[84] The ambient discourse was identical among all contemporary ideologies: from Lacordaire to Michelet, the merits of chastity and of limiting sexuality to marriage were praised. Two ideological currents, one moral code. As for bourgeois youths, they too began to respect the propriety of their social milieu: as an adolescent, Schnitzler "severely admonishes" his (French) maid, who changed her corset in his presence, "perhaps not entirely inadvertently."[85] Better still, he made paid but chaste visits to prostitutes, whom he tried, apparently in vain, to guide down the path of virtue; he was sixteen years old at the time and was neither a mystic nor a moralist. We should note, finally, that in order to understand the nature of relations among students, it is imperative to grasp the difference in the expression of feelings between the highly expressive nineteenth century and ours: the correspondence that young men would exchange, including brothers like the Garnier-Pagès, or Charles and Jules Ferry, reflected a keen sensitivity toward one another along with a purity of sentiment and an unambiguous use of the word "love."

THE PARIAHS OF HUMANITY

There remains the matter of the education of girls—the case of these "pariahs" of humanity must necessarily be treated separately. Everywhere in Europe, the German three Ks—*Kirche, Kinder, Küche*—formed the boundary of the female horizon. The entire ancien régime and a good part of the nineteenth century functioned according to a postulate stated in the fifteenth century by Gerson: "All teaching for women must be considered suspicious."[86] We will not revisit the reasons (religious, moral, and social) for such a position, but the consequence was a long delay in education for girls. While in France Condorcet or Diderot might have argued in favor of their schooling, we know what Rousseau wrote about the question; his thoughts on inequality were echoed by writers as late as Proudhon,

Auguste Comte (who spoke of a "natural inferiority that nothing can destroy"), and Renan ("The woman is in charge of goodness, truth is none of her business").[87] The Church, for its part, remained attached to the idea of the woman as the special messenger of Christianity for the generations yet to be born. This position was ultimately fairly close to that of Michelet, Hugo, Enfantin, even that of Flora Tristan, who assigned a privileged moral role to the woman: in all these cases, with some variation, she incarnated the redeemer. The subjugated woman of the Napoleonic Code was also, logically, forgotten when it came to the creation of the university. And despite the advent of feminism in about 1830, despite the forty-eighters (Désirée Gay, Pauline Roland, Jeanne Deroin) and George Sand, the question of secondary education for women was not seriously addressed until 1867, when, with the support of the empress, courses were established by Victor Duruy.[88] However, the creation of such courses naturally raised the question of their purpose: what was the point of schooling that was unsanctioned by diplomas and ultimately would never lead to employment? To stick to our chronological framework, the birth of this secondary education occurred, in France, only at the end of the period we are addressing: on December 21, 1880, thanks to the Camille Sée law, secondary education for women was officially established. Previously such education was not legally recognized, although it existed nonetheless, in various forms. In 1848 Hippolyte Carnot launched a project that didn't reach fruition until the days of June. Not until the Falloux law of 1850 were communes of more than 800 residents obliged to open primary schools to girls, with the result being a sizable increase in their literacy rate. But these girls had a hard time crossing the line into secondary school, a world reserved for boys.

Throughout Christian Europe, women themselves sometimes offered staunch resistance to the attempts at developing education for girls: "Nature, which ranked us second, prohibits our education from raising us to first," writes the mother of Charles de Rémusat in 1819.[89] The few scattered initiatives remained without a future: such was the case of the Smolnyï Institute in Russia, founded by Catherine II in Saint Petersburg in 1764 for about 200 daughters of the nobility, who were subsequently joined by 240 upper-class girls. In France, in the 1820s, the courses of Lévi-Alvarès were popular in Paris—mothers and daughters took them together. There also existed boarding schools and nonreligious institutions; it was in one of these that Balzac's two sisters learned English, the piano, sewing, embroidery, whist, a little chemistry, and a few texts by classical authors. But such schools were uneven as a whole when it came to the quality of the teaching. They would be among the first victims of the Falloux law, which, by expanding the freedom to choose one's form of schooling to the secondary level, would spur a spectacular development of religious schools. Under the Second Empire, the professional classes of Elisa Lemonnier, who sought to train qualified artisans, were highly successful. But whereas in the United States Elizabeth Blackwell became the first woman medical doctor in 1849, in France it was not until 1861 that the first high school degree was granted to a woman, Julie Daubié, who enrolled in the university ten years later. And the phenomenon remained rare: from 1861 to 1873, France granted only sixteen high school degrees to women, of which twelve were *ès sciences* (we see here the gap between "noble" literary subjects and scientific subjects). In 1858 Russia developed gymnasiums for girls; altogether, there were 190 such secondary schools in 1873.[90] In Germany, the positions of Fichte and Jean-Paul, of Campe and Basedow were not particularly progressive on the question.[91] Protestants were nonetheless ahead of the game in terms of the emancipation of women, with the development of a network of secondary schools starting in the early nineteenth century. Private or municipal institutions followed in Munich (1822) and Berlin (1838). By expelling the teaching congregations of Prussia (1875), the Kulturkampf reinforced the importance of the Protestant and secular ones. By around 1870, there existed a network of so-called advanced schools for girls (more than 45,000 of whom were taking classes in these institutions at the time of German unity), which were privately developed, both religious and nonreligious, but it was not until 1889 that the first real high school for girls was created in Berlin. Only in 1891 could women take the *Abitur:* Hildegard Ziegler would be the first German woman to pass this exam, which was administered at the end of secondary studies and was mandatory for enrolling in a university (in 1906 there were 111 female students who passed it). In Austria, the first gymnasium for girls was created in 1892, but girls' high schools received official status only in 1900. In Italy, aside from the predictable importance of religious congregations, advanced schools for girls began to open—in Milan in 1861, then in the other large cities. In England, private institutions were founded, such as the Queen's College of London, in 1848, which accepted young girls age fourteen and over (but they could not receive grades until 1878), and Bedford College, founded in 1849. The activities of Miss Buss (North London Collegiate School, 1850) and of Miss Beale (Cheltenham Ladies' College, 1858) are also familiar. After passage of the law of 1869, secondary establishments for girls grew more numerous: thirty-six public schools for girls were in existence in 1891, including some within the male fiefdoms of Oxford and Cambridge.[92]

In France, the Camille Sée law was adopted following scathing debates, as the Church feared losing its traditional clientele to the republican schools. Under the Second Empire, a polemic raged between Monseigneur Dupanloup and the minister of public education, Victor Duruy, who in 1867 had created secondary classes for girls: Dupanloup became the defender of the girl raised "in the lap of the Church," and mobilized the clergy against the Duruy classes. But the activities of the Society for the Study of Educational Questions and the Society for the Propagation of Education among Women were important. Michel Bréal, founder of the Alsacian School and of the Sévigné middle school (with J. de Marchef-Girard), played a capital role in this struggle. Such figures as the rector Maggiolo, Paul Bert, and Octave Gréard should also be noted. Within the republican camp, however, not everyone was convinced of the need to create middle and high schools for girls. Jules Ferry, in a famous speech given in 1870, explained how the education of women—future wives and mothers—formed the basis for the clerical power he denounced: "Women must belong either to science or to the Church." But he also returned to an argument previously developed by Legouvé in 1849: what was a couple, even if it was united on the basis of love, if only one of the two partners was educated? Ferry contrasted the "marriage of souls" with "intellectual divorce," in which men were forced to seek satisfaction for their intellectual needs outside the home, notably in clubs. It was an argument corroborated by many testimonies of the period, but which nonetheless did not support a thesis placing women on equal footing with men. Camille Sée himself specified that it was not a matter "of turning women away from their true vocation, which is to raise their children and keep a household." Furthermore, there was no parity between girls' high schools and their male homologues: no baccalaureat degrees were granted; at best, a young woman might receive a secondary school completion diploma. At the end of the century, forty-one girls' high schools and twenty-nine middle schools were in operation, some of which, such as Fénelon in Paris, quickly developed good reputations. But attendance grew rather slowly faced with competition from the religious schools, which continued to attract girls of the upper and middle classes. The laws of 1901 (on associations) and 1904 (on Church-run schools) would play an indirect role in the shift of middle and high school girls toward public and secular establishments. In 1881, a total of about 6,000 girls attended the various types of secondary establishments; in 1891, 12,000; on the eve of the First World War, about 35,000 girls were counted—versus twice as many boys.[93]

Almost all of these girls' schools functioned quite differently from the boys' schools: the accent was placed less on passing exams and more on the content of the material, which was "adapted" to the "feminine" virtues (modesty, sensitivity, simplicity, and the like). Nothing was really dealt with in depth, no Latin or Greek was taught in the watered-down humanities courses. There was little science, and little or no physical education. Instead, one studied "easy" authors, history, geography, and sometimes cosmography; drawing, writing, the inevitable needlework, singing, music, and sometimes dance. Girls' educations were often less sustained than those of boys, and only a minority finished their schooling. Many attended only a few classes and did their homework by correspondence. The students were more socially homogeneous than in the boys' schools: in the public establishments, the lower-middle and middle classes dominated. This included commercial and industrial families but also those in the liberal professions and in public service, as well as the daughters of teachers, who monopolized the rather parsimoniously distributed grants. There were few lowerclass girls, and the upper-class was also little represented, given its preference for Catholic schools. The pool of teachers was sometimes wanting in quantity and quality, which led to the creation of the Ecoles normales supérieures (in Fontenay and Sèvres), which accepted the best students from the public schools. If they didn't marry, the graduates then went on to teach in middle or high schools; many remained single, living their profession as a sacred trust.

Aside from the public high schools and private secular schools, there existed two additional solutions for providing girls with an education beyond the rudiments of reading, writing, and arithmetic: home teaching and the education received in religious teaching communities. Home education was the more common, but was less well documented. Sometimes it was a sibling who provided the rudiments of culture. The brother of the future Saint-Simonian Suzanne Voilquin was a defrocked seminarian who taught his sister snatches of ancient and contemporary history.[94] As a high school student in Bastia, the young Lanfranchi decided to teach his sisters a little natural history and French philosophy.[95] But the task usually fell to the mother. How can we evaluate what mothers brought to this teaching or transmitted to their daughters, aside from basic religion? Some were cultivated women who held occasional salons and proved to be real educators. This was the case of the German mother of Marie D'Agoult, whose curriculum for her daughter included Grimm, Schiller, Mozart, Haydn, and cosmography, while her French father proposed Horace and Ovid, Rabelais and Montaigne, La Fontaine and Voltaire.[96] This well-educated bicultural family provided their daughter with an aristocratic education completed by French dance and arms instruction. When it came time to move on to serious things, the task was entrusted to a French abbot who taught Latin, grammar, history, geography, and the rudiments of mathematics to the young girls and boys of the Faubourg Saint-Germain (in coed classes, a rarity)[97] and to a private German teacher. An advanced education, all in all, and thus relatively exceptional, even in the circles in which Marie d'Agoult belonged.

The convent also educated, with the clearly defined mission of turning the young girls it accepted into good Christians. The Ursulines, the Visitandines, the Community of Notre-Dame, and later the Institute of the Sacred Heart were some of the most common teaching communities. A cloistered life was not obligatory, as evidenced by the Ladies of Saint-Maur. Starting in the seventeenth century, the community of Saint-Louis, founded in Saint-Cyr in 1686 by Madame de Maintenon and influenced by Fénelon, author of the *Traité de l'education des filles* (Treatise on the Education of Girls), was created to give a true education to girls of the nobility. Following the Revolution's elimination of convents, private boarding schools developed. The Napoleonic state established the Maisons de la Légion d'Honneur, at which Madame Campan (who had opened a boarding school for girls of high society in Saint-Germain in 1795) and Madame de Genlis (who had been the "governess" of the future Louis-Philippe) would distinguish themselves. But beginning with the Consulat, religious schools, such as the Sacré-Coeur founded by Sophis Barat in 1801, returned and sprang up in large numbers. The Restoration ushered in the golden age of the convent: Sainte-Clotilde, l'Assomption, and les Oiseaux were intended for an upper-class clientele. After 1830 and the advent of liberal Catholicism, a reaction favored giving women more sustained instruction so that they could become the pillars of the Christian faith, which seemed threatened among the new generations.

Life in convents was generally fairly harsh: the material severity, austerity, and monotony of daily life were worse than in the boys' boarding schools, as was the lack of contact with the outside world: "We were cloistered in every sense of the word. We only went out twice a month and we only slept out on New Year's." These are the words of the young Aurore Dupin (George Sand), educated by the English Augustines of Paris from 1818 to 1820.[98] As for Marie d'Agoult, she did not seem to suffer from this confinement. After an early youth marked by a real education, but also by real liberty, living "in great freedom, improvising new amusements every day, sometimes alone, sometimes with children from the area," at the age of sixteen she entered the Ladies of Sacré-Coeur, where her name and rank earned her a few modifications in the rules: a private room, a piano and piano teacher, extra outings, and so on. In addition, the quality of her previous education allowed her to pass directly into the advanced class—signified by a belt of black ribbon worn by the students—which was limited in size to six students, all nobles. Convent life was not unpleasant for this young girl, who was warmly welcomed by her classmates and sensitive to the religious aura of the site.

Yet criticisms abound in her testimony, about the mediocre—if not dangerously unhealthy—food and the near total lack of cleanliness, similar to the conditions in boys' schools but with the religious and moral dimension of disdaining the flesh. "We took baths at Sacré-Coeur only under doctor's orders, in case of illness."[99] Ten minutes of morning washing with a basin of cold water, and no mirror. Though this regimen produced "a halt in life," the cessation of her menstrual cycle, no doctor was alerted and no treatment was offered. Something else she decried was the practice of informing and the constant denunciations, which fell to the Children of Mary, a small group of the smartest and "most Christian" of the students. The relationships among the girls also had a violent side: one ugly, simple-minded pupil was persecuted by her fellow students until Marie intervened. Emotional tensions among students or among teachers and students were repressed, but they surfaced sometimes following minor incidents. As for the quality of the education received, it too was harshly judged by Marie: Athens, Rome, antiquity and the Renaissance, the Ladies of Sacré-Coeur knew nothing about them. Everything was watered down, everything was dulled, including religious teaching, which was based on sensation, close to mysticism. There was no scientific teaching, no natural history—"nature is Satan." These were no doubt the thoughts, in retrospect, of a woman of letters who was subsequently exposed to "true" culture, which is to say the culture ordinarily reserved for men. But she did not have militant, hostile words for the convent as a system: Marie d'Agoult was basically happy there. The relatively free regimen under which these upper-class girls lived allowed for contact with the world, of which the young Aurore Dupin was deprived. This was evidenced by the visiting room, where every Thursday the families of boarding students assembled in circles, including brothers, male cousins, "middle schoolers, students from the Saint-Cyr military academy, from the polytechnic, and page boys": the world of men was not entirely absent from the life of the young ladies of Sacré-Coeur. And ultimately there developed a fear of the void upon leaving the convent, to which Marie d'Agoult returned on several occasion for religious ceremonies.

CONCLUSION

At the twilight of his life, Vallès again addressed the theme of high schools: his flamboyant style found material for expression in a subject that had remained dear to him. He launched into a merciless critique of the system of secondary education, harping on the military-style discipline that reigned: the militarized high school, the enlisted student, trained to be absolutely obedient and to fit a single mold. "The high schooler, according to the formula, will be a foot soldier by the age of twenty, and will remain one everywhere, always, in offices or academies, with children or crowds, in the face of budding sciences and of new literature, before every libertarian movement."[100] There was only one solution: "The high school is another Bastille to tear down." His was a losing battle, however, and Vallès knew this better than anyone, being a pure product of these schools. But beyond the polemical and political spirit that prodded him on, beyond words and resentment, there remained this constant return to his youth, to his past as a primary school, secondary school, and university student. This youth filled with humanities and written punishments, but also with friendship and hope, had left an indelible mark.

This is ultimately what comes through in Vallès's many writings, and this is also what he has in common with those of his contemporaries who left their memoires: the middle school or high school was a place of social formation, education, and instruction. Whether loved or hated, feared or longed for, left regretfully or joyfully, middle and high schools made a lasting impression on those who attended them. These students formed a privileged class, or caste: they clashed with and sometimes adapted to a same culture; they grouped together into alumni associations—at Henri IV beginning in 1833, at Louis-le-Grand in 1839—to prolong the feeling of belonging to an elite bourgeoisie—which, taking as its own the principles of 1789, launched itself toward the conquest of economic and political power in France and in Europe. School was important to this strategy. In the case of primary school, its role was indirect: by giving the rudiments of education to the people, it was intended to "civilize" them and allow them to recognize the supremacy of the "superior" class. In the case of secondary education, its role was direct: even more than higher education, it was a stepping-stone to a social position that family heritage (through transmission of a trust, a clientele, or a patrimony) did not always provide. It was thanks to their success in secondary school, to their absorption of the system of values conveyed by its teaching, that Pasteur, Gambetta, and Ferry, among others, became emblematic figures of the republic. More broadly, and on the scale of Europe as a whole, secondary teaching was the training ground for the sons of the conquering middle classes. It is striking to note the parallels between the creation of national systems of secondary education and the rise of these middle classes, which, through economics and politics, took the reins of already thriving and sometimes budding states. This "fabrication" of states required the "fabrication" of elites; of the latter, it has been said that they received more of a practical education than a gentleman's education in the nineteenth century; that the shift from the ancien régime to the contemporary period was marked by this reversal of values. But this vision is too schematic. Middle and high schools were as much places of education—which was passed through the teacher as well as the classmate—as of training, and ultimately they produced individuals educated according to the values of this "new" society: effort, merit, competition, success, and so on. If, in the end, secondary education became an issue of national importance in the nineteenth century, it was less for the social promotion it offered than for its role as an educational agent, a shaper of youth, which was confronted with a system of values that subsequently had to be applied, passed on, and defended in life. The high school was ultimately a normative agent, which is what Vallès, the rebel, forcefully denounced.

CHAPTER 6

YOUNG REBELS AND REVOLUTIONARIES, 1789-1917

Sergio Luzzatto

It's the Revolution that brought old age to the world.

GEORGE SAND

In every European country, throughout the nineteenth century, a heterogeneous but clear image emerges of a restless or rebellious youth: the French and Italian Carbonari of the 1820s and the majority of the Russian Decembrists were young; the students and workers at the Parisian barricades in July 1830—at least those whom Delacroix depicted in his famous painting—were young; those who followed Mazzini and his "Young Europe" of the 1830s were, by definition, young, as were so many heroes and martyrs of the European revolutions of 1848; the "sons" who revolted against their "fathers" in the Russia of the 1860s—the Russia of Turgenev and Dostoyevsky—were young; so were the intellectuals who came to the defense of Captain Dreyfus in the France of the 1890s, and the members of the Wandervögel who, after the turn of the century, attacked the tranquil Wilhelmine bourgeoisie and its labored certainties. The history of the early twentieth century would further confirm the permanence of this equation between youth and rebellion in France, Germany, England, and Italy, where so many spokesmen for the youth of Europe invoked the regenerative virtues of war—a call to arms to which the generation of 1914 would respond with great discipline.

Young against old: the nineteenth century was constantly tempted to see protest movements as merely the effects of regrettable generational conflicts. At first sight this seems to be a paradoxical temptation. It was at the very moment when youth lost the role it had played in traditional societies—a culturally recognizable role and a factor in social cohesion—

that it began making political demands and thus became the object of political denunciation. But this temptation, if one looks harder, does make sense. In the "new regime" that the ten years of the French Revolution and fifteen years of Napoleonic power bequeathed to posterity,[1] in a century marked by the "discovery" of the family,[2] it was especially urgent to give new definitions to the respective roles of youth, adulthood, and old age. It was no accident that, from Masonic lodges to the Carbonari sects, from the Saint-Simonian church to Cabet's Icarians, reformers and revolutionaries, converts and utopians were so concerned with finding an associative formula that could reconcile the egalitarian aspirations contained in the idea of fraternity with the hierarchical order guaranteed by the recognition of paternity.[3] In any case, the temptation to celebrate or deounce, in moments of crisis or rupture, a youth that was determined to intervene is sufficiently present in the political culture of the nineteenth century to merit serious consideration by the historian.

Many will object that this image of nineteenth-century youth as perpetually in revolt has been disproved, or at the very least blurred, by the best research in the field: highly attuned to the factual reality, social historians have shown, for example, that the revolutionaries who climbed onto the Parisian barricades in July 1830 were not young lads but, for the most part, artisans of all ages employed in traditional trades; they have pointed out as well that in June 1848, youths served the cause of order far more than that of revolution. The fact remains, however, that young people inspired fear throughout the nineteenth century. Everything seemed to conspire to make youths appear untrustworthy: the corporative system of the ancien régime was no longer in place to harness their efforts while the urbanization that accompanied industrial development upset their geographical distribution; nor should we overlook the novelty of a familial and social context in which primogeniture was being questioned and the average period of bachelorhood was lengthening. Hence the urgency of instituting a kind of delaying tactic, of postponing the moment when young men could assume political and social responsibilities.[4] This was indeed what the electoral laws strove to do, basing the distinction between the voting and nonvoting citizen on the criteria not only of property but also of age. Of the vicissitudes and effects of such a delay, the heros of the bildungsroman are our literary witnesses, while bohemianism was the living incarnation.[5] But for describing its logic, no contemporary found more incisive words than Ludvig Börne, the poet in whom the German youths of the 1830s saw as the symbol of their contesting of philistine values: "It is because every man is born a Roman that bourgeois society seeks to de-Romanize him," said Börne. What was the point of gambling and society games, gazettes, novels, operas, casinos, tea salons, "the years of apprenticeship and novitiate," life in the garrisons, the changing of the guard, the ceremonies, the courtesy calls, the efforts to be fashionable, if not to deplete youth of its strength and ambition?[6]

But the revolutions of 1848 demonstrated to the European bourgeoisie the insufficiency of such measures, and highlighted the fragility of a world undermined by crisis in its entrenched hierarchy. After two years of terror, the leading classes of continental Europe regrouped, determined to defend themselves as much against the revolt of their sons as against a proletarian revolution. During the second half of the century, in the most advanced countries on the Continent, the combined mechanisms of obligatory education and military service would assure social discipline, more than compensating for the potential disorder deriving from the granting of universal suffrage.[7] The schools were modeled on the barracks: the literature of the period abounds in reports of arbitrary punishments inflicted on young students by teachers who were stricter than any sergeant. In the end, the pedagogical efforts of two generations of educators would have the desired effect: the youth rebellion of the late nineteenth and early twentieth centuries was different from what had preceded it, aiming to serve the interests of the nation rather than yearning for a revolutionary transformation of society. That is why it escaped the control of the socialist parties even more than that of bourgeois organizations.

Whether they involved action or were limited to mere words and gestures, the youth protests of the nineteenth century reminded contemporaries—and remind historians today—of the incontrovertible novelty of the revolutionary legacy: youth had ceased to exist in its traditional form, as an age group with its own social and cultural function, (see

Chapter 3 in this volume), and as compensation for this break took on enlarged proportions in people's imaginations. It is thus not so much the *real presence* of youth in the various European revolutions that I am proposing to study here as it is its *presumptive presence:* the protagonists of the pages that follow are not so much, or not only, the youths who actually mounted barricades or belonged to political protest movements as they are rebels or revolutionaries who, whatever their age, felt young, and fought like young people. They will be joined here by the political adversaries of this so-called youth, insofar as the latter felt that the conflicts were above all generational. So far as the geographic terrain of this study is concerned, it seems appropriate to recognize the central place of the French, and especially of Parisians, in the revolutionary activities and legend of the Continent, at least for the period from 1789 to the Commune. Other major personages—whether Italian, German, Austrian, Rumanian, Swiss, or Russian—are naturally part of the story, but if they are, it is mainly because they spent their youth confronting the revolutionary myths and rituals of France.

Rather than myths and rituals, in fact, one could also say parodies and fashions. The more foreign France was to them, the sooner these other revolutionaries recognized, starting with the Directoire and the "sister republics," the extent to which the force of the French revolutionary tradition was problematic, and how much its cumbersome past weighed on the course and outcome of other revolutions: hence Vincenzo Cuoco's well-known harsh critique of the "passive" Neapolitan revolution of 1799, of which he was nonetheless one of the protagonists, and Marx's vicious remark in *The Eighteen Brumaire of Louis Bonaparte* that the tragedies of history are destined to repeat themselves as farces. The revolutionaries of the nineteenth century, at least the most perceptive ones, were also able to see the extent to which their own respect for Parisian primacy was reverential homage or simple mechanical and pedestrian reverence: "You can translate popular Russian fables, Swedish family sagas or English stories about crooks: we will still have to look to France for everything that is important to the masses, not because it will always be true, but because it will always be the fashion," wrote Karl Gutzkow, a disenchanted publicist with an illustrious past as founder of the literary movement baptized Young Germany, in his 1842 *Letters from Paris*.[8] In 1849 a leader of the moderate liberals in the Frankfurt parliament would say: "Our revolutions, like our fashions, must come from Paris."[9]

In a particularly dense page of his study *Paris, Capital of the Nineteenth Century*, Walter Benjamin considered that the categories of "fashion" and "aging" were essential to an understanding of the fundamental difference between the tradition of the dominant classes and that of the oppressed: for him, the proletariat lived more slowly than the bourgeoisie, or at least lived more slowly than the bourgeoisie in its incarnation as the dominant class. The movements and ideologies of the bourgeoisie, which have constructed something that serves as its tradition, depend closely on fashion, because they must periodically adapt to whatever social conflict is occurring, deny that it is conflictual, and, instead, prove its harmony. Conversely, these waves of fashion break against the mass of the oppressed, whose militant leaders do not age, or at least do so more slowly than the major figures of the bourgeoisie.[10]

The idea that the bourgeois tradition ages rapidly is even more pertinent to this study than that of fashion. It is a notion that is open to discussion, no doubt, for we know that many of the proletarian movement leaders of the nineteenth century were of bourgeois origins, and that it was through the "bourgeois" channels of printed matter (books and brochures, newspapers and memoirs) that most of the revolutionary tradition was passed on from one generation to the next, through a complex process that included oral transmission and increased literacy. But it is also a very pertinent notion, at least in the French context: from 1793 to the days of July, from 1848 to the Commune, the transmission of every revolutionary experience required that veterans and new recruits meet, and these encounters often led to conflict, the stakes of which resided not only in the political currentness of each side's ideas, but also in the age group that each side attributed to the other. It is difficult to understand fully the history of nineteenth-century French revolutionary youth without studying its conflictual relationship with those who preceded it on the path to revolution. Among the young, the arrogance of the neophyte went hand in hand with the cult of the "great ancestors"; among the old, gratitude for the heirs was inseparable from a pioneer's pride. In the memory of each was the sometimes stirring, sometimes annoying memory of the Declaration of the Rights of Man of 1793, which states in Article 28 that "one generation cannot subject future generations to its laws." Thus the genealogy of those recognized as ancestors and those who were excommunicated, of masters and monsters, was ordered according to complex formulas. And sometimes the old people ended up more "to the left" than the young.

Roman Jakobson demonstrated this brilliantly with respect to the generation of Maiakovskii: the relationships between the biographies of a generation and the march of history are curious, while "the age at which a generation's call to service comes, as well as the length of its service" are different for different periods; in some generations, history mobilizes "youthful ardor," in others, "tempered maturity or old wisdom."[11] It would be wrong, then, to try to write the political history of young nineteenth-century Frenchmen as if it had occurred in a world as devoid of adults as that of Linus and Charlie Brown: the history of young revolutionaries is also the history of middle-aged and even older men; the path is long, and everyone runs and stumbles. We must therefore avoid any teleological approach to the history of France in the nineteenth century, which would tend to see in it the progressive and logical realization of the Revolution's promises, from one revolutionary generation to the next. But the French Revolution must nonetheless be our starting point. For some historians, it was there that the modern concept of the generation was invented.[12] Undoubtedly, the Revolution inaugurated a political rhetoric around young people that had lasting repercussions: that youth, in its liberality and exuberance, is a permanent danger to the political and social order.

GOLDEN YOUTH, WASTED YOUTH

"Revolution is to the human spirit what the sun of Africa is to vegetation; the influence of freedom makes every fruit *precocious* and every institution easy!"[13] To demonstrate to his colleagues of the Convention how necessary it was to create a military school that would train the most promising French youth in the art of war, Bertrand Barère, the regular spokesperson for the Committee of Public Safety during the Terror, had recourse to his usual metaphorical and baroque language. Yet these words, spoken in February 1794, furnish an excellent definition of the Jacobin wager, which the Ecole de Mars would concretize a few months later: while young people from eighteen to twenty-five were fighting courageously on the country's borders for the defense of republican freedoms, why not select several thousand youths aged sixteen and seventeen, from every department, gather them in Paris for some weeks, and inculcate them once and for all in the secrets of the martial art, hatred of tyranny, wariness of prejudice, sincere patriotism, and the fraternal instinct? After Thermidor, the Convention deputies felt equally confident about the possibility of training a generation of schoolteachers in identical criteria, and it was on the model of the Ecole de Mars that the Ecole normale supérieure would be founded. But perhaps it is more interesting to focus on the Ecole de Mars, whose history, better than that of any other revolutionary project, reveals both the Jacobins' attitude with respect to youth and the extent of their failure.

It all began auspiciously; the provinces responded encouragingly to Barère's report of 13 Prairial, year II (June 1, 1794), which served as the basis for the founding of the military training school. Several districts proposed more candidates than the law provided for. A selection was made with all due attention, and care was taken to give preference to young people of limited resources and, especially, to those whose families' political orientation seemed safe. In more than one case, the national agents in charge of recruitment were pleased to note a laudable republican zeal among the candidates: the six students from the district of Limoux, for instance, had the promising idea of taking nicknames from the saints of the new calendar: Basil, Laurel, Tulip, Oak, Mushroom, Rake! As tutelary figures of the new military school, the Convention had (not surprisingly) chosen Bara and Viala, two young martyrs of the Revolution upon whom republican lore had quickly seized: their busts were enthroned on the plain of Les Sablons, at the outskirts of Paris, where the 3,400 recruits of the Ecole were assembled. In short, there was ample justification for Barère's optimism in his report of Prairial, in which he took care to emphasize (in purely Jacobin language) that the job of raising free men lay with the great family of the nation, even more than with each individual family. He said he was certain the Ecole de Mars would produce a race of true republicans, and that it would count neither a single "dandy" *(muscadin)* nor a single "hermaphrodite" among its ranks.

Barère's words are instructive for the historian, for they are merely an embroidered version of the stereotypical political discourse of the period. The rhetoric, or ideology, that underlay the creation of the Ecole de Mars was that of virility. The students were sixteen and seventeen years old, sixteen also being the age at which the creators of revolutionary festivals considered that young Frenchmen could be awarded weapons and be called to participate in the parades under arms, the true rite of passage in the new republican liturgy.[14] From this point of view, the Ecole de Mars experiment was meant to be the most sophisticated and most successful of all possible festivals of virility: at the borders, young people who had trained on the plain of Les Sablons would prove themselves real men. Barère's negative reference to dandies (*muscadins*, affected youths who were unrepentant opponents of the Jacobin regime) and hermaphrodites was no accident: to the intransigent revolutionaries, these were individuals who wished to hide from the virile struggle to defend the Republic.

But this cult of virility contradicted the fundamental moralism of the Jacobin imagination—the kind of moralism that led the Ecole de Mars doctor to caution students against frequenting women, not only to avoid illnesses but also to show that they were different from "those depraved peoples who seek pleasure in a life of debauchery and libertinage." The students were thus invited to steer clear not only of prostitutes but also of women who too openly proclaimed their revolutionary faith, or who were too enthusiastic, too masculine in the way they lived this faith: they too were whores, if one really thought about it, because politics implied the use of body and spirit, and it was said there could be no seduction without prostitution. When Barère railed against hermaphrodites, he was thinking not only of the femininity of certain men but also of the masculinity of certain women. It was hard to reconcile the independence of bachelors and the assertiveness of women with the conservatism of the Jacobin mentality, which cultivated the myth of the father and was equally wary of ardent young men and militant women, whom it branded transvestites.[15]

After the fall of Robespierre, in the new political climate of Thermidor, the *muscadins* swelled the ranks of what was referred to as the "golden youth," gangs of young men who attacked the Jacobins with canes at the Palais-Royal, who invaded the Parisian theaters and forced the actors to sing counterrevolutionary tunes, who destroyed the busts of Marat in public places and finally ensured that his ashes were ignominiously excluded from the Pantheon. All this was done with the friendly complicity of the Committee of General Security, firmly controlled by the Thermidorians, who, at least initially, praised the patriotic virtues of these young men: "Never has it been easier to be a hero," Charles Lacretelle, one of the leaders of this golden youth, would say decades later with laudable sincerity.[16] Faced with this phenomenon, prorevolutionary historians have merely repeated the Jacobin argument, tending to see these youth gangs as a late eighteenth-century version of fascist squads. But the young men of year III were as little cut out to be heroes as they were to be monsters; their protests simply illustrated the resurgence of a part of civil society that the Revolution had disdainfully rejected, that of young bachelors (and it was no accident that Thermidor was also, in certain respects, the revenge of women).[17]

The Ecole de Mars episode clearly reflects the price that Jacobinism ended up paying for its naïve belief in the possibility of shaping youths according to the Spartan model cherished by the adult revolutionaries. A few weeks after 9 Thermidor, the Ecole encountered a crisis: the students were proving increasingly indifferent to military discipline; not surprisingly, these adolescents began longing for the comforts of family life and objecting to their almost complete isolation from the rest of the world. As for the Thermidorian deputies, they claimed to be skeptical about the political loyalty of an institution founded during the most glorious days of Jacobinism. Louis-Stanislas Fréron, whom everyone considered to be the authentic patron of the golden youth, had no trouble convincing his Convention colleagues to send the Ecole de Mars recruits home, taking advantage of the occasion to again magnify the contribution of the *mus-*

cadins to the cause of the Republic. A few months later, when the offensiveness of the golden youth had impressed itself on the sansculotte movement and the Convention understood the urgency of restoring peace, the same Fréron took it upon himself to sound the requiem for these young gangs, which he had manipulated so skillfully: "It pains us to realize that children had taken it upon themselves to maintain order and ensure the triumph of justice," he wrote in *L'Orateur du Peuple*, in the spring of year III.[18]

This was also, more generally speaking, a requiem for the Jacobin wager that young people, if properly trained, could precociously adopt an adult republican identity. The Revolution was preparing for another wager, this time on the psychological and social moratorium to be imposed on adolescence viewed as distinct from childhood and adulthood—thus, on the kind of "quarantine" that boys should undergo before fully assuming their roles as fathers and citizens. Time was therefore the issue. The Jacobins had counted on the miraculous effects they expected to achieve, in barely a few weeks, by both removing youths from corrupt society and adequately indoctrinating them. The Thermidorians, for their part, were more realistic. While promoting a cult of old age—which didn't prevent them from also organizing an annual youth festival, as it provided a spectacular forum to demonstrate clear age distinctions[19]—they were preparing to subject youths to a far longer period of separation.

In the spring of year III, the Convention began the debate on the new constitution and invited republicans from throughout France to send their views on what needed to be done. It is immaterial whether the initiative for this popular consultation was based on pure demagogy, on respect for tradition (this had been the procedure in 1791 and 1793), or on a sincere wish on the part of the representatives to know the political will of the electorate. What matters most, from our point of view here, is that among the hundreds of citizens who addressed more or less detailed letters to the Convention, many took the trouble to discuss, among other things, the problem of youth. For these ad-lib legislators, the question of what age the constitution should set for the right to vote and the closely related question of the age required for citizens' eligibility to hold public office were the best occasions to take a stand on the issue. Whether they declared themselves favorable to maintaining the constitutional disposition of 1793 (the right to vote and eligibility for office conferred at twenty-one) or to returning to the delay provided for in the constitution of 1791 (right to vote at twenty-one, eligibility at twenty-five), the correspondents to the Convention proved unanimous in their desire to link the question of voting to that of civic status. Like their representatives, the constituents were convinced that a direct relationship existed between an individual's age, his marital status, and his trustworthiness as a citizen.[20]

But what counted even more, from our point of view, was the Convention's final decision: aside from different property requirements [which also were a way of differentiating by age, as young persons rarely had the necessary patrimony], the new constitution of year III provided that all Frenchmen would be nonvoting citizens from the age of twenty-one; that they had to wait until they were twenty-five to exercise their active right to vote within electoral assemblies, until they were thirty to be elected to the Council of Five Hundred (which initiated laws), and until they were forty to be elected to the Council of Elders (which approved or rejected laws). To belong to the latter chamber, one also had to be married or widowed. These measures were momentarily tempered by a clause in the constitution stating that for the first two elections, the minimum age to be eligible for the Council of Five Hundred would be lowered to twenty-five: the Revolution did not want to immediately reject all its sons. Putting aside these transitional clauses, and the brutality of the events that destined this 1795 constitution to a lifespan of only four years, the fact remains that the Thermidorians opened a new chapter in the political history of youth. According to the logic the Thermidorians would transmit to the nineteenth century, the interval separating the ages of twenty-five and forty (later it would be thirty) represented the quarantine, or delay, to which each "youth" had to be subjected before being recognized as a full citizen (see chart).

As for the Jacobin diehards, they were reduced to writing for increasingly clandestine papers and were hunted down as former agents of the Reign of Terror throughout Paris and in the depths of the provinces— when they were not already in Thermidorian prisons. For them as well,

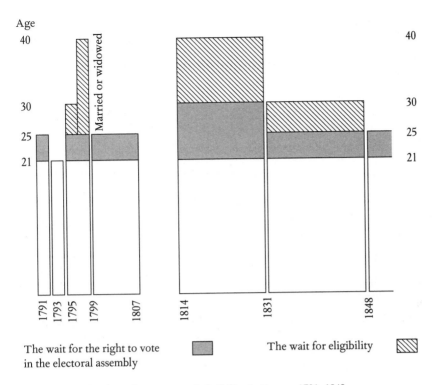

The wait for the right to vote
in the electoral assembly   The wait for eligibility

Minimum ages for the right to vote and eligibility in France, 1791–1848

the time had come for disenchanted reflection on the role and destiny of youth in the Revolution. For those who did not die in combat, for those who did not honor Saint-Just's precept—according to which a good revolutionary never dies in his bed—mounting a revolution also meant surviving it: in other words, it meant in a certain sense surviving oneself, when the new world (or the world one had tried to change) adjusted, and when the fire that burned in the mind of every revolutionary died out. For those who had thrown themselves into the fray when they were young, this ashen period would last a lifetime. This is what awaited Marc-Antoine Jullien, a figure who is central to the pages that follow, for though it cannot be claimed that he was typical of the young revolutionaries who survived the Revolution, he was without a doubt a fascinating witness.

At the tender age of twenty, Jullien was already stagnating in his Thermidorian prison cell, with a long past as a militant in the service of the Terror. He had arrived on the revolutionary scene as an exterminating angel. The son of a member of the National Convention, at barely eighteen he became Robespierre's confidence man, in which capacity he carried out delicate and cruel missions in the provinces during year II. After 9 Thermidor, he was chased down, along with all of Robespierre's agents, and he remained in prison throughout year III, until he received the amnesty that followed the monarchist plot of Vendémiaire, year IV. While in prison, he learned of the sacrifice of so many republicans, the horror of the White Terror, and the progress of the counter revolution. He wanted to find a means of opposition, but his political techniques were ill adapted to the new times.

More than a document of the factional struggles in the France of 1795 (year III), Jullien's prison writings (the letters, scattered notes, and diary pages that survived) are of interest to us as a spontaneous expression of the state of mind of a young revolutionary who grew up too quickly and aged prematurely. "I was born in a volcano, I lived in the midst of its eruption, I will be buried in its lava": such is the hyperbolic style of a young man fresh out of school, marked by the pain of an adult who realizes his youth has been spent. "My life is a dark and terrible story, but one that is touching and educational for inexperienced youth," writes Jullien, on the same page of his diary on which he wonders who will be the "savior" who will restore freedom to the beleaguered Republic. If his life is an educational story, it is because youth can learn how to protect itself against revolutionary fever. Finally liberated in Vendémiaire, year IV, Jullien jots down this Rousseauist reflection: "I am leaving, I never wish to see Paris again, I want cows, milk . . . I am twenty-one years old, may the dawn of my life no longer be clouded by dark images."[21]

By the coup d'état of 18 Brumaire, year VII (November 9, 1799), the "savior" invoked by Jullien, and many others, was incarnated in Napoleon Bonaparte. Jullien didn't waste any time: a few weeks after the coup, he anonymously published an overtly Bonapartist *Entretien politique sur la France*. Moreover, contrary to his initial intention on being released from prison, the three preceding years of freedom had been not a bucolic interlude but a political adventure as he had followed Napoleon's army from the Cisalpine Republic to Egypt and the Neapolitan Republic. He had moved in the entourage of Bonaparte himself, to whom he had made known his critiques. Putting aside the political opportunism that may have pushed Jullien to take up his pen in Frimaire, year VII, what is striking in his *Entretien* is his constant reflection on the destiny of youth, and more generally on the generations who are fated to live through a revolution.

For Jullien, the current generation was incurably corrupt. A strong government was therefore needed, one that was sufficiently sturdy to hold up until a new generation had matured. In the meantime, children had to be placed in state boarding schools at a tender young age, where they would receive long, strict training in academic subjects, work, and war. According to Jullien's plan, for ten or twenty years they should be placed "as if in quarantine, and sequestered from society, to safeguard them from contagion and to train a new generation."[22] We have before us, in many ways, an updated version of the Spartan dream, present at the heart of so many political and pedagogical reflections during the second half of the eighteenth century: bathing newborns in new wine, combining physical exercise with study, and, especially, taking children away from their families to entrust them to the exacting care of the state.[23] But it is not so much the century's optimism about education that we should note in Jullien as it is a kind of despairing pedagogical rage: we are far from the Ecole de Mars or the Ecole normale endeavors, far from the belief that a few months or weeks of training will triumph over universal vices. The experience of the Revolution had proved the futility of concentrating pedagogical training into a few months; for Jullien the Jacobin, as for the Thermidorians, young people had to be separated from the city for their entire youth.

Luckily for the "children of the century," projects such as Jullien's remained dead letters, at least in the short term. In his famous "confessions," Alfred de Musset was content to exaggerate only slightly the dark spots in a picture otherwise faithful to reality.[24] The history of youth under the Empire encompasses high school students as agitated as adults would have them austere, overzealous sons of Grand Army officers, polytechnic students impatient within their four walls; during the Hundred Days, if so many students followed Napoleon, it was less out of enthusiasm for the imperial military legend than out of a hope that the dictator would return to the republican values of his youth.[25] The history of youth under the Empire must also take account of scientific study that was evolving so rapidly, and a social sphere so fluid, that the university, in its growing pains, was hard pressed not to refuse professorships to thirty-year-olds. This continued until 1808, when Minister Fontanes attempted to bring the young generations back to the Catholic faith of their fathers, or at least of their grandfathers.[26]

It was in that same year, 1808, that Marc-Antoine Jullien set back to work, producing his *Essai général d'éducation physique, morale et intellectuelle; suivi d'un plan d'éducation pratique pour l'enfance, l'adolescence et la jeunesse* (General Essay on Physical, Moral and Intellectual Education; Followed by a Practical Educational Plan for Childhood, Adolescence and Youth). The method he advised provided for a strict division of the day into hours for sleep, study, and physical exercise, varying according to the age of the student. In addition, students would be required to compose a kind of daily report, on the model of those written by military men for their superiors: they would receive three notebooks at the start of the year in which they were to record, with the greatest introspection possible, the most minute details of their physical, affective, and intellectual life. But unlike in the military world, this report was to be shown to no one and carefully kept secret. And, to shuffle the cards even more, each young writer was to invent false identities for the individuals he named and to speak of himself "as a stranger," designating himself in the third person and by various fictional names.[27]

Jullien's pedagogical work did not go unnoticed at the time. As Alain Corbin has pointed out, this work gives significant testimony on the evolution of the relationship between the public and private spheres at the dawn of the new century.[28] This treatise is all the more impressive as we know that its author was something more than the "retired military man" of which Corbin speaks. Jullien had been a great admirer of Saint-Just, among other things: under the Directoire, he had worked to bring out several as yet unpublished texts on republican institutions from Saint-Just's *Fragments*, without revealing their authorship.[29] But nothing could be more paradoxical than the lesson Jullien drew from Saint-Just's political and moral project, with its dream of absolute transparency among individuals in a republic, of total communication between the I and the Other. The ultimate objective of the kind of interior monologue Jullien recommended for pupils was in fact to make oneself unknowable to the Other. The myth of transparency became praise of opacity.

Let us jump ahead a dozen or so years to 1820, to an ardent young man in search of work and mentors, who knocked on the door of the editor-in-chief of a well-respected review: Jules Michelet has recounted his meeting with Jullien, then at the helm of the *Revue encyclopédique*. To his great disappointment, the seventeen-year-old Michelet discovered a sad little man, prematurely withered, his gaze turned more to the chimney fire than to the face of his visitor, and whose conversation was monotonic and didactic.[30] Jullien had sent his own children to Switzerland to test Pesta-lozzi's educational techniques: proof that concern for pedagogy continued to stir the old Jacobin. But he had a difficult relationship with the youth of the Restoration. By the time Michelet visited him, a quarter century had passed since Robespierre's former aide-de-camp had lamented his destiny—destroyed in the lava of the times—from his Thermidorian cell. No doubt he had survived the revolutionary volcano, but his life, like that of others, had been forever scarred. In the faces of these survivors, the youths of the Restoration, like Michelet, had the impression of confronting the living dead.

THE GRACE OF A LATE BIRTH

The year 1820 was an important one in the history of the Restoration: the assassination of the Duke of Berry and the fall of the Decazes government marked the end of the liberal experiment and the beginning of a decade of reactionary politics, reinforced by the Spanish crisis and French intervention on the peninsula. In 1821, the death of the titan at Saint Helena provided young French officers, as well as many Italian and Polish emigrants, with a legend sufficiently glorious to tempt more than one into conspiracies. Other young Frenchmen, less tempted by risk, decided instead to follow the advice given, after the fall of the Decazes cabinet, by an intelligent moderate, Pierre-Paul Royer-Collard: "write books." This was the case for two young counsels from Aix-en-Provence, Louis-Adolphe Thiers and François-Auguste Mignet, both barely more than twenty years old. When they weren't gathered with their comrades in the warmth and privacy of Mignet's father's smithy, discussing politics and deploring the excess of reactionaries, these underemployed lawyers (the market was saturated) worked on composing a history of the extraordinary years that followed 1789. In their respective histories of the Revolution, Thiers and Mignet invited readers to consider the revolutionary events from the necessary historical distance, which required overlooking the Revolution's errors and considering even the crimes of the Terror as having been inevitable. Their works marked an important step in the history of the revolutionary tradition and were commercially quite successful: the politically apathetic middle classes of the Restoration were hungry for historical novels and history books that would gratify their incipient national sentiment.[31]

Giving historical meaning to the sadly famous year 1793 did not mean restoring political dignity to those responsible for the Terror. The reaction of the still living members of the National Convention, faced with the public success of Thiers and Mignet, is instructive: the regicides saw these works more as the product of arrogant young pedants than as a demonstration that their own rehabilitation was evolving.[32] One document that is revealing of the distance that then separated the old from the young (or fathers from sons, if one prefers) is the brochure published in 1820 by a certain A. F. Carrion-Nisas and entitled, simply, *De la jeunesse française* (On French Youth). The author, the twenty-five-year-old son of a former member of the Tribunate, cultivated, bright, and sensitive to the intellectual heritage of the eighteenth century, had set himself the task of collecting the works of Volney, the great *idéologue*. Carrion-Nisas's first concern was to convince his peers to break away from the conflicts that had driven their fathers apart. Anyone born too late to participate in person bore no responsibility for the excesses to which those conflicts had given rise, but was fully entitled to reap the benefits of their positive results: "This new generation, which was born and raised amid new institutions, owes to its age the precious advantage of inheriting from the Revolution without having participated in it."[33]

It is tempting to compare the situation of the "sons" of revolutionaries living during the Restoration to that (nonetheless quite different, for an infinite number of obvious reasons) of the "sons" of Nazis in Germany,[34] and to compare this text by Carrion-Nisas with Chancellor Helmet Kohl's unfortunate statement regarding the "grace of a late birth."[35] In 1820 too, the soothing evidence from the registry office was there to help all who wanted to transcend their sense of guilt. Yet it was not simply a matter of sleight of hand on his part: Carrion-Nisas had the courage to ask that judgment on the founders of the Republic and their violence be suspended, considering the extraordinary circumstances with which they had been confronted; he had the honesty to write: "None of us can say what he would have done in their place." But the gap between the men of the Republic and the youth of the Restoration was nevertheless impossible to bridge: it was the difference between those who begin a revolution and those who find it already finished.[36] Rather than looking backward and revalidating the revolutionaries of the previous century, the young people of the Restoration preferred to look ahead. Few generations in the history of France have felt so strongly that it was their responsibility to turn the page in the book written by the previous ones.[37] The demographic evolution of the country only encouraged this: beginning in 1824, the majority of the French male population was born after 1789.[38] But political life in the form of parliamentary debate was quite unattractive to them: it was difficult for young people with strong feelings, seeking examples of exalted undertakings, to feel passionate about the mannered liberalism of the "constitutionalists" and to find leaders in their cautious spokesmen. It was easier, all things considered, for them to content themselves with a romantic rally to the legitimism of the elder branch of the Bourbon dynasty, as the young Victor Hugo and several others would do.

We can therefore understand the docility with which some of the best representatives of the Restoration generation responded, beginning in 1825, to the call addressed to them by the prophets of a new gospel: the good news of Saint-Simonianism. Saint-Simon had spent the last decades of his fallen aristocratic life in a vain effort to convince scholars and philosophers that politics would dissolve into political economy and that the future lay in industry. Shortly after the count's death, several young men (but not kids: Enfantin, Bazard, and Buchez were old enough, in fact, to have "done" the Hundred Days during their student youth)[39] took on the mission of spreading his doctrine. After an initial timid phase, Saint-Simonianism found more fertile ground: the failure of conspiracies at the start of the decade had shown that the sectarian path, while not entirely ill adapted to the goal of changing the regime, was nonetheless insufficient. The time had come to seek consensus. It is significant that, aside from the works of the master himself, the followers of the new school had high regard for the books of Ballanche, the Lyonnais philosopher who wished to found the theoretical bases of social regeneration on a renewed Christianity.[40] But religious minds were not the only ones to flock to Saint-Simonianism; there were also many hopeful and impatient young adherants who were suffering from the glut of professionals and therefore feeling personally concerned by the battle waged by *Le Producteur*, then by the *Globe*, for a softening of the banking and credit systems. Appreciating its political content, radicals and democrats also followed Saint-Simonianism. In about 1830, Filippo Buonarroti himself, the Nestor of revolutionary historical memory, envisaged—at least for a moment—forming a strategic alliance with the Saint-Simonians.[41]

The historical significance of Saint-Simonian ideology is always a matter of debate. Those who see Saint-Simonianism's associative thesis as significant in the development of an embryonic class consciousness among the workers of France are in opposition to those who focus solely on the fierce productivism promoted by Enfantin and Bazard, and see them as the bourgeoisie's "Salvation Army"; and to those who emphasize the importance, in Saint-Simonian economy, of the very secular confidence in the possibility of human emancipation, others respond by highlighting its deism and taste for hierarchy. Those who insist on the antimonarchic and antifeudal aspects of the doctrine are countered by those who see antidemocratic, antiparliamentarian, and antiegalitarian Saint-Simoniansm as the cradle of contemporary totalitarianism.[42] This is not the place to take a stand on the ultimate meaning of the Saint-Simonian experiment. From our perspective, that of the dynamics of the generations that organized themselves around the revolutionary tradition, or, to use Benjamin's expression, that of the forms of aging in this tradition, the problem of Saint-Simonianism presents itself, above all, as the problem of the relationship between Saint-Simonian youth and the heritage of the French Revolution. It is therefore appropriate to consider for a moment the most important historic-political work produced by the Saint-Simonian school, the *Réfutation de l'"Histoire de France" de l'abbé de Montgaillard* (Refutation of the "History of France" by the Abbé de Montgaillard), published in 1828 by Uranelt de Leuze (the pseudonym of Laurent de l'Ardèche, one of the leaders of the movement).

The book starts off with Laurent's homage to the courageous work, even the moral greatness, of many members of the National Convention, and above all of Robespierre.[43] Historians are right to see the *Réfutation* as the most obvious sign of the opening of a new ideological season, marked by a will to reconsider the historical meaning of Robespierre's experiment.[44] But it seems important to distinguish between the historical and political dimensions of the revolutionary heritage. If Laurent was inviting his generation to show indulgence toward "the inflexible democrats" of the Convention, it was because the Revolution itself had pronounced the funeral oration for democracy, a "system . . . that is essentially transitory in nature," soiled forever by the blood spilled, and ultimately crushed by the popularity of Bonapartism. The dozen years that separated Waterloo from the current era were for Laurent the proof of the "identical sterility" of the political alchemists of both camps—the legitimists and the "ontologists" still naïve enough to believe in popular sovereignty. But fortunately for France, Auguste Comte, with his *Catéchisme des industriels,* and the men of the *Producteur* had used every possible means, after Saint-Simon, to stop the outpourings from the "revolutionary arena, where only ghosts were left to fight." Laurent asked his readers to collaborate with the Saint-Simonians in the organic work necessary to destroy the final vestiges of the ancien régime, and in the establishment of a new link that would guarantee the unity and harmony of the social assembly.[45]

The revolution proposed by the young Saint-Simonians was neither violent nor, in general, political. Their aspirations went far beyond liberty and fraternity: they wanted to honor the most enterprising and capable producers, society's only real elite, and were opposed to both the feudal privileges of a parasitic nobility and the idle liberal chimera of the "doctrinarians" and "constitutionalists." Thus Enfantin applauded the financial opuscules of a barely thirty-year-old Swiss publicist, James Fazy, who had settled in Paris after a lengthy experience as a Carbonari conspirator and a Buonarroti partisan. With greater eloquence than others, Fazy argued that France's credit system had to get with the times and guarantee the most skillful entrepreneurs fortunes on the scale of those being accumulated by certain English or American capitalists.[46] In the Paris of the 1820s, Fazy was one among many more or less penniless youths whose reading was good but haphazard, and whose economic reformism was perhaps only a way of seeking a place for themselves in the sun. Fazy was descended from an important family in Geneva, and he was preparing to play a role of first rank in the history of that city in the nineteenth century, in which capacity he is well known to Swiss historians.[47] He nonetheless merits the consideration of all historians interested in the political culture of Restoration Europe.[48] The papers of his youth as they have reached us—a shapeless mass of notes, drafts of small literary or moral works, and ambitious editorial projects—are highly representative of the intellectual landscape of a young man born with the century: a landscape as rich as it is jumbled, with smatterings on the horizon of Rousseau and Voltaire, Sismondi and Fourier, Lamennais and Saint-Simon, Buonarroti and Lafayette.[49]

In 1828, Fazy published a savage and highly successful pamphlet with the provocative title, *De la gérontocratie* (On Gerontocracy).[50] The entire generation of the 1820s would applaud its brilliant and irreverent expression of its own unease, idiosyncrasies, and predilections. The first words were searing: "What spirit of domination got into the turbulent generation of '93! It began by banning its fathers, it ended by disinheriting its children." Not satisfied with having witnessed the loss of the most intelligent and vital men of the era—who were decimated by executions and weakened by war—this generation still wanted to occupy every government post: in its thirst for power, it had decided that no one could be a deputy before the age of forty and without possessing a great fortune. Thus France was "reduced to the seven thousand to eight thousand 'eligible,' but asthmatic, gout-ridden, paralyzed individuals, their faculties weakened." The young and the full grown were excluded from public deliberations, and the real France, the immense majority of the country, watched in dismay as its old men engaged in stupid and vulgar quarrels, was subjected to their drivel on monarchic legitimacy or English-style freedom instead of seeing them undertake what was truly urgent: the reform of public administration, justice, and the fiscal system—and above all, the reform of credit, which would have brought them all into agreement, because it would have shown that the growth of wealth was infinite, and that the principle according to which one could not acquire assets without depriving someone else of them was false.

At the end of the 1820s, Fazy was still in contact with Buonarroti, who contributed to the financing of his publishing initiatives. But the distance between the two men was enormous, as much in terms of mentality as of political jargon. In the writing of the Swiss revolutionary, one would seek in vain a trace of the moralism that was the basis of the ideas and texts of the former companion of Babeuf; and the magic formula of *De la gérontocratie,* "get rich," was apt to horrify Buonarroti. Fazy's text reads like a summary execution of those that had lived through the Revolution, whichever side they were on: "You exhaust yourselves in old battles, while youth agrees, from the young peer to the shop assistant; you still fear the word 'revolution,' and already youth has changed this word, which you have so variously interpreted. It is civilization that is propelling today's youth, and no longer revolution; what you call upheaval, it calls progress."[51] In another text, written two years later, Fazy reads like a hymn to credit; he sings the praises of discount banks, insurance, and joint stock companies.[52] When the July revolution erupted, Fazy was in the front lines with his newspaper, *La révolution de 1830:* the Orleanist revolution had to be prevented from turning into a farce organized by "the decrepit old generation that is on its way out" at the expense of the new generation; the change of regime should not be allowed to become simply a replacement of the ancien régime aristocracy with a financial oligarchy.[53]

We now know that the revolution of July 1830 was neither a noble revolt of youth against the gerontocracy, followed by a painful defeat, nor an act put on by a cunning elite at the expense of the popular movement. On the one hand, judging by the number of victims among the combatants during the July revolution, the glory of victory seems to belong more to the veterans of the Empire than to the young men of the Restoration. On the other hand, it is also true that the change in regime created conditions that were favorable for a new social stratum, the "bourgeoisie" or the "middle class"—the name matters little—to replace the aristocracy at the helm of the country. The years that followed 1830 did indeed witness an evolution of the Orleanist regime toward authoritarianism, culminating in the persecution of and trials against militant republicans. But the early 1830s were nonetheless a moment of great intellectual and moral effervescence that, among other things, would allow the growing working class to put its stamp on the new formulation of democratic doctrine.[54]

However, the reconstructions of today's historians do not necessarily correspond to the contemporaries' perception of the event, and even less so to the perception that young rebels or revolutionaries of bourgeois backgrounds may have had. These individuals were foreign, by vocation, to the spirit of initiative that a new generation of entrepreneurs would demonstrate throughout the reign of Louis-Philippe, and foreign as well, by virtue of their social origins, to the workers' movement that was then developing a new political strategy based on the solid groundwork of its corporative tradition. Thus the fact remains that, when faced with the patent mediocrity of the new citizen-king and with the moral grayness of the "happy medium," many young people (whether they were really young or just considered themselves so) who had believed in the July revolution said they were played a bad turn and had wasted their youth.[55] One of them, Edgar Quinet, described the painful plight of his generation as shifting to adulthood in a matter of a few months, then going gray overnight.[56] But not everyone was content with rhetorical metaphors: for the refined Jeunes-France, of which Théophile Gautier emerged as the spokesperson, or for the more popular *bousingots*, experimenting with an eccentric or scandalous lifestyle was a way of dramatizing what they felt to be the psychological and social ambivalence of their own identity.[57]

In his works collected under the title *The Human Comedy*, Balzac, as well, told the story of French youth in the period from the Restoration to the July Monarchy. Was he writing fiction or nonfiction? In the early 1830s, he was still more of a journalist—a bitter, cutting journalist—than a novelist, as well as an unsuccessful candidate in political elections. The dominant themes of his articles that appeared in *La Caricature* were the distressing capacity of the gerontocracy to reestablish itself after the failures of 1830; the ridiculous spectacle of the "old clowns pulled off the stage of the Revolution, the Empire and the Restoration," who were nothing more than genuflecting skeletons; the scandal of the "fake young men" and "young old men" who had seized power at the expense of the legitimate aspirations of the new generation. The Orleanist regime misjudged the merits of youth, denigrated it, wanted it out of the way: youth was not in fashion, lamented Balzac in *La Mode*.[58] In a certain sense, this is the basis for the author's entire body of work, in particular *Illusions perdues*, which begins with an exceptionally lucid reflection on fashion and its effects on the perception of an individual's age. Indeed, the new bourgeois system was not content to prohibit youth from assuming political responsibilities. In Balzac's vision, in his nostalgic denunciation, the acceleration that capitalism imposed on the social dynamic also acted on the dynamic of generations, for the young were so caught up in the whirlwind of fashion that it consumed their entire lives.[59]

There is no point going into too much detail and attempting to distill the parts played by fiction, journalism, politics, and myth in this 1830s melting pot. It was not unusual, in the salons of Hapsburg Venice or czarist Russia, for men and women to assign themselves the roles of characters in *The Human Comedy* and to attempt to model their lives on those of Balzacian heroes![60] And what the myth and fashion from Paris could not do (the "pink gauze" that was capable of blurring the colors of the harshest

Parisian reality, according to an image by Heinrich Heine),[61] the geographical distance and diversity of the political and social contexts could: thus, whereas Saint-Simonianism was declining rapidly in France in the early 1830s, after the break between Enfantin and Bazard, the doctrine continued to fascinate young foreigners living sometimes thousands of kilometers away. Among them was a young Sardinian naval officer, Giuseppe Garibaldi, second commander of the ship headed for the Orient upon which Emile Barrault and other disciples of Enfantin had embarked to seek the female messiah, the redeemer of the Western family; the strangeness of the project was not enough to destroy the vitality of Saint-Simonian humanism in the eyes of Garibaldi.[62] Also among them were two young Russian aristocrats, barely twenty years old, who were convinced they had been entrusted with a revolutionary mission ever since their childhood when, one day, on Sparrow Hill in Moscow, they had sworn to seek revenge for the sacrifice of the Decembrists. For Aleksandr Herzen and Nicolas Ogaryov, becoming followers of Saint-Simonianism, in about 1833, meant detaching themselves from the French Revolution, critiquing democracy, seeking new bases for the socialist ideal.[63]

If it is worth insisting on the contrasting episodes of the Saint-Simonian experiment, it is precisely because of the doctrine's influence on European youth in the 1830s, at a time when the movement was in crisis in its country of origin. Its strong influence helped many to distance themselves from the French Revolution and to define a landscape of expectations in which the principles and values of 1789 and 1793 played only a limited role. The path taken by Young Germany is typical here. Until 1832, Karl Gutzkow could recognize and proclaim that the true duty of the new generation was to construct a democratic republic in Germany on the model of the French republic that Robespierre and Saint-Just had wished to create. But after 1832, under the influence of his friend Heinrich Laube and of Heine, both imbued with the spirit of Saint-Simonianism, even more than under the pressure and censure of the Prussian government, Gutzkow ended up proposing an entirely different ideal for Young Germany (a philosophy of history, literary experimentation, religious regeneration), leaving behind the political battle. In 1835 he had the courage to publish, though in abridged form, the extraordinary *Mort de Danton* (Death of Danton), in which Georg Büchner expresses his moral revolt and political denunciation. But even to a young man of Büchner's temperament, Gutzkow advised turning toward literature rather than to a radical contesting of the system.[64]

The encounter with Saint-Simonianism seems to have been equally decisive in the intellectual itinerary of Giuseppe Mazzini. In his first years of exile in Marseilles, which began in 1831, the Genoese lawyer, the "young fanatic" who so worried an informer for the Austrians,[65] still applied a Buonarroti-inspired concept of class struggle to the French political situation, to which he added his own generational conflict theory: a merciless war should set in opposition the rich old France and the poor young one. But already in 1832, strongly impressed by his reading of *L'Exposition de la doctrine de Saint-Simon*, Mazzini preferred to speak of democracy directed from above, of intelligences, of geniuses. He insisted on viewing the distinction among generations as affecting the political struggle, in addition to seeing it as a tool of historical analysis, and he went so far as to oppose it with the class struggle. "Let us abhore fraternal blood":[66] for Mazzini, the offensive against the father was a way of sublimating the elementary prospect of a struggle among brothers in a superior form of class collaboration.

The political movements created and led by Mazzini in these years, Young Italy and later Young Europe, set forty as their membership age limit. The historian interested in the political representations of youth in the nineteenth century, or in the myth of youth as a revolutionary force, could not find more evocative testimony that this: to recognize the capacity for progressivist political action only in youth under forty is to manifest with near scholastic precision one's revolt against the quarantine imposed on the new generations by the Restoration when it set eligibility at forty. But this reversal of the meaning given to the age-forty cutoff also had the result of alienating many patriots who had passed that age and who, after decades of political activism, suddenly found themselves being treated like "senile old men of the Argonaut era."[67] The competition into which the partisans of Mazzini and of Buonarroti entered in the early 1830s to determine who should head up the revolutionary movement in Italy was also based on this opposition of generations.[68]

Nonetheless, we mustn't exaggerate the reach of the appeal the Genoese exile launched to those under forty and see it as the basis of the entire history of Mazzini's movement. For the greatest difficulties encountered by Mazzini's creations lay elsewhere, and were eminently political in nature—including those encountered by the liveliest among them, his Young Germany (not to be confused with Gutzkow's Young Poland and Young Switzerland)—in their attempt to define a common line of action: all feared that Mazzini would wish to replace the traditional French role of leader with a sort of Italian hegemony in the European revolutionary arena. Among the minor difficulties encountered by Young Europe, one is of particular interest here. Between 1834 and 1835, Mazzini's most prestigious counterpart in Switzerland, and also his most determined adversary, was none other than James Fazy, who had become the leader of the so-called National Party.[69] The machinations of Young Europe in Switzerland would be crushed against Fazy's firm opposition, Fazy having already been the standard-bearer of the young Restoration Frenchmen in their struggle against the gerontocracy. It was eminently clear to whoever wanted to see that the problem of the revolution could not be posed solely in terms of a generational approach: for more than one European revolutionary, the time was ripe for an approach based on class struggle.

DANGEROUS BOYS

Among the young English revolutionaries of the 1830s, in any case, the time seemed ripe for true class consciousness. The 1820s, inaugurated by the "massacre of Peterloo" (the bloody repression of a popular riot in Manchester), had been calm in appearance only. In fact the decade was one of the most important for the development of trade unionism and for the struggle in favor of freedom of the press. In the 1830s, the worker movement, increasingly self-aware, was ready to go on the offensive against what remained of William Pitt's antidemocratic edifice and, more generally, against what were being discovered to be the ills of the industrial capitalist system. In an England whose economic advancement over the

Continent was considerable, though class struggle may not yet have been the clearly formulated objective of the worker movement, the class identity of the movement was already established.[70]

The maturity of the English revolutionaries, however, should not make the historian blind to the generational dynamic also at work in this country, nor to the individual itineraries of youth within the broader class conflict. It goes without saying, for example, that in fighting "Old Corruption," the English radicals meant to combat not only a corrupted but also an aged system. What are more difficult to detect are the tensions and generational conflicts that could emerge within the worker movement, in relation to the activists' strategies for instilling political responsibility. There is no doubt that the radical propaganda promulgated in cafés, nonconformist churches, mutual aid societies, and trade unions was designed to reach the illiterate masses. But the time was also characterized by enthusiastic autodidacts for whom, as expressed by the title of William Lovett's memoirs, education was an essential ingredient in the struggle for bread and freedom.[71] Yet these autodidacts had to confront the distrust of older workers confident enough in the force of their corporative culture not to see the urgency of spreading to the people a form of culture perceived as irremediably bourgeois.

A trade union leader like James Burn, who spent his childhood amid Glasgow's underworld, had a hard time understanding how the older men could continue to work like slaves half the day just for the meager satisfaction of getting drunk the other half, instead of using their free time to educate themselves in order to be better equipped to demand their rights.[72] But Burn-style autodidacts were rare (at least so long as the propaganda of the chartist movement hadn't found a happy medium between its "literary" component and the more immediate demands of the political struggle). Even among young men, the attraction of the bottle ended up winning out over the fascination of the book: one sign of the silent resistance with which youth attempted to oppose industrialization, which gathered factory laborers into indistinct masses, without regard for age. It was also a symptom of the more or less conscious attempt on the part of youth to preserve something of the margin of independence it had had in traditional society. And when the progress of the radical movement and the electoral reform of 1832 brought about a profound modification in the landscape of English political life, it was no accident that Benjamin Disraeli would found a movement baptized Young England, with the intention of capitalizing on the "carnavalesque" nostalgia of English youth for conservative ends, thereby earning him Marx's sarcasm.[73]

In France, as the 1830s faded into the 1840s, the nation experienced an explosion of publications on the social issue, the product of the profound questioning that the 1831 revolt of the Lyons silk weavers had inspired among republicans. In 1840, Louis Blanc's *L'Organisation du travail*, Étienne Cabet's *Voyage en Icarie*, Pierre-Joseph Proudhon's *Qu'est-ce que la propriété?*, Pierre Leroux's *De l'humanité*, and *Agricol Perdiguier: Compagnon du tour de France*, the first social novel by George Sand, were published.[74] The following year, two twenty-year-old boys, Théodore Dézamy and Albert Laponneraye, launched *L'Humanitaire* and *La Fraternité*, the first communist periodicals in Europe. They were followed, shortly thereafter, by Victor Considérant's *Manifeste de la démocratie*. It is not surprising, then, that when Marx, Arnold Ruge, and other German revolutionaries arrived in Paris in 1843, they felt as if they were at the heart of the burgeoning European revolution.

This impression was quickly dispelled, however. The disappointment of the German revolutionaries resulted from the failure of their *Deutsche-franzosiche Jahrbücher* (German-French yearbooks), on which the major signatories of Parisian socialism refused to collaborate.[75] The arrogance on the part of the French socialists, their rock-solid certainty of the superiority of their revolutionary tradition and their lack of interest in the propaganda initiatives of exiles, triggered a reaction of pride among the Germans: whether or not they had a past as "young Hegelians," they knew they too could boast of a prodigious philosophical heritage—that of Kant, Fichte, Schelling, and Hegel, a patrimony no less rich than the French one. What prompted them in this direction were the teachings of Heine, who was increasingly convinced of the revolutionary potential of modern German philosophy, and ever more critical with respect to the French Revolution, which he denounced as exclusively political and not social. Another source of pride was the memory of Young Germany, though in its time it had been disdained by some, like Bruno Bauer and Moses Hess. For Friedrich Engels, Gutzkow was a model of politico-literary journalism, and Börne, the idol of Young Germany, seemed to him an exemplary figure.[76]

During his years of exile in Paris, from 1843 to the first months of 1845, Marx was in personal contact with Heine, and it was at this time, when he was so close to the greatest German thrasher of the French Convention myth, that the twenty-five-year-old revolutionary from Trier undertook to write his a "History of the Convention" (which he never completed).[77] Obviously the young Marx had sufficient intellectual energy to make his way by himself, and it would therefore be unwise in his case to imagine excessively mechanical connections between his encounters and his choices, between his human experiences and his ideological responses. After the intense journalistic activity of his Rhineland years, during his two years in Paris Marx was especially eager to learn; his different biographers agree in emphasizing the role of the books he read during these years in the maturation of his doctrine. Yet it is not a matter of cheap psychologizing to propose that certain of the works he read in Paris— *Einzige und sein Eigenthum* (The Ego and Its Own) by Max Stirner, for example—may have particularly affected the young Marx for personal reasons. Though the work is philosophically and anthropologically weak, Stirner's description of the vital childhood-adolescence-maturity cycle is fascinating in many ways. He depicts this cycle as a series of revolts by "sons" against "fathers," until the rebel sons discover that it is the fathers themselves who are at the origin of the rebellion. Later, when in London, Marx took Stirner seriously enough to refute him: in *German Ideology* he turns around Stirner's idea that maturity is an individualist retreat from life, considering it instead to be the moment when the individual fully accepts his socially appropriate role. But the Marx who accused Stirner of creating a self-portrait of his own youth rather than a picture of youth in general was the Marx who sought, in turn, to escape from the weight of the relationship with the father. By rejecting any psychological interpretation of the relations among generations, by affirming the primacy of social status, Marx was attempting to transcend his own youth.[78]

Fathers and Sons: the fame of Turgenev's novel is such that the historian risks confining the father-son relationship to the realm of literature or imagining it only metaphorically. And yet, particularly in France—land of revolutions—the succession of generations implied, strictly speaking, the existence of a delicate relationship between revolutionary fathers and sons who were more or less invested with the paternal role: without necessarily journeying into the depths of psychology, this relationship must therefore be taken into account. The story of the sons of the members of the National Convention,[79] for example, is directly linked to the problem of the aging of a revolutionary tradition: to have a father who had been a deputy of the Convention, and to see him age under new and often hostile regimes, forces the son to measure himself against a political heritage of which the father is, for better or for worse, a living incarnation—or of which he is, more frequently, a frozen incarnation,[80] even when his greatness is admired. For understanding the human and ideological tribulations that awaited the sons of the members of the Convention, the writings of Jean Améry on the general human experience of aging are priceless. No one asks the old revolutionary, or any elderly person, "What will you do?" Instead the initial and instinctual impulse is to say, "This is what you have already done." After others have taken stock of his life, the old revolutionary is presented with a tally with which he must identify.[81] Sometimes the father's tally is placed back on the market of political life to be cashed in (thus Walter Benjamin was able to speak of the nineteenth-century French revolutions as so many "liquidations");[82] sometimes it is the sons of the old revolutionaries themselves who perform the operation.

In this context, one revealing episode was the conflict between the Blanqui brothers in 1846. Sons of an obscure former deputy of Girondin sympathies who became subprefect of a village in the Var during the Empire, Adolphe and Auguste Blanqui spent their adolescence in the Paris of the early Restoration: in this culturally vivacious metropolis, the two boys quickly broke away from their father, a debonair but colorless man.

Adolphe, a brilliant student, the elder brother by a few years, took care of Auguste materially like a son, and he had himself gotten his brother involved in the militant opposition to the Bourbon regime. But after 1830 the two brothers' paths diverged: while Adolphe went on to a highly successful career as a professor of political economy, Auguste devoted himself to the more thankless career of a professional revolutionary.[83] As a governmental candidate in Gironde under Guizot, in the elections of 1846, Adolphe Blanqui believed he would win the approval of the citizens of Bordeaux by reminding them that his father had been a Girondin militant: in a campaign letter, he went so far as to make him the initiator of the petition of protest of the so-called Seventy-Three against the purification desired by the members of the Montagne on May 31, 1793. Auguste was then in the hospital in Tours, where, for health reasons, he had been transferred by the government from his Mont Saint-Michel prison. He wrote to Ferdinand Flocon, editor of the republican newspaper *La Réforme*, to unmask his brother's electoral propaganda: "The version of the candidate from Bordeaux is a fiction." He explained that their father's involvement with the Girondins' counterrevolutionary plots had been small; as for the printer's proof of the declaration of the Seventy-Three, which Adolphe boasted of possessing, supposedly corrected by the hand of his father, he said it was a complete fantasy, since the declaration had never been printed!

Auguste added in his letter to Flocon that his father had converted, late in life, to the Montagne camp (after the July revolution). Jean-Dominique Blanqui had allegedly seen in the conservatism and corruption of the Orleanist *grande bourgeoisie* an updated version of the *"moderantisme"* and the *"négociantisme"* against which the Montagne men had fought. The old revolutionary had thus seen the error of his forty years. Wrote Auguste, "How many times did I hear him cry, 'They were right,' in speaking of his former adversaries, 'Now I side with them.' And this old Girondin, who had nourished my youth with his resentment against the men of the Montagne, died a *montagnard.*"[84]

Naturally it is impossible to verify the version of the facts given by Louis-Philippe's prisoner. Jean-Dominique Blanqui died in 1832. During the July revolution and the years that followed, Auguste had been in and out of prison; there is therefore reason to suppose that he did not have many occasions to hear the paternal retraction. But what is interesting in this episode is that Auguste Blanqui, the flag bearer of neo-Jacobinism in the nineteenth century, was brought up on the resentments of a Girondin father. And we should also note the aggrieved protest of the son faced with his elder brother's "liquidation" of the father's political image. Nothing is more likely and yet unprovable than Sartre's statement that when fathers have a project, sons have a destiny.

Louis-Philippe had already been on the throne for fifteen years, and the democrats were still awaiting the end of Orleanism, which had long been announced as imminent. Thus the years that immediately preceded the revolution of 1848 were experienced, by some, as years of great lassitude. "We are tired, young and old alike," recognized Michelet in *Le Peuple* in 1846.[85] Yet Amédée Jacques, Jules Simon, Ernest Renan, and the other studious young men who the following year created a pugnacious periodical, *La Liberté de penser*, hardly seemed tired. These literary youths had been trained in the secular and democratic ideal by Michelet, Cousin, and Quinet; it is significant, however, that in the first installment of their journal, they pondered the reasons why an embittered indifference had taken root among French youth.[86] A tired France, an indifferent youth: no doubt it took the fresh energy of a foreign student (in this case Dumitru Brătianu, future liberal party leader of Romania) to feel "younger, stronger, better" upon reading Michelet's *Peuple*.[87] But if the Collège de France historian was enthusiastic about the Moldo-Wallachian students' dreams of freedom, he did not put the same energy into defending the cause of the Polish independence fighters, who in that same year, 1846, were once again abandoned to their unfortunate destiny by a France renowned for its Rights of Man. Many were still in the romantic habit of thinking of peoples in terms of age, as if countries were like individuals, as evidenced by many pages of Michelet, Quinet, and others: how old the countries of Western Europe were, while the peoples of the North and the East were fresh with youth! These ideas were even more confused in the mind of the Parisian lady who, upon being introduced to students from distant Danubian regions in a prestigious salon of Polish exiles, exclaimed, "So young, and already Moldo-Wallachian!"[88]

As Sir Lewis Namier has shown, the revolution of 1848 was a revolution of intellectuals. There was something literary about it, at least in the way the first leaders of the Second Republic confronted the question of old and new peoples, revolutionary traditions, and "nationalities": either they exhumed an old decree from 1790 as justification for the French refusal to intervene in Europe, as did Lamartine, or they pointed to the precedent of 1792 and the Revolution to push for intervention, as did Blanqui and Barbès. In preaching class war, those like Blanqui and Barbès paid the price for their abstract thinking, for they proved insensitive to what was most rooted in the collective mentality: in the cases of Poland and Hungary, they invoked the revolutionary principle of the right of peoples to self-determination and did not understand the community of interests that existed with respect to the "subject races" among the Magyars, the Poles, and the Germans.[89]

Literary prejudices and the weight of the revolutionary tradition influenced not only the foreign policy of the French revolutionaries of 1848 but also their domestic policy. In some ways, the tradition inspired both the popular revolt in Paris of late spring 1848 and the harsh repression that followed. The blood spilled in June 1848 demonstrated the contradiction between the two central principles of revolutionary memory in France: that of the right to resist oppression, which workers of the outlying districts could consider a heritage of the rich insurrectional history of the years 1789 to 1795, and the principle according to which exercising this right was unjustified when popular sovereignty had not been usurped, a principle on which the National Guard was founded, under General Eugène Cavaignac, to whom the legitimate authorities of the republic had entrusted the task of restoring order. Beginning in June, interested observers, such as Marx, understood that many aspects of the Second Republic harked back to the First. But it was not so much a Marxist-type class struggle that occurred on the streets of Paris in June 1848 as it was a new conflict around the enigma of popular sovereignty, which the French Revolution had transmitted to posterity without fully resolving.[90]

Here again the story of two sons of a member of the National Convention illustrates the drama, this time of 1848. In moving to initiate the massacre of workers in revolt, General Cavaignac took the occasion to put an end to a contradiction pernicious to the revolutionary legacy: that between the popular right to insurrection and the republic's aspirations to stability. As for the workers of the outlying districts, they could not have forgotten the revolutionary lesson that another Cavaignac son, Godefroy, the charismatic leader of the republican movement, had taught them for nearly twenty years. Sometimes one page of a book, a few words related through the oral tradition, can convey the most intimate and wrenching moments of history: one day Godefroy had said of his brother Eugène, "He's my son, I'm raising him for the Republic."[91]

We know, however, that it was more the Mobile Guard—a creation of the Second Republic—than the National Guard that was in the front ranks of the June repression. The high daily rate of pay is not enough to explain its soldiers' eagerness during these days of civil war. Nor is the bleak legend convincing that the Mobile Guard was a subproletarian army ready to do anything to avoid unemployment; the social composition of the Mobile Guard did not differ significantly from that of the National Guard. The real difference was in age: the average officer's age in the Mobile Guard was twenty-two.[92] And while the Mobile Guardsmen also chanted republican slogans, in the worker milieu from which they hailed they had had little time to absorb a heritage of democratic values. They also were not old enough to have internalized the principles of solidarity characteristic of worker corporatism. Born under capitalism, they knew only the most degrading aspects of the working world. Some have also pointed to their mostly provincial origins, and it is perhaps true that, during those days, the officers of the Mobile Guard became representatives of the confused and fierce hatred that the French provinces manifested toward the capital in moments of crisis.[93]

If the insurrection in the Parisian outskirts made apparent to the country's bourgeoisie the existence of a "red peril," the fury of the Mobile Guard was a reminder of the permanent threat of youth. Throughout the first half of the century, the working class had been denounced as danger-ous because it was composed mostly of young men.[94] Here let us put our faith in Honoré Daumier, keen social analyst that he was: one of his caricatures from 1848, entitled *The Dangerous Boys*, depicts a bourgeois couple that cannot hide its fright at seeing the young Mobile Guard in control of the streets of Paris. The events involving the Mobile Guard were also proof, for lucid contemporaries, of the basic emptiness of a certain republican rhetoric, which could be twisted in every direction. Here is what Natalia Herzen, wife of the illustrious Russian exile in Paris, had to say: "After the massacre, which lasted four days and four nights . . . the jubilant drunken troops of the Mobile Guard sauntered down the boule-vards, shouting, 'To die for one's country'; sixteen- or seventeen-year-old kids were bragging of the blood of their brothers that had dried on their hands."[95] And it would take all the sensitivity of a Maxime Du Camp, the good-heartedness of a man who frequented the bohemian world on occa-sion—not to mention his pride as an officer of the National Guard, wounded in the February 1848 combat—to get sentimental about the memory of the "little Mobile Guardsman" who was fatally wounded, and whose final wish was to taste Madeira.[96]

More of a regular in the circles of Parisian bohemia than Du Camp, Alfred Delvau was barely twenty-three in 1848, but that was old enough to be the right arm of Alexandre-Auguste Ledru-Rollin, the leader of the parliamentary extreme left. He was also old enough to take up his pen, following the battle, to attempt to reconstruct the dynamic of events too serious to be drowned out in bitter discouragement. The *Histoire de la révolution de février* (History of the February Revolution), published by Delvau in 1850, was intended to contribute to a renaissance of the demo-cratic movement. But disenchantment seeps through from the very first pages. Thus, with respect to the decree that made every citizen over the age of twenty-five eligible for elections, without stipulations as to property or domicile, Delvau spares no sarcasm in describing the patriotic zeal of all the under-forty candidates in the upcoming elections who begged La-martine or Béranger to give them letters of recommendation, which were always granted: "The little guys placed themselves under the patronage of the greats, who, in turn, for the voters, invoked their close relations with the humble."[97]

Despite his intentions, Delvau's work is that of a young man profoundly pessimistic about the results of political action and the dynamics of revolutions. The pages devoted to Blanqui are fabulous: he describes a pale little man with the face of a monk, "worthy of the brush of Holbein or Ribera," graceful in manner and yet so strong, so determined to attain the goal he had set for himself—the foundation of a new world—at any price, determined not to look back, never to retrace the path already taken, which he knew to be littered with ruins, violence, sacrificed friends.[98] In these years, only a poet, Baudelaire—a friend of Delvau in fact and, like him, a regular within bohemian circles and an activist on the side of the people in '48—could be so incisive in his description of all that was wearing in the business of being a revolutionary, from one generation to the next.[99] When, in the years 1850 to 1860, Delvau chose to bear witness to the lowest strata of Parisian life, he was only extending his pessimism to what was already the protest of the bohemians, even comparing Henry Murger, the personification of the bohemian, with the boys of the Mobile Guard in the days of June. Murger was a bourgeois who had spit on the bourgeoisie, just as the Mobile Guardsman had shot at the people among whom they belonged.[100]

FROM THE GUILLOTINES TO THE AXES

In the aftermath of 1848, many Frenchmen attempted to address the recent, dramatic past of the nation, with the idea of finding its logic and perhaps diagnosing its ills. The "retirees" of the Orleanist generation—Barante, Broglie, Tocqueville—dove into this exercise with as much passion as Delvau. And while Ledru-Rollin's former secretary was working on his *Histoire de la révolution de février,* a former seminarian of about the same age, Ernest Renan, was fine-tuning his own assessment of the events as he had witnessed them, initially full of sympathy and then full of horror.

A history of youth and revolution in the nineteenth century cannot fail to mention *L'Avenir de la science (Pensées de 1848)* (The Future of Science

[Thoughts from 1848]). This book by a young man barely twenty-five years old is perhaps the richest work in themes and ideas of nineteenth-century French literature.[101] But it must be noted that Renan waited forty years to publish it (as if he himself wished to impose a moratorium on his vigorous young intellect),[102] and that when he finally decided to bring it out in 1890, hardly anyone would read it. But it is a work Renan drew on abundantly, at least during the quarter century that followed the feverish moment when he had written it, and thus *L'Avenir de la science* became an integral part of the lesson conveyed by Renan to the generations of the second half of the nineteenth century. Despite all that is cumbersome in this book—personal confessions, appeals to the nation, erudite digressions, and pedantic polemics—its thrust is unequivocal: politics is sufficiently repellent to be left to politicians. Universal suffrage, which the Second Republic had inherited from the First, was also hardly presented in an enthusiastic light, since, as Renan put it, "stupidity has no right to govern the world." The future of the human race belonged to religious and moral reform, which could originate only with an intellectual elite. Putting aside all reference to what was beyond nature, this elite had the task of "scientifically organizing humanity."

Like the most disenchanted young men of the period—Flaubert, for example—Renan saw only boredom in contractual democracy and only absurdity in socialist utopias. But like the most brilliant minds of his generation, such as Hippolyte-Adolphe Taine or Marcelin Berthelot, he placed his bets on a theocracy of men of science as representing the best of all possible governments. Yet the young Renan did not aspire to an entirely gray, domesticated, socially pacified society. He felt within himself a confused and restless desire to experience fascinating historical moments, "to be a soldier lost in the immense army advancing to conquer perfection." It is pointless to emphasize all that was "modern" in this; more than one page of the *Pensées de 48* may seem quite disturbing to us as twentieth-century readers, given our awareness of certain developments of "reactionary modernism." But there is no question that Renan's work constitutes a kind of moral history of French generations from the eighteenth century to 1848. Renan spared no criticism of the pedagogical dream the

Enlightenment had passed on to Jacobinism, of the quest for procedures to accelerate the moralization of man, "like fruits one ripens in one's hands! People of little faith in nature, leave them in the sun!" He was nonetheless forced to recognize that the sun of progress did not send the same heat to all generations.

Like many others before and after him, Renan gave in to the temptation of believing he belonged to a sacrificed generation. What was lacking for the men who had begun thinking after 1830, unlike those who had come of age in 1815, was a true and noble combat in which to invest their youth. Born under the sign of Mercury, the men of Renan's generation had settled too much into a comfortable and ordinary life: "Woe betide the generation that has seen only a regular order, that conceived of life as repose and art as pleasure!" But the young Renan, who had nonetheless seen the bloody battles of June 1848, found hardly more enviable the fate of the generations to which revolution fell; sensitive too to the favor of a late birth, he exclaimed: "Woe betide those who create revolution! Blessed is the man who inherits it! Blessed, in particular, are those, born to better days, who will no longer need irrational and absurd means to bring about the triumph of reason!" As we can see, Renan's thought followed a vicious circle, without his making many efforts to get out of it, convinced as he was that he was writing the prophetic panegyric of a happily progressive humanity. This conviction, which the former seminarian deliberated in his *Pensées de 1848*, would be reproduced, with more or less venom, in his subsequent works: revolutionary periods are a malediction, those of repose a damnation; political society is a hunting ground for immoral creatures, civil society the paradise of frivolous beings. And while Renan's historiographic vigilance and critical genius made him the master of generations of linguists and psychologists, ethnologists and religious historians, for the young people who would read him with a political eye, Renan would play a very different role: to Georges Sorel and Lucien Herr, to Charles Maurras and Léon Blum, he would transmit an attitude of fascination for politics together with a revulsion toward it.

Nothing could be more foreign to Renan than revolutionary violence, whether that of the workers of 1848 or of the terrorists of year II. And yet he knew that "when it is a matter of founding the future by striking down the past, you need these formidable pioneers, who never allow themselves to be softened by the tears of women and never spare the blows of the ax."[103] Like so many Jacobins before him, Renan disdained the masses but admired those who could be their representatives, whether a handful of men or a unique individual. Indeed it was also through Renan that the French Revolution transmitted to the men of the Third Republic its most important Jacobin legacy: wariness with respect to a civil society recognized as pleasure seeking or incompetent, and the conviction that it fell to a handful of intellectual heroes to sacrifice their lives in the mud of political society for the good of future generations.

It is now time to consider the fact that, faced with the revolution of 1848, the French were not the only ones to reflect on their "ills" and the prospects for revolution in Europe. Key to the future of the revolutionary tradition would be Aleksandr Herzen's reflection on the deep-seated meaning of the days of June and the prospects for French socialism in the context of the European democratic movement. In a now classic essay, Isaiah Berlin highlighted the extraordinary current of antidogmatism animating a book like *From the Other Shore*, Herzen's elegy to the illusions of 1848 and simultaneous denunciation of the aberrant Jacobin logic that asked current generations to sacrifice themselves for generations to come, "like caryatids forced to hold up a room where, one day, others will dance."[104] In his admirable study on Russian populism, Franco Venturi emphasized the political consequences of Herzen's meditation on the rubble of '48: recognition of the irremediable "old age" of Western Europe, and the decision of exiles to return to the East, an East from which they had come, an East "young" enough to escape the ossification of Western ideals and perhaps to avoid some of the stages of economic development for which Europe was in the process of paying so dearly.

Louis-Napoleon Bonaparte's coup d'état, his new stranglehold on France, could only reinforce Herzen in his diagnosis. And suddenly, in the mid 1850s, two major events occurred in Russia: the Crimean War crumbled the myth of the immense autocratic empire's military invincibility, and the death of Nicolas I in 1855 sounded the end of the thirty hard years that had followed the failure of the Decembrists' plot. "We're drunk, we've become crazy, we've become young," exclaimed Herzen at the announcement of the czar's death. In a large meeting in London, on February 27, 1855, before the finest of Europe's political emigrés—Louis Blanc, Marx, Mazzini, Lajos Kossuth, Worcell—he confirmed that the moment for Russian renewal had come.[105] In terms of his French counterparts, the Russian exile Herzen was in touch with all the great exiles of the Second Empire: Proudhon, Quinet, Hugo—all proud opponents of Napoleon III. It is true that these were not young men anymore, rejuvenated though Herzen may have felt by the death of Nicholas I. But the correspondence between these men in their forties or fifties is relevant to our subject, because it was to such great figures of emigration that all revolutionary youths turned, whether Russian or French, in the 1850s and 1860s. It should also be added that, with regard to the young generations, these illustrious exiles spoke in terms of incomprehension: if the practice of revolution wears out revolutionaries, waiting for a revolution—even a moral revolution—had no less devastating effects on these exiles, whom we often find frozen in bitter solitude and precociously aged.

What is highly significant in this respect is the reaction of the Second Empire exiles to the literary tastes of French youth in the 1850s and 1860s, the decades that witnessed the publishing explosion of the novel. The exiles had already shown true disdain for the masses—who were too docile in the face of Bonapartist propaganda—and they did not understand how, instead of being interested in political and social history, the brightest of the young generation could be happy reading novels. Deep down, Napoleon III's adversaries shared a moralizing conviction with the imperial censors: youth had to be protected from excesses of sensuality and material appetite.[106] Our exiles felt like Tacitus and Seneca faced with Petronius and Martialis: "It is not with novels that France shall be saved," wrote Edgar Quinet to a friend.[107] The arrogance of the mentors also brought great suffering, and the most sensitive among them, in their defense of inalienable principles, realized that they displayed a kind of rigidity, a sad affectation, in the eyes of youth. "I cannot help but see that in times of decadence, sullied, degraded consciences are infinitely more at ease, and thus more *natural* in the artistic sense, than are the few sincere individuals who continue to write." Thus wrote Quinet, when faced with the success achieved by authors whom he had once esteemed and even counted among his friends, beginning with George Sand.[108]

No one is a prophet in his own country. While Quinet, Blanc, and sometimes Michelet had the impression of being neglected by the cream of French youth, they could not say the same of Russian revolutionary youth. The more or less clandestine reading of historical works that Napoleon III's opponents had devoted to the French Revolution constituted—along with Filippo Buonarroti's *Conspiration pour l'égalité*—an obligatory stage in the political apprenticeship of young Russian populists between 1855 and 1870. Conversely, the polemical target of the populists was increasingly Herzen himself, proudly perched on his London pedestal. The author of *From the Other Shore* was no doubt a mythical enough figure to still push certain courageous young men, such as Nikolay Chernyshevsky, to undertake the journey to London to visit him, despite the distance and the czarist police, but these visits were always a great disappointment for the travelers, for reasons that had to do not only with their youthful impatience but also with the roughness of the "old man." Herzen, like so many other European exiles of 1848, clung to his exile status as a way to be in the right, alone against everyone else.[109]

The letters by Quinet already cited, on the role reserved for political writers in the arid moral climate of France under Napoleon III, must be considered in the context of what Herzen was then writing about the plight of the "superfluous man" (the expression is Turgenev's) in Nicholas I's Russia. When Herzen undertook to defend the existential choice of the so-called superfluous man—in other words, the intellectual of noble origins courageous enough to accept physical and moral alienation as the price for following the path of his ideals—it was obviously a way of defending his own life choices, faced with the severe critiques that the populist leaders Chernyshevsky and Nikolay Dobrolyubov had brought raining down on the chief of the nobiliary intelligentsia. And yet the London exile saw this superfluous man as being in "one of the most tragic situations in the world." Most difficult was the ingratitude of the revolutionaries of the young generation with respect to those who had paved the way for them. At the end of his life, Herzen would compare the "Bazaroïdes" (another term borrowed from Turgenev, referring to the famous hero of *Fathers and Sons,* Bazarov) to "those inhabitants of Kamtchatka who kill their old people."[110]

The lack of understanding between revolutionary "fathers" and revolutionary "sons" was less than total, however. In 1861 and 1862, following the abolition of serfdom in Russia, when the students from Moscow and Kharkov began their conspiratorial activities, they circulated Herzen's London publications, which shows that the influence of Iskander (Herzen's pseudonym) was still strong in younger circles—not to mention the success of the command launched at the time by another London exile, Nicolas Ogarev: "One must go to the people." But in the summer of 1862, the young authors of the manifesto *Young Russia* attacked Herzen with unprecedented violence, reproaching him not only for his wait-and-see policy but also for what they saw as the stupidity of his constitutionalist positions. What was worse, Zaitchnevski and the other creators of *Young Russia* based their rejection of Herzen on a political and historical judgment of the French Revolution, bragging of having closely studied "the great men of the Terror," comparing them to the "poor revolutionaries of '48," and of having arrived at the conclusion that to revive Russia, even more blood had to be spilled than in France between 1792 and 1794. In Russia, it would be up to the axes of youth to assume the role of the holy guillotine.[111]

In 1863, with the failure of a new Polish insurrection, to which the young Land and Freedom Russians had hoped to be able to contribute thanks to Herzen's London funds, the gulf with Iskander widened. In 1866, the founder of the first Land and Freedom organization, Aleksandr Serno-Solovievitch, was exiled in turn, in Switzerland, and it was he who launched the final offensive against Herzen. According to him, it was not the London exile, with his Lamartine-style humanism, who could rally Russian youth: his admiration went instead to Chernyshevsky, who was paying in Siberia for his plot against the czarist regime, and to the socialism of *What Is to be Done?,* Chernyshevsky's famous novel. It was toward the one confined in Siberia that "truly young Russia" turned, without giving another thought to Herzen and his "pretentions" of being young. These were not merely words: Serno-Solovievitch was actively working for the International, seeking to reconcile the positions of Marx and Bakunin; he played a primary role in the social conflicts in Geneva, as is the great strike of building workers in 1868, which had repercussions throughout Europe. This polemic in the name of youth, embellished with quotes from Proudhon and Marx, was not directed solely against Herzen. In *La Liberté* Serno-Solovietvitch explained that, to become an independent force, the International had to put away any idols, whether they be "Fazy, Garibaldi himself, or any other god." Like James Fazy forty years earlier, Serno-Solovievitch seemed to believe in a kind of biological law favoring youth. He expressed his confidence in the "strength . . . of young organic tissues," in "young will, which dried out, old, broken-down tissues could not resist."[112] Herzen was horrified at the arrogance of this second generation of unpolished and fanatical Russian revolutionaries: "Turgenev's Bazarov is a God next to these pigs," he wrote to Ogarev in May 1868.[113]

More encouraging, in the eyes of Herzen, was the attitude of the other great figure of Russian emigration, Mikhail Bakunin, toward the programs and plots of the young populists. But a rift would develop between these two, becoming irreparable in 1869, with the appearance, on the gray emigrant horizon, of a barely twenty-two-year-old Russian agitator, Sergei Netchaiev, a figure whose thunderous energy Bakunin would recognize but in whom Herzen would see only moral and ideological ambiguity. The disagreement between Herzen and Bakunin was already germinating by 1866, after Karakasov's failed attempt against Alexander II, as we see in Bakunin's letters to Herzen. "Herzen, you can say what you will, although these pioneers of a new truth and a new life may be dirty, awkward, and often unbearable, they are a thousand times better than all your proper cadavers," launched Bakunin. "Do not get old, Herzen, there is nothing good in old age." While Herzen clung to his exile, Bakunin clung to other people's youth. When they spoke of the future, Herzen and Bakunin envisaged the prospects for the economic evolution of the Russian agrarian community and the tactics suitable for politically mobilizing the peasant masses, but their debate bore mostly on the past: it was the great debate of the century, the debate on the French Revolution and the Terror. In defense of the "Bazaroïdes" generation, Bakunin explained to Herzen that the entire problem with youth was this search for a new morality, which they never managed to find: "Hence the uncertainties, the contradictions, the baseness, and often the indecent scandals. It was the same thing in '93, except that the guillotine purified and left no time for the buds that never reached maturity to rot."[114] In Bakunin, we are faced with the extreme form of the Jacobin wager on the precociousness of fruits warmed by the "African sun" of the Revolution: the guillotine is the ultimate guarantee for a delicate biology, for a problematic maturation.

When Netchaiev, in 1869, decided to write his *Catéchisme d'un révolutionnaire,* it was Bakunin who inspired him. Each paragraph begins with the same phrase, "The revolutionary is a lost man,"[115] and this became the leitmotif of the maniifesto. This expression drew from the most famous interrupted speech in the history of parliamentary government: on 8 Thermidor, year II, when Robespierre had taken the floor to ask the Convention for new executions, he had wanted to speak of his generation as "a generation of lost men." But, tired of listening to him, the Convention preferred to silence Robespierre, and Saint-Just along with him, before sending them to the gallows. These dramatic circumstances had turned Robespierre's words into a kind of testament of the Incorruptible for those who saw themselves as his heirs. For the militant French republicans of the early years of the July Monarchy, this speech of 8 Thermidor had become "a gospel," Heine tells us, with his usual skepticism, especially "for the very young and the very old."[116] In 1869 Herzen's comment about Netchaiev's recipe for a new Terror (with its likely train of new severed tongues, new murders and betrayals, and new mass exterminations) picked up on Heine's idea: "They are the vicious dreams of those too young and those too old."[117]

They were sufficiently seductive dreams, nonetheless, to turn Bakunin into one of the leaders of European socialism. With regard to France, he was then disputing with Auguste Blanqui for the premiere place in revolutionary leadership during the final gray years of the Second Empire. And Blanqui, in turn, was taking advantage of several years of freedom to foster a handful of young zealots of the Jacobin cult. A pedantic, anti-quated troop of men turned toward the past rather than the future?[118] Perhaps. But there is something moving about the serious way certain university students dwelled on the French Revolution, composing short monographs for the benefit of the old Blanqui. What is especially moving is the lucidity with which the most intelligent among them perceived the social limits of their political actions, as we see in Gustave Tridon's letters to Blanqui between 1866 and 1868. Born in 1841 to a wealthy landowner from Dijon, Tridon was the most intellectually gifted of the group of young Blanquists, and the most generous in the time he gave to militant activities. His studies in law and the philosophy of history, the newspapers he ran, and the trials and incarceration that were the inevitable conse-quences, still left him time to think about the fundamental ambivalence "of a revolutionary movement led by young men of the bourgeoisie." Tridon appreciated better than Blanqui the distance separating the ranks of Blan-quists—men of letters or jurists—from the working class for which they claimed to want to fight. What irritated Tridon most was the "bohemian" strain (that of Jules Vallès, he specified) of certain revolutionary youths who thought only of joking, chatting, drinking, mocking everything and everyone, and whining: "This whole group of youngsters are disgusting rabble":[119] No verdict could have been harsher.

Some time later, the Paris Commune, in some aspects, would reveal itself to be a bohemian adventure: not only because it would give the highest responsibilities to Raoul Rigault and Jules Vallès, but also because it claimed to be a final attempt at conciliation between rebellion and moralism, between emancipation of the individual and society's need for order. It was not so in the eyes of Tridon and his lean group of followers, of course: for them, the Commune was the long-awaited opportunity to reawaken, or pursue, the Hébertist dream (of political liberty and social equality propounded by the journalist Jacques-René Hébert during the French Revolution—*trans. note*) which they had learned about in their books on the Revolution. Nor was it so in the eyes of the workers on the outskirts of Paris, for whom the Commune signified something quite different. But for more than one bourgeois revolutionary, adherence to the

Commune was based on the anxious quest for a happy end, for the long-awaited crowning (as Vallès said in 1867) of the reconciliation between "artists" and "bourgeois," between the "sons" and "fathers" who had been separated too long.[120]

WHITE BEARDS, GRAY BEARDS, BROWN BEARDS

Like the generation of the National Convention, like that of the forty-eighters, the generation of communards can be considered a generation of survivors. The diverse destinies of the Blanquist squad, after the Commune, are particularly illuminating. Tridon left Paris right before the "Bloody Week" of May 1871, heading for Brussels, where he died in utter solitude at the age of thirty. Blanqui, once again imprisoned, began work on his *Eternité par les astres,* a staggering cosmology whose function as a stage in the evolution of the revolutionary tradition was emphasized by Walter Benjamin. In it, Blanqui disenchantedly contemplates the obstacles that stand in the way of progress, the "flesh and bone mimicry artists" who interpret the history of humanity.[121] As for the other Blanquist leaders who escaped the firing squads, they dispersed all over Europe, returning to France only after the amnesty of 1880. They then seemed to have no difficulty translating the traditional Blanquist chauvinism into nationalism, or even swelling the ranks of General Boulanger's troops.

In Russia, 1871—the year of the Paris Commune—was the year of the trial of Netchaiev and the other members of the group People's Will. It was the first political trial in the history of the czarist regime, the consequences of which would be as important to the internal development of opposition movements (depending on the level of student adhesion to the Netchaiev catechism) as to the role of Russian exiles in the revolutionary movements in Europe. In the 1870s, in fact, the theory and practice of populism, crowned by twenty years of struggle and sacrifice, attained the status of a tradition, as can be measured by the success of the Chernyshevsky's political novel *What Is to Be Done?,* translated in Belgium by César De Paepe, one of the most prestigious personalities of the International, and published in serialized form in France, in the 1880s, in the Blanquist bulletin *Ni dieu ni maître* (Neither god nor master) as well as in

Benoit Malon's *Revue socialiste*. The person responsible for the first French translation, published in Lodi in 1875, was none other than Jules Guesde.

Even more than to the growing authority of the Russian revolutionaries, the prominence of Guesde points to the recognition on the part of the French of a revolutionary primacy in the social democracy developing beyond the Rhine, at a time of "German crisis" among the French extreme left.[122] Yet we know how difficult it was for Guesdist Marxism to get a toehold in the French left, as much on the level of worker organizations as on that of the political and intellectual avant-garde. Guesdism was confronted with the solidity of an indigenous revolutionary tradition—the richest in the world, and one that was endowed with an authentic worker vein. In addition, the inevitable anti-German reflexes of Jacobin ideology, which Gambetta and the national defense government had wanted to resuscitate following the defeat at Sedan, the long-lasting impact of the military experience, which the royalist and republican armies had shared on the battlefields of 1870–71, the rise of a dream of revenge for the annexation of Alsace-Lorraine, and several years of alliance between the classes in consolidating the Third Republic against monarchist maneuverings[123] all explain the limits of the French revolutionaries' attraction to the German social-democratic model, whether those revolutionaries were young or old. What worked better, in fact, than the concept of class was the concept of race found in the political culture beyond the Rhine, and which, in the 1880s, was capable of impressing some of the more restless Frenchmen of the young generation, aided by the local support of the writings of Taine and Drumont, as well as of Tridon's posthumous work, *Du molochisme juif* (On Jewish molochism), and many articles from the *Revue socialiste*.[124]

The intellectual apprenticeship of Lucien Herr, the future librarian of the Ecole normale supérieure and a charismatic figure who would be at the origin of the socialist careers of so many French intellectuals (from Jean Jaurès to Léon Blum), demonstrates the relative weight of the Russian revolutionary tradition on French youth in the late 1880s, compared with that of the German tradition. After receiving his philosophy *agrégation* at the age of twenty-two, Herr wasn't content to make the traditional journey to study in Germany: in 1886–1887, perhaps under the influence of Gustave Monod, Herzen's son-in-law and a great teacher of positivist history, Herr headed for Russia. On returning to France, he developed contacts with the most representative figure of Russian political emigration in Paris, Pyotr Lavrov, the already middle-aged author of the *Historical Letters,* which had had a profound influence on the populists of the 1870s.[125] Lavrov's cultivated political elitism was hardly to the taste of the French proletariat, but this was not the case for an intellectual like Lucien Herr, whose education, like that of many French youths of the Third Republic, had been under the moral auspices of Renan, and who had been prepared by the long Saint-Simonian and positivist tradition to particularly appreciate the idea of a party of intellectuals that was so dear to Lavrov.[126] It was through Herr's influence that the slogan "One must go to the people," which had mobilized the Russian populists of the 1870s with varying degrees of success, would be revived in fin de siècle France and would translate, notably, into achievements such as the so-called popular universities and popular socialist publishing—but at the price of a heightened recourse to abstraction in a country that made less and less of peasants and more and more of "Frenchmen."[127]

Lucien Herr was too intelligent to depend on only the word of his teachers, and too young to reject the idea of a revolutionary mission for youth. One of his notes of the time seems to be an exact reply to the famous page of *Réforme intellectuelle et morale,* in which Renan deplores the absence, in the political and social history of France, of a link that would join the dead to the living, one generation to the next, ensuring the stability of the future. Herr wrote, "All modern political life presupposes the negation of heredity, of solidarities among successive generations . . . As the average man is frozen in his ideas and his interests when he reaches maturity, progress requires the initiative of younger generations." Nonetheless, Herr agreed with Renan's intellectual moralism and Lavrov's elitist socialism on the essential question: in this same note he went on to argue that "insurrection and revolt" went hand in hand with "examination and criticism."[128]

Several years hence, Herr would find in Renan's *L'Avenir de la science* [The Future of Science]—when it was finally published—the most complete expression of a revolutionary project transmuted into a revolution of intellectuals. It is no accident that fifteen years later, Charles Péguy (who in the meantime would be Herr's right arm in the Dreyfusard mobilization of the Latin Quarter) could speak of Renan's early work as key for anyone wishing to understand the modern world.[129] But one needn't wait until Péguy launched his *Cahiers de la Quinzaine* in 1900—an extraordinary display case for the ideals and obsessions, hopes, and traumas of an entire generation of intellectuals—to detect the common moral attitudes and political culture that, through Herr, connected the fin de siècle, socialist, Ecole normale supérieure students with the Renan of 1848. One need only follow the itinerary of another of Herr's "students," a classmate of Péguy's at the Ecole and a Dreyfusard activist, who, as a young twenty-five-year-old teacher at the *lycée* of Montauban, on July 31, 1899, harangued his students in the school's traditional awards ceremony speech, an important ceremony in the republican liturgy.[130] The teacher's name was Albert Mathiez, and he would become the leader of the "prorevolutionary" historians.

If this speech is worth quoting at length, it is because in it Mathiez recited the credo of the radical or socialist intellectual of the Belle Epoque faced with the problems of youth, its emancipation, and revolution. This credo would remain stable throughout a season destined to end precisely fifteen years later, on July 31, 1914, with the assassination of Jaurès on the eve of the declaration of war. As historian Zeev Sternhell has maintained in a solid, much discussed book, it is not appropriate to attach too much importance to the choice in favor of war, nor later (for those who had survived the trenches) to the "socialist" or "fascist" choices of the most brilliant representatives of Mathiez's generation: Péguy and Berth, Challaye and Bourgin, Isaac and Benda.[131] One may nonetheless disagree with Sternhell in that the common language that united all these intellectuals did not necessarily entail the historical devaluation of the French Revolution: it was entirely possible, as in the case of Mathiez, to cultivate its myth while sharing with one's age group, on the right and on the left, the boredom and disdain that liberalism, individualism, and materialism inspired.

In Montauban in 1899, Mathiez began his speech as follows: "There are . . . various ways to be young" but "there is only one good one, only one that is in keeping with a given time and a given society." And he quotes, of course, the lesson of 1793. He recalls how the lower-middle-class men from the provinces who became ministers of the Republic, how the farmers who became generals of victorious armies, had received their training more through life than from books: emerging from the depths of France, they had endured all of its suffering and shared all of its hope. If these young men ended up winning out over allied European monarchies, explained Mathiez, it was because they hadn't hesitated to sacrifice their own lives, fully aware that in their battle for France they were fighting for the regeneration of humanity as a whole. And the generals of the Empire were no less valiant, and so many young people of the Restoration and the July Monarchy no less admirable, even if many of them, "those that had eaten mad cow for too long" had remained "bohemians." But the others, the scholars, had performed forty years of scientific miracles, and had brought about in France a revolution that was no less beautiful or fruitful than the revolution for the rights of man. On the other hand, under the Second Empire, one saw only degraded young men, a hundred times more calculating and coldly materialistic than their fathers, and it was they who were responsible in many ways for the defeat at Sedan and the mutilation of the national territory.

Mathiez then moved into the present, and invited the young students of Montauban to consider the risks that the Third Republic itself was running, threatened as it was by "these youths who live only for themselves," these grotesque esthetes "who perfume themselves and live like women," devoting half the day to studying the color of ties—a republic threatened further by the cursed race "of unscrupulous climbers, of profiteers and of pleasure seekers," hypocritical fools in times of calm, but vicious and greedy when the time was right. "It is they," he said, "esthetes and social climbers, who brought into vogue this literature that falsifies

and corrupts the national soul, this literature of byzantines and degener-
ates," these decadents and symbolists enclosed in their ivory tower, culti-
vating only "'their I,' as they say, the immense 'I' that hides them from
the rest of the world, these young people who, in their stupidity, go so far
as to proclaim themselves *uprooted*." Faced with such debauchery, Mathiez
invited his students to pay an all the more respectful homage to the
generation of men who had fought the French Revolution, to those young
apostles of a new gospel, who, even when they had been martyred or
forced to face a counteroffensive from a past they thought they had
abolished, had nonetheless never doubted or been discouraged, to those
men whose soul "radiated an eternal youth, because they were filled with
truth and justice."[132]

What Mathiez was expressing at this awards ceremony was mainly a
form of populism common to many radical and socialist graduates of the
Ecole normale supérieure at the end of the nineteenth century. His speech
revealed the tenacious will of a teacher who had "arrived" to remain
faithful to the working classes from which he had sprung; Mathiez was
determined not to allow the improvement in status he had attained to
become the pretext for a kind of social betrayal.[133] In addition, it was a
conviction among the leftist intelligentsia of the Third Republic that liberty was inherently internationalist when it was exported at the tip of a
French bayonet, whereas it was nothing but insidious imperialism when
imposed by the arms of others.[134] We find as well in the newly appointed
professor's speech the lessons of Renan and the entire positivist culture of
the second half of the nineteenth century: the real modern revolution was
the one that was taking place in the calm of laboratories and libraries. But
Mathiez also updated the old sansculotte antipathy for corrupt boys and
corrupting women, for the *jeunesse dorée* and the *merveilleuses* of the
French Directoire period, who threatened social morality. He shared the
republicans' distaste for the pleasures of life, for "enjoyment," for which
the Jacobins had reproached Danton's partisans to the point of punishing
them by death, which Renan too had look upon with a scandalized eye,
and which Lavrov had seen only as the dark and anonymous appetites of
a purely "zoological" existence. Mathiez's words also suggest the scholar's

horror for bohemianism, past, present, or future, when it becomes an individualist retreat from life; and beyond his transparent attack on Barrès, the teacher demonstrated the order-loving revolutionary's visceral wariness of art and literature when conceived of as free exercises in fantasy and the refuge of an "I" that claims opacity with respect to the collective's scrutiny. Finally, and perhaps above all, Mathiez's words (like the pages that Jaurès was preparing to publish on the French Revolution)[135] reflected fin de siècle philosophical idealism and its rediscovery of voluntarism in politics. In this commendation of revolutionary subjectivity, which took on an eighteenth-century tone, the Montauban teacher gave the impression of sharing the Jacobin dream of a world regenerated through purity of conscience even more than through solving the material problems of the popular classes.[136]

During these same years, while the young Mathiez saw in the historical events of the French Revolution the best proof of the primacy of subjectivity in revolution, the young Lenin was transforming this same assertion of primacy into a political philosophy. But his point of departure was more a reflection on the Russian revolutionary tradition than an adoption of the French tradition.[137] Before his exile in Switzerland, what had been critical for Lenin—far more than any book on the Great Revolution—was his meeting with Pavel Akselrod and his epistolary dialogue with Georgy Plekhanov, two veterans of populism who had alighted on Marxism. Though certain exegetes have continued to emphasize Lenin's debt to Jacobinism, Vladimir Ulianov's ideological trajectory shows the growing lack of currency, outside of France, of the heritage that for a century had been the obligatory point of reference, whether positive or negative, for the revolutionaries of the entire world. When Lenin turned toward militant action in the early 1890s, the generations of Russian populists and nihilists that had preceded him in revolutionary opposition to the czarist regime had already sufficiently toiled and sacrificed for him to be obliged to take account of what they represented, outside of any foreign revolutionary experience and even outside of the cumbersome precedent of the French Revolution.

In 1902 Lenin published his own *What Is to Be Done?*, borrowing the title from Chernyshevsky's novel, and in it we find a great deal of what the author had learned from Akselrod: that the method of capitalist production does not have such a constraining impact on social development as to leave no room for individual and collective voluntarism, for revolutionary intervention. But it is important to note the primacy of the generational question in the teachings of Akselrod and Plekhanov, who forcefully opposed the scholastic interpretation of Marxism of the young Russian recruits—as blind in their faith toward the proletariat as the populists of the 1860s had been toward the muzhiks. Thus at the moment when he was learning from the "elders" to turn toward socialist action as the greatest way to make up for the historical indifference of the Russian masses, Lenin became practically foreign to his own generation. And this when European social democracy in general, and that of Germany in particular, was attempting the impossible by endeavoring to counter the success of bourgeois-inspired youth associations with the creation of parallel socialist associations, while denying any theoretical relevance to the dimension of age, which was inevitably subordinate to that of class.[138]

From the point of view of youth—and especially from youth's point of view, one might say—the decade that preceded 1914 was dominated by the idea of war, a specter for some, a mirage for others. Perhaps for this reason, the most subtle analyses of the political dynamic of these generations come from Otto Bauer and the other Austrian socialists in their attempts to understand the success of the student movements in non–German speaking Hapsburg territories, where they oscillated between reactionary patriotism and democratic nationalism. In 1908, a Viennese worker demonstration against the high cost of living brought about a kind of student counterdemonstration, at which time Max Adler bitterly noted the difference between these Viennese street scenes and the "grandiose spectacle" of Parisian youth in 1848, the memory of which had been transmitted to him through the European revolutionary tradition. Once again, students and workers took over the streets and public squares, but this time, far from working together, "they were separated by an abyss of reciprocal hatred and rage," armed against one another. Sixty years had not passed in vain: the bourgeois *Bildung* had succeeded in turning the ideals of liberty, citizenship, and patriotism into concepts apt to shine in the eyes of students but which elicited distrust on the part of working-class youth.

The theory and practice of the Viennese avant-garde of the early twentieth century were no less lucid than the political reflections of the greatest Austrian theoreticians of Marxism. The expressionists resisted the temptation to affirm their identity in terms of conflict with their fathers and renounced reestablishment of the generational tension that had marked the cultural and ideological life of Austria in the second half of the nineteenth century, from the Wagnerian protests against the old liberals to the Jung-Wien movement and the destructive criticism of the "secessionists." In these years, while Freud (who belonged to the preceding generation) asserted that the Oedipal revolt was at the core of the individual and of society, Schiele, Kokoschka, Trakl, Musil, Schoenberg, and Wittgenstein chose to reflect on the condition of man in general, rather than organize their discourse in terms of the opposition of fathers and sons, of the past and modernity. It even became possible to show indulgence toward fathers, in an unprecedented awareness of the otherness of their condition: thus Robert Musil, who in 1906 published *Young Törless,* wrote, "My father was younger than I."[139] During the first half of the nineteenth century, the bildungsroman had brought into play the restlessness of youth and the wisdom of adults, and now, at the turn of the century, in its ultimate incarnation, it was telling the story of youths who no longer aspired to become adults and even wanted to transform the natural biological course of growth into a regression toward adolescence, preadolescence, or beyond.[140] To Egon Schiele's painted figures, for example, maturity seems physically out of reach: their bodies are young but dry as sticks, inert, sterile.

"Our children are not our age," said Charles Péguy in France, but this was a truism in appearance only. What he meant was that sons were both younger and older than their fathers, younger than what their state-issued birth certificates said, older than those issued by humanity. Péguy too, at the age of forty, obsessed by the failure of the "Dreyfusard revolution," by the aging of people and things, by the problems of the imprint of history on life and of life on history, saw only sterility in the modern world. And he ended with a kind of wager as to the virtues of the filial curse that sons can cast at their fathers, through war. While Péguy's journal was a model for the young Italians gathered around Giuseppe Prezzolini and *La Voce*,[141] Péguy, for his part, drew symbolic inspiration from Ernest Psichari, the young heir to an important intellectual and bourgeois family, who had chosen to abandon his studies to enlist in the colonial artillery, and who, in his poems, expressed the ethical and aesthetic unrest of his generation. Péguy's choice was no accident: Ernest Psichari was Renan's nephew on his mother's side, and, in Péguy's eyes, the living incarnation of Renan's generational theory, according to which young and old should unite against middle-aged men. As for Psichari, from the depths of his garrison he wrote to Péguy "like a son to his father."[142] Both considered that youth and old age were difficult but fertile times, and that the worst age was middle age—one's forties—a time condemned to irremediable sterility.

Thus "brown beards" and "white beards" (the expressions are Péguy's) must mock the "gray beards" of those such as Lucien Herr and Jean Jaurès. The time even came, beginning in 1911, when the managing editor of the *Cahiers de la Quinzaine* wouldn't hesitate to say, in old revolutionary style, that those who had brown beards and white beards should cut off, as did the members of the National Convention, those heads that were framed by gray beards.[143] Jaurès's head would indeed fall on July 31, 1914, just in time for the socialists to develop with impunity the myth of the Great War as the last and most indispensable combat of the revolutionary wars. Another few weeks and Péguy, like Psichari, would in turn be mowed down, along with thousands and thousands of comrades and adversaries, in the slaughters of the Marne or the Somme. It was only a few months before soldiers and young officers, whether French, English, German, or Italian, realized how little the current war resembled the clean regeneration of humanity in which so many of them had believed. The announced regeneration of the world was developing into the inhuman massacre of an entire generation. Those who returned would be men who had survived their own selves—mere shadows—even when the memory of the daily battle against death in the trenches remained sufficiently intoxicating for them to describe it with the verses of Wordsworth, who, speaking of the French revolution, had exclaimed: "Bliss was it in that dawn to be alive / But to be young was very heaven!"[144] In the meantime, the literature of the war would follow different paths from those of history and ideological imagination. In France at least, the human and political costs of the conflict would force socialist intellectuals to completely revise the myth of revolutionary war.[145]

The consequences of the Great War on the future political choices of the young Europeans who had participated in it were so varied as to discourage any attempt at synthesis. Let us simply cast a glance at the correspondence of Romain Rolland, Péguy's old friend and the illustrious contributor to the *Cahiers de la Quinzaine*—until world conflict sent Péguy into the trenches and Rolland into his Swiss exile to fight the battle of pacifism. A letter Rolland received in early November 1917 informed him that the "brutal law" formulated in *Jean-Christophe*, according to which each generation would be obliged to reject the one before it, had now been surpassed; the law had lost its relevance after the Great War and the Bolshevik challenge: "There are no longer any ages . . . Romain Rolland, my dear friend, I am forever a part of our ageless generation." And several days later, the same correspondent wrote to Rolland, "Tell me, truthfully, whether you find in me, [one] who is from another generation and could be your son, the same distress and the same enthusiasm that you experience, the same weariness with nonetheless the same passion."[146]

The author of the letters was twenty years old; his name was Jean de Saint-Prix. He had been exempted from military service for health reasons, but he felt sufficiently concerned by the prevailing tragedy to devote himself, from 1916 on, to internationalist and revolutionary propaganda. Rolland had met him briefly during the summer of 1917 and had seen this "little Saint-Just" (the young man was a direct descendent of a Saint-Prix who had been a member of the Convention) as the best representative of the new generation.[147] Written under the shock of the news from Petrograd, the words of Rolland's young correspondent constitute an excellent epilogue to our story: on the one hand, the young Saint-Prix returns to the dream of a reconciliation without compromise between fathers and sons, a reconciliation that would in no way detract from the revolution, and on the other, the great-grandson of a member of the Convention resigns himself to passing on the flame: "We are not a young country like the country of Gorky. The wing of death passes over our finest days."[148]

CHAPTER 7

THE MYTH OF
YOUTH IN IMAGES:
ITALIAN FASCISM

Laura Malvano

> Youth, youth,
> Springtime of Beauty!
> The intoxication of life,
> Your song sounds out and away.

Through the concise paraphrasing of symbolism and the wordy redundancy beloved of fascist phrasemakers, *Giovinezza* (Youth), the anthem of the Mussolini regime, expresses in exemplary fashion the twofold relationship fascism maintained with the concept of youth. The "fine song of bold youth" designates, above all, a social segment that, thanks to a clever symbolic device, becomes universal and all-encompassing. Rather than to any historical or generational cut-off, this notion refers to an ideal lifestyle: "Within the ranks of fascism the Garibaldian or Avanguardista can be young so long as he understands Mussolini's model of life."[1]

Indeed, "Our youth is a symbol that transcends the bounds of space and time; it sums up love and beauty, strength and song." The notion of youth covers a huge spectrum of civic, moral, and aesthetic values: "The base and vile cannot be young; as Il Duce so well understood, the base and vile are what is old and decadent. 'Youth' implies the soul of a hero."[2]

But most of all, the fascist anthem expresses the central, indentifying model of fascism:

Fascism is youth, but the inexorable law of time is that of aging; what will become of fascism as it ages? . . . Men grow old, but the Race, unless condemned to extinction by some degenerative defect, perpetually renews itself. Fascism, born of the most vibrant energies of our Race . . . so as not to degenerate and age in turn, must shed any element of weakness and frailty . . . and follow nature, identifying itself with the Race, and every year drawing the vigor of life from upcoming generations.[3]

The eternal youth, then, of an eternally young nation, translates into the political choice of a regime that makes youth the touchstone of its activities, the key to its own organizational system.

This youth is also that of the fascist state, vigorous heir to the fascist revolution, itself "young and fresh." It is a "young," "innovative" state and, in the Duce's words, one "in full possession of all its energies," disrupting the values of "the old government of Italy," whose ideal was "financial politics with Nitti and Giolitti . . . Clearly, we have one fatal defect: that of being too young. Thanks to the irreducible, youthful restlessness that brought us out onto the piazzas of Italy with bombs in hand in 1919, we have always had innumerable enemies."[4]

Of course the destructive force of this youth, still imbued with the violence of 1919 ("When it comes to the Motherland and fascism, we are ready to kill and to die"),[5] would be carefully channeled into the rigid military discipline of the regime's organizations. The young madcaps who sang *Giovinezza* and casually handled bombs and daggers would find themselves institutionalized by the military ritual of the regime, becoming the Young Fascists who, by virtue of the Duce's decree, "had to faithfully and silently serve in positions of obedience before being able to command."[6]

These few examples show how the discourse was able to adapt itself closely and flexibly to the multiform and polyvalent notion of youth, to the point of becoming its basic building block. Thanks to clever manipulation of this discourse, the concept of youth could be stripped of all historical or sociological connotations and assume a purely symbolic dimension, thus fusing its various implicit meanings. In taking up the study of images, one might well ask to what degree they were able to represent the multiple implications contained in this concept of youth.

One cannot help but recall how Ernst Gombrich, a great familiar of symbols, often warned against the difficulties inherent to the use of images when one wishes to express a clear, unequivocal message: "the signified is a fleeting element, expecially when applied to images and not to verbal formulations."[7] The problem is all the more significant when we consider the fundamental role played by images as a special vehicle for the regime's ideology throughout the two decades of fascism in Italy.[8]

"Fascism is youth, hence beauty, fire, harmony."[9] It was thus the classical image of the vigorous, athletic "ephebe" that would come to symbolize the fascist "new man," indeed that would become the symbol of fascism itself. "This handsome, young man, confident in bearing, direct in gaze, is called Mussolini's Italian. You can spot him a hundred yards off. He stands solidly in his all-black uniform, the external sign of his faith . . . An ethic of dress must correspond to a personal aesthetic."[10]

THE HANDSOME YOUNG MAN

Appropriating this seductive model of discourse, so meticulously detailed, was a much more awkward task with images than with words. For in his suggestive all-black uniform, there was a risk that the young man, the ephebe, would be relegated to the category of "low" art as a propaganda image, and would thus find no place in the rigid formal esthetic governing "works of art."

Furthermore, emphasis had often been placed on the unbreachable demarcation line separating the two different categories of images: painting and sculpture, "noble" art, on the one side, and all the rest on the other—images, no matter the format, intended to fulfill a "social function." Margherita Sarfatti, for instance, though she had tried to shift the aesthetic parameters, declaring the art of the 1900s an expression of "Italian modernity," did not neglect to underline that "the immediate representation of contemporary events was incompatible with the traditions of our great art, which is by nature mystical and legendary."[11]

It is interesting to note that the same preoccupations afflicted the upper echelons of the fascist regime. The party secretary himself, Alessandro Pavolini, raised the troublesome question of the pertinence of "propaganda art" during a meeting of the Syndicate of Professionals and Artists.

His answer was clear: "Propaganda is an entirely worthy and useful thing, but Art is something quite different."[12]

When monumental sculpture was set against public demand in the 1930s, the problematic relationship between art and propaganda became intensely topical. The handsome young man was summoned up to translate into the majestic language of sculpture the complex symbolism of "Mussolini's Italian." The metaphor of the all-black uniform was thus reserved for verbal discourse, while the monument could unreservedly exalt the athletic nudity of the young ephebe, heir to an illustrious tradition immortalized by Michelangelo's *David*. This was an important point of comparison that legitimized the model while giving the work a cultural value, an unchallengeable artistic prestige; the *David* of Savonarola's Florence was a guarantee of incontestable "Italianness."

The elaboration of this representation, hovering between culture and symbolic references, was not easy and followed anything but a straight path. We can trace it among minor, common, nonmonumental artifacts— highly diverse images as regards their nature, format, and intention. The young and handsome character who advertised the merits of the National Insurance Institute, for instance, was doubly effective, symbolizing and flattering both the beneficent fascist state and the citizen who would be its beneficiary. The abstraction of its symbolic language was softened by the context of the image, whose reading was facilitated by a series of clear references: the harking back to a vaguely mythical, pastoral society; the fasces associated with the harvest (fig. 1).

In another image, the same agrarian, idyllic universe, brimming with the flowers of spring ("Youth, youth, springtime of beauty!") serves as the backdrop for a surprising group of adolescents, legs still encased in their black uniforms but bare-breasted, accentuating their incongruous, somewhat faunlike aspect ("Youth of Italy! Lovely, fresh youth that erupts into our time as a flaming spring in the Motherland's sky!") (fig. 2).[13] One can measure the effectiveness of the image, part of an unusual propaganda campaign based on mail orders,[14] by its ability to present the young fascist (then still oscillating between early fascism's myth of violence and the regime's call to order) in folksy, cheerful atmosphere, whose flowering trees and waving flags temper the aggressive echoes of the *arditi*, the strong-arm commandos of fascism's beginnings.

At this point one might reflect on the acrobatic capacity of the image, in the early 1920s, to erase troublesome elements: while constantly recalling the myth of its origins (the revolution, the hard-core fascism of 1919), figurative representations eliminated any trace of violence. In those years, in fact, the "look" of young fascists underwent a significant transformation: a more respectable uniform took the place of the "inspired" and nonconformist wardrobe of the *ardito*, the early militant so admired by Filippo Marinetti. Gone, too, was the panoply of skulls, the dagger between the teeth, now replaced by the abstract and Romanizing symbolism of the new "Italian youth." We thus find the deeds of the early *squadrismo* related through a great variety of formats: the helping hand, the cheerful outing, in which the disquieting presence of "Saint Manganello," the "holy bludgeon," is camouflaged behind flasks of wine; the exuberant youths and budding heroes joyfully gathered amid waving flags.[15]

In 1932, the Exhibition of the Fascist Revolution opened in Rome. In the shrine to the first ten years of the regime, extensive use was made of images, all cleverly stage-managed to achieve various aims, illustrating and visualizing the "Revolution," but especially offering "plastic and visual symbols" the exceptional opportunity to "definitively sculpt the history of our time in eternal matter."[16]

In Brescia that same year, the brand-new Piazza della Vittoria, brilliantly designed by Marcello Piacentini, inaugurated another celebratory space. There, the rhetoric of the buildings merged with the ensemble of monuments to doubly ensure the presence of the fascist message. On Piacentini's Tower of the Revolution, Romano Romanelli's equestrian bas-relief of Mussolini sought to translate "into eternal matter" the epic of fascist discourse. Opposite, on the walls of the Arengario, the tribune, Antonio Maraini's bas-reliefs celebrated the *History of Brescia*.[17] In the center of the square rose the "enormously proportioned mass" of Adriano

Dazzi's marble ephebe.[18] In true Roman form, the outsized figure displayed its nakedness and athletic youth with unconcealed arrogance (fig. 3).

This unquestionably emblematic figure, which evokes in various and not entirely innocent ways its illustrious antecedents, was anything but explicit as to the exact meaning of its presence. The message it bore was seemingly situated on several levels. First of all, it expressed those "eternal qualities of the race" that the propaganda bible had turned into a product of mass consumption: what Bottai called the "vital energies of the race forever renewing and revivifying itself . . . by the very power of its tradition."[19] Yet the title of the work, *Fascist Era*, hinted at a more complex message than the dense physicality of the monument would suggest.

One may, in fact, question the capacity of this vigorous sculpture to become an image that is "alive and speaking" of the multiplicity of meanings suggested by the title. As with every work that has a social purpose, the context of its display, in this case so unmistakably fascist, left no doubt as to the ideological meaning of the mysterious young man. But to judge from the reservations expressed about this sort of representation, the difficulty of reading the work justified the uncertain nature of the choice.

Above all, one cannot overlook the provocation that the radiant presence of the nude, ostensibly pagan, athlete represented vis-à-vis the sensibility of a Catholic country, in which the wishes of the Church were carefully attended to by the fascist state. That the same kind of representation could readily be adapted to a different political and cultural context is demonstrated by Arno Breker's famous nudes. Their uninhibited physicality, their glorification of a mythical pagan past, became the transparent metaphor for the Aryanism of a people. The muscular heroes of Valhalla depicted by Breker were thus transformed into efficient propaganda instruments straight out of Nazism's racial eugenics.

Unlike fascism, Nazism would have ample recourse to an abstract and all-encompassing symbolism, in which the pagan and hedonistic exaltation of the young body would become integrated with the immaterial symbolism of space and light found in the Wagnerian sets created by Speer on the occasion of major Nazi celebrations. Italy, on the other hand, preferred a symbolism that was more directly accessible to the public. Such discourse found its place within a broader strategy, inherent to the whole of the politics of imagery established by fascism.[20] The emblematic imagery associating fascism and youth was fragmented into a vast, composite iconography with a wealth of formal and symbolic manifestations. Thus avoiding the dangers and limitations of an abstract and symbolic image of uncertain interpretations, fascism would opt for a clever and pragmatic articulation of the image drawn from a living social reality. This did not prevent the image of the ephebe from making regular appearances during the two decades of fascism, however, notably at highly celebratory events that were more receptive to the presence of images with powerful symbolic potential.

One such occasion was the projected Universal Exposition in Rome, unrealized because of the war; the famous "E 42" was designed to celebrate the glories of the "Third Rome," Mussolini's Rome.[21] The sculptor Italo Griselli, who had been commissioned to produce an imposing "figure of a youth" to stand before the Palazzo degli Uffici, had sculpted a nude athlete, two meters high, his body rigid in a Roman salute. The pedestal was inscribed with the words *"Roma aeterna,"* punctiliously and redundantly emphasizing the significance of the gesture. Despite this clear interpretation, despite the gesture that was to express the fascist discipline of the youth "who drinks in the words of others,"[22] the hesitations concerning the choice of a title for the monument indicate the difficulties connected to this sort of representation (fig. 4). The artist had first, cautiously, chosen a literal title, *GIL, Gioventù Italiana del Littorio* (Lictorial Youth), a subject the artist had undertaken before.[23] The director of the exposition, however, preferring the universality of the symbol, opted for *Il genio del fascismo* (The Genius of Fascism), a title that, after the war, was prudently camouflaged as *Il genio dello sport* (The Genius of Sport).

While risky in the area of sculpture the timeless figure of the ephebe was better adapted to painting. Thus we find it bearing the most varied attributes, especially where painting sought to follow the path of rhetoric and epic. We encounter it in the work of Achille Funi, for example, but even more in that of Mario Sironi, who renews this archetypal image by inserting it in archaic and solemn settings. The ephebe became *The Athlete, The Builder,* or, more generally, *Work (Il lavoro),* which affirms its social vocation on the walls of the Fifth Triennial in Milan (fig. 5).[24]

Another figure belonging to the same category—that of major symbols of the regime—unexpectedly found its way into the Twentieth Venice Biennial of 1936. For several years Antonio Maraini, a sculptor and national commissioner of the Fascist Syndicate of Fine Arts, had been introducing into the program of the exhibition a special section reserved for "works that deal with the various aspects of our family and political life."[25] On this occasion the party secretary, Augusto Turati, had sought to give a greater presence to this section by proposing a prize reserved for works that "bring to light the contemporary art we are all awaiting . . . that modern sensibility . . . our sensibility, that of the Italian fascists of the Mussolini Regime."[26] Despite the appeal, the galleries of the Biennial revealed a scant following for this "modern sensibility." In a 1936 publication, however, Maraini nonetheless saluted "the return of art to life" with a long article. Nonetheless, in the main gallery of the Italian Pavilion, pride of place went to the *Bronze Bust of Mussolini,* a futurist-inspired work by Ernesto Michaelles (better known as Thayath), and to a less "synthetic" and "essential" sculpture, "the powerful mass of a striding athlete, an image of Fascism on the march."[27]

THE ATHLETE, SYMBOL OF "FASCIST STYLE"

This *Fascism on the March* by Domenico Ponzi represented a solidly built runner (fig. 6). Yet nothing, apart from the title and the context of the exhibition, predisposed this sculpture to such politically charged symbolism. Despite its mediocrity, the piece represents an interesting moment of iconographic transition, the artist having circumvented the impasse of the ephebe by substituting the athlete "in action." Thanks to this visual metonymy, what had originally been no more than a simple connotation became the constitutent elment of the symbol itself, thus allowing for an easier reading.

The best-known example of this symbolic promotion of the young athlete is no doubt the group of marble athletes crowning the stands of the Foro Italico in Rome, the work of the architect E. Del Debbio (fig. 7).[28] That these famous nudes (the object of prudish and discreet intervention on the part of the censors) were able to take on broader symbolic significance is evidenced by their presence at the heart of the Foro Italico, called the Mussolini Forum, the magnum opus of the regime, designed to evoke all the pomp of imperial Rome via the plastic language of fascism. Yet this high-minded purpose did not prevent the nudes' original athletic calling from being fastidiously illustrated with a panoply of skis, rackets, and balls, unmistakably indentifing the nature of the throng.

During these years, the theme of sport took on particular importance within the written and figurative language of fascism. We are familiar with the emphasis, especially in the 1930s, that the regime's policies for the masses placed on sport as a means to organize and train the Italian of tomorrow: "The motor of fascism is the playing of sport."[29] Sport became—notably during the ritualistic Starace period—a synonym for a "fascist manner of conceiving of and living life . . . of forming the fascist character."[30] Sport as a sort of mythical fountain of youth would therefore unite young men and old, as well as a few female elements (despite some reticence). In the Luce news reels of the period, we see young adult men shedding their city clothes for a day to don the glorious garb of athletes.

While "the step of the young was supposed to be elastic and quick, expressing energy, athleticism, and perfect physical fitness," the "quick step" or running procession *(sfilare di corsa)* was not just a tonic sporting practice. Indeed, it possessed far more political implications: "Racing involves not only speed and the achievement of harmony, but it is also the symbol of rapid action, of the irresistible nature of fascism."[31]

Fascist discourse would push this taste for sport into some of the most thankless areas of daily life, managing to impose a new "dynamic and virile" image even on ordinary, far-from-heroic civil service. For in the fascist era, it was said, "state employment does not imply a life in slippers," much less "a peaceful life, the odious, peaceful life of flabby organisms." On the contrary, "far from the mentality of the sinecure and the prebend," the civil servant will incarnate "the plenitude of youth, the will to act, speed, and dynamism," because, it was argued, "office hours do not make you age, do not make your blood stagnate or lower your energy."[32]

This image was promoted enthusiastically and with indisputable success in constructing the flattering self-representation of the new Italian: dynamic and muscular, he was called on to chase away both the frustrations of daily life and those of the nation, thanks to the bearing and combativeness of the athletic model. Photographs, whether still or moving (I have already mentioned what a potent instrument of visual propaganda the Luce newsreels could be), were called on to portray the athletic glory, whether amateur or professional, of Italians, who were "young in body and mind." Soccer, the famous *calcio nazionale*, even more than cycling (another popular sport), became a powerful part of the national identity in a country with little sporting tradition. This transformation became a success most notably in the late 1930s when, after a series of international victories on the part of the Italian soccer team, the emotional impact on a people who participated little but were willing enthusiasts was amply applied as a "glue" in the construction of national myths.

Outside of propaganda, myriad images of varying status became obliging vectors for this national mythology. Its most important vehicle was the specialized youth press, which assumed a clear didactic function and glorified athleticism, the special symbol of values dear to fascism: the exaltation of physical activity, self-discipline, the virtues of effort, and the importance of teamwork (for which soccer was a powerful model). The covers of *Gioventù fascista*, the youth magazine under Starace's direct control, offered a vast gallery of young athletes; the heading, invariably, would be a phrase from Mussolini, in large capital letters like a monumental inscription, lending the axiomatic certainty of words to the image, emphasizing the duty and combat inherent to "athletic practice" (fig. 8).

"The spectacle of youth strong in mind and body," so easily visualized, enabled the communication of less innocent messages: "the clear proof of the vigor of the race"[33] as expressed in sport served as a vehicle for the racial theories that would be promoted toward the late 1930s.

Painting and sculpture were also solicited to express, in the solemn language of art, "the passionate care the regime devotes to this branch of human activity."[34] For the Rome Quadrennial of 1935, it was suggested that artists work around the theme of "sports seen through the art of its time," an unquestionably topical theme but one that was not terribly constraining given the "athletic nature of Greek and Roman art." A few sculptors did indeed seize on this reference to Roman times as a convenient antidote to the troubling intentions of the regime. Thus while Fontana presented an *Athlete in Repose* and Maraini, a boxer, Romano Romanelli took refuge in the timeless *Hercules Strangling the Lion.*

The painters were in a more difficult position, as they were less adept in the myths of ancient Rome. Few, in fact, responded to the invitation. Furthermore, as was noted, "rather than the athletic element," the artists generally preferred "the male or female nude," turning the supposed athletes into either "bathers or fishermen."[35] Among the few courageous painters who confronted the suggested theme head on was Carlo Carrà, with an irreproachable *Soccer Game* (fig. 9). The abstract volumes characteristic of Carrà's poetical world here give way to a deliberately representational clarity of line: the work balances precariously on the boundary line that, at the time of the Novecento movement, had been drawn between "the representation of contemporary events" and "true, great art," which was supposed to transpose "material and passing events into the realm of eternal and spiritual images."[36]

"True art" was thus invested with the privilege of transmitting the great messages of the regime through its solemn language, "ever elevated, aristocratic, grandiose, and controlled in thought as in form." One may well wonder (and the question must have been asked at the time when the response implied a choice of cultural strategy) to what extent the representation of a contingent and passing event (a game of soccer) could reveal what Panofsky calls the "hidden symbolism" of the image. To what extent was it possible to "make the concept palpable"[37] through the sporting event, to make sport "the key to the physical and moral regeneration of the race"?[38]

In any event, the theme of sport had the advantage of bearing a clear, immediately exploitable message, readily adaptable to those for whom it was destined. The speed, efficiency, and physical bearing at the basis of the sporting myth could become efficient means for designating "the young fascist state," a dynamic and "modern" state. It was a visual metaphor to which the publicity image had frequent recourse. Sport was also insistently promoted in the many women's magazines as well, for women and "the mothers of Italy," as a model of health and family hygiene.

The attractions and gratifications of sport were a recurring motif in the great variety of publications for children (all carefully calibrated by age and sex). For the huge audience of *Il Balilla* (the official paper of "the boys of Italy," published under the aegis of the national Balilla organization), the model was the petulant and enterprising Lio, who embodied, via his comic strip, the advantages that the Spartan camping life could bring to a vigorous people: "Our teams are full of solid kids: they can even sleep on nails when they've done their duty."[39]

For little girls, the benefits of sport were presented in less peremptory fashion. *Piccola Italiana*, "a paper dedicated to the little girls and young women of Italy," gave its audience a more discreet and nuanced image of sport. While urged to be "healthy, strong, and beautiful," these girls and young women were not to forget that their vocation was still to keep house, to maintain a household. The little black, pleated uniform skirts would be shortened or lengthened modestly according to the demands of the sport, which was always limited to rhythmical exercise or light athletics, thought to be "more suitable to young girls and adolescents" (fig. 10). Toward the end of the 1930s, however, the same girls and adolescents are attired more freely, and in a way more suitable to sport—hence the appearance in the pages of the feminine press of a few attractive swimmers in bathing suits. This was probably due to the influence of their less-inhibited German sisters of the Hitler Youth, but also, in Italy, to the increasing accent on biological eugenics, as officialized from 1937 onward by the racial policy that gave new direction to the politics of youth in general (and of young women in particular). The creation of the GIL bears evidence of this orientation, as does the inconographic material of the period. But this hypothesis would merit a more in-depth study.

THE YOUNG WOMAN WARRIOR

The strong young man had a feminine double of high symbolic value: the comely, monumental young woman, emblematic figure of the combined concept of fascism and the nation. The vast success of this image went beyond any mere historical contingency; it rose to prominence as the center of a symbolic representation that was distributed nationwide.[40] In fascist iconography, this young woman, disdaining the necessarily ephemeral fashions, was always nobly draped, her head topped by a pointed crown. This Mamma Italia first represented Italy; ever reassuring and maternal, she was tremendously popular within the universe of children's images (fig. 11). But on occasion she could show herself to be strong and determined in the face of foreigners' cowardly aggression.

As one might expect, this image came to the fore in reaction to the "iniquitous sanctions" (the economic embargo imposed by the Society of Nations following the war in Ethiopia). In the *Rivista Illustrata del Popolo d'Italia,* for example, we find this Mother Italy evoked by Sironi. Her monumental body is barring the passage of a grim rabble, their "faces contorted by trafficking, speculation, the slimy faces of businessmen, jaundiced with gold . . . their breath stinking of the back shop, of drugs and gasoline." In the center, Italy is brandishing her menacing sword with one hand while with the other she supports a tired olive branch in her skirt. "Leave the symbol of peace where it may fall on fertile ground" was the message; "in your hand it is better to carry the sword" (fig. 12).[41]

This powerful female image was adapted, with some slight iconographic variations, from a more aggressive and warlike version, the model for the innumerable "winged Victories" celebrating the glories of the regime, a celebratory cliché that sculpture compliantly interpreted in public monuments of high symbolic potential. Examples abound: the winged figure carved on the face of the victory monument erected by Piacentini in Bolzano,[42] and the colossal victory statue erected in the Turin Remembrance Park by the sculptor Rubino, an early version of a model that became common in the course of the 1930s.[43]

Naturally, we also find this theme of the winged goddess at the 1932 Exhibition of the Fascist Revolution. In this particular context the figure took on a specific connotation: she embodied "armed Italy . . . vigorous and severe, outstretched as though in flight."[44] She was the high point of the part of the exhibition focused on the symbiosis of Italy and fascism. Sironi imposed his presence in the middle of the Galleria dei Fasci with a huge, five-meter-high statue.[45] Marino Marini adapted into plastic language a symbol that was denser still, the Italian "victory" in the Great War, intended to signify not only the continuity between Italian history and fascism, but also "the simple, heroic purity of our eternally young race versus certain sick and artificial cerebrations produced by decadent races" (fig. 13).[46] One curious example of a "militant" interpretation of a symbol generally held to a rigid, formal code was the monument to *Victory in Africa*, born in the climate of the "Empire" and colonial wars, and the work of an unknown artist of the GUF, the Gruppi Universitari Fascisti (University Fascist Groups) of Rome. Reproduced on a full page in the *Rivista Illustrata del Popolo d'Italia*, it offered an emphatic example to the "warrior youth" absorbed into the youth structures of the regime.[47] Set up as it was inside the courtyard of the University of Pavia, there was no doubt regarding the audience to whom the monument's message was addressed. An expression of militant enthusiasm more than a shrewd manipulation of the symbol, the "winged goddess," a fragile adolescent dressed in an outsized robe, her hair blowing in the wind, seems stripped of her usual haughty solemnity. In the arms of this angry, modern Diana the allusive language of symbolism is materialized via the presence of a threatening rifle in one hand, and in the other an equally menacing Roman fasces (fig. 14).[48]

Thanks to the adaptability of the symbol, the female image of Victory could, in a different cultural context, recover its original role: stripped of her wings and her warrior aspect, we find her once again the majestic and solemn allegory of fascist Italy, legitimating by her presence the pompous rhetoric of mural painting, which was the special sign of the "national" vocation of great fascist art. Thus Italy, in her toga, would have the honor of presiding over the frescoed assembly in *Italy among the Arts and Sciences*, painted by Sironi for the *Aula Magna* of the University of Rome.[49] This difficult semantic compromise brings together the signs of the nation's twofold identity: a nation at once "very young," according to the founding myth of the "revolution," and also heir to a distant past that, even before Roman times, found its roots in uncertain temporal zones where the myth of the "Italic race" was forged.

A YOUNG AND PROLIFIC PEOPLE

The representation of the Italian people according to the regime, and by virtue of that notorious fascist tautology, is "young" and, consequently, overflowing with an aggressive and prolific vitality. Among the notions that were apt to elicit the enthusiasm of a collectivity entirely devoted to youth was, of course, the "fine Italian family," the "solid and living pillar" of the fascist state, the object, as we have noted, of "great care" on the part of the regime and, especially, of an intensive birth campaign, given that "the fate of the nation [was] linked to its demographic power."[50]

On the level of political discourse, this "youth" of the Italian people was associated with the expansionist notions of fascism; Italy's "historic destiny" found a more current manifestation in the mirage of the "spaces beyond the seas" that awaited a "young and prolific" (and consequently numerous) people. The image fulfilled its role effectively in this flattering national self-representation. Rather than relying on eloquent speeches, the state had recourse to a vast body of images that directly touched on a "vague" sensibility, using popular cultural codes drawn directly from the everyday mythology familiar to Italians. From this mythology was drawn a proliferation of images that unabashedly embraced the vision of exuberant national procreativity: broods of children (preferably in uniform) attentive as much to the political as to the commercial message (fig. 15); official exploitation of the Italian cult of the "family photo," celebrating the domestic glories of a nation with strong family traditions. The father (usually in uniform), the ostentatiously posed "vigorous offspring," the obligatory grandparents (mark of the unchanging, traditional extended family), were symbols of the passage from generation to generation (the middle-aged were strictly excluded). In fact, the continuity of time, which the presence of "elders" valorizes in simple and familiar terms, enables this ordinary image to convey the notion of the continuity of a race both "young" and "very old": "a hard-working and warrior race, heir to its remotest ancestors, linking Romulus's plough to Garibaldi's rifle."[51]

Fascism's incessant birth campaign played not only on economic incentives but also on the prestige associated with the "fine Italian family," a hagiography of procreation celebrated by the press through innumerable photographs. In this exaltation of fecundity, the written word played no small part, as evidenced by the letter sent by a "German colleague" to the happy Roman father of twenty children, and Mussolini's more modest "message of sympathy" to the prolific mother.[52] Further evidence is provided by the triumphant self-proclamations that appeared in letters from readers. Thus *Mamma e Bimbi* published the "Secrets of a Mother of Ten," from a rural homemaker in Cicognolo who was proud of having "borne twelve children, ten of them living and flourishing. A nest of Avantguardisti, Balilla, Piccole Italiane, and Figli della Lupa."[53]

In this area, the earth metaphor as a synonym for healthy fertility would be amply exploited. This is of course by no means exclusive to fascist discourse, but the image of the rural family as the archetype for society as a whole took on a special relevance during these two decades, due not only to the Italian social reality but also to the importance of the rural world fascist ideology.

The "earthy, popular, rural" family, that "noble and pure" expression of the race, was a ductile and easily accessible symbol validating a mode of life that happily united the production of children with that of bread, "the fruit of the earth," and it would serve as the driving force behind national mobilization in the "Battle for Grain." As Manlio Pompei, a prominent fascist and sometime writer declaimed:

Work and song—we need song as much as we need work . . . and your song drifts back to the house where your wife and children await you and all day long keep alive the ties that bind your marvelous family . . . You are and will always remain the king of the open fields . . . with a pure source to slake your thirst and warm-smelling bread to satisfy your hunger: and the children who swarm about you in a throng, the living bread and butter of your modest riches, are your reward for every pain, for every deprivation.[54]

This mythical family Eldorado would of course be adapted to the most varied publics, the youth of an entire people expressed in a profusion of images of happy sowers and reapers, forever fixed in vigorous action or seated at the "family table." This kind of easily digestible social exoticism was well suited to the world of children, but also to those less young. Let us cite once again the gentle refrain, as both written and illustrated in comic books: "There's gold in the bowels of the earth and one ear of grain yields up a hundred . . . And when the lovely sheaves on the threshing floor spread their golden sparkle / raise your flail singing! Fatigue is joy, / and blessed is the fruit of labor!"[55]

After 1935, we find these same young men now saddled with children and some modest baggage, still joyous and exuberant, hugging their families good-bye on the bridge of a ship. The photographs, generously reproduced in the press, showed them leaving Italy for the promised lands of the empire "beyond the sea" (fig. 16).

FIGURATIVE COMMUNICATION: A PLURALITY OF REGISTERS

Of course on the level of high culture, painters and sculptors were highly circumspect; they were in no hurry to abandon the privileges of their status to flatter the "modern sensibility" and take on "the realities of fascist Italy" so dear to exegetes of "fascist art." We find a less allusive symbolism, however, among the artists directly caught in the wheels of the system, among whom aesthetic quality unabashedly came to terms with a militant calling. It is at this "intermediate" level that production in conformity with the artistic criteria of the regime was situated, and it was this art that would feed the vast network of syndicalist, regional, and national exhibitions. One of these groups that defined itself as "militant" was the famous Cremona Prize, founded by Roberto Farinacci in 1939 as "a first attempt to bring Italian artists into the historical reality of the Mussolini era."[56] It was a tall order, since adhering to this "reality" demanded a careful balance between the contingent, descriptive aspect of Mussolini's Italy and its symbolic translation.

This delicate feat was more or less successfully achieved in the first two exhibitions, the themes of which were, respectively, "Listening to the Duce's Speech on the Radio" (1939) and "The Battle for Grain" (1940). Both exhibitions were occasions for an avalanche of images exalting the Mussolini era through depictions of a people clearly young and clearly surrounded by solid, reassuring, and generally rural families (fig. 17).

The problems of "this difficult encounter between art and celebration"[57] were revealed quite clearly at the third exhibition, whose subject was the GIL, a theme described as "one of the most noble, but also one of the most complex."[58] Even the most irreducible defenders of the exhibition regretted that the artists had limited themselves to "flat illustration": worse still, "many fell into vulgarity or empty rhetoric; others revealed the mediocrity of their concepts, notably in the area of 'morality'; still others attempted to illustrate our flourishing fascist youth active in GIL sports without having any notion of sport at all," showing discus throwers "who looked like rachitic puppets."[59]

Thanks to their universality, of course, certain themes (such as that of the family) were treated at different levels of interpretation, either as a theme for ideological mobilization, or as a simple pretext to develop purely formal ideas. The theme of the family, in fact, which acquired potent ideological overtones during the fascist period, was nonetheless associated with an illustrious and ancient cultural genealogy. These models were to be ably addressed by the critical discourse of the time.

Thus Margherita Sarfatti said of Sironi's *Family*, shown at the Quadrennial in Rome in 1931, that it was "as grandiose as a fragment of antique painting."[60] Backed by the context of the exhibition, which guaranteed its cultural status, the timeless quality of the work could be the basis for a simple yet essential message founded on antique models, and present the family effectively, thanks to archetypal and "eternal" figures (fig. 18).

I should emphasize once again that the extraordinary wealth and variety of these images illustrating the myth of fascism's splendid youth all bear witness to the symbol's great capacity for adaptation to diverse iconographic references. The symbol of youth was thus fragmented into myriad images that for twenty years bombarded the Italian people.

Still, it was necessary to have recourse to more totalizing symbolic forms that could gather under a single sign both fascism and youth, without allowing the visual metaphor to obscure the quality of the message. But above all, it was necessary to find a symbol capable of seducing both the public commmited to high art and those who were accustomed to "mass" images.

IL DUCE, "THE YOUNGEST OF US ALL"

From the 1920s onward,[61] at the initiative of Mussolini's press office, the "cult of the Duce" became one of the most important themes for national mobilization, which reached its peak in the 1930s. Indeed, thanks to attentive, meticulous staging, Il Duce became a cult object.[62] A charismatic as well as familiar and reassuring image, its obsessive, repetitive nature expressed more than an homage to and veneration for the leader. "The omnipresent and dominating figure of the Duce" became an interpretive medium that allowed one to symbolize fascism itself without a cumbersome conceptual intermediary. The spectacular 1932 Exhibition of the Fascist Revolution had already demonstrated the "spiritual unity between the Duce, Italy, and fascism."[63] In truth, the "Exhibition of the Revolution was him, was Mussolini. The exhibition palpitated with his giant presence, which dominated men and things . . . artistic creations and symbolic figurations" (fig. 19).[64]

The "spiritual unity" between the Duce and fascism required close coordination of the various elements. The eternal youth of fascism had to be inseparable from that of its leader. The image of Il Duce therefore had to reflect all the attributes that the "springtime of beauty" could bring to fascism: dynamism, strength, enthusiasm, efficiency, physical superiority, and a bold, combative spirit. "The Duce is the youngest of us all. What wonderful youthfulness is his!" The "wonderful youthfulness" of the leader also had to bear witness to the youthfulness of the political system and its administrators. But the youth of Il Duce also extended "beyond space and time": his was an eternal youth that provided reassuring certainty of the everlasting nature of fascism.[65]

We have already seen how fascist discourse managed to create an endless stream of metaphors, of lyrical evocations and mystical transports

1. Advertisement for the Istituto Nazionale della Assicurazione (National Insurance Institute), in *Rivista Illustrata del Popolo d'Italia*, July 1927, p. 1. The handsome young ephebe.

2. *"Giovinezza, Giovinezza!"* (Youth, Youth!), in *Buon senso e tricolore*, a catalogue issued by the National Propaganda Institute (Florence: n.d.), p. 27. The "springtime of beauty," the idyllic vision of the "primeval power of the New Italy."

3. Adriano Dazzi, *Era Fascista*. Brescia, Piazza della Vittoria, 1932 (*Rivista Illustrata del Popolo d'Italia*, November 1932, p. 63). Roman-style sculpture to feed the fascist myth.

4. Italo Griselli, *Il genio del fascismo*. Rome, 1939. The statue was to have dominated the great E 42 exhibition, which, due to the war, never took place.

5. Mario Sironi, *Work*. Genoa, 1931, private collection. Thanks to the many meanings it contains, the ephebe, symbol of youth, appears in turn as *Work* (here), *The Builder*, and *The Athlete*.

6. Domenico Ponzi, *Fascism on the March*, 1936. The muscular athlete made his appearance at the Twentieth Venice Biennial in 1936. A redounding symbol of the "fascist style."

7. E. Del Debbio, Foro Italico. Rome, 1929–1932. Mussolini's "Third Rome" was celebrated in this magnum opus of the regime.

8. *Gioventù fascista*, April 30, 1932.
Sports: "A spectacle of youth strong in
mind and muscle," used as a model for
fascist youth.

9. Carlo Carrà, *Soccer Game*, 1935
(*Rivista Illustrata del Popolo d'Italia*,
April 1935, p. 37). Carrà's rigorously
formal painting adapted itself to the
sporting myth of the regime at the
Second Quadrennial in Rome.

10. *"L'educazione fisica delle nostre camerate"* (*La Piccola Italiana*, October 14, 1928,
p. 4). "Healthy, strong, and beautiful": the physical education of the Piccole Italiane,
or Young Italian Girls.

11. *"Mamma Italia"* (*Il Balilla*, May 29, 1930, p. 5).

12. Mario Sironi, *La spada che corregge i pastori* (*Rivista Illustrata del Popolo d'Italia*, December 1936, p. 25).

13. Marino Marini, *L'Italia armata*. Exhibition of the Fascist Revolution, Rome, 1932 (catalogue, p. 97).

14. *Victory in Africa*. University of Pavia (*Rivista Illustrata del Popolo d'Italia*, November 1936, p. 28). Born of the "imperial climate" of the time, this work, created by a young artist of the Gruppi Universitari Fasciti of Rome, offered young university students a modern fascist version of the classical Nike.

LA NIDIATA "500"

cco una esemplare e automobilistica famiglia italiana: la famiglia del rag. Tarcisio Giacomini, di Milano, agente per la Lombardia della Casa Editrice F.lli Treve
dolto cortesemente egli autorizza a riprodurre questa fotografia eloquentissima e questi dati anagrafici: il babbo 30 anni; la mamma 26; i piccoli Giacomini un
d'anno: Giorgio 6 anni, Lucio 5, Gianni 4, Gisella 3, Franco 2, Jorna 1.
Josella FIAT 500 ha già fatto migliaia e migliaia di chilometri, e per il suo animatissimo contenuto questo sempre, ove passa, un vivo interesse e un subixo (
tomando. «Sono spesso costretto — dice il rag. Giacomini — a ripartire in fretta e furia per non intralciare la circolazione!».

15. *La nidiata "500"* (*Mamme e Bimbi*, October 1938).
Automobile advertising and demographics.

PERIODICO MENSILE ANNO IX
NUMERO 9 - LUGLIO 1942 - XX E. F.
SPED. IN ABBONAM. POST. - GRUPPO 3

16. Leaving Italy for the "lands of the Empire" (*Famiglia Fascista*, July 1942).

17. *Italia in piedi: Une famiglia di colini ascolta alla radio del fattore la parola del Duce.* For the Cremona Prize of 1939, an anonymous "militant-artist" showed this epiphany of peasant fertility.

18. Mario Sironi, *Family*, 1929. Rome, Galleria d'Arte Moderna. Eternal archetypes of the "youth of the race."

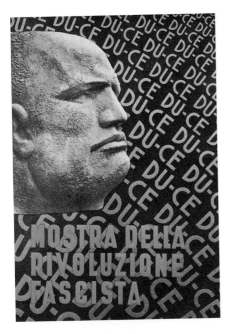

19. *"Du-ce, Du-ce."* Catalogue cover, Exhibition of the Fascist Revolution, Rome, 1932. The exhibition was an affirmation of the "spiritual unity of Duce-Italy-fascism."

20. Ferruccio Vecchi, *The Empire Springs from the Duce's Brow,* 1939 (*Rivista Illustrata del Popolo d'Italia,* July 1939, p. 45).

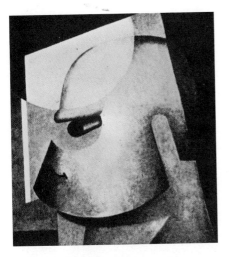

21. Enrico Prampolini, *Sintesi plastica del Duce,* ca. 1926. Art at the service of the Duce's "eternal youth."

22. *"I Figli della Lupa"* (*Rivista Illustrata del Popolo d'Italia*, May 1935). Sons of the Wolf: "The sparks from the great forge of fighters."

23. *Romulus Fed by the Wolf* (*Rivista Illustrata del Popolo d'Italia*, April 1936, p. 12). Romulus nourished by the She-wolf: the mythic models.

24. The rural supervisor, Maria Italiani, of Montagnana (Perugia) with her five-month-old twins (R. De Felice and L. Goglia, *Storia fotografica del fascismo* [Rome: Laterza, 1982], figure 92).

25. *"I futuri Balilla"* (*Il Balilla*, August 29, 1929, p. 10). "Vigorous offshoots of a prolific race."

26. The Balilla Fiat (*Gioventù Fascista*, April 20, 1932). The fateful stone thrown by the "heroic kid" in Genoa and the launching of a publicity campaign for the new Fiat.

27. *"XXIV Maggio: Il premio del Duce al Balilla"* (*Rivista Illustrata del Popolo d'Italia*, May 1935). The Duce bestows a prize on "Italy's little soldier."

28. *"La guerra di Lio"* (*Il Balilla*, May 30, 1929). In a popular comic strip, Lio represented the bold and reckless Balilla.

29. *La Piccola Italiana* (February 5, 1928, p. 16). The Piccole Italiane (Young Italian Girls), judicious and domesticated, were the "little swallows of Italy."

30. *La Piccola Italiana* (October 14, 1928). The careful little mothers.

31. Advertisement for a sewing machine (*Gioventù Fascista*, April 21, 1933). "Little sister, you are right to prefer the Necchi machine."

32. *"I figli della Rivoluzione"* (*Rivista Illustrata del Popolo d'Italia*, April 1935, p. 21). Sons of the revolution.

33. "Credere" (L. Schiava), *Mattino di festa: XXVIII ottobre,* Cremona Prize, 1939. Morning of the festival, October 28: the domestic image of a fascist family as seen in a painting by an anonymous "militant-artist."

34. Racial instruction in school. *(Rassenkunde)*. Here one is choosing "conformity" (to the "Nordic-Aryan race") and excluding those who are different (the "non-Aryans"). Bilderdienst Süddeutscher Verlag.

35. "Adolf Hitler Führer and Chancellor of the German Reich—Reich Chancellor Hitler loves children—Heil Hitler!" A page from a reader. Stuttgart, Württembergisches Landesmuseum.

ADOLF HITLER

FÜHRER KANZLER

DEUTSCHES REICH

REICHS-KANZLER

HITLER MAG DIE KINDER GERNE

HEIL HITLER!

36. Emil Dielmann, *Hitlerjunge*, n.d. Munich, Zentralinstitut für Kunstgeschichte.

37. "The NSDAP protects the popular community. Comrades, need advice and help? Come to the local office." NSDAP propaganda poster. London, Wiener Library.

38. "Youth serves the Führer. All children over ten in the HJ." Propaganda poster, 1936. Koblenz, Bundesarchiv.

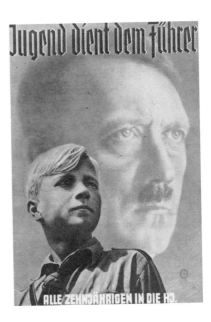

39. Jürgen Wegener, *German Youth*, fresco, 1937. Munich, Zentralinstitut für Kunstgeschichte.

40. "We affirm a healthy culture of the body." From Ferdinand Hoffman, *Sittliche Entartung und Geburtenschwund* (Moral degeneracy and falling birth rate) (Munich and Berlin, 1939), "Politische Biologie," issue 4.

41. Uniforms of the Bund Deutscher Mädel [League of German Girls]— Subregional *Führerin* in the winter uniform; Jungmädel [Young Virgin] in summer dress; Subregional *Führerin* in summer dress. London, Wiener Library.

around the image of the leader, of bold or fantastical, historical or literary associations. "That best son of our great Italy" became "the new Aeneas," the "hero who surpasses human boundaries." Professional writers enthusiastically participated in this Mussolinian epiphany. The futurist Mario Carli intoned: "Mussolini, outstretched canvas of our wings and sails / shock of manhood, willing and able seed."[66] Elsewhere, Mussolini figures as "the Sower," who in his morning smile "had a fatal beauty."[67]

Naturally the plastic arts had some difficulty incorporating these verbal acrobatics without lapsing into the grotesque. The former *ardito* Ferruccio Vecchi, turned sculptor, attempted a laborious allegory titled *The Empire Springs from the Duce's Brow* (fig. 20). Atop the head of the thinking Duce ("his eyes are half shut . . . but behind the apparent calm of his mask, the miraculous power of his mind reduces twenty centuries into a day, into an instant, to begin a new era") bounded a muscular figure of the Empire, "climbing the steps of a well-constructed mind." The association was dangerous, bold: "The very face of the Empire resembles that of its Founder: could it be otherwise?" The two emblematic faces bear the same youthful, passionate features. The physical vigor of the one ensures the youthful spirit of the other: "The lips are heavily pronounced, as if Il Duce is sniffing out treachery, the eyes burn menacingly, open, wide open, fixed on the ground, on reality. And the sword is visible to whoever wishes to see it, as well as to those who don't, solid in his tight grip, a synthesis of the noble certainty of his face."[68]

The "manly and willing" jaw, the "lofty brow," the "magnetic eyes," such was the Mussolinian typology—reduced to a few recognizable signs, immediately accessible to all, an unchanging symbol, the eternal image of the youth of Il Duce (fig. 21).[69]

YOUNG PEOPLE IN UNIFORM

The figure of youth was a powerful symbol of the entire nation, but it also took on another meaning: youth's role as a social protagonist and the special reference point of the regime also had to be emphasized. This highly codified, ritualized model was offered directly to the young through the intensive and strongly visual pedagogy present in the vast number of newspapers and magazines aimed specifically at Italian youth, "the pupil and hope of the regime."

A well-defined set of stereotypes, transmitted in words, of course, but most of all through the elliptical and concentrated language of pictures, aimed to define and to impose the wide repertoire of models that, classified by age and sex, formed the "legions" and "maniples" of the ONB, the National Organization of the Balilla, and, after 1937, of the GIL, the Lictorial Youth. Once again the image was the preferred medium for the regime's youth organizations, the best instrument for communication and mobilization, capable of touching the farthest reaches of the social fabric as a whole.

The portrayal of fascist youth obviously led to the modification of some representative stereotypes, insofar as the "new, warrior" youth included not only the young, but also the very young. This was a forward-looking measure on the part of the regime, which was "thinking of tomorrow" in order to build "the grand network of fighters" in time (fig. 22).[70] In fact, "the party and the regime [gave] themselves the task of educating the minds of children by training their bodies and by gradually fortifying both for the demands of combat."[71] This is why, at the fascist vacation "camps," designed to complement the family, "the maternal overseers [gave] this tender youth, the breeding ground of the nation, a fascist education."[72]

Images would thus linger over the numerous "sprouts of our fertile stock," harking back to the mythical "sons of the wolf," the vigorous twins breast-fed by the she-wolf of Rome, the emblem of the Roman origins of fascism (fig. 23). An astonishing series of male infants (little girls were strangely excluded from this ritual), dressed in black shirts and the obligatory black berets and proudly held up to the camera, would also appear in newspapers, a convincing and domestic manifestation of the "everlasting race," the reassuring "certainty of fascist Italy" (figs. 24 and 25).

Nonetheless the most pertinent symbol of that "magnificent," "irresistible" fascist youth was provided by the Balilla, which made up the "new fascist age group" and ensured the "recurrent wonder of eternal youth."[73]

They were the descendants of the "heroic kid," the Balilla of the popular districts of Genoa whom the hagiography of the Risorgimento had immortalized in the act of throwing a stone at an Austrian officer, a daring act that was to bring about a "victorious insurrection of the people" against the invader (fig. 26). It was with this mythic hero that Mussolini's *Balillas* indentified, "dressed in their black shirts, black berets perched on their little whimsical heads . . . small but indomitable soldiers."[74]

The symbolism of the uniform was carefully calibrated to lie between the easygoing and exuberant nature of the original model and the militaristic rigor consonant "with young girls and boys already adopting the pattern and bearing of foot soldiers" (fig. 27).[75] Less relaxed, and certainly less warlike, was the uniform of the Piccole Italiane, the Young Italian Girls: their discreet and austere black skirt, the white blouse, the little beret perched on their head and the obligatory white tights were intended to highlight the moral and civic qualities of "Italy's little swallows."

The more reserved style with respect to the men's uniforms sets the fascist version apart from its Nazi or Stalinist counterparts, which seem less differentiated by gender. This was probably due to the twofold ideological objective of fascism's politics for the masses: the reference to the family (of clearly Catholic origin) for the women, while for the men, the warrior-like mobilization that after 1935 would take on an increasingly militaristic tone.

As for the Balilla, their slightly subversive founding myth made them a generation of bold, reckless, resolute, and courageous kids to whom the state offered "a manly education that doesn't just crystalize in the head" and that would make them ready to "love risk and dare anything."[76] Their emblematic hero, besides the ever-present Lio (fig. 28), was the valiant Cuordiferro (Ironheart), an intrepid Balilla always ready for the riskiest adventures: "Thought and deed are / for him but one / in a flash he flies / twixt cloud and thunder."[77]

With considerable skill these suggestive models were adapted to specific audiences: a world of adventure (carefully linked to the essential message) for the youngest Balillas, while their older brothers were treated to examples of devotion and discipline, of exaltation through competition, of the sporting life, of "healthy training" in outdoor camps: "a military week at Camp 'Dux,' a reality like a flash of steel."[78]

Far less suggestive were the models offered to the weaker sex: girls and young women were rigorously excluded from the adventurous world of the boys. Instead they were offered carefully selected, "exemplary" reading matter: *Love Nests, The Soldier's Guide, The Flight of the Butterfly,* "novels particularly apt for modern young women, devoid of that brazen realism that so harmed the young" (fig. 29).[79] In the many publications devoted to them, images aimed to point up the positive aspects of the Piccole Italiane: they were judicious young ladies, diligent at "the small chores of young girls," ready to mend the trousers of their roughneck brothers, to rock their dolls to sleep, budding "little mothers" of future children, and most of all "the helpers of their own dear mothers in the holy mission of the family" (fig. 30).[80]

The opposite of this edifying model was the scatterbrained and irresponsible Carotina Zuccalessa, a model of naughtiness whose insipid frivolity was stigmatized in the pages of *Il Balilla,* where we see her stealing fruit from the kitchen: "Two cherries for a hat / A fine example is that!"[81] Whereas everyone knows that even in her leisure time the well-behaved Piccola Italiana never forgets her role as a future housewife: "Little girls of Italy! Tell your parents to give you something useful for Christmas!" suggested an advertisement from a company that "specialized in making miniature copper and aluminum toys, reproductions of kitchen implements" (fig. 31).[82]

The images of the Giovani Italiane, Young Women of Italy, in their sober black and white uniforms, emphasized their discreet roles, which were highly unwarlike but undeniably efficient, both inside the home and in the womens' organizations of the regime. Fascism, in fact, made them "worthy of participating in society, of leading an intense life of work and politics," the ultimate goal of which, nonetheless, was to be "good wives, excellent mothers, and perfect housekeepers" because "nothing is more appealing than a young woman intent on humble, necessary domestic tasks."[83] This was a sublime mission, despite its seemingly thankless nature, since "nations, like men, are formed at their mother's knee."[84]

Fascism proposed to forge a warrior nation by basing the formative structures of fascist youth—"magnificent, organized, irresistible"[85]— on harsh discipline and rigorous military training: "Youth marching with a military step in closed ranks, as if emerging from long barracks training . . . soldiers of the motherland and of fascism, with their will trained to obey."[86]

This vast job of militarization would engage a broad spectrum of age groups, making the myth of the "eternal youth" of fascism possible through the passing of generations. The Balilla, "the future legionnaires of fascism and soldiers of Italy" would become the "'Legion of Recruits' who are entering the Party and the Militia today, radiant with pride, vibrant with impatience and male exaltation, in perfect military order. If you close your eyes for a moment and think of the future, there rises before you the vision of a dense and infinite forest of rifles, of cannons, of machine guns saluted by a storm of tricolored banners, whirling and roaring in the skies" (fig. 32).[87]

This apotheosis of rifles and tricolored wings is concentrated in a more defined, more precise iconography: the figure of the Balilla (or the Avanguardista), rigid in his all-black uniform, along with the ever more visible panoply of war as he parades before Il Duce or gives a Roman salute, a symbol of fascist youth and of the youth of the regime.

In the face of all the warlike exaltation of a nation in uniform, the procreating function of the woman-mother exonerated her from any open participation in the political life of the regime. It would thus not be necessary, nor even desirable, to see "the shiny fascist badges" glimmer on her dresses, since "the time has passed when school and politics destroyed everything that the tender and holy mothers had affectionately constructed in the souls of children." Fascism "wanted women to be good mothers and nothing more."[88]

The *mamma* was thus the symbol of the youthful fertility of the people; she was the bride of a warrior and the mother of heroes, the

"Roman mother" by antonomasia, since, in Mussolini's words, "the fascist mother is the Roman mother." She was "devoted to the highest ministry of the woman, to the idyll that breeds and strengthens the race."[89]

The ideological change with which the maternal figure—the keystone in fascism's family component—was invested consisted precisely in this absence of the woman as a political subject. Hence the hypervalorization of protective, maternal aspects, heavily emphasized in written and figurative representations: "Leave your mother alone. Even if she doesn't have a party card, she is already, in her ideals and worthiness, among the women of our faith. She brings her children up to work hard, to be religious, to do their duty; she gives them a daily example of sacrifice . . . she is devoted to the fields, to the family, to her duties . . . What more do you want from her?" (fig. 33).[90]

The fall of fascism brought about a general revision of the various support structures on which the ideology of the regime had been constructed. At the heart of this operation were the images that, at different levels and in different styles, had helped to construct the edifice on which the consensus of the regime had been built. With the fall of fascism, the symbols that had celebrated eternal youth crumbled.

Nonetheless, certain images were recycled, adapted to new messages. Those of the splendid youth of fascism fell into oblivion, condemned by scorn or irony as evidence of the folly of fascism. But some works of unquestionable quality could be redeemed, transcending as they did any time-bound, embarassing message thanks to their formal value.

In this general questioning of a period in which images played a decisive role, that of the mother constituted the element of continuity that enabled the passage from the fascist era into postwar Italy. In the process, of course, many components of the image were modified or abandoned: the mother lost the banner of her ancient "Romanness," and the merits of her "prolific family" were no longer exalted. What remained, however, was the archetype of the protective mother "without a uniform." Thus the "Roman mother" became *"la mamma,"* a figure omnipresent in the literature, film, and painting of the postwar years.

SOLDIERS OF AN IDEA:
YOUNG PEOPLE UNDER
THE THIRD REICH

Eric Michaud

Push yourselves, old boys!" hollered Gregor Strasser, organizational chief of the Nazi Party, in 1927.[1] "Get lost, old men!" repeated Baldur von Schirach, the head of the Hitler Youth, in 1934. "Only the eternally young should have a place [*Heimat*] in our Germany." One had to understand, according to Schirach, that "youth is an attitude [*Haltung*]," and that "men who are internally old are the scourge of a healthy people," because they doggedly oppose "any new ideas."[2] Under the Third Reich, *youth* did not refer so much to a social group, or even to a moment in the biological development of the individual. To be "young" meant first and foremost to belong to a new *idea,* the National Socialist weltanschauung, which sought to incarnate itself in struggle: "He who walks in the ranks of the Hitler-Jugend is not a number among millions of others, but *the soldier of an idea.*"[3]

This is why the battle that the Hitler Youth was to lead did not simply graft itself onto an ordinary generational conflict; it did not identify itself solely with the struggle against the "Weimar system" that had preceded Hitler's taking of power on January 30, 1933. This struggle was inscribed in history, but it did not belong to it. It was merely a transitory form of the "eternal struggle" led by the Aryan race for the purity of its blood—in other words, its Idea. Hitler had written this in *Mein Kampf:* while "all other problems of life . . . are limited in time, . . . the question of preserving or not preserving the purity of the blood will endure as long as there are men."[4]

Herein lies the difference between the everyday existence of youth under the Third Reich and that of Italian youth during the same period. For while it is true that Hitler and his ideologues drew inspiration from the fascist model, with its much-admired youth organizations, its Balillas and its Avanguardisti, they differed distinctly from the Italians in the central place they accorded racism in the formation of the New Man.

Because the task of formation *(Bildung)* and education *(Erziehung)* was primarily the responsibility of the racist or "ethnic" *(völkisch)* state, family and school would gradually become secondary authorities, subordinate to the paramilitary youth organizations. But this widespread recruitment into the "State Youth" became effective only on the eve of the war, when terror finally reinforced the laws and their decrees, making enrollment in Hitler Youth obligatory.

Thus school, although it was less immediately and regularly controllable ideologically, remained—especially in the early stages of the new regime—the only place where the racist state could hope to leave its imprint on the *whole* of German youth.

On this point, as on many others, *Mein Kampf* served as a program:

> The crown of the folkish state's entire work of education and training must be to burn the racial sense and racial feeling into the instinct and the intellect, the heart and brain of the youth entrusted to it. No boy and no girl must leave school without having been led to an ultimate realization of the necessity and essence of blood purity. Thus the groundwork is created by preserving the racial foundations of our nation and through them in turn securing the basis for its future cultural development . . .
>
> For the rest this education, too, from the racial viewpoint, must find its ultimate completion in military service. And in general, the period of military service must be regarded as the conclusion of the average German's normal education.[5]

Between the declining authority of the family and the new "way of life" of the nation, which Rosenberg defined as that of a "marching column,"[6] school was at a critical juncture in the formation of youth, whose mission was to give concrete reality to the "Reich ideal." *(Ideales Reich)*.

At a conference on June 12, 1933, Alfred Bäumler, professor of philosphy and political pedagogy at the University of Berlin, defined the New Man as a *political soldier* who would be created by a transformed educational system: "By political soldier we mean a type: the historical type of today's soldier, the man who feels he is the soldier of a concrete idea, the missionary of a historical fact." This system of "soldierly education," said Bäumler, "must encompass all Germans, whoever they are and whatever they do." Such a conception only took on meaning and historical import when based on the presupposition that, to assume the "Aryan" essence of its "Germanity," Germany had to live out the Spartan ideal to which it was the natural heir. Asserted Bäumler, "By making the soldierly type the goal of our education, we are merely fulfilling the law that governs our essence . . . The technical instruction given by the army completes the soldierly education of the young man."[7]

THE APPRENTICESHIP OF SELECTION

It was on September 13, 1933, that "racial science" was introduced into the schools. But since the law of April 7, 1933, on the "reconstitution of public service" (excluding Jews) and the July 11, 1933, decree demanding that teachers obey the *Führerprinẓip*, the principles of the fürher, racism had been rapidly taking over all disciplines: "The crowning of all national-socialist teaching of history consists in only one thing: allegiance to the Führer."[8] Once one accepted that "science, like any other product of humanity, is racial and conditioned by blood,"[9] it became clear that the Nazi weltanschauung should infuse all teaching, habituating the pupil to discerning what was useful to his "race" from what threatened it. Even the teaching of arithmetic could be closely connected to that of racial selection, as seen by this problem, which was given to hundreds of thousands of primary school *(Volksschule)* pupils to solve: "The Jews in Germany are of a foreign race. In 1933, the German Reich numbered 66,060,000 inhabitants. Of them, 499,682 were practicing Jews. What percentage did they represent?"[10]

But it was mainly during "racial science" class that pupils were truly initiated to what was "racially foreign" to them. Although the new *Rassenkunde* manuals, as well as countless brochures, reflected the Nazi ideologues' myriad and contradictory concepts of the notions of a "people," a "race," and a "nation," all prompted the student to reconstruct the racial myth himself though image and text. Among the exercises proposed under the heading "How we can learn to recognize someone's race," one of these manuals required that the student gather various descriptions of "ethnic" personages, taken from poems, novels, and short stories.[11] The pupil was supposed to underline the terms describing expressions, gestures, and movements in order to draw "conclusions on the behavior of the soul of the race," and relate them to the character's "physical features." Next, one had to "apply this mode of observation to the people one knew." Caricatures, propaganda posters, cosmetics advertisements, pictures of great men cut out of magazines, monumental busts, and sculptures were employed to give the student practice in distinguishing the Jew from the Aryan by "his way of walking, his bearing, his gestures and his movements when he speaks."[12]

Thus the decree of the Reich Ministry of Education, instituting this teaching "from which applicable conclusions in all the areas of public and private life will be drawn," was followed to the letter. The decree, which aimed to lead the pupils to "actively cooperate in everything that would reinforce the German people's Nordic belonging," itself reproduced the passage from *Mein Kampf* quoted earlier, almost to the letter: "All this must be put into practice beginning with the first school years to respond to the desire of the Führer, who has demanded that in the future, no student, whether boy or girl, must leave school without having realized the essence and necessity of blood purity" (R. Min. Amtsbl., 1935 S. 43 RU II C 5209).

To respond to the desire of the führer was thus everyone's main and constant task, from the author of the decree—the Minister Bernhard Rust, member of the party since 1922—to the *Volksschule* pupil and his teacher. To respond to the desire of the führer was thus a racist act of faith, and the teacher became almost an equal to his most zealous pupils in this task, which was increasingly overseen by the Hitler Youth.

In addition to this basic work seeking to give the child practice in "judging foreign faces," there were more "practical" sessions on skull measuring, which students performed together in the classrooms. Sometimes the lesson consisted of learning to describe the "cowardly and cheating expression" of their Jewish comrades, sometimes of learning to recognize the most beautiful specimens of the "nordic" or "Aryan" race. (fig. 34). But the fact that someone fit the correct physical norms was not to exempt him from the suspicion of his classmates: "Of course," wrote Franz Lüke in the textbook *Das ABC der Rasse*, "one mustn't confuse race and simple appearance. Race means soul. And there are men who present real signs of belonging to the nordic race externally, but who are Jews in spirit."[13]

Thus, though the body told the truth of the soul, it was also apt to lie: such contradictions constituted the heart of Nazi ideology, because they enabled the creation of a climate of general suspicion and, soon, of terror, penetrating the most intimate spheres of private life. If anyone could be a "Jew in spirit," denouncing someone, even a family member, in case of doubt, became a sacred duty.

The extensive bullying and humiliation that were inflicted on Jewish pupils (who were forced to sit on separate benches, insulted, publicly deprived of milk during recreation periods, and so on) served a *pedagogical* function: that of maintaining each individual's passion for combat led by the community of the people *(Volksgemeinschaft)*, to protect themselves from the "antipeople" *(Gegenvolk)*. And until November 15, 1938, the date on which Jews were declared temporarily excluded from teaching establishments (a measure that became permanent on June 20, 1942), all were encouraged and overseen in this "sacred" struggle by their Hitler Youth comrades, whose brown shirts had grown ever more numerous on classroom benches since the spring of 1933.

In this way, school became the place where one learned "racial selection," understood in the broadest sense. Distinguishing the "Jews in spirit" required constant vigilance, before and after class.

The young German, reported Erika Mann, performed the Hitler salute 50 to 150 times a day. On leaving home in the morning, he saluted with a "Heil Hitler!" the "leader of his building block" as he passed him on the stairs, the classmates he met on the street, and the tram conductor; he repeated this same salute, which had become law, with his teachers at the start and end of every hour-long class period, with the baker or the stationer when school let out, with his parents when he came home for lunch. Anyone who did not respond with the same "Heil Hitler!" was guilty. Whether a neighbor, a friend, or even a parent, no one escaped risk of denunciation. While some were occasionally tempted by mockery, pronouncing their "Heil Hitler" as "Drei Liter" (three liters), they knew that this barely perceptible alteration did not affect their *Haltung* (attitude) and allowed nothing of their *Stimmung*, their frame of mind, to show.[14]

Still, because the "Idea" of Nazism was symbolized by the person of the führer, the Hitler salute, with right arm raised (or the left in case of injury or handicap), was far more than an automatic act of allegiance: it was a sign of aptitude for the permanent struggle that, from the age of ten, the "soldier of an idea" was to lead. And it meant this even more after Rudolf Hess, during the gathering of the party in Nuremberg in 1934, launched the slogan *"Deutschland ist Hitler, Hitler ist Deutschland."* The "German salute" signified not only the young German's salute to Hitler, but also his salute *by* Hitler, the "Doctor of the German people," the Savior of Germany, whose "vision" or "idea" of the pure and eternal Reich would become a reality one day.[15]

It was to hasten this day that the child kept a bust of the führer in his bedroom (a reduced version of those present in classrooms); ever since he had learned to read, he had known that the führer "liked children" (fig. 35). It was so that the führer's "vision" would become a reality more quickly that he chose to keep among his toys not little lead soldiers but little SA men (Brownshirts) or SS men, geological survey maps, drums, and flags with the colors of the National Socialist Party (fig. 36).

"RESPOND TO THE DESIRE OF THE FÜHRER"

In addition to learning in school about the continuous scrutiny to which he had to subject those around him, the young German also learned competition within paramilitary youth organizations: he discovered that he himself was undergoing a rigorous selection process, administered by his superiors through a variety of highly competitive activities.

According to their leaders, Hitler Youth groups had to be the real "schools of the nation."[16] In fact, their function was not only to supplant school and family in their educational tasks, but also to encourage a process of "permanent education," in the sense suggested by Hitler in the speech he delivered to "his" Hitler-Jugend in September 1935 at the congress of the National Socialist German Workers' Party (NSDAP) in Nuremberg: "We have undertaken to educate this people in a new school, to give it an education which begins in youth and shall never come to an end. In future, the young man will be raised from one school to another. It begins with the child and ends with the old fighter of the Movement. *No one may say that for him there is any period of life when he can devote himself exclusively to his own interests.*"[17]

In 1938, when he was assured of his power, Hitler gave additional details regarding his successive "schools" by declaring more bluntly that *"in all their lives they shall no longer be free."*[18] The comment by Baldur von Schirach—for whom "youth is an attitude"—takes on meaning in this context:[19] it was a matter of freeing everyone from any responsibility other than that of *responding to the desire of the führer*—in other words, of subjugating and infantilizing an entire people so that it would remain "eternally young."

A new "social contract" was being established with the *Volksgemein-schaft* by Hitler and the NSDAP, whose eagle symbolized the protective and "eternal idea" (fig. 37): it guaranteed the security of each individual, provided that each in turn devoted all of his time and spirit to it, in order, as Hitler said, to guarantee eternal youth for the German people. More than a social contract, it was thus a kind of new Faustian pact, with no expiration, between a "people" and its führer—who was in the role, whether consciously or not, of Mephistopheles.

At the end of 1932, the Hitler-Jugend (HJ) numbered 108,000 members—a low figure relative to the total of 4 million youths who were members of the various political, religious, sports, and leisure organizations.[20] One year later, it counted 2,300,000 members, then 3,500,000 in 1934 and 5,400,000 at the end of 1936. This massive increase was not the result of enthusiasm alone but was due, first, to the seizing of control over the Committee of Leagues of German Youth in Berlin, on April 5, 1933, and the dissolution of those groups that did not submit (that same month, Schirach illegally took over the large network of youth hostels, the *Jugendherberge*). Second, it was due to the absorption of the 600,000 members of evangelical youth groups and other Protestant leagues, an act proposed by Reichsbischof Müller and signed in November; and third and most of all, it was the result of the social and political pressures and threats that weighed on the professional lives of parents, as well as on the activities, whether school-related or not, of the children.[21]

In June 1934, Saturdays were declared "national youth days": young HJs were excused from class to perform their "civic" service, in uniform, while the others had to attend "classes in national politics." In addition, Wednesday was declared the "day of vigil." But without sufficient supervision, most boys and girls wandered the streets aimlessly. In 1936, this day of vigil was therefore replaced by two afternoons a week. Many members having been trained in the meantime, thanks to the creation of the *Führerschulen*, this new arrangement reinforced the HJ's possible appeal to youths wishing to escape from educational and family demands.

The HJ was initially placed under the auspices of the Sturmabteilung (SA), the Brownshirts, which selected many of its recruits from it (before the taking of power, the shift from the Hitler-Jugend to the SA occurred automatically at the age of eighteen). But after the purge of June 30, 1934, put a brutal end to the "social" revolution represented by Röhm's SA, Schirach won his autonomy and chose instead to conclude an agreement with Himmler's Schutzstaffel (SS): he would educate his youth to join the SS forces and would collaborate with the latter in controlling all youths through the establishment of a patrol *(Streifendienst)*.[22] He wrote at the time that the unification of youth had to occur "through an idea, a weltanschauung, which had to be lived as a life principle by the young generation. Only the HJ," he added, "carried this idea."[23]

Schirach had placed his organization under the rule of this statement by the führer: "A great Idea can only achieve its goal when a solid and rigorously disciplined organization, led with the proper severity, gives the weltanschauung its form."[24] He knew, since meeting Hitler years earlier in the Wagnerian circles of Bayreuth, that he could count on his support. In the course of the struggle for control over youth that pitted him against Rust, the minister of education, he had no difficulty getting the führer, to whom he reported directly, to sign the Law on Hitler-Jugend of December 1, 1936, stipulating that *all* German youth were to be regrouped within the HJ, which was transformed into a "state youth group." Schirach could then write: "The struggle for the unification of youth is over." He knew, nonetheless, that 40 percent of German youth were resistant and still eluded him, but hoped that they would join voluntarily. Such was not the case in the short term, even though a stint in the HJ was required for attendance at a university and, after November 1935, for entrance into public service or certain liberal professions.

It was only in March 1939, more than two years later, that the decrees enforcing the 1936 law were made. It then become obligatory for parents, under penalty of a summons or prison, to declare their children to the HJ authorities when they reached the age of ten. The same penalties were established for those who said they wanted their children to avoid HJ service—which the local police were permitted to compel by force.[25]

This increasingly fierce rivalry with parental authority—or, at least, with those parents who continued to resist the "will of the führer"—had the effect of destroying in youths any private vision of authority in favor of the collective image of the führer. "I have no conscience! My conscience is named Adolf Hitler":[26] this famous statement by Göring ultimately represented the ideal goal of the *Erziehung*, the education and training through which the Nazis sought to shape the New Man. Whoever then followed the moral norms transmitted by the family instead of giving in to the "will of the führer," of responding to the desire of the führer— "who likes children"—was guilty. A new version of the "categorical imperative in the Third Reich" was developed beginning in 1936 by Hans Frank, legal director of the Reich: "For each decision you make, ask yourself: 'How would the führer decide in my place?'" He would reformulate this question in 1942: "Act in such a way that if he knew of your actions, the Führer would approve of them."[27] Thus the higher interest of the *Volksgemeinschaft*, represented by the will of the führer, often demanded that the child wage battle against paternal or family authority. The regime's policy toward youth was generally adept at taking maximum advantage of Oedipal conflicts.

Enrollment in the Hitler-Jugend occurred at the age of ten: after undergoing certain athletic tests, the Pimpf (a member of the ten- to fourteen-year-old age group) entered the Deutsche Jungvolk (DJ, the German Young People) for a period of four years, during which time a record book indicated his physical and ideological progress. A ceremony took place every year on Hitler's birthday (April 20), so that everyone would know that he "belonged to the führer" (fig. 38). The young boys swore an oath during the "consecration of the flag": "In the presence of this banner of blood, which represents our Führer, I swear to devote all my energy and all my strength to the Savior of our country, Adolf Hitler. I am ready to give my life for him, and place myself in the hands of God."[28]

Then the young person's true education began, leading him to "think German" and "act German"[29] in order to identify with the now legendary ideal portrait that Hitler provided as a model: "The German youth of the future must be slim and slender, swift as a greyhound, tough as leather, and hard as Krupp steel. We must educate a new type of manhood so that our people does not go to ruin amongst all the degeneracy of our day."[30]

He therefore had to toughen his body ("Your body belongs to the nation," "You have a duty to be in good health"). Physical exercises, for which the length of time had already doubled in the new school programs, were organized to promote endurance and competition. At the age of ten, boys had to cover eight to ten kilometers a day on foot; at thirteen, eighteen kilometers, at least two-thirds of them in the course of a "long march." "In the beginning," writes Hermann Rauschning, "these marches passed for a strange hobby of national socialism. It was only much later that one discerned here, too, a subtle will, which had quite cleverly found a means suited to its ends . . . Marching kills thought. Marching kills individuality. Marching is the irreplaceable magic rite, whose mechanism would shape the popular community even in its subconscious . . . The measured step brings the feeling of community into the body, so to speak."[31]

It was also at the age of ten that girls entered the Jungmädel (JM, literally the Young Virgins). During their first year in the DJ or JM, boys and girls had to study the "Gods and heroes of the Germans"; the second year, the "great Germans" (from Frederick the Great to Bismarck); the third year, "twenty years of struggle for Germany" (the years of struggle of national socialism); the fourth year, finally, "Adolf Hitler and his companions in the struggle."

At the age of fourteen, the young people entered the Hitler Youth proper. At eighteen, other party structures awaited the young men: The Work Front (Deutsche Arbeitsfront, or DAF), the SA, or the SS. The girls stayed on in the Bund Deutscher Mädel (BDM, League of German Girls); they remained in the Faith and Beauty section (Glaube und Schönheit) from the ages of seventeen to twenty-one, for intensive training dominated by physical exercise, household tasks, and, according to Schirach's formula, "specifically feminine objectives," the content of which we shall see further on.

The ideological training of the fourteen- to eighteen-year-olds included courses on "the struggle for the Reich," from the ancient Teutons to Hitler by way of the relations between the emperor and the papacy, on "the people and the heritage of the blood" and "vital space," as well as on problems concerning "the future of the Movement," "the work of the Führer," and "Germany in the world."[32] These themes were developed each week in the HJ centers, which were supplied with films as well as prepared commentary, and the lessons were reviewed during radio programs specifically intended for youth, such as the weekly *Hour of the Young Nation* (Schirach spoke on Wednesdays at 8:15 P.M.) and the *Rundfunk-Morgenfeiern der HJ* (The HJ morning radio show). But most of all they filled the pages of innumerable publications supervised by the HJ Press and Propaganda Office. Every journal corresponded to a specific category of organized youth: *Der Pimpf, Die Hitlerjugend* (which would become *Junge Welt*), *Das Deutsche Mädel, Wille und Macht* for the leaders, *Das junge Deutschland* (more immediately "political"), *Jugend und Heimat* for those who frequented youth hostels, *Die junge Dorfgemeinschaft* for young peasants, and so on. And finally, these same themes were the subject of conferences held at camps.

The camps played a major role in the life of the HJ, taking up the heritage of the dissolved Jugendbewegung, which at the turn of the century had enabled its members to discover the *Wandervögel* (migratory birds), mountains, and gorges deep in the German countryside, along with the country's traditions, ancestral rites, and popular songs. But under the direction of the HJ, the camps became sites for genuine military training, lasting from one to three weeks when they took place during vacation periods. With its vertical hierarchy of thirty-two titles and grades and geographical breakdown into five sections, the HJ's very structure was a copy of an army's. Each of the camps boasted the same slogan: "We are born to die for Germany."[33] The activities were akin to a military preparation: training in open and close formation, in camouflage, in baiting the enemy, in protecting a walking column, in reconnaissance operations, pitching tents, cartography, and shooting, as well as in all sports tending to develop a sense of performance. The length of the hikes increased with the age of the campers, as did the weight of the packs. Finally, as Göring wished to make Germany into a nation of aviators, gliding and flying lessons were added, as well as airplane model construction (fig. 39).

The girls of the BDM received comparable training, though requiring a lesser degree of performance (fig. 40). In addition, they were supposed to acquire "advanced knowledge of first aid" and "passive defense," in case of an aerial attack or a chemical war. But of all the "specifically female objectives" targeted by Schirach, the most essential, without a doubt, was the teaching of motherhood and its "vital" function for the future of the young Germany.

Hitler had written in *Mein Kampf:* "The goal of education for girls must invariably be the future mother."[34] He reminded German women of the duty of their sex in a speech delivered in Nuremberg on September 8, 1934: just as on the battlefield man must show proof of heroism, so "every child that [the woman] brings into the world is a battle she wages for the survival of her people."[35] In December 1938, he created the Cross of the Mother, which Himmler asserted was the most important distinction of the great Reich to come: it was awarded in bronze for four children, in silver for six, and in gold for eight. In 1926 Gregor Strasser had asked that a multiple vote be given to mothers of large families; though this bold suggestion of a "vote for newborns" was forgotten, the idea of considering motherhood the equivalent of mens' military service remained.[36]

Girls had to be inculcated in their duty to the race as soon as possible. And here again they were being asked to *respond to the desire of the führer,* as was overtly signified by the slogan, "Give a child to the Führer." Only with motherhood did they truly become "soldiers of an idea," with the mission of giving concrete reality to the "ideal Reich." Before each gathering of the BDM and HJ "units," on the occasion of camps or excursions, the captain would address the troops: "You cannot all find husbands, but you can all become mothers."[37] On October 28, 1935, "biological marriage" was officially adopted, recommending sexual relations outside the bonds of marriage between boys and girls united by the same ideal of conserving the race. Several months later, more than a thousand girls returned home pregnant from the Party Congress held in September 1936 in Nuremberg.[38] This impressive figure shatters the received notion that paramilitary and athletic training diverts youth's libido from its sexual ends. To those parents who remained attached to traditional moral values, the girls sometimes wrote letters of warning: if such parents balked at their daughter's giving a child to the führer so soon, they would denounce them immediately for opposition to the politics of Bevölkerung, the settlement of Eastern Europe intended to create the "vital space" *(Lebensraum)* for Germany. "From a National Socialist point of view," the *Reichsjugend-führer* Baldur von Schirach had said, "youth is always right." Thus the Bund Deutscher Mädel rather quickly earned the nickname *Bald deutsche Mutter,* "soon-to-be German mother." To the omnipresent slogan enjoining girls to "give a child to the Führer" was added the term *Führerdienst*—service of the führer—the name by which biological marriage was ordinarily designated. From the National Socialist "point of view," the führer was therefore the symbolic father of all those children born under the rule of the racial ideal; it was he who engendered them by the power of the "National Socialist idea" and by virtue of his "unshakable will." As for the unwed mothers, whose ranks—after 1937 especially—increased rapidly, and who had the right, through a special ordinance of the Ministry of the Interior, to be called "Mrs.," they appeared as heroines infused with the "National Socialist idea," fighting on the "birth front" to ensure the reproduction of "human matériel" *(Menschmaterial)*.

GENERAL VERSUS PARTICULAR INTERESTS

Yet the implementation of racial politics—with youth constituting both the means and the end—produced numerous "adverse effects" that the "Doctor of the German people" had not envisaged. The sacrosanct principle, inherited from the "years of struggle," according to which "the general interest took precedence over the particular interest" was going to be put to a harsh test.

The "rural year" *(Landjahr)*, instituted by Rust to bring children back to the living sources of the peasant world, as well as the "rural service" *(Landdiesnt)*, which put the HJs to work in the fields, cleverly dovetailed the *"Blubo"* ideology (*Blut und Boden*, blood and soil) with the problem of the lack of agricultural laborers and the exodus from the countryside. But this forced contact between the farm world and working-class or student milieus often inspired either incomprehension and disdain, or a decline in the "values of the earth" when farm youths were faced with the example of the young city dwellers. One study showed that nearly all young peasants between the ages of ten and fourteen wanted to live in the city,[39] despite its stigma as the source of all the physical and moral decay striking Germany. Moreover, the influence of the HJ was especially difficult to maintain in this farm world, where the time given to the führer was necessarily time that would have been spent working on the farm or in the fields.

The presence of BDM girls' camps in the vicinity of Work Front boys' camps also favored the expansion of the "birth front" into the countryside; in homage to the leisure organization of the Work Front, Kraft durch Freude (KdF, Strength through Joy), the following popular couplet arose: "In the fields and in the bushes / I lose Strength through Joy."[40]

In addition to a limited kind of "passive resistance," which expressed itself mainly through an often resigned humor, some freedom, albeit relative, was made possible in the early years for young people (in particular girls and working-class boys) by the autonomous principle offered them by Schirach: "Youth must be guided by youth" Schirach. Moreover, to counter "Judeo-bolshevism," the HJ and the Work Front liked to project the image of organizations intended to train the German people in "socialism." The best way to abolish classes was to accustom "the son of the [factory] director and the young worker, the university student and the farmhand [to wear] the same uniform, to set them the same table in common service to Volk and Vaterland."[41] Shirach himself devoted an entire chapter of his HJ program book to the question of socialism: "A single flag floats before the HJ. The son of the millionaire and the son of the worker wear a single and same uniform. For only youth is capable of being free of this type of prejudice, is capable of an authentic Community; yes, Youth is Socialism."[42]

While it was true that some children of the "proletariat" who had been promoted within the Hitler Youth hierarchy could, in the early stages of the regime, permit themselves to give orders to the children of the aristocracy or the industrial bourgeoisie, this reversal of the social hierarchy did not last long: beginning in 1936, the movement's leadership slipped out of the hands of young workers, apprentices, and salaried employees, passing progressively into the hands of the young, educated bourgeois and aristocrats.[43]

Beginning that same year, a certain apathy became perceptible among the HJ, who often deserted gatherings at the organization's center to escape the monotony of ideological oral reports and "discussions." Also beginning that year, employers began to show a certain wariness toward former HJ cadres who were seeking work: they knew that the responsibilities within the state youth group were incompatible with a "normal" education and that the little führers were generally bad students. Moreover, few employers rejoiced at the idea of hiring a stool pigeon to work in his business or store. Faced with the breadth of these rejections, and in the name of the führer, Rudolf Hess had the minister of education adopt a secret ordinance (in June 1937). It forbade any "notice of the activities of a student in the NSDAP or one of its branches" from being mentioned on certificates or diplomas.[44]

Four years had already passed since the educational system had been transformed: in keeping with the program outlined by Hitler in *Mein Kampf*, instead of "adjust[ing] its entire educational work primarily to the innoculation of mere knowledge," it aimed first to "breed . . . absolutely healthy bodies. The training of mental abilities is only secondary."[45] But for this rearing to produce an elite,[46] the HJ was assigned the task of organizing a selection process, with a series of competitions aimed at stimulating youths' athletic performance and ideological discipline. Beginning in 1934 ("the year of training") the *Leistungabzeichen,* or badges of performance, levels I and II, were created for both boys and girls, along with "German athletic badges," the attainment of which became the primary goal of every newly enrolled age group. The term *Leistung* (performance or attainment) invaded the language of the HJ and of the two institutions that constituted its main extensions: Himmler's SS and Robert Ley's Work Front. Competition was fierce not only for the best athletic or professional *Leistung,* according to the postwar testimony of a former HJ *Führerin,* but each "unit" also fought for the finest decorations, the best choirs, and best theatrical performances: "Already in peace time, this incessant struggle for *Leistung* introduced an element of unrest and of artificially forced activity into the life of the groups. . . The leaders [*Führerschaft*] of a youth group, thus prepped for action and for *Leistung,* gradually became quite original in their style of managing. They ran from one activity to the next and made their 'retinue' [*Gefolgschaft*] do the same."[47]

This competitive dynamic extended to all branches of the organizations: starting in 1933, the Work Front—which had replaced the outlawed unions—instituted a Reich Professional Competition (Reichsberufswettkampf) for young apprentices, workers, artisans, and employees. "Winners were treated like Olympic athletes or film stars, brought to Berlin, and photographed with Ley and Hitler himself."[48] The intense propaganda surrounding these competitions (the importance of which was ever increasing) presented them as reflecting "the socialist concept of selection." The young laureates were often given real promotions; as the winners generally had come from modest backgrounds, this reinforced the feeling that the new regime gave everyone a chance, whatever his social origin.

But as soon as they left the Hitler-Jugend for the Deutsche Arbeitsfront, the Work Front (instead of continuing their studies or entering the SS), the "soldiers of an idea" all became, as Robert Ley put it, "soldiers of work" whose "marching orders" were given by Hitler and whose "company was called Deutschland!"[49] This national version of "socialism," which spectacularly glorified its few worker promotions, clearly contrasted with the rapid rise of the "managers" in the various SS power mechanisms. But everywhere, from the Jungvolk to the ranks of the SS, *responding to the desire of the führer* also meant entering into a lovers' rivalry with one's "comrades" to satisfy that desire. Thus a perverse dynamic was created with respect to this vital "idea" for which everyone was to be a soldier: "the general interest takes precedence over the particular interest" *(Gemeinnutz geht vor Eigennutz)*. And it was always in the name of the general interest, symbolized by the figure of Hitler, that all selections occurred, as well as the ferocious rivalries that internally undermined the regime.

SWING VERSUS WAGNER

But what was the nature of the führer's desire? If it was able to hold most young people in its thrall, it was no doubt because they understood that they were its privileged object. By early 1939, almost 9 million youths had accepted the ultra-Faustian pact proposed by Hitler (to preserve eternal youth), whether by choice or by force. Whatever the constraints involved—and they were often strong—this mass adherence cannot be understood without reference to the specifically material nature of the love bond that united youth to their führer.

Aside from the program of "independence, freedom, and happiness" that Hitler proposed, "something else seduced us," a young woman who had entered the HJ reported after the war, "which for us had a mysterious power: young people marched in close ranks, flags waving, to the sound of drum rolls and chants. There was something invincible about this community. It's not surprising that Hans, Sophie, and all of us soon found ourselves enrolled in the Hitler Youth."[50] The "mysterious power" of the spectacle was its ability to prompt a desire to join in, as in a great collective work of art, that which Wagner had named "the common work of art of the future"; only by means of this common work of art could the redemption of the entire people occur:

> More and better than an old-fashioned religion rejected by the public spirit, more effectively and more strikingly than a State wisdom that has long doubted itself, Art, eternally young, ever able to find freshness in itself and in what is most noble in the spirit of the time, can give to the current of social passions, so prone to wash onto wild reefs or down to the lower depths, a beautiful and elevated goal, the goal of a noble humanity.[51]

"Anyone who wishes to understand National Socialist Germany must know Wagner" declared the führer.[52] Of this passion for Wagner and for the army, which Adolf Hitler shared with Baldur von Schirach (in Bayreuth they had attempted to write an opera together), was born a gigantic and permanent military operetta, which the Hitler-Jugend performed on the scale of the nation. Just as he had overseen all costumes and scenery at the Bayreuth Festival since 1934, as well as the evening wear of the SS officers, for which he corrected Benno von Arent's designs three or four times,[53] Hitler commissioned the designs for the HJ outfits (fig. 41), which he refashioned on the stage of a Germany whose entire set he was striving to remodel.

These costumes, marches, and songs, this constant staging of a collective life of heroism, punctuated by the many National Socialist festivals, was not, as is too often claimed today, the most spectacular aspect of a propaganda of lies whose function was to camouflage a disastrous reality. Like Baudelaire—and herein lies the formidable aspect of Nazism—Hitler and some of his close collaborators believed that "the idea that man possesses of beauty is imprinted in all his attire, rumples or stiffens his dress, cultivates or orders his gestures, and even subtly penetrates the features of his face" over time: that "man ends up resembling what he would like to be."[54] Propaganda was no more intended to fool people than art; neither one masked or beautified anything. Far more radically, both were entrusted with *heroically transforming reality*. Beginning with his speech on full powers, on March 23, 1933, Hitler had emphasized the central place of art in the new regime: "Art will always remain the expression and the reflection of the longings and realities of an era. The neutral international attitude of aloofness is rapidly disappearing. Heroism is coming forward passionately and will in future shape and lead political destiny."[55]

From one gathering to the next Hitler constantly repeated to "his" youth that they represented the future of the eternal Germany. Their very presence anticipated the total realization of his "vision" and began giving substance to the ideal Reich. Like the romantic Schleiermacher, for whom "the greatest work of art is that made of humanity,"[56] Goebbels, the apostle of the "romanticism of steel," saw politics as "the highest art," which had "the high responsibility of creating, from a raw mass, the solid and full image of the people." And, he immediately added, "The mission of art and of the artist is not only to unite, but goes much farther. It is their duty to create, to give form, to eliminate what is sick and to pave the way for what is healthy."[57] This also supposed the right to do violence to the human matériel *(Menschmaterial)* when it resisted being transformed according to the "idea."

The task of selection and elimination was at the heart of the National Socialist "idea," just as, since the Renaissance, it had been at the heart of the theory of art and of the "idea of the painter": it was a task of purification inseparable from the production of an ideal beauty.[58]

This is why Hitler expected "his" youth to display the same "fanaticism" that he considered to be indispensable to the artist: the soldiers of an idea, whether students, apprentices, or peasants, were all the artists of the eternal Reich, as well as its incarnation, by means of their uniforms, gestures, and voices. They were thus being called to the noblest of tasks, and it was this nobility that so attracted them. And this task was especially stirring, as it constituted its own end, its goal being the production of the New Man: "But most of all we ask of you, German youth, that you fashion the German people of the future, and in yourselves be for it a model."[59]

By calling on youth to become the artists of the German people and, simultaneously, to be the work of art that would serve as its model, Hitler, wittingly or not, adopted one of the boldest presuppositions of modernity, according to which the possible and the real change status. Or, as Jan

Patočka wrote, "the possible is no longer what *precedes* the real; rather, it becomes the real itself in its creative process."[60] But—and herein lies the "archaism" of Hitler, who inherited the "classic" theory of art—the goal of this staging of youth was to break free of history and reach eternity through "Art, eternally young" (Wagner). "The German way of life has been precisely determined for the thousand years to come," said Hitler.[61] Since 1934, the year that brought a halt to the "revolution," such was the nature of the eternal youth that Hitler promised young people, providing they were capable of self-producing themselves into works of art, exactly as he, their führer-artist, had been able to create his own immortal image, with hair that never grayed.[62]

What Nazism presented as a great movement of self-production *(Selbstgestaltung)* on the part of German youth was also to be a self-purification: to respond to the desire of the führer was not only to engage in self-selection through songs, uniforms, tests, and marches; it was also to wish oneself purer, or to realize the pure essence of one's eternal soul through the elimination of all "otherness." Rosenberg, in *Der Mythus des XX. Jahrhunderts* [The Myths of the Twentieth Century], provided the model for this self-love, which he believed he had found in Master Eckhart: "To be one with oneself."[63]

Nonetheless, the National Socialist line also reflected the types of resistance that arose in response to the process of unification by and in the eternal work of art: it was said that the Jew, or rather "the Jew in spirit," was always attempting to break this perfect circularity of love, which was the only means by which the race could be assured its eternal youth. It was not enough to exclude this "plastic demon of humanity's decadence," as Wagner put it,[64] from the production of "the common work of art of the future," for the contamination had infested the German body itself. Starting in 1938, an ideologue of "political biology" put the *Volksgemeinschaft* on guard:

> Today, as in previous eras, our love life is continually determined by Jewish influences. These Jewish influences are, as we have seen, particularly evident in the first bloom of youth through the dislocation of barriers between the sexes . . . Anyone who laughs at the behavior of a

young virgin must be declared against nature, as should be anyone who disdains masculine bravery or heroic commitment, or the values that, in the construction of the people's morality, play a powerful and even determinate role . . . *So long as we have not abolished the Jew in ourselves, so long as our survival is in question, the Jewish problem can in no case be considered resolved.*[65]

This exhortation to "abolish the Jew in ourselves" was essentially targeting the youth who gathered in often informal groups, chose their own signs of recognition, their own music, and their own songs, who "strolled around" but didn't march, and who, for the most part, were sexually promiscuous. Quite remarkably, far from responding to the desire of the führer, the members of these groups, with their provocative attire— and whose number would grow considerably with the war—offered a most "dissonant" spectacle in the face of the ideal of harmony, of the great common work of art of the future.

While the HJ sang the unavoidable *Vorwärts! Vorwärts!*, which Baldur von Schirach had written and composed for the film *Der Hitlerjunge Quex:*

> Our flag flies before us,
> We enter the future one by one.
> We march for Hitler in night and misery
> With the flag of youth, for bread and liberty.
> Our flag flies before us.
> Our flag is the new day,
> And the flag leads us to eternity.
> Yes! the flag is greater than death![66]

some, in the first years of the regime, sang it to the tune of an old melody:

> We are criminals in your State
> And we are proud of our crime.
> We are the Youth guilty of high treason,
> Servitude can't break us . . .[67]

After their dissolution in 1933, the youth organizations associated with unions and left-wing and extreme left-wing parties made numerous attempts to rebuild themselves clandestinely. But the arrests and trials that were on the rise until 1937 gradually got the better of this immediately political form of resistance. After 1938, once the Catholic associations had been dismantled, the hostility of youth manifested itself increasingly in the form of lifestyles that were radically incompatible with the aims of the regime. The latter, having destroyed all traditional forms of authority and established a monopoly, now found itself alone, faced with *youth's* "desire." Unable to capture all of these libidinal forces and make them work solely to its own ends, the regime instead inspired a splintering and dispersion toward various models, which it then attempted to gather under the heading of the "single enemy," or "Judeo-bolshevism."

Thus in October 1944, Himmler, chief of the SS and the police, composed a memorandum regarding "the struggle against youth cliques"[68] in which he distinguished three marginal categories. Those who were "criminal-asocial" in nature manifested themselves via various misdemeanors, such as loutish behavior, fighting, breaking police rules, collective thefts, and indecent assault. The second category of youths was politically oppositional in nature but had no defined program, and manifested itself through rejection of the HJ and its duties with respect to the *Volksgemeinschaft*, indifference to the course of the war, listening to foreign radios broadcasts, attacking members of the HJ, circulating rumors, and often penetrating Nazi Party organizations to carry out "their destructive activities." Finally, the third category was referred to by Himmler as "liberal individualists": its members adopted "English ideals," English language, behavior, and clothing, and preferred jazz and "hot" music, swing, and the like. They usually hailed from the "better social classes" and were seeking only to satisfy their desires, sexual or otherwise, through excess, which quickly led them into conflict with the National Socialist weltanschauung. Two years earlier, Himmler had already advocated radical treatment for the leaders of these gangs: it was his opinion that work camps or youth camps were insufficient, that "these good-for-nothings" had to be sent to concentration camps, so that they would receive a "thrashing" before being vigorously put to the hardest labor.[69]

In working-class milieus, gangs recruited youths who had left school at the age of fourteen and couldn't yet be enlisted in the army. Preferring to be masters of their own time, rather than giving it to the upper-class leaders of the Hitler Youth, these young workers shared with the young "swing" high schoolers of the leisure classes the same hatred of the HJ. And within the HJ itself, a hostility developed that could take various forms, from the widespread adoption of "peasant shoes" (prohibited due to their dangerous evocation of the Peasant Wars) to the beating up of the local leaders.

Among these "cliques," "mobs," or "wild" groups, one of the most important, beginning in 1938, was the Edelweisspiraten.[70] In 1942 the police estimated their numbers at about 750 in the Ruhr and Rhine regions, distributed among twenty-eight groups in Düsseldorf, Duisburg, Essen, and Wuppertal. Other groups included the Düsseldorf Kittelbachpiraten and the Cologne Navajos. In 1940, the OK-Gang and the Haarlem Club, were tried in Frankfurt; they had existed since the beginning of 1939, and were followed by the Ohio Club and the Cotton Club. In Munich, the Buschwölfe, with their seven-pointed star, committed collective thefts, while the Charlieblase organized meetings with young girls in the shelters. In Hamburg, the "swing" youth organized tremendous dance parties; the boys had long hair ("up to 27 cm" specified a police report) and the girls wore makeup—which was prohibited for members of the BDM—and outfits considered extravagant; an "uninhibited" sexuality reigned, in which "giving a child to the führer" was not the primary goal.

It is interesting to note that the ideal of reproducing the "creator race" promoted by Nazism triggered both a widespread "marginal" sexuality, which proved dangerous for the "realization of the racist weltan- schauung," and, for opposite moral reasons, the only street demonstration seen by the regime.[71]

While one would have thought that, with the onset of war, the mass mobilization of HJ boys and girls, their forced enrollment in agricultural service (2 million in 1942), and the displacement of the youngest to protect them from bombardments (800,000 in 1944) would have irreversibly de- tached all young Germans from the control of parents and school, the many-sided opposition of the countless "cliques," "gangs," and "mobs" revealed that Hitler's "vision" had failed to be fully realized. More pro- foundly perhaps, and aside from any specifically political hostility to the

Nazi dictatorship, these youths seemed to reject the regime of *Leistung*, of performance and attainment. They "knew," in their way, that the *desire of the führer* symbolized his faith in a vision of the possible that no longer preceded the real, but which, again recalling Jan Patočka, "instead became the real itself in its creative process." In the first years of the regime, this prospect seemed to many a promise of liberation. But it gradually turned out that this *creative process* delivered those who submitted to it to the most extreme servitude. It demanded of them an ever-greater *Leistung*, to which they had to devote themselves entirely to make the "vision of the führer" tangible and legitimate. This process, which made them "soldiers of an idea," demanded that war become a permanent state, and thus that the *creative process* be entirely confounded in the negation of reality.

CHAPTER 9

YOUTH AS A METAPHOR
FOR SOCIAL CHANGE:
FASCIST ITALY AND AMERICA
IN THE 1950s

Luisa Passerini

In Mussolini's Italy, in the eyes of the regime, youth was considered to be the avant-garde of the fascist "revolution"; in the United States in the 1950s, public opinion and the media considered youth a "risk group" for social order. The exploration of these two debates on youth—different in their content but structurally related—is meaningful in the context of the deconstruction of the concept of youth that began taking form during the romantic period and ended in the 1980s, when the image of the child tended to supersede that of the adolescent. Clearly, the various phases of this period were not the same in all countries, but common dates exist. On the one hand, the decade from 1895 to 1905 was determinant for the invention of adolescence—it was during this period that the idea of youth was reformulated in psychological and sociological terms as turbulence and rebirth; as the seed of new wealth for the future, capable of annihilating the misery of the past; as the promise of individual or collective regeneration. On the other hand, in the 1960s, we encounter the final stage of this conception, whose last hurrah (so far as the idea of youth goes) was the student movement. The critique that the students of 1968 made of such a conception of youth, on a theoretical as well as a practical level, when they forcefully rejected all sociological interpretation of their revolt as youthful rebellion, encountered strong limitations in practice and in the imagination: the same students showed great indulgence for the emblematic figure of the young androgyne, a rebel against the existing order and a key to the future, and for the belief in an equality based on belonging to the same age group.

Discussions on youth and adolescence that occurred between these two dates were marked in particular by an accent on middle-class males, who were considered the most pertinent youth segment; while this was not the only group taken into account, its image was considered a privileged model. To analyze Western society's complex discourse on youth and adolescence in its main variants, it is appropriate, initially, to partially analyze certain significant moments. The two stages that we will study here can be considered such moments because they were imbued with an ideological vision of society and resulted either from a will to train "elites" within a totalitarian system (fascist Italy), or from the intention to ensure the peaceful renewal of the ruling classes in a democratic society with a high level of well-being, a nation convinced that it was the beacon of Western values (American in the 1950s). In both cases, we are faced with a crisis in patrimonial transmission, with adults doubting that their natural successors were capable of pursuing their work. In the case of Italy, youths were ascribed the power to accomplish a mission of salvation for the Fascist Party and state; in the American case, it was feared that they possessed a dark and hostile force, which threatened to interrupt the progress of American society.

Methodologically, many factors, such as the discordance of sources (essentially primary in the study of the Italian fascists, and mainly secondary in that of America in the fifties), prohibit considering this essay as the draft for a comparative study. Rather, we should view it as the kernel of a work that sheds light on different moments in different countries, stages in the two national, though discontinuous, evolutions of the discourse on youth. Here too, my goal is more aimed toward deconstruction than toward the classic historiographic objective of reconstruction. I am therefore not trying to suggest that the American democratic system is directly comparable, much less similar, to Italian fascism, nor that the fascist regime was in this case the precursor, on a global level, to a form of modern socialization. What was true for Italy, even with respect to a distortion in modernization, could not be true for the United States.

The fact that the two systems resulted from capitalism, and that they shared, in clearly different ways, the values of the West, created similarities in the ideologies proposed to resolve different problems in different contexts. There was the same illusory will, in both cases, to return to old values—such as family, community, nation—but the content of these illusions differed, despite resemblances in the practical solutions they produced. Thus while the two systems may have been similar in their hatred of all that was foreign, considered a factor in alienation and in the shattering of the social bond, the fact remains that in the case of fascism, this rejection did not realize its full meaning, for it became integrated into a precarious and incomplete attempt at modernization, into an experiment without the resources (such as a minimum level of democracy) that would have allowed for long-term action. In the case of the United States, however, we find the contradictions of Enlightenment thought fully expressed, with the debate on youth demonstrating the profound crisis of a system of values, positive and negative, conceived as the bulwark of the West. While the debate on youth in fascist Italy uncovered the weakness of totalitarianism at its roots, that which took place in the United States in the 1950s was related to a critique of Western society and its limits.

THE DEBATE IN FASCIST ITALY

Fascism and Youth

Fascism inherited the problem of youth from the Great War, and it was a problem that would accompany the regime throughout its domination of the country. But the primary issues were already posited before Mussolini took power in 1922. The First World War, and the years leading up to and following it, constituted an important stage in the establishment of a certain concept of youth. The youth movements from the early part of the century in Germany and England had strongly posited a connection between youth and patriotic values and, at the same time, between youth and emancipation, far from family and bourgeois society. The confluence of these two conceptions account for the enthusiasm with which war was greeted, seen as it was as the vehicle for allowing new energies to be liberated from the existing system, enabling the rediscovery of the country's abandoned traditions.[1]

Also in Italy, a certain group consciousness, which at various times had animated school-age youth, acquired new vigor during these years. The question of Italian intervention in the war played an important role as well: in the south especially, university students were the ones pushing for intervention in response to the economic and social crisis. Toward the end of the "Giolitti period," thousands had to make do with jobs inferior to their original social status, their expectations, and their degrees (university students belonged in the main to the various levels of the bourgeoisie, with only 7 percent coming from the lower classes).[2] (The Piedmontese Giolitti was council president almost without interruption from 1903 to 1914. His adversaries spoke of this long period of power as a "parliamentary dictatorship." *Trans. note.*) At the same time, this student population was progressively breaking away from its previous position of sympathy for the worker movement, while the Risorgimento period's patriotism was degenerating into nationalism. It should be recalled that the Socialist Party at this time was entirely cut off from the schools, that it was terribly wary of the student movement, and that only certain progressives from Turin showed a sensitivity to the themes it defended.

Before becoming the object of power, youth was thus first a subject of upheaval, which the fascist movement would turn to its profit by attempting to represent it. In the immediate postwar period, it was mainly a matter of students from the urban lower middle class, hit by the economic crisis that affected those social categories of workers on fixed salaries. Once again, these young people had to confront unemployment or underemployment, a situation that was especially hard to accept given their veteran status. Thus we observe a convergence between their situation and the eagerness Mussolini showed to support their demands, either through his newspaper, *Il Popolo d'Italia,* or by the creation, in 1919, of the Fasci di combattimento, or Combat Units and the Avant-garde Students (Avanguardisti), which provided a military framework for the students. We find them at the sides of the fascist squads in all the violent acts of the two years that followed.[3]

But aside from this social segment, the correlation between youth and fascism found its basis in the relative youth of many of the movement leaders: in 1922, Mussolini was thirty-nine, Italo Balbo twenty-six, Giuseppe Bottai and Dino Grandi twenty-seven, Roberto Farinacci thirty, Cesare Maria De Vecchi thirty-eight; the oldest of the *quadrumvirs* of the March on Rome was Emilio De Bono, at fifty-four.[4] All these leaders therefore belonged to the war generation, that of men who were between the ages of eighteen and forty in the years 1915 to 1918, born during the final two decades of the nineteenth century. To narrow it down even further, as Camillo Pellizzi has pointed out, the leaders of fascist activities throughout the country were born between 1890 and 1900.[5] Even if the adhesion of youth was not as complete as the propaganda would have it, the participation of youth was sizable in the early years of fascism: in 1921, youths under the age of twenty-one represented 25 percent of the movement's members; in 1924, 146 fascist deputies out of 220 were under forty.[6]

Fascism used these statistics to claim that it coincided with the fighting men of Italy and represented not only the generation that had waged war but also the aspirations of youth in its entirety. Nonfascist veterans protested, pointing out that fascists represented but a minority of the 300,000 members of their association in 1924. But this association between fascism and veterans, even if it could not be validated, was vigorously put forward throughout the 1920s, with the fascists portraying themselves as the defenders of generations of soldiers "betrayed" by the results of the war.

Thus there was a revival of many concepts and images already present in European culture, but now tinged with fascist implications—such as the link between youth and war, and its connotations: the generosity, the restless, anxious sensibility, and finally the heroic death for one's country. The theme was already extremely popular in the Italian literature of the first twenty years of the century, and was an outgrowth of romanticism. From the futurists to D'Annunzio, it had passed through many manifestations, all of which were material for the political usage fascism intended to make of it. By a kind of typical fascist process involving the degradation of the symbolic into the political, what had been a mere artists' aestheticism would be transformed into an operational myth in the Mussolini era.

Luigi Russo defined this process as a mixture of "triumph and practical debasement of D'Annunzio's old themes," and he added, "In the first twenty years of the century, we all wanted to be 'young' poets . . . but Mussolini ordered that the myths of our aesthetes be transformed into a *"mythurgy"* of politics, and that the literary game become a full-blooded and bloody political reality."[7]

Among these themes, another attribute of youth played an essential role: *masculinity,* a term used by Giovanni Papini in 1915 as the title of a collection of his writings. Virility was considered to be intrinsically linked to warlike violence and passion, as opposed to comfort, money, and the "armchair soul."[8] Fascist writers harped on this theme a great deal, especially when the advent of war offered them an unassailable argument: the trenches would bring together the three determinants (youth, male, and warrior), which would also be the basis of the image of Il Duce, who was idealized to the point of preserving an eternal youth.

The antifascists countered these myths with a critique that aimed to deny the very concept of generation. For a long time the left considered, as Norberto Bobbio (a major antifascist figure) wrote as late as 1960 in response to an inquiry by the journal *Il Paradosso,* that the term "generation" denoted "a situation that is largely irrelevant, sociologically and politically," and that "political problems were not generational problems but problems of individuals or groups."[9] The antifascists highlighted the limits of the fascist categories, but usually did not consider putting them to alternative use, attentive as they were both to the social reality and to the coherence of the mythical elements employed. As Renato Treves has pointed out, it was rare for the antifascists of the time to consider themselves as belonging to a specific generation, with the exceptions of Pero Gobetti, who spoke of belonging to a "generation of historians," and Alberto Cappa, author in 1924 of an essay on this theme, published by Gobetti's own publishing house.[10]

In the case of those who became antifascists while at the same time being "younger" than fascism, the question presented itself in a different fashion. While they could not help but consider themselves members of the same generation, they felt alienated by the propaganda and manipulation of the regime and its mass organizations. For more than twenty years, fascism continuously proclaimed its special attention to youth, physically and spiritually, superimposing and confusing the various levels of signification, with particularly painful consequences for all those whose adolescence and youth coincided with Mussolini's dictatorship. The drama of this situation has been told in the autobiographies of many who went from a more or less convinced acceptance of fascism to antifascism and resistance.[11]

As is often the case when it comes to ideology and the imagination, fascism shows a repetitive circularity, certain developments and novelties notwithstanding. In the case of youth, the phenomenon is particularly evident: on the one side, we note the iteration of already well-known themes, and on the other, a reformulation necessitated by the circumstances, a degradation or aggravation of the problematic. In many respects, the debate on youth was one of the themes through which society reflected on itself when it couldn't do so more openly. For the young, the debate was also an occasion for self-recognition, albeit in a roundabout fashion, as imposed by the fascist atmosphere. This was evidenced by the flowering of journals for youth in the period from 1923 to 1943, whose writers included many of the most interesting postwar intellectuals and artists.[12]

The political treatment of the question of youth that the fascist regime established in the twenties through its youth organizations reveals a two-pronged attempt to achieve totalitarian socialization and to effectively educate a new political elite. In 1926, the fascists created the Opera Nazionale Balilla (National Organization of the Balilla), which in 1937 became the Gioventù Italiana del Littorio, or GIL (Lictorial Youth), and which would remain under the control of the Fascist Party even when it was attached to the Ministry of National Education. [The emblematic hero Balilla was a young Genovese who had given the signal for revolt against the Austrians in 1746. (Trans. note.)] All boys between the ages of eight and fourteen were enrolled in the Balilla, those from fourteen to eighteen, in the Avanguardisti; girls between six and twelve joined the Piccole Italiane, or Young Italian Girls (one of the regime's novelties was the inclusion of girls in youth organizations). These institutions were obligatory in each district, while other youth organizations, in particular Catholic ones, could exist only in areas of fewer than 20,000 inhabitants. The system was not to be a substitute for school, but it extended into workshops and factories when youths entered the working world. In fact, it ended up colonizing the schools, as total collaboration was expected from educators, particularly in primary schools.[13]

This system of youth enrollment was a way of controlling and channeling social impulses, and it also played an internal role within fascism, as a tool for training party members. Thus the University Fascist Groups, created in 1920 for students between the ages of eighteen and twenty-eight, were never formally included in the Balilla organization nor in the Lictorial Youth: they remained a special section of the party, under the direct authority of the national and provincial secretaries. Beginning in 1927, enrollment in the Fascist Party was reserved for the "fascist levy" (then reopened to others, at frequent intervals, under special circumstances), enrollment being possible at the age of eighteen. Every year on April 21, the transition was ritualized with a ceremony, during which all members of the youth organizations took a step forward to pass into the next age group, or, in certain cases, into the party.[14]

The system was based on a paramilitary structure, as shown by the Roman terminology used for the various formations (centuries, cohorts, legions); the mystique of action and violence was always strongly linked to this concept of youth, with its connotations of virility and heroism. In his *Amonimentio ai giovani e al popolo*, Arnaldo Mussolini (Il Duce's younger brother and director of the *Popolo d'Italia*, the main fascist newspaper) reminded Italian youth of "the male poetry of adventure and danger."[15] But what the regime proposed for girls was characterized by a significant contradiction: while constantly vaunting an ideal of motherhood and aid to the warrior, it offered a means of emancipation through sports and mass organizations. The leaders were concerned with "not distancing young girls too much from their families" and "with not inspiring great illusions of knowledge, but with teaching them to be good housewives and good mothers." And yet they offered courses in infant welfare, hygiene, and domestic economy, visits to the poor and to hospitals and libraries, encouraged them to read, to see films and plays, and to participate in annual excursions, competitions, and hikes. But when it came to ideals and models, it became impossible to avoid the old paradox that consisted in "telling young girls about our past glories, about Italian genius and heroism," in which women had played only a secondary role.

For girls and young women, fascism had decreed eight commandments. These commandments were hardly new, especially not the first one: "To do one's duty as a daughter, a sister, a pupil, and a friend with kindness and cheer, even if it is sometimes hard"; nor the fourth, "Obey one's superiors joyfully"; nor the seventh, "Flee stupid vanity but appreciate fine things." The third commandment, however, "Love Il Duce, who made the country stronger and greater," shed a slightly different light on the second, "Serve the Country like the Mother Superior," in that it gave the nationalist sentiment shades of a personal relationship, which could be infused with a sublimated eroticism. Other formulations of civic and moral duty— "Have the courage to oppose whosoever recommends evil and mocks honesty," or "Teach your body to triumph over physical exertion and your soul not to fear pain"—illustrated by examples of heroic little girls and promoted by sports, were somewhat closer to the precepts concurrently imposed on boys, but they did not diminish the fundamental contradiction. The final commandment, "Love work, which is life and harmony," merely restated an established credo, but it could not help but bring to mind, at least by association, the many social norms that discouraged or prevented women from performing certain tasks.[16]

The outline chosen for the present essay itself reflects the contradictions of fascist Italy faced with female youth: it is significant that women were nearly absent from the political debate, which was widely broadcast by the fascist press, and that, on the contrary, their presence was so strong in film, which reflects in its own way the problematic issues that surface in society. I have chosen two partial analytical perspectives, two points of observation, for the period from 1928 to 1933, in order to define certain images. On the one hand, we will look at the discussion surrounding the themes presented by *Critica Fascista*, a journal in which the fascist regime's confused aspiration for the renovation and rejuvenation of fascism was expressed through the adoption of political positions on the problem of youth; on the other hand, we will consider a segment of cinematographic production as a mirror on society (an equally distorted perspective, at times, though in its own way) and a place where the hopes and fears of youth were reflected. The starting point for this two-pronged analysis imposes itself, from the perspective of political history, not only from within fascism's development, but also in its relationships to potential adversaries. Prior to 1928, wrote Aldo Capitani in his book on youth and antifascism, "youth was not yet subject to the fascist pressure that was later to grow, forcing itself on almost everyone. My friends and I could still, quite peacefully, be whatever we were, unless we went to a specifically antifascist-related activity."[17]

As for the end date of the era under discussion, it is also easy to determine: 1934 was the year when the fascist program began to be realized, with the creation of the *littoriali* (special annual courses leading to competitions on particular themes, prepared for throughout the year), schools of political training, and special classes for young fascists, accentuating the dynamic that was budding during the preceding period and reinforcing tensions. The first products of these initiatives would appear in the years 1937 to 1939. Here we will address this intermediary period, during which fascist evolution was almost suspended, at the intersection of the 1920s and 1930s, a period when young people appeared on the public scene who had neither participated in the First World War nor in the March on Rome, and who thus felt a particular need to launch into politics, to express themselves, to take their place among those who would "make Italy greater."[18] It was a period when the fascist illusions, which would crumble in the five years to come, were still present; a time when what Alfassio Grimaldi defined as "the solitude of youth" was never so heavy to bear, and when consciences were never so confused. Among those who described it after the war, this period would always be referred to as one of ambiguity and illusory certainties: youths, it is argued, thought they were fascist because they believed that fascism was something other than what it really was, that it was a step beyond socialism.[19] Many would pay dearly for this persistent illusion, such as Sigieri Minocchi, who went off to Libya to "commit suicide," perfectly aware that it was absurd to die for this colonial enterprise, or Teresio Olivelli, "lictor" in 1939 on the theme of race (he had presented a Latin and Catholic interpretation contradicting Nazi doctrine), who was killed at the camp at Hersbruck for having defended the Jews. It will be necessary to examine certain aspects of this central period, when such illusions were formed, to attempt to understand their genesis.

"Young, Younger, Youngest"

The polemic on youth suffered from the start from being determined by formulations inherent to the internal oppositions within fascism.[20] The debate reached its greatest intensity after mid-1928, when Giuseppe Bottai reprinted in his journal, *Critica Fascista*, two of the many articles on the subject already published in the fascist press, launching the provocative slogan "Give the power, all the power, to the young generations."[21] At the time, Bottai was undersecretary of state for the minister of corporations (that is, the fascist-oriented trade unions), a post to which he had been appointed by Mussolini in 1926, at the age of thirty; in 1929 he became the minister of corporations, and he remained in this position until 1932, when Mussolini dismissed him for his "dangerous dynamism" and because employers showed an aversion to the young minister.[22] At the time of the debate, Bottai was therefore a qualified representative of the generation, one whose role in the war and in the "revolution" had earned him positions of command unusual for his age. He himself had declared, in 1926, that fascism had succeeded "in violently shattering the monotonous succession of generations" and in speeding up the replacement of one generation by another in the posts of command, in a break with the policy that had been followed "for ages and ages."[23]

The debate on youth followed two, often confluent, currents that created ambiguities and irritation always masked by the superficial harmony typical of totalitarian regimes. To begin with, the debate presented itself, in large part, as a comeback to those who manifested displeasure with the "question of posts." As Bottai himself learned, the assignment of high posts was an essential tool in Mussolini's power structure, but in the long run the system would emerge seriously weakened. Submission to the will or the whims of the leader, the preponderance of backbiting and complex love-hate games among associates or among Il Duce and his faithful, the presence of so many new men, these were all factors that broke with the traditions that up until then had regulated political careers—although such elements of instability nonetheless opened many possibilities for hope on the part of climbers and ambitious men of all stripes. The title of one of the articles that triggered the polemic put its finger on just this aspect of the problem, on this kind of mad dash on the part of young men for prestigious, responsible positions: under the title "Cariche ai giovani ouvero giovani alla carrica" (Young People in Charge, or Rather, Young People Charging), Gian Paolo Callegari attacked the "rabid, eleventh-hour youths" who graduated from the university obsessed with the idea of being given a post: "If they find one (for example that of Vice-Secretary of the local leisure center for some sort of wonder-working manufacturer, as my friend Longanesi would say), you find them all inflated like blimps, proclaiming themselves 'hierarchs.'"[24]

Such an interpretation of the problem was obviously reductive, and it was no accident that it was promoted by those who rejected Bottai's idea that the assignment of posts was a means of politically and culturally renewing fascism. As the *Bibliografia Fascista* asserted, displaying a certain impatience with Bottai's positions, "the terms of the debate concern the replacement of men in leadership functions and the valorization of young fascists."[25]

This question of youth was therefore apt to raise another issue, that of the internal renewal of fascism, though the former issue tended to overshadow the latter. Within the first polemic, and on the outside, Bottai and his collaborators found occasion to criticize the regime's creations in the name of ideals attributed to youth. In doing so, they contributed to the establishment of a myth of youth, and to placing youth at the heart of the political debate, using young people as the symbolic performers of a task essential to the society and to the single party. This explains why in these same articles dealing with youth, we find harsh words about freedom of expression and the state of the fascist press:

> We all know today what the party press has been reduced to, especially in the provinces, with a few rare exceptions: it is nothing but a pointlessly declamatory and adulatory chorus; it has become exasperatingly monotonous.[26]

> [There is a] terribly uniform tone to the fascist press, from which one seeks to banish every effort at reasoning, criticism, and peaceful disagreement, the only way in which convictions can be born . . . [so that] well-founded, reasonable critiques are transformed into expressions of anger, which, through subterranean channels, spread into gossip, denigrations, systematic and anonymous ill will, into crude and vicious irony, until they resurface in the form of a diffuse anxiety . . . that risks turning the living Italy into a mass of well-dressed automatons.[27]

Bottai and his clan attacked not only the "regime zealots" and the "declamatory and adulatory chorus of party people,"[28] they also attacked those youths hungry for posts. It was not to young people as such that "all the power" should go, but to those who showed real proof of warriorlike nobility, of devotion, of "restlessness." This last term was used in a positive sense, as a characteristic of youth, even if, in "a young country such as ours," it represented an entirely different thing than in "old dissatisfied Europe."

When it rose to the level of this broader perspective, the polemic offered an occasion to sharply criticize the creations of the fascist state and the people in power; this was a way of giving more meaning to the provocative assertion that the young generations should have all the power. But the poor training of the fascist youth could not help but be noted: as Emilio Settimelli wrote in *L'Impero*,[29] several studies had already indicated that often the successor had turned out to be worse than his dismissed predecessor. According to Bottai, who thus reduced the first aspect of the problem to the second (whereas to reduce the second to the first was already for him a symptom of the crisis of fascism), the key to solving the problem of high posts lay with the party, whose essentially political nature had to be affirmed if it did not want to lose itself in the tortuous paths of administrative action.

This attitude meant that the difference between "real youth" and "fake youth" had to be clearly determined, hence the confusion and mystification typical of fascist thought and language (the dead are alive, the absent are present, the young are old, and the old are young), and the many variations on the same theme: one's youth does not depend on one's birth certificate but on whether one expresses the spirit of fascism; "youth in the political and national sense means having taken part in the revolution"; "the young person is he whose age is accompanied by adequate fascist seniority"; a fascist is physically unsuited to win an election, because fascism is aristocratic.[30] Here the debate on youth linked up with that bearing on the reestablishment, however partial, of an electoral system: certain functions could be accepted as elective, one read in *Critica Fascista,* in which a writer, who was quickly reprimanded, courageously hoped for the end of the "alleged 'dictatorial period' and the return to 'normal methods,' in other words, to a state of freedom."[31]

The generation that had not participated in the war was referred to as the "generation of Mussolini"; as it was educated during the fascist era, it could not compare itself to the preceding generation. The obligation not to take opposing viewpoints but to sacrifice to harmony made it more difficult for youth to fulfill the innovative role demanded of it. A generation had been in power for eight years (which was not very long), and the entire fascist ruling class, wrote Bottai, was in its thirties. The generation that began to appear on the public scene liked to say (and sometimes not only out of ambition) that "by the age of thirty a man is worthless." This was the expression used by a Florentine "journal for the very young," *L'Universale,* and in the eyes of Bottai it referred to a state of mind and not an actual state.[32] But we might now also consider that this state of mind revealed, in a global and diffuse manner, a wish to liquidate fascism and its values. Here we are touching on the specifics of the problem under a dictatorial regime: youths were already in power, and younger men had to be won over, either by the promise of being included within the power structure or by that of modifying it. The fake youths, those who "are political by their birth certificates," were happy with the first promise, but the real youths, "those who are really active within the party, beyond a simple ambitious desire to obtain the right to take a competitive exam," were expecting something from the second. But to thus distinguish between fake youths and real youths, one also had to accept that there were "old old people" and "young old people," as when someone like Giovanni Giurati was named to a high post, a man "who is over fifty years old but who is younger than many of us in spirit and in action."[33]

To those who accused it of forging a myth of youth, *Critica Fascista* responded that, on the contrary, it was the others who were putting forth a "myth of experience and old age" in order to defend their interests, a myth that was highly beneficial to individuals whose mentality and past records should have cost them their jobs long ago, but who couldn't be budged because they had their party cards, which they had "acquired during those happy days of early 1926 to mid-1927" (an ironic allusion to the fact that in 1926 the Fascist Party decided to recruit through simple enrollment, which attracted many opportunities—*trans. note*). Their behavior had not been modified but simply copied by young people who were "burning with the frivolous desire for a quick fortune," yet who had "little desire to prepare for it rigorously, and were flighty to the point of impudence."[34]

We nevertheless see the emergence of a mythical definition of youth, to which certain "natural characteristics" were attributed, namely "enthusiasm, impulsiveness, promptness, and active passion," intuition, ardor, and pride, added to which were other qualities, induced by fascism: culture, political training, and the ability to control one's passions. Here the debate intersects with another—one that increasingly obsessed Mussolini—on the natural characteristics of the Italian, "pragmatic, easy, intuitive, intelligent," but with little concern for the state, for the destiny of Italy, for moral renewal.[35]

The partisans of the status quo were scandalized to see twenty-eight-year-old boys named to university posts or to managerial functions within the party and its press. Camillo Pellizzi of the newspaper *Il Resto del Carlino*[36] condemned the myth of youth, which, according to him, was far more a pose than a merit. Alessandro Pavolini replied that a people in the midst of renewal needed myths more than bread, and that in the meantime, the truth was that young people were not taking up all that much space: "Youths, with their black hair and curly locks, are greeted with sympathetic smiles on the front pages of the dailies, but when you get down to reality . . . with great courtesy and without great fanfare, doors are shut in their faces." Everyone agreed, nonetheless, on the mythical duo of "youth and training," so vaguely defined and so difficult to put into concrete form.[37]

In early 1930, Mussolini published his *Punti fermi sui giovani* (Firm Ideas on Youth), which *Critica Fascista* immediately hailed as encouragement for its theses, but which, as always, lent itself to divergent interpretations. The firm ideas included: 1) a youth policy for the regime; 2) totalitarian training for the young; 3) political apprenticeship; 4) their spiritual formation in the moral climate of fascism.[38] But the formula "with equal merits" introduced into the first "idea" a condition that was rather difficult to meet, due to its vagueness, whereas the principle of stability introduced in the fourth, "learn obedience in order to gain the right, or rather, the duty to command," was merely a received idea, with which the debate was overflowing and on which no one could disagree. Similarly, all agreed that the education of youth should be totalitarian (idea 2), though they might diverge on the practical means and ideals of political apprenticeship (idea 3).

Once again, the ambiguity of Mussolini's formulations aimed to maintain balance between various strains within the fascist movement: partisans and adversaries of "liberalization," revisionists like Bottai and Massimo Rocca, hard-line partisans such as Malaparte and Maccari. Mussolini did not mean to give the new generation a truly creative role, nor to grant real political importance to their ideas and proposals, which would have meant reopening the political debate within the party, thus favoring democratization over submission to the state.[39] Pleased at seeing Mussolini intervene, *Critica Fascista* returned to the theme of biological youth as an insufficient guarantee of merit, and thus to the theme of real and fake youth, clarifying as follows:

When Mussolini asserts that the regime "is and intends to remain a regime of youth," he wishes to confirm that the continuity of the fascist revolution is entrusted in the young, on the condition, however, that this desire for will, for creation, and for political tangibility is not extinguished in them, features that distinguish the real youth from the fake youth, in other words, those whose age seems to give them the right to an easy irresponsibility.[40]

As we see, Bottai's journal was fighting on two fronts, that of the internal conflicts of the political apparatus and that of entreaties from society. It was the latter that often pushed the journal to stigmatize the greed of the "old youth," those who thought only of jobs, as for example in an "Editor's Note" addressed to "a young comrade from Milan," who had proposed giving many old people a "well-deserved rest" and resisting "the ever-increasing invasion of women":[41] the comrade was accused of confusing the problem of leadership with that of employment. For Bottai and his colleagues, presenting the problem of leadership in adequate terms also required making connections between youth from different social classes as well as, and especially, between the institutions they attended. It was necessary to get students to participate in the working world, which in fascist terms meant, for example, that the University Fascist Groups began signing agreements with the Confederation of Unions. It was thus always an organic conception of power relations, but with interesting ideas on the question on youth, that they would attempt to put into practice in the second half of the 1930s.

What ended up bringing everyone together was a preoccupation with the widespread feeling among youth of "being foreign,"[42] a feeling that would be described remarkably by those who had lived through it after the fall of fascism, but generally not before the second half of the 1950s and the early 1960s. Only historical perspective would allow these youths to understand the complexity of what they had experienced. In the early 1930s, things were often confused and full of ambiguity. The very formulation of the problem in terms of generations was misleading and reductive, which explains the wariness of the antifascists with respect to the matter. It also explains the firm, courageous, and highly significant reaction of Luigi Russo in January 1930: "We are not among those who love youth in and of itself. We want young men only because we want to become men, or to be men . . . We have always associated the word "youth" with an idea of lack and immaturity; and while we have never been ashamed of youth, we have never bragged of it either."[43]

Next came words of disdain for those who played the part of "lifetime youths" (a transparent allusion to the fascist apparatus), in the first rank of whom was Marinetti (the creator of futurism, who rallied to fascism from the start), who "sings the hymn of eternal youth to young fifty-year-olds." The reference to Marinetti was particularly significant, as Russo meant to insist on the degeneration of the literary myth, and above all he denounced the political myth of youth as an instrument for justifying violence and the abuse of power. Among those who embraced the decaying myth, Russo included "the popularity fanatics, surrounded by hypocritical applause, the miracle-criers of perpetual youth, the inventors of newer and newer styles and remedies, and those who corrupt minors," and he mocked "the twenty-five-year-old Italian of today," so different from the ideal of which D'Annunzio had dreamed, happy to besiege the editorial departments of newspapers and publishing houses, demanding a post as inspector, a mayoralty, or the management of a hotel or a girls' school, "anything, so long as there is something to manage." Thus reemerged the desire for "the modest conquest of a place in the sun," the inevitable result of fascism's system of power.

In October 1930, the discussion started up again with the creation of the Youth Groups, conceived as a preliminary step toward entering the party. Bottai was against this, fearing that the groups would become a simple recruitment structure, instead of bringing to the party "youth's heightened spirit of subversion": he was wary of a party of the masses and its inevitable bureaucratization, and remained faithful to the idea of the party as a select group of activists.[44]

In any case, 1930 marked a turning point in the debate on youth: while during the preceding years the discussion had reflected a desire to normalize relations among the pioneering generation of fascism and those that followed, the economic crisis served increasingly to link the question to the debate on fascist unionism and the economic crisis.[45] This was also the moment when the fascists began to openly express themselves regarding the moral consequences of the economic crisis and to transfer to youth all the pioneering generation's hopes of renewal. The same year saw the publication of the novel by Mario Carli, *L'italiano di Mussolini,*[46] whose hero was part of the shock organizations of early fascism: his incapacity to become the new man, and his death in an airplane, left only his newborn son, "the Italian of tomorrow," to continue the work. The disillusionment and discouragement of diehard fascists that the novel expresses could just as easily have applied to the ideology of the new man, which was recurrent in fascism and always connected to the idea of youth.

We find the same profession of pessimism in a polemical exchange between Bottai and Ojetti (a fascist journalist) in early 1931, on the results of the policy of training a fascist ruling class: Bottai set his sights on 100 to 200 individuals, while Pellizzi, who immediately got involved in the debate, wanted even fewer.[47] A few months later, the same Pellizzi was at the center of a new debate on youth, with four letters published in the journal *Il Selvaggio* (The Savage) and commented on by Mino Maccari, its editor.[48] These letters were part of the polemic that set *Il Selvaggio* in opposition to *Critica Fascista,* and Pellizzi did not fail to attack Bottai's journal, and in particular Gherardo Casini, who in it had called Bottai's discoveries on corporatism "incontestable truths." In the tirade that followed, Pellizzi did not claim that Bottai was wrong (they had been very close in the twenties) but ended up attacking young people, asserting that youths' sympathies tended toward communism and that, in recent times, "nothing contributed to developing in youth the feeling of spiritual autonomy, of freedom." This was one way of saying that the hopes Bottai placed in youth were unjustified, and that if one day youth decided to act, it would not be to renew fascism but to get rid of it.

Until 1929 *Il Selvaggio* had maintained a clearly negative position with respect to youth, but starting in 1930 its attitude evolved, faced with the appearance of what was referred to as "the third wave" of young volunteers ready to rally for the "revolution."[49] It was within this new perspective that the comments of Pellizzi and of Mino Maccari must be situated. But despite good intentions, it was difficult to determine from their writings how it was that "the naturally subversive instincts of youth" could succeed in finding "a method of noble transformation and its use toward fascist ends."

The discussion triggered by Pellizzi's letters bore on the second point of the debate on youth and attacked the ruling class, which, according to him, "not only doesn't exist within the regime, but there is nothing to indicate it is forming." The truth, lamented Pellizzi, was that "a new, insular class of party and union functionaries had begun to form," and that the regime could be summarized in three words: "Mussolini, teamwork, bureaucracy." In such a political climate, it was therefore not surprising that the effects on youth would be negative: "They teach them not to doubt or discuss anything, which isn't bad at all; but when they begin wanting to think for themselves, we see clearly that they have neither the necessary character nor the training, and that they fall into the most vain and ridiculous heterodoxies. Hence, during a second phase, they evolve toward an attitude that oscillates between lethargy and hypocrisy, beneath a facade of discipline."

This lethargy, hypocrisy, and external discipline were spontaneous reactions to the mystifying and unrealistic discourse of writers like Pellizzi himself, when he spoke of "fascism as freedom" (in a letter from London dated April 1932 and also published in *Il Selvaggio*). Such a position forced him into paradoxes and verbal extremism that had no relationship to reality. One of the paradoxes, for example, was what he said of Benedetto Croce, who, because of "personal resentments" had made freedom "unfree"; as for verbal extremism, it was manifested in his desire to see "the replacement of all 'hierarchs' . . . who, at best, are stuck in the psychology of fourteen years ago."

Bottai's tone was entirely different. He did not believe that the question had to be posed in such dramatic terms, and said as much in response to the 1932 survey in the journal *Il Saggiatore* (The Essayist) devoted to the new generation, in which it asked such questions as: Could one find "a well-defined spiritual attitude" among young people, "capable of providing a breath of fresh air to culture and life?" Bottai's conclusion was that three generations were in conflict, the prewar, the war, and the postwar generations,[50] but that it was wrong to think that this discord implied a desire to do away with all that fascism had achieved since coming to power. The solution he proposed functioned via corporatism: "The new generations can accomplish a great task by going from the current phase, in which the political organization and the syndical-corporative organization are juxtaposed, to a phase of integration and interpenetration, in which the various institutions work together."[51] This optimism was one of Bottai's typical contradictions, but was also one of the reasons many young people saw him as a guide and were attached to the "corporative revolution."[52]

Judgments about Bottai differ, but most historians agree that even the adoption of total revisionism would not have been enough to guarantee the survival of the regime. On the one hand, the most serious and most politically committed youths criticized almost all aspects of the political, economic, and social reality.[53] On the other hand, the regime itself proved incapable of any concrete liberalization of the party or the administration.

In 1933, Giulio Santangelo considered the youth polemic to be "dusty," and contrasted the "clear affirmations of Il Duce" with Bottai's "nebulous uncertainties." But both were in agreement when it came to rejecting as ridiculous and absurd the positions of those who attempted to substitute the generational struggle for the class struggle (even if they disagreed on all the rest). Bottai had irritated Santangelo by ironically speaking of those who had been "hauled along from the first hour," and by adding one of his usual provocative remarks: "The problem of youth is the central problem of fascism." Youth as a "particular state of mind and awareness" was always for him a metaphor for the primary duties of "political, spiritual, and moral education" assigned to those in power in Italy, but "these sad, wilted boys one finds hanging on" were unworthy to be included in this category.[54]

One of the collaborators closest to Bottai, Agostino Nasti, took on the polemic in turn: out of 100 students who had participated in a debate on "youth and the regime" at the National Fascist Institute of Culture in Rome, he had found no more than 3 or 4 who were suitably educated. As for the others, said Nasti, one could see the effects of the "superficial and bombastic speeches" on "Roman eagles, consular roads, the universal mission, the salvation of civilization in danger," which taught youth only a banal journalistic rhetoric.[55]

This was a regular theme in *Critica Fascista*, where it was often lamented that there were "no more ideas. We seek them in vain in the great swamp of rhetoric." The problem was even more dramatic when one thought of the future of the young generations: "Do we want even our youngest to be fed on the mash prepared by the so-called thinkers of fascism?" mused another contributor to the journal, Giuseppe Lombrassa: "Shamefully, we must confess that we no longer have the training, the political culture of many young liberals or socialists of twenty years ago, who knew in depth—from the point of view of their specific doctrines, that is—the political, social, and economic questions of Italy or of foreign countries."[56]

To these images of youth as "fresh and strong, impetuously enthusiastic and exuberant" as well as "inventive, original, and creative," was increasingly contrasted the reality described, somewhat autobiographically, by Romano Bilenchi in 1933: "I am speaking of those of us between twenty and twenty-four, and who are, somewhat comically, youths, extreme youths, promises, dawns, etc."[57] According to Bilenchi, young people did not listen at all to what was said about them: "They couldn't care less about the discussions, and worse still, about those who were doing the discussing." Youth couldn't care less about anything, he insisted: "They've forged a new, rather convenient 'so what' attitude," so that "getting into a position not to care about anything" has become the fashionable goal. Faced with such analyses, the sentence the author placed at the end of his book, even if it was written in good faith, rings particularly false and incongruous: "Our life must be one of faith and emotion."[57]

In the years that followed, by one of the paradoxes common to fascism, the creation of the *littoriali* would turn out to offer rich opportunities for youths, and in particular university students, but it would also have the effect of producing many antifascists.[58] What many had said in the years from 1928 to 1933 out of indolence and careerism would be replaced by more specific symptoms of unrest and renewal, which were themselves perhaps only symptoms of attitudes ranging from apathy to protest, with the same intolerance for predecessors, whoever they were: "The impossibility of having masters is one of the essential conditions of our youth and perhaps the proof of its naturally revolutionary spirit," wrote Giaime Pintor (born in 1919), who counted on learning from his comrades, and not from his elders, the "progressive asceticism" that would lead him to new forms of opposition and antifascism.[59]

Images of Modernity: Youth in Cinema

While this debate on youth was taking place in the political and cultural world, Italian cinematic production was giving increasing attention to the same theme, even though, for reasons intrinsic to the history of cinema, the films concerned were made mostly in the years 1932 to 1934.[60] In these films, the young characters were called on to embody the novelty and difficulty of the times, the crises specific to modernity, the uncertainty of values, the force of the changes, and confusion those changes brought about. The equation between youth and modern times took various forms, but the dominant theme was the ambivalence of modernity, the duality of the choices being offered youths in a terrain as yet unclaimed. Depending on the case, "modern" could mean lacking in roots and community or, conversely, being resolutely, "fascistically" determined to change oneself and the world. The question of youth was thus posed initially through the recurrent theme of the choice of lifestyle, which according to old stereotypes rejuvenated by fascism often contrasted dissipation and eagerness to work. The choice was not presented in the same terms for male and female characters, but the former were always flanked by the latter, who played determinant roles in the existential choices of their companions.[61]

In one of the Italian movies that marked the transition from silent films to sound, *Rotaie* (Rails) by Mario Camerini (1929), the two heroes, in love and out of work, evolve within the modern, expressionist landscape of a large city at night: the geometry of the signage, chimneys, intertwining rails, and luminous advertisements (all lessons drawn from cubism and futurism) seems to be a most suitable setting for the presentation of two young rebels dissatisfied with the order of the world. The girl leaves her family to follow an unemployed good-for-nothing. They escape the temptation of suicide only to succumb to that of luxury and dissipation. The discovery of a wallet (in a train station) and luck at gambling lead them to a grand hotel, where the girl gives in to the persistent advances of a middle-aged fop, a negative model of the vain, parasitic, amoral rich. Two traps await our young heroes: theft for him, the selling of her body for her. A wave of disgust stops both of them in time, and they end up on a train once again. The tracks reappear on the screen as an image of destiny, of promise for the future, of the hardness of mechanization and the shortsightedness of its methods, of the bond between youth and technology. On the same train, a working-class family (a nursing mother, a child who offers an apple to the heroine, a father in worker's clothing who accepts a cigarette from the boy) offers another model. The two young people must choose. As in many other films, the working class is represented in a state of healthy dirtiness, strong and laughing, in perfect contrast with the lazy do-nothings and their affected elegance. The images in the film are quite beautiful, referring at times to the work of the painters Sironi, Carrà, and Rosai, and are evidence of the cinematographer's effort to take in the social reality.[62] *Rotaie* ends with a factory outing in which, amid the crowd of workers, the viewer encounters the two heros: surrounded by her coworkers, the girl approaches the boy, and the radiant couple sets out on a life devoted entirely to labor.

"Modern" can also mean indifferent to all values, old and new, according to a model whose prototype is found in a novel by Moravia, *Gli indifferenti* (1929), which was attacked by the doctrinaire theorists of fascism.[63] As the fascists, and others, could plainly see, the meaning of the story was that young people were not finding enough in fascism to escape indifference. But the fascist critics pointed out that the indifference was a problem for young people from good families and living in large cities, the only setting possible for this syndrome. The cinema would often return to this theme. *Come le foglie* (Like the Leaves) by Camerini, a 1934 film adapted from a comedy of the same name by Giuseppe Giacosa, portrays, and contrasts, an upper-class family (and its entourage) and a poor, working cousin who is honest and noble. Unlike what is shown in most films, the cousin does not possess the typical "youth" physique: he is a bit chubby, more adult than childlike, "a little bearish," as he says himself. He speaks English, but only at work, and never drops English words like "weekend," as do the young affected snobs who are his cousin Nennele's contemporaries. The unabashed young heroine proves capable of making up for her false start in life by opening herself up to work (she gives private lessons) and to the love of her cousin.

The emphasis placed on work, which unites the rich and the poor, refers in a light-handed manner to fascism's stress on capitalist values. What is remarkable, on the other hand, is that the type of individual commitment glorified in these films is miles away from political commitment. And the words by which Ugo Ojetti justified his advice to a twenty-year-old youth could easily be applied to these young characters: "The most obscure local doctor who saves the life of a child, and the most humble peasant who, through work and forethought, increases the fruit of his field, are engaged in healthier, more direct politics, which is to say they increase the force of the Nation better than if they went to orate or applaud at a political gathering."[64]

Work was thus at the center of the debate on the idea of youth, both within the fascist apparatus and outside of it; the insistence placed on praising work, while generally meant to confirm the established order, could nonetheless take on an anti-conformist sense at times, when the values of work were contrasted with political values.

The films I have just discussed were considered very moderately fascist, and were quite different from those more openly intended to celebrate the regime, which constituted, overall, a fairly small portion of cinematic production. This was the case of films such as *Camicia nera* (Black Shirt) by Giovachino Forzano, *Acciaio* (Steel) by Walter Ruttmann, both from 1933, as well as of *Vecchia Guardia* (Old Guard) by Alessandro Blasetti (1934). These three films focus principally on the relationships among generations, which had become a crucial problem at this time when tradition no longer held sway. With their strongly ideological backdrops, these films represent youth in a highly symbolic manner, while the images are realistic. *Camicia nera*[65] takes place in the Pontine marshes (which are still insalubrious at the start of the film), and the theme of life choices is first incarnated by the hero's young sister, a victim of all the illusions of youth: she dreams of "seeing the world" and would do anything to emigrate with her fiancé, who has no money. On their return to Italy (a box on the screen announces "And they found a country in order") they are amazed to discover the changes the regime has made: in the now drained Pontine marshes, rationalist architecture has replaced the former shacks, and we hear the famous fascist song, *Giovinezza, Giovinezza,* (Youth, Youth) in the background. But at the heart of the film's story is a two-pronged relationship between male characters: on the one hand, between the hero, a blacksmith (a predestinate trade in an Italy where Il Duce was often called "the son of the blacksmith") and his father; on the other hand, between the blacksmith and his own infant son, whom he tenderly bathes on Sunday mornings (his wife is a marginal character).

The theme of generations is also at the heart of *Vecchia Guardia* by Blasetti. The story takes place in October 1922, in the context of a general strike that includes hospitals and schools. Here again, we have three male heroes emblematic of the three ages of life: the old doctor, his son who fought in the war and is the leader of a fascist squad, and finally the doctor's youngest son, a lively and intelligent boy, who will be the victim of the "reds" in a fight triggered by the forced reopening of his school, ordered by the fascists. The women have secondary but fairly well-defined roles: the mother-wife, an anxious type from whom everything must be kept secret; the courageous young teacher who becomes engaged to the fascist son, and little Lucette, to whom the young son entrusts the task of painting his face black to improvise a fascist uniform. The middle generation is the one that saves Italy from corruption and the inertia of public powers as well as from socialist violence: the other two envy this role and seek in vain to imitate it.[66] But the youngest dies—and he represents the generation that, in the early thirties, would be at the heart of the debate. As for the oldest, a man of order who attempts in vain to employ legal channels, he is first rejected by the fascists because of his age, then ends up joining in the March on Rome, with the illusion that he will be able to resuscitate his son: "To Rome, to Rome! No one can stay home today. Mario, you're here, come with us, to Rome, to Rome."

The film was not well received by the dignitaries of the regime, for whom the violence of the shock organizations from the early days of fascism were a little to dangerous to be recalled, despite the fact that the film presented a watered-down version, transforming into student pranks a scene in which a robust fascist single-handedly forces a group of socialists to ingurgitate castor oil, and in another showing a fascist barber only half trimming the beard of a greedy leftist parliamentarian. Though the antifascists are presented in the worst light possible, and the consequences of the strikes are exaggerated in the extreme, the film was initially blocked by the censor; the intervention of the critic Corrado Pavolini, who presented the film to Il Duce, was required to obtain its release. Mussolini emerged from the film quite moved and gave the order to show it not only in Italy but also abroad. In Berlin, it was screened for Hitler.

It is within the centrality of the father-son relationship that the reference to youth takes on meaning in the film. Of the three generations present, none represents youth in the strict sense: we have at once the child, the adult, and the middle-aged man, all of whom are affected by the call to youth. Youth, here, is the capacity to see beyond the present, to be ready for sacrifice, for war, to defend one's country, it is youth as generosity as opposed to petty shortsightedness.

Another type of juxtaposition, opposing two characters of the same age but unequally endowed with fascist virtues, can be seen in *Acciaio*.[67] This film was intended to be a great work of fascist art and the filmmakers spared nothing to that end: the subject came from Pirandello, Malimpiero wrote the music, Emilio Cecchi and Mario Soldati collaborated on the screenplay, and Isa Pola was in the cast. The objective was to deprovincialize the Italian cinema, to give it a new luster, while attempting a realist approach to daily life capable of validating talking cinema. It is the story of Mario, a young Bersagliere (or sharpshooter, the branch in which Mussolini had served) who, after his military service, can't seem to find a place in everyday life. His girlfriend, Gina, prefers Pietro, one of his fellow workers at the steelmill. A confrontation between the two boys occurs in the factory, and Pietro is killed by a white-hot steel ingot, which his rival passed on to him too quickly. The competition between the two boys therefore ends in victory for Mario, who is an impetuous adventurer, the incarnation of physical strength, masculine beauty, and presence, and in the defeat of his rival, who never left the house and placed sentimental values above the loyalty due his fellow workers and his age group.

Mario is presented as an impulsive character who disdains order and dreams of being a successful cyclist. But what is most pronounced in him is his attraction to the factory and to work, a theme that is abundantly developed in the film, with the support of documentary details. Thus an emphasis is placed on the relationship between the machine and virility, not as brut force, but as intelligence, as if youth were the master of technology. Waterfalls and running water (in many of the film's shots) are used to show an affinity with youth; they are symbols of power and destiny, but also of energy in work, and partial acceptance of paths already traced.

Today, with the ideological pressure no longer operative, the symbolic charge of the images seems quite thin and the cinematographic language incoherent: the realistic elements, as well as the effort to accentuate spoken language and everyday gestures, are not enough to give it documentary value. The internal contradictions of its ideology prevent the young character from becoming a true figure of innovation. He is not confronted with real choices but only with those of the regime, and the idea that faith in fascism is capable of instilling youthfulness in all generations ("the youngest of all" always being Mussolini) is not convincingly demonstrated.

The sensitivity to the theme of generations displayed by the film industry also illustrates, through the diversity of the works produced, a complex relationship to fascism that combined adherence and indifference. On the one side, we note the near-schizophrenic separation between ideological cinema and "escapist cinema." On the other, it is impossible to ignore the many ideological connivances of this cinema, which was adapted to the social and political order of the moment—as in the case of the films we have just analyzed dealing with the relationships between youth and modernity, and between youth and existential crises. Yet the treatment of these themes was not the same in films with clear political intentions and as in those that merely suffered the dominant ideology, even when they had the involuntary effect of reinforcing it.

Among the nonfascist films that carried fascistic ideology (with many contradictions), we should mention in particular *Gli uomini, che mascalzoni* (Men, What Dirty Bastards) by Camerini (1932) and *Treno popolare* (Popular Train) by Raffaello Matarazzo (1933). In both cases, youths are represented as going through a waiting period before plunging into "serious" life: even if they work or keep themselves busy, they can allow themselves to be more open, jokey, irreverent, irresponsible. We also see that they are capable of renewing certain old forms of mentality, behavior, or interpersonal relations. *Treno popolare* tells the story of two girls who head off on a day-long excursion with their admirers, the one, Lina, with a young office worker, the other, Maria, with an older man. It is the Lina character who pushes innovative behavior the farthest, since she switches dates in the course of the excursion and is shown on the train home tenderly enfolded in the arms of someone she hardly knows. As for Maria, she breaks away from her older admirer and returns on the train with the boy dropped by Lina: in each case, the girl's will asserts itself in the form of a choice.

Treno popolare was received as a "a youth film" with "the qualities of twenty-year-olds: freshness, simplicity, spontaneous interest in things, impulsive sincerity in talking about them."[68] But it is mainly the light tone, with its touch of irony regarding "popular" tourism, that allows for the innovations and gives the public the feeling of a new climate, in which youths can be relaxed without being stupid. The film also emphasizes differences among youths, a group within which we encounter not only "real" youths—vigorous, active, and joyful, like the young man with whom the heroine falls in love—but also pedantic, conventional young men who fear novelty, such as the little office worker with whom young Lina embarks on the excursion. Ridiculing the weak, the timid, the nonathletic, as well as those who were cultivated or too hungry for knowledge, was a recurrent theme in fascism.

In *Gli uomini, che mascalzoni*, which was Camerini's first major commercial success and was well received at the first Venice festival in 1932, the character who does as he pleases is, on the contrary, a young mechanic (a new association between youth and machines) played brilliantly by Vittorio De Sica: he abandons a girl in a bar far from the city, smashes into a cart with his boss's car, and gets fired from several jobs. His character therefore belies the concern for modernity, the "laborious vitality" of film (which had struck the critics):[69] it was the first time one could see Milan in a film, the Milan of the great annual fair, rich in new trades, inventions, and technologies. The slogans used to launch the film spoke of a "modern work," of a "story with the scent of youth," set in "the most significant and most complex demonstration of work."[70] What was really "modern" was the use of realistic spoken language, which represented an innovation in the comedy genre and "demonstrates the possibility of a precise and critical representation of society."[71] The gestures of daily life become meaningful: we see the girl leave her house, buy a newspaper, take the tram, and so on. Our young mechanic at first seems to like running after girls better than working, but he is quickly transformed into the obedient son-in-law of a taxi driver whose daughter he loves, thus resolving the contradiction between his initial cheeky manner and "worker vitality." As is often the case in these films, the heroine is presented as "different from the others," from the perfumed saleswomen who require their admirers to have a car and money. She, on the contrary, is ready to give up her work and stay at home to marry the penniless mechanic, thereby becoming the ideal wife and mother. She is the key to the boy's transformation.

The images of girls proposed by the cinema of these years also reflect, in certain aspects, the stereotypes adopted and manipulated by the regime. Some are both old and new, such as that of uncontrollable girls: a group of girls, often very young—say, middle school students—and undifferentiated from one another, whose facetious and cruel remarks are to be feared. Is this a female version of the spirited male student, or an imaginary figure of subversive femininity, dangerous, uncontrollable, not yet strongly identified by traditional sexuality, but generally mocking of the dominant virility? Whatever the case, it is a vein that would continue to be exploited in the postwar period, and which can be found, in the thirties, in *La telefonista* (The Telephone Operator), in the schoolgirls in *Vecchia guardia*, who mock the socialist deputy with his tinted hair, and in the saleswomen united against the male world in *Gli uomini, che mascalzoni*.

The choices offered girls are thus even more difficult and dramatic than those offered boys: in their case, the theme of work is often associated with that of single motherhood. The first Italian talking film, *La canzone dell'amore* (The Song of Love) by Gennaro Righelli (1930), which was presented for Mussolini in a private screening at the Supercinema of Rome and was also produced in French and German versions, revolves around this theme, introduced in the context of an unlikely story: a young girl abandons her fiancé, a promising musician, with the sole purpose of taking care of a love child to which her mother (who has just died) gave birth late in life. (The father of the child was unable to live with the mother and child because his own wife is paralyzed and he has major financial problems.) Thus the heroine cares for the child with all the love she has in her, gives up her studies to take a job as a salesgirl, and refuses to explain things to her ex-fiancé. The fiancé finally replaces her with another woman, played by Isa Pola—a light and whimsical singer, the archetype of the "other," so different from his beloved. The return of the child's father, now a rich widower, enables the fiancés to reunite. The film, a free adaptation of a novella by Pirandello, was enormously successful, no doubt because it was based on the traditional theme of motherhood as a supreme value, while evading the thorny problem of the unwed mother.

The stereotype of the passionate and naively anticonformist girl is the female version of the enthusiasm, readiness, and radicalism attributed to youth. The unwed mother thus becomes a convincing incarnation of youth, and the fascist politics of childbirth at any price encouraged the depiction of her triumph. The attempt to erase the traditional stigma associated with unwed motherhood nonetheless reflects the contradiction, within fascist ideology, between a desire for modernism and the more conservative tendencies of clerical-fascism, defender of family virtues. This contradiction explains the over-the-top sentimentality and the unlikelihood of many of the stories treated, such as that in the *La canzone dell'amore* or in *La maestrina* (The Little Schoolteacher) by Guido

Brignone (1933). The latter was an adaptation of a play by Dario Nic-codemi that had been attacked by the young participants in the Lictorials of Culture and Art as an example of facile sentimentalism with harmful effects on the education of the people. At the same time, the film was favorably received by *Il Popolo d'Italia,* which praised "the powerful passion" of Andreina Pagnani, who played the part of the schoolmistress.[72]

The film is set in a small village in central Italy in 1911, and the heroine is a young schoolmistress who has just left her job in Turin to return to the local elementary school. The pupils adore her right from the start, while the female director hates her: she projects an image of independence, of almost transgressive autonomy in the slavish Italy represented by the little village, with its dismissiveness, its gossip, its hatred of whoever is different and avoids rigid social control. What is unbearable in Maria, the teacher, is her happy solitude, the fact that she is content to be by herself. Only the beadle, a singer in the choral society, and the mayor, an intelligent and cultivated man, appreciate her personality. But Maria is a woman with a past, a little girl love child, and that is why she had to leave Turin. When she reveals that she is a mother, the village capitulates, the director gives in to a moment of tenderness, the mayor declares his love. In short, all prefer an illegitimate child to Maria's solitude, the real social stigma. The mother and daughter head off together in a calash, soon followed by the mayor, who abandons his automobile, the village, and all its pettiness. Praise of maternity, even outside of wedlock, is coupled here with the image of a strong and sentimental young woman, a loner who is capable of great devotion, and who, in her need for affection, fell victim to a vile and weak seducer. This heroic journey toward motherhood ends up moving men of greater dignity, who are won over not only by the seriousness, knowledge, and grace of the young woman, but especially by her devotion to her daughter.

The same situation is identically replicated in Camerini's 1933 film *T'amerò sempre* (I Will Always Love You), an exemplary film from many points of view. Though not as moving as the previous film, its apology of motherhood is quite touching. The beginning of the film is extraordinary, with images that read like UNICEF propaganda: newborns in a hospital, with nurses bathing and powdering them in a precise, efficient, and affectionate manner. The critic Nicola Chiaromonte instantly declared this opening sequence "almost admirable," with "these maternity ward scenes, the little bodies still damp from the darkness, still animals, powdered, weighed, catalogued, followed by a shot of a woman's face, dark and unhappy."[73] The face is that of the heroine who just gave birth to a little girl, and whose loneliness inspires pity in her roommates. A flashback explains how it happened that this young, beautiful, and virtuous woman ended up in this situation: after the death of her mother, a miserable and immoral woman, she was raised in a religious school, and she believed the promises of a young aristocrat who swore he would never abandon her. But he left her at the moment of birth, and he does not reappear until five years later. The two main characters say they are twenty-two and twenty-three years old, but as in almost all the films analyzed here, the young people have no physical characteristics to distinguish them from adults, as they would in the cinema of the fifties. The heroine rejects her former lover, telling him, "I live from my work, alone with my daughter, and I'm happy"—a true manifesto of the young working mother. This attitude finds its reward in the person of the accountant in the store where she works as a salesgirl: when both are laid off, we see them walking amid the sound of honking horns as night falls on the city. He invites her to dinner, offering to stop and pick up her little girl: "My mother would be so happy to see her." The film was a great success; the critics praised "its sincere humanity and remarkable workmanship,"[74] representing as it does a successful balance between ideology and narration. The fact that the story is situated in a big city—unlike *La maestrina*, which places its young heroine in a small, stifling, prejudice-filled world—allows for a new narrative solution: the final scene, in the streets of Milan, announces the possibility of a more humane and more "modern" union between the sexes.

Cinema thus reflects the multiplicity of work choices with which young women were confronted: work as sporadic activity or as a mere stage before marriage *(Gli uomini, che mascalzoni; La telefonista)*, or as a life choice for personal autonomy *(La maestrina; Vecchia guardia; T'amerò sempre; La canzone dell'amore)*. It is true that even in the latter case, affective choices in the form of a child or a man push the decision to work to the back burner, but they do not entirely void it, as in the first case. For the woman, the fundamental choice is between seriousness and frivolity, and here again she is in the position of interpreting modernity: either superficially, as opening the way to a pleasant life of clothing, admirers, and fun, as in the first case; or in a profound sense, as a possible reformulation of traditional femininity, as in the second case. *La telefonista* by Nunzio Malasomma (1932) presents an extreme opposition between vain and flighty seamstresses (who become agitated around clients and order lobster and champagne at restaurants), and the honest and simple telephone operator, who is invited out by her boss: she accepts his invitation to dance, but not to dine. The way these stereotypes are presented shows that they have been modernized: the representation of work "is dulled, 'feminized,' so to speak, in order to reduce the tension, to rescale the threat" represented by women at work, and to inscribe its social novelty within the value system established by the old order.[75]

The cinema thus played out the diffuse worries and innovations, the uncertainties of youth and the uneasiness of society faced with the unknown that youth represents. So many illusions and fears were projected onto youth, which became almost the symbol of alternatives within or outside of the regime, alternatives that would reach maturity in the years 1938 and 1939. In the early thirties, the antifascists themselves had enthusiastically believed in the hopes incarnated in the "young generation." In 1932, *Giustizia e Libertà* gave an account of the suit brought against the students of Turin, aged seventeen to twenty-five, who had joined the movement: "It's the new generation that is talking to the tired and discouraged old one, and indicating the path of revolution."[76]

Such fermentation was at work in cultural life in a more complex and discreet way in than in political life, but the former bore witness more strongly to the breadth of a problem that affected all social classes and both sexes.

The Metaphorical Nature of the Idea of Youth

On the question of youth, fascist Italy was like a two-faced Janus: on the one side, we note the persistence of the image of youth as a preparatory phase to adult life (even if the impatience of youth threatened this concept); on the other hand, the modern, and postmodern[77] idea was beginning to develop of a prolonged and restless youthful condition, a summation of the crisis in society (this was especially true for the image of youths from the relatively wealthy and educated classes, but it progressively extended to the working classes). In short, fascism revived the vitalist myth of a sacred youth that knew everything by instinct, was capable of obeying and fighting, but was also capable of commanding and governing, and it adapted this myth to justify and enliven a political apparatus composed of young men with a sense of full entitlement. Youth was thus both a metaphor for fascism and its tool, since it enabled the fascist regime to present an image of strength and power, of historical determination, of destiny.

Fascism adopted the literal and traditional representations of youth just as it appropriated the traditional behavior of young people, in particular that of hot-blooded student youth,[78] using them to its own ends, from the constitution of a political elite, in the full sense of the word, to the simple assignment of posts. In both cases, the operation took on a "modern" character, in that it introduced programmed procedures to behaviors that previously belonged to the domain of primary socialization and were relatively spontaneous.[79] All this enabled it to respond—albeit in authoritarian fashion—to the requirements of the period: the need to enter into political formations, the taste for collective and ritual demonstrations, militarism, the supremacy of young males, and the taste for public exhibition.[80]

In the face of these open efforts on the part of the regime, Italian society and culture of the years 1919 to 1939 offered more complex responses. The few examples taken from cinema show that the aspirations of youth, and especially of girls, broke the mold assigned by the regime. While the most clearly fascist cinema insisted on the generational problem as one between males centered around politics and war, another area of production highlighted the uncertainties of young women faced with choices in life and work. These films clearly demonstrate the changes in ideals and behavior occurring in the lives of their female characters, presenting the themes of solitude (often not in a negative fashion), work, motherhood, consumption, freedom, and pleasure. The fact that the cinema of these years still presented young girls as only partially distinguished in their physical aspects from mature women indicates that the process of identifying youth and the young body was only just beginning;[81] this process would not develop fully until the postwar era.

Through all these representations, the idea of youth became overdetermined, absorbing all the problems of the society. Youth and its symbols crystalized social anxieties—ranging from unemployment and alienation to a desire to live life to the fullest—and became a model for the future, both threat and hope. Its fragility was equally accentuated, for it was the repository of values that the society had been unable to realize, and its marginal status enabled a relatively selfish critique of the existing order. Real young people, youths of flesh and blood, internalized these images through a process that would reach its peak in the postwar era: in the fifties, the emphasis would be on the deviance of youth, a kind of delirium within the utopia it represented, the result of the social illness with which it was infected. In the sixties, on the contrary, a certain optimism would prevail, the idea of a new universalism, of a new capacity to redesign the world along the lines of freedom and justice. But as demonstrated by the debate that began under fascism, these two aspects have always been connected. Ultimately, the prolongation of schooling and the creation of a market for youth would form the bases of a real youth culture,[82] founded on a democratization of consumption—a leveling instrument, at least in appearance. The generational conflict would end up seeming as pertinent as the class struggle, even on the left. Considering these subsequent developments, the images of youth in fascist Italy are both archaic and forward-looking symptoms of a concept of modernity as acceleration, anomy, technology, and mastery.

AMERICA IN THE FIFTIES
The Birth of the Teenager

The theme of youth as a social problem was present in the United States beginning at the end of the nineteenth century; one of the major stages in its development was the publication in 1907 of a book entitled *Adolescence,* by the psychologist G. Stanley Hall, who saw himself as the "discoverer" of the American adolescent. Hall attributed antithetical qualities, borrowed from Rousseau, to this phase of life (hyperactivity and inertia, social sensitivity and egocentrism, heightened intuition and an infantile disordered state) and insisted on the idea that all forms of pressure and conditioning meant to push the adolescent toward adulthood had to be eliminated, and that one should instead help the adolescent to realize all the possibilities of the phase he was experiencing. For him, adolescence corresponded to what prehistory had been to collective history, with its large-scale migrations: it was therefore a period of profound regeneration, almost a new birth. Despite this starting point, Hall nonetheless considered military training to be the best means for realizing the potential of this age and for respecting its specificity.[83] Throughout the century, the debate on youth in America would navigate between these two poles: on the one end, the obligation to guarantee the adolescent's freedom and potential for autonomy, and on the other, that of unifying, collectivizing, and restoring the creative momentum of youth to society.

Historians consider that the progressive codification of adolescence as a distinct phase reached full maturity right after the Second World War.[84] They also emphasize the contrast between this immediate postwar period and the seeming absence of adolescents during wartime, when the accent was placed either on soldiers, whether young or adult, or on children.[85] In 1945, in an article by Elliot E. Cohen for the *New York Times,* the word *teenager* appeared as part of the everyday language,[86] but it was only in the 1950s that the term would assume full force and that the debate on its meaning and implications would extend to the society as a whole. Many consider 1955 to be a crucial date: the generation that was then in adolescence was born between 1934 and 1940. It is significant that the works considered to be most symbolic of this generation were written in the early 1940s and widely circulated only ten years later; to give only two examples: *On the Road* by Jack Kerouac, written in 1941 under the title *The Beat Generation* and rejected by editors until late 1956, when it was finally published to immediate success (to Kerouac's great horror, the term *beat* began to be used not in its original sense of "beatific," but to designate disorder and delinquency), and *Rebel without a Cause* by Robert Lindner, published in 1944, but whose popularity dates only from 1955, after the novel was made into a movie starring James Dean and Natalie Wood.

At the end of the 1950s, the process reached its conclusion, and adolescence became a legal and social status that had to be disciplined, protected and given its own institutions. Its legal recognition resulted from governmental creations: in 1951 the Youth Correction Division was established (by the Federal Youth Corrections Act) to provide for the treatment and rehabilitation of delinquents under twenty-two; in 1953, the Senate Subcommittee on Juvenile Delinquency; in 1954, the Division of Juvenile Delinquency in the federal Children's Bureau; in 1961, under the initiative of President Kennedy, the Committee on Youth Employment; and numerous research programs launched by various federal administrations to address the problems of youth, such as the large conference on childhood and adolescence organized by the White House in 1960 with the participation of 7,600 delegates, 1,200 of whom were between the ages of sixteen and twenty-one.[87] The premise behind all these governmental initiatives was that young people represented a danger, both to themselves and to society, and that they needed specific protection and aid. Inevitably these initiatives ended up inciting behaviors that confirmed the correctness of their premises, or that at the very least made it difficult to define or to think differently about the social phenomena they were intended to treat. Kett pointed out that the thinking that created the delinquent as a social type was similar to that which created the adolescent as a type: one began by defining certain physical or mental traits, and the definition was then used to explain the behavior of the youth.[88]

Thus a debate on youth developed in the United States, bringing together psychologists, teachers, sociologists, and education and justice administrators, and it continued into the sixties. An enormous amount of documentation is available on the subject, but simple polls provide us with the main themes that are of interest to our research on youth as a metaphor for society, providing the elements of a debate that society was also having about itself and its worries. The debate was carried on not only by societal and, increasingly, youth professionals (psychologists, specialists in urban problems, teachers, parental advisers) but also by many simple citizens, whose words emerge from letters to newspapers or the reports of social workers. In the early sixties, the atmosphere began to change, and with it the tone of the arguments: the term *juvenile delinquency* was replaced by other expressions, such as *youth culture,* and in some universities and publications a strong opposition began to sprout against the old manner of positing the problem. In 1968, the government reorganized the Children's Bureau, which lost much of its power. It can therefore be considered that the debate was most virulent between the years 1950 and 1964, the year of the first student demonstrations in Berkeley and when the American "escalation" in Vietnam was becoming accentuated.

The fifties saw the appearance of "teenagers," who were different from their predecessors due to their numbers, their high level of resources, and their group consciousness. This was the first generation of privileged American adolescents, but it was also the first to demonstrate a cohesiveness, an awareness of constituting a distinct community with particular interests. The image of the adolescent that then emerged was associated mainly with urban life; his habitat was the high school, which became a world unto itself, with clubs, sports activities, fraternities and sororities, dances, parties, and other extracurricular activities that had their own sites: the local drugstore, the car, and other sites frequented by youths. With this association between youth and high school, now attended by almost all youths of all social classes,[89] adolescence seemed to become an increasingly autonomous world; there developed a segregation of social roles as a function of age that some considered to be without precedent in the history of the country. Young people now spent most of their time among themselves and without adults, whether in school or in the working world, which was governed by a hierarchical structure. But most important were the new forms of interaction: it was no longer the parent-child relationship or the student-teacher relationship that generated social rewards, but the interaction among peers. In a study conducted in the spring of 1955, and which would become one of the main references in the debate, sociologist James Coleman analyzed the emergence of "a youth subculture in industrial society" and justified his research with worrisome observations: "These young people speak a different language . . . and the language they speak is becoming more and more different."[90]

The "difference" in youth could translate into apathy and passivity (one sometimes spoke of the "silent generation") or into a more or less open rebellion. In both cases, it induced a separation, a feeling of both alienation and otherness. This attribution by the public of an "alien" character to youth, confirmed by countless writings and debates by experts, gave the adolescent a centrality analogous to that held by other social and political figures in the past. The psychologist Edgar Friedenberg, author of seminal works on youth, observed that the teenager seemed to have taken the place of the communist in public debate and in the vision of the society's future. Many pointed out that a terminology had come to be adopted that accentuated the adolescent's foreign nature with respect to society: terms such as *cast*, *tribe* or *subculture* all came out of ethnographic studies on peoples who were "different," who did not share Western society's ideas as to what should be considered central.[91] The terms *underculture* or *subculture* were commonly applied to youth, because they did not seem to imply too severe a judgment yet they emphasized a state of difference and subordination. Youth symbolized both the underprivileged and the overprivileged, a process of symbolization in which, as we shall see, the cinema of the period is rich in examples.

Friedenberg's analysis (to which we shall return) was founded on an interesting diagnosis: what appeared to be an accentuation of adolescence also represented its end, at least in traditional terms. The title of one of his most famous works, published in 1959, *The Vanishing Adolescent*, referred to the disappearance of an intermediary age, now compressed between childhood and a precocious maturity, which meant that the adolescent was sexually active, a consumer, and a member of associations far earlier, while the period of education and of professional training was constantly getting longer. This diagnosis would be supported by David Riesman, who wrote an introduction to Friedenberg's work when it was reprinted in 1964. This approbation was the sign of a more widespread convergence: many of those who wrote on youth based their views on the works of a few sociologists from the fifties, who had essentially set the tone. Figuring among these, unfailingly, was *The Lonely Crowd,* a collective work on "the changes in the American character," but whose author was primarily Riesman. It held that American society now produced individuals who were "hetero-directed" as opposed to being directed by tradition or, as in the American past, "self-directed"; children were taught that the unity of the personality was no longer founded on competency or on the development of one's own desire and ideals, but on the satisfaction of others' expectations, which meant that everything depended on social approbation; thus, in a society characterized by abundance, bureaucracy, and permissiveness, the individual was directed toward passive enjoyment, consumption, and conformity.[92]

In his book *Childhood and Society* (which would play an important role in formalizing the American vision of childhood), the psychologist Erik Erikson asserted that to protect themselves against anxiety, young Americans learned not to involve themselves in what was happening around them. The same idea was present in Friedenberg's diagnosis: adolescence was becoming obsolete because personal integration could no longer connect with the old ideal of maturity, which was now unrealizable; the adults themselves were the ones who were communicating to adolescents their anxiety and hesitation as to the definition of roles. The ball was cast back into the court of the parents and teachers, defined as "individuals with insufficiently formed characters," rendered anonymous by the process that was transforming the crowd into a mass. Parents had changed before the children, observed psychologists, who nonetheless attempted to reassure "American parents in mutation" that every educational choice allowed for elasticity. At the end of the 1950s, in a discussion organized by the journal

Daedalus, Erikson returned to certain fundamental aspects of the debate: his interlocutors were mainly people belonging to the "other" generation, that which was between forty and fifty years old; they pointed out that the emphasis had mainly been placed on the "alienation" of youth, forgetting that there were also many peaceful, determined, well-formed adolescents; and that, finally, women had remained largely outside the debate, both as a subject of discourse and as participants.[93]

The Difference of Youth:
Responsibilities and Remedies

As for the manner of confronting the "difference" and the separation of the adolescent world, the debate took two directions: there were those who saw its origin in an education that was too permissive and in the crisis in traditional values, particularly the "disintegration" of the family, while there were others who were concerned with understanding, anticipating, and finding the proper institutions to remedy it.

Let us consider the first position for a moment, taking as a representative example of a long list of studies the book by the Hechingers, *Teen-Age Tyranny.* The second position, which is more interesting for our purposes, will be the subject of a more developed analysis. In and of itself, the title of this book by Grace and Fred Hechinger (a work that acknowledges the analyses of Coleman and Friedenberg but uses them to its own ends), echoes the diffuse fears of the public, which we see appearing in letters to newspapers and in interviews between parents of teenagers and experts. "Tyranny" represents an exaggeration of the terms of the problem, which was spread throughout the society: "American civilization . . . is in danger of becoming a teenager society, with permanently teen-age standards of thought, culture and goals. As a result, American society is growing down rather than growing up."[94]

What preoccupies our authors is not so much the excessive freedom of young people as the abdication of adults' rights and privileges in favor of immature youth, which they blame on a permissive doctrine of self-expression pushed to the extreme. This favored the equation individualism and egotism within the educational system, thus generating personal insecurity and a lack of goals. The Hechingers insinuate that American teachers sinned through an excess of goodwill when, perhaps out of a reaction against fascism and communism, they discredited all forms of leadership. Their tone is stern: the first years of adolescence have been built into an institutional empire, the adolescent subculture is tribal-like and characterized by many aberrations, the cult of the cheerleaders in schools is obscene, rock and roll idols are depressing. But in their opinion, the sexual issue is the biggest problem: in order not to lose face, one is obliged to have sexual relations from the age of sixteen on (the legal driving age in most American states, and thus the age at which one may have a car available, a site that lends itself to sexual intimacy), and teenage pregnancy continues to grow among the white middle classes.

Such assertions led to a strategy for restoring the family and its values. James S. Coleman pointed out that this strategy risked linking the adolescent too much to his family, and wondered what would happen in the case of delinquent homes. Herein appeared one of the most common underlying fantasies: that of juvenile delinquency as a "lower-class" culture set to conquer the undefended zones of the middle classes—in other words, their most impressionable children, those with the most confused ideas. The remedy proposed by Coleman was more subtle, because it depended on the use of criteria adopted by the separate society that adolescents had created for themselves in order to flee that of adults. His major study of high schools (in five rural and five urban or suburban areas of Illinois, thereby covering a large social spectrum, from the children of farmers to those of industrial executives and working-class families) showed that it was precisely among the students that made up the elite of the academic population that detachment from the parents was most marked; he also emphasized the fact that adults were misinformed about their childrens' schedules. Adolescent society's values accentuated the importance of appearance (clothing, popularity, external attributes), with the greatest popularity falling to football players and athletes in general, while the most intelligent students, especially the girls, refused to adopt a smart image that would risk hurting their popularity among their friends. These "surface" values were encouraged by the parents, who were concerned with the "happiness" of their children, even if, in principle, they would have preferred the old model of the studious and obedient adolescent. Coleman thus emphasized a schizophrenia of values among adults, and an inconsistency in their educational principles.[95]

The remedy proposed by Coleman was to take advantage of the very spirit of competition that characterized youth's separate society, which was striking in its harsh exclusiveness, the rigid hierarchy of its groups (necessary for "self-protection"), the partial maintenance of class distinctions combined with cruel status-based discrimination: just as sports offered an outlet for violence, so competition should be introduced into the academic arena, not on an individual basis but on the level of the group and the school. To this end, intellectual competitions should be organized, centered around scientific, musical, and theatrical projects. Computers should be used to simulate problems of strategy and organization (on the model of those already used for executive training) until a system of group competition was achieved in all areas.

Thus America in the fifties was rediscovering a recipe very similar to that of the *littoriali* in fascist Italy in the thirties. The idea was also proposed of extending this remedy to teachers—the weak link in society, increasingly discouraged by a difficult, poorly paid profession affording little social status, poised in the front ranks of a struggle for which they were not armed. Many experts accused them of falling prey to the anxious passivity of petty bureaucrats,[96] of inhibiting students' creativity and rewarding conformity. But the cinema of the day presented the image of a teaching corps terrorized by violent and delinquent adolescent gangs, as in the popular movie *Blackboard Jungle* (1955), which the American ambassador to Italy, Claire Booth Luce, had withdrawn from the Venice film festival because of its portrayal of adults entirely stripped of authority. For Coleman, the question of teachers could also be resolved by competition, with the reward being a salary increase.

A vicious circle became apparent, characterized either by the dream of restoring the past or the wish for reform: the two strategies were seeking to reintegrate adolescent society into American society, after diagnosing that the former had been created as a reaction to the latter. Such a circle revealed the projective nature of many of the opinions advanced in the debate (youth as a group onto whom repressed fears and desires were projected) and the aspiration to find a solid and known point of departure. There was a constant need for reassurance: despite their scandalized tone, many arguments highlighting youth's habits of consumption—this huge new market open to Coca-Cola, chewing gum, candy, records, clothes, cosmetics, used cars, and automobile accessories—perhaps reflected a secret complacency at finding confirmation of the philosophy of consumption that represented an American credo of well-being. Bruno Cartosio points to various examples of arguments that begin with "negative" considerations only to turn them into "positive," reasonable, and justifiable facts in order to convince readers that youths, whether apathetic or rebellious, could still develop into active executives and trustworthy fathers, or else (and the reasoning itself was quite meaningful) that this youth with so little enthusiasm for war would nonetheless do its duty in Korea. The reassuring tone of articles published in *Time* magazine in 1951 and 1952 in fact dissimulated what would be revealed only later: the psychological crumbling of many youths in Korea in the years 1950 to 1953.[97]

Let us recall that this decade, despite America's prosperity and its proclamations of a glorious future as the leader of the free world, was one of profound anxiety created by the cold war and the execution of the Rosenbergs: many Americans feared the imminence of an atomic war. These teenagers with their own separate societies were also the first generation to grow up with the bomb: they were accustomed to daily drills, to sirens interrupting class, and to the presence of fallout shelters in residential areas. This underlying vein of anxiety in American society found hidden expression in the question of adolescence, but the fear of war, whether a cold war or the real thing, was accompanied by other racial and sexual terrors as well.[98]

It was quite natural that the debate on juvenile delinquency should graft itself onto all this. On the one hand, an attempt was made to show greater understanding of the social dimension of the phenomenon, an attitude that would lead, under Kennedy, to the adoption by Congress of the Juvenile Delinquency and Youth Offenses Control Act (1961), which was based on the recommendations of the president's Committee on Juvenile Delinquency and Youth Crime. The law recognized that economic and social factors could be causing the deliquency problem, and authorized the government to finance prevention programs. But on the other hand, the association between delinquency and adolescence had the effect of considerably enlarging the notion of delinquency: any irregular behavior, even any form of unconventional language, the use of curse words for instance, was considered a step toward delinquency.[99] As a correspondent to the Senate Subcommittee on delinquency put it, Elvis Presley had adopted lower-class attitudes and hostility to schoolwork: "Elvis Presley is a symbol, of course," he wrote, "but a dangerous one . . . The gangster of tomorrow is the Elvis Presley type of today." Elements of adolescent subculture, such as rock and roll music, cars with souped up engines or customized bodies, Elvis-style haircuts or long hair, and clothing styles borrowed from black Americans or gangs, were considered forms of aggression. The definition of the gang was so elastic that it placed real gangs that were committed to violence, vandalism, and theft, on the same footing with groups that were more like clubs or associations.

These gangs, whether delinquent or not, were opposed to adolescent organizations overseen by adults, such as the Boy Scouts, but the protagonists in the debate were hardly attentive to the similarities between the two types of groups: the use of their own jargon, the emphasis on the values of loyalty, physical courage, and precocious maturity. In his book *Delinquent Boys: The Culture of the Gang*, Albert Cohen showed that the culture of delinquency was a tradition in certain groups of American society. Such groups were originally situated in the lower classes but were in the process of spreading into the middle classes due to parental errors in children's education. Cohen demonstrated that a gang was a little society unto itself, whose values were defined by opposition to those of the middle class, and was thus a kind of vengeful countersociety, but that such a phenomenon merely confirmed the dependency of the gang members on traditional society. In another book, *Growing Up Absurd*, Paul Goodman considered that it was the unfinished nature of the American Revolution and the country's inability to keep its promises that explained youth's nihilism;

beatniks on the one hand, delinquents on the other, were all manifestations of lost potential.[100]

Public opinion and experts agreed in partially attributing the increase in juvenile delinquency to the mass media preferred by youths—comic books, radios (present in cars), and movies (the telephone might be added to the list, the prime instrument of cohesion among youths and a source of irritation to adults)—whereas television was reserved for the family universe. In 1954 Frederic Wertham published his *Seduction of the Innocent,*[101] in which he maintains that mass culture could be more powerful than family, social class, tradition, and history. That same year, the Senate subcommittee looked into the role of comic books in juvenile delinquency, and the publishers of these types of works adopted a moral code to eliminate obscenity, vulgarity, and horror. But what aroused the most indignation were the radio, cinema, and popular press intended for young people, which broadcast or defended music that gave youth culture a sense of cohesion and identity. The main targets were rock and roll and its stars Elvis Presley and Bill Haley, who had absorbed the transgressive nature of black music, with its allusions to sexuality, alternative lifestyles, and different ways of experiencing one's body.

There is reason to wonder whether these violent reactions to the penetration of black music (even if some wrote that Presley was adopting a black style that was in turn inspired by white music)[102] were not indirect responses to the major racial problems that were beginning to surface during this same decade. In 1954 the Supreme Court delivered a judgment in *Brown v. the Board of Education* that destroyed the educational doctrine of "separate but equal" schools, considering that such a racial distinction violated the Fourteenth Amendment of the Constitution, and ordered courts to accelerate procedures to admit black children into all public schools. The decision triggered a series of conflicts, the most famous of which occurred in Little Rock, Arkansas, in 1957, where the struggle for school desegregation ran into opposition from the state governor, and where the intervention of federal troops was required to protect black students on their way to school. In many sectors of society, and in many areas of American culture, the racial question was operating below the surface, in typical fashion for the period, requiring any inclination toward alternative cultural choices to exist on the sly.[103]

Sexuality, Sexes, Cultural Polymorphism

The debate on youth often tackled questions dealing with sexuality and the sexes, even though the implications of what was found in the studies were little addressed. What is most striking is that women were often absent from the debate, or silent. This fact was recognized by everyone (in particular by Erikson, as mentioned earlier), but they considered it to go without saying, or to be insignificant. Even those who noted this absence mentioned it only in passing, insisting that the problem was mostly a boys' problem, either because it was on boys that the strongest pressures were being placed to maintain an American way of life, while motherhood was sufficient self-justification for girls, or because adolescent girls seemed less aware than did boys of the institutional pressures placed on them by school.[104] Friedenberg, who developed an analysis in which the theme of sexual repression occupied a place of central importance, considered that the marginal position of women in the culture and in American bureaucracies (where they were excluded from important functions) ensured them "greater subjectivity," greater freedom, and an image that was less threatening to society as a whole.

In reality, the crux of Friedenberg's analysis was the following diagnosis: it was the adult male's fear of homosexuality that placed boys at the heart of the problem, and this did not implicate girls. The stereotype of the teenager included many sexual elements, from tight jeans to provocative gestures and the practice of coitus interruptus with which teens were often associated. Adolescent sexuality awakened erotic conflicts within the adult world, which masked them beneath a show of concern. Added to the repression of desire was a fear of disorder and loss of control resulting from the growing democratization of relations between young people and adults, an envious view of youth resulting from a fear of aging and from the observation that young people were enjoying a sexual freedom far greater than anything their parents could ever have imagined, and a certain adult self-hatred that sprung from not having gotten what one wanted in one's youth. Recent research has confirmed that it was an era of particular hostility toward the expression of male homosexual desire, which can be seen in the different behavioral criteria applied to the two sexes in the fifties: while girls were permitted many physical manifestations of reciprocal affection (they could dance together, swap clothing, or dress alike), any physical contact other than during sports activities was forbidden among boys.[105]

Whether they ignored or highlighted the question of male homosexuality, many studies from the fifties gathered important data on the theme of the differentiation between the sexes—a theme that would come to light only later on—and the data are therefore particularly interesting from a retrospective point of view. Many of the findings showed that the female question was indeed at the center of the debate, whether it was a matter of the conflict between the sexes (for some, boys were disoriented by the aggression of girls) or, more generally, of the "feminization" of the image of the adolescent. This image was alleged to have developed slowly between the end of the century and the 1950s, resulting in the attribution to all youth of a vulnerability, a passivity, and an awkwardness previously reserved for girls.[106] Many of the most prestigious experts, from Riesman to Whyte, were in agreement that male and female roles had come closer together, especially among the middle classes, an idea that was considered self-evident by studies such as Coleman's.

James Coleman had nonetheless discovered that there was a notable difference between the behavior of boys and of girls: the former preferred sports and outdoor activities, while the latter preferred to stay at home with their friends, watch television, read, listen to records, and especially to organize activities in the countless clubs and associations that were at the heart of high school life in the fifties. Being "popular" in the eyes of the opposite sex was as important for girls as sports achievement was for boys, and since boys preferred active girls (cheerleaders) to "passive" girls (good students, well-behaved toward parents and teachers), the middle-class high school girl was "popular" only insofar as she reproduced the model of the adult American woman with all her outside activities, from the club to religious organizations or charities. While in the high schools attended by working-class children, good grades were considered to be more the purview of girls than boys, the higher a girl advanced on the social ladder, the more she refused to be categorized as a "good student"; this was true of even very intelligent girls, because it would be a strike against them in terms of their "popularity." Many hid their intellectual capacities, allowing less gifted students to achieve better grades.[107] Coleman's study was certainly quite revealing, even though it did not question the idea of a decreasing differentiation between male and female roles in the classes, whereas in reality a separation most certainly did exist in certain key areas, such as housework, which was reserved for women.

All participants in the debate, without necessarily sharing the Hechingers' horrified reaction, recognized that sexual behavior had undergone a profound mutation. Much discussion revolved around the new custom of "going steady," this promise of sexual fidelity among adolescents, and here too, Riesman's theses were invoked:[108] it was a need for affective security, but also the desire to combine responsibility and sex, that prompted American youths to seek stable relationships early on, and thus to marry earlier and earlier. In 1955 a Catholic journal deplored the fact that there were 1 million married teenagers, and blamed it on the practice of going steady. The age at which the first amorous relationships were formed was constantly decreasing: in the 1950s, middle-class girls began meeting boys at the end of junior high school: the first flirtations occurred in the form of group dates. These romantic gatherings included "petting" and "necking," practices considered to be perfectly respectable. This was not the case of certain other practices such as "heavy petting," which nonetheless allowed girls technically to remain virgins. It was in the 1920s and 1930s that the frequency of premarital sexual relations had begun to increase: in the 1953 Kinsey report, 50 percent of women respondents admitted to having engaged in them, even if unbeknownst to their family and community. All this showed that the sexual behavior of boys and girls had become more similar, resulting in a broader debate on sexual freedom within American society. Sex was exalted and commercialized by the mass media; "sex appeal" was presented as an ideal one could achieve through adequate efforts and codified techniques, while the topic of female frigidity was also frequently discussed (the fashion for large breasts and for "falsies," which were sold in large quantities, was only one of the more widespread concessions to "sex appeal").[109]

This underestimation and devaluation of women in the fifties has been contested by many autobiographical texts and by recent studies that also indicate the strong limits of the supposed liberalization of morals. Thus it has been shown that girl gangs existed, apart from male or coed gangs,[110] and, most important, that despite androgynous themes, this youth culture was in reality based on a strong opposition of the sexes. The female body was divided into parts of varying accessibility to a partner and was the subject of cold war–style negotiations. The condition of women was bound up in a profoundly contradictory system: in theory they had unlimited possibilities before them, but in reality the only truly legitimate outlet remained a future as wife and mother. The obligation to save appearances at all costs weighed not only on women: all adults had to be heterosexual, married, and happy about it. As Wini Breines has written, the true symbol of the times was ultimately Rock Hudson, whose virility made him an adolescent idol, but who was in fact homosexual, as the entire world learned upon his tragic death from AIDS in the 1980s. Significant, too, was the song by the Platters, *The Great Pretender*, which was very popular at the time, according to which pretending was the only way to explore new possibilities short of openly rebelling.[111]

The importance of sexuality in the fifties was also connected to its central place in the youth rebellion, within which it partly compensated for the sexual obsession at work in the repression of female behavior with its repercussions on the behavior of men. Sexuality became a symbol of authenticity, of reality, of the "real life" from which youths of both sexes felt excluded, imbued as they were with the oppressive feeling that their environment, and they themselves, were deprived of reality and consistency. For girls, especially, sexual freedom was a manner of expressing revolt, at the price of a contradiction in their process of identity formation. Male figures were exalted who were entirely improbable as husbands—James Dean, Marlon Brando, or the beatniks of Greenwich Village—and this despite their macho and sexist behavior inspired by "lower-class" virility and a rejection of white middle-class sexuality. Girls dreamed of being the ones to propose or embody other lifestyles, even if they ended up simply in the codified role of the "girlfriend." This was why personalities like Elvis and James Dean, with their androgynous features, were such a hit.[112]

Considerations of the differences between the sexes tended to reintroduce a sense of diversity in a debate previously devoted to "youth" as a uniform group. As we have said, some authors considered the debate itself, or rather the form it had taken, as a manifestation of a generational conflict. For Kett, the dominant ideas being discussed were too strongly ideological to truly reflect the social and psychic tendencies of the majority of youth: "Small groups of influential adults single out the experiences of small groups of young people and pronounce these experiences as archetypical, uniquely important, and harbingers of all future tendencies."[113]

The result of this state of affairs was that the basic feature of the condition of youth was forever, and increasingly, evading the analysis of experts: social perception never focused on this polymorphism of young society, which was, all in all, its most characteristic feature.

It is significant that certain more recent works by historians who use innovative categories and methodology, such as microhistory and categorization by sex, have highlighted precisely this polymorphous character. Graebner, Breines, and Doherty—each in his own way—have emphasized the multiplicity of youth cultures, their differentiation by sex, ethnic group, education, religion, social class, and neighborhood. The adolescents of the fifties were a highly diversified group, these authors insist, with contradictory tastes and values, and with violent internal conflicts. But polymorphism is something more than multiplicity: it is the willingness to adopt different representations, even those designated by one's own culture as irredeemably "other." It was no doubt this characteristic that allowed the youth of the fifties to break, or at least tend to break, the racial and sexual barriers, to choose idols who scandalized adults because they were "ambiguous," androgynous, with attitudes borrowed from blacks or the "lower classes." Most often, the break was below the surface, symbolic, or partial (but no less significant), born of an impulse to find another identity for oneself. Audre Lorde expressed this impulse in her "biomythography" of a young black lesbian living in New York in that era: "Gay girls were the only Black and white women who were even talking to each other in this country in the 1950s, outside of the empty rhetoric of patriotism and political movements."[114]

"Teenpics"

The American cinema of the fifties is also a source of primary importance for a history of youth. In about 1955, a type of cinematic production appeared that not only depicted adolescent heroes and their problems but also was specifically intended for teenagers. Before then, films were intended for all generations: going to the movies was a family ritual, which justified strict control over the morality of films. This "juvenilization" of the content of films and of their public, and the accompanying decline of the classic Hollywood production, made movies intended for viewing in theaters a medium increasingly geared toward youth, while the expansion of the suburbs increased the adult consumption of televised programs, and subsequently of videos. These films intended mainly for adolescents were called "teenpics" (an abbreviation of teenage pictures). Good filmographies and interesting interpretive hypotheses have already been produced on this phenomenon.[115] I will limit myself here to outlining certain characteristics of the films—useful for a future analysis of the image of youth and of its pertinence for a history of the debate on youth in the West in the last two centuries.

Unlike in fascist cinema, here the figure of the young hero was treated fully independently of that of the adult. The images proposed were highly diverse. *On the Waterfront* (1954), by Elia Kazan, presents a Marlon Brando who is clearly younger than the other members of the mob to which he and his older brother belong (everyone calls him the kid).[116] He is also the only one who finds the strength to revolt and denounce a murder to which he was an involuntary accomplice: he thereby runs the risk of being killed in turn, but he succeeds in shaking off the apathy of the other longshoremen being extorted by his mob. The scenario pairs him with Eva Marie

Saint, a blond, religious girl, accentuating the contrast with his dark hood-
lum looks (the only scene in which Brando wears a tie is the one in which
he must testify at the trial against his fellow mob members). When he tells
his life story to the girl (including his childhood in an orphanage and his
escape) she observes: "Maybe they didn't know how to handle you. That's
what makes people mean and difficult, people don't care enough about
them." These two youths stand out because of their beauty, but also
because the difference in their styles; as a couple, they perfectly embody
the adolescent desire mentioned in the preceding section. The boy is wild
and insolent, but deep down he is good, and if he attacks the established
order and its injustice, it's thanks to the love of the young girl. The role
of the girl—along with that of the priest—is in fact crucial in bringing
about this conversion in Brando, who is caught up with his group of
delinquents and alienated from the great American values: sincerity, courage, individualism.

East of Eden (1955) opens with images of Monterey, California, in
1917, the period being revealed by the architecture of the homes and the
dress of the passersby. Ladies are wearing dark colors, dresses down to
their ankles, and hats; men are wearing jackets, with ties and vests; and
suddenly Cal (James Dean) appears in white jeans, a light-colored sports
shirt and a beige sweater: his dress is exactly that of a teenager in 1955,
the year when Elia Kazan shot the film, adapted from a novel by John
Steinbeck. The heroine (Julie Harris), the girlfriend of the hero's brother,
is dressed in a hybrid fashion, generally following the silhouette of the
fifties—a wide, long skirt, a tight waist emphasizing her bust. The difference between the two characters, thus presented, will be developed in the
course of the film, which effects a distinct division between the good and
the bad in the social sense: the former are incarnated by the "too pure"
father and Cal's brother, the latter by Cal himself and his mother, who
couldn't stand her cloistered life with a husband "who wanted to keep her
all to himself," and abandoned him for the lucrative position of madam in
a brothel. It is she whom Cal, the bad son, resembles; his father reproaches
him for "not being interested in anything," and he rejects the paternal
credo, "You can make of yourself anything you want." The girl mediates

between the good and the bad with the explanation she gives for the origin of evil: "It's awful not to be loved. It's the worst thing in the world. Makes you mean, violent, and cruel." In fact, Cal's entrepreneurial spirit proves better than those of his father and brother, but they refuse to praise him; to get revenge, he informs them of the mother's new profession. The news destroys the father; the brother decides to join the American troops fighting in France.

All this naturally helped the teenagers of 1955 to identify with Cal, and with the girl, who understands him and dares to transgress social codes and fall in love with him. The entire story is treated in a somewhat exaggerated fashion (especially the figure of the mother, if one thinks of the fifties), but the tragic climate of the film expresses the dark and unspoken anxieties of the decade. On September 30, 1955, James Dean died in a car crash, at the wheel of his Porsche, on a California road. He was twenty-four years old. For many car-crazed adolescent speed demons, this accident and death bore the seal of their difference: breaking the rules of the road, whether seriously or not, was high on the list of illegal acts of which young delinquents were guilty.

Another film with James Dean, *Rebel without a Cause* by Nicholas Ray, which came out shortly before his death, would participate in the debate on juvenile delinquency in its own way by showing that these deviant behaviors were due in reality to the suffering of children faced with parents who were weak, incompetent, or lacking in affection. Forced to accept the rules and rituals of a society that, in their eyes, reflected only the laws of the jungle, adolescents reacted by forming small groups founded on a demand for total loyalty. Their difference was manifested in behaviors expressing despair, disgust, and apathy, as we see in the first scene of the film, in which the young protagonists meet, at night, at the police station: one (James Dean) is drunk, he sneers, totters, pounds on the desk; the other (Sal Mineo), who is less white-skinned, remains obstinately silent and trembles from the cold (to the point that Dean offers him his jacket). On learning that his parents are separated, the policeman asks in a serious tone if the boy ever talked to a psychiatrist; meanwhile the girl (Natalie Wood) tearfully explains that her father doesn't love her, which is perhaps why she is the girlfriend of the gang leader who steals cars and demolishes them in the course of dangerous competitions. Even the images accompanying the titles (Dean playing with a cymbal-crashing windup bear, setting it next to himself before going to sleep curled up in a fetal position) are allusions to the childish nature of the hero and to the vain automatism of society. The behavior of the young heroes throws this society violently into question. The motives for revolt may very well be benign, connected as they are to the "American way of life" of those years (the absence of the Mineo character's mother on his birthday, the girl being forbidden to wear lipstick), but the dialogue accuses the society as a whole: "If I had one day when I didn't have to be all confused, and I didn't have to feel that I was ashamed of everything, if I felt that I belonged someplace," declares Dean, who adds, speaking of his family, "How can a guy grow up in a circus like that?" The heroine, for her part, says that life "is crushing in on me," but he comforts her: "We're not going to be alone anymore, ever, ever." The tragedy is sealed with the death of one of the three adolescents, due to a police error (the boy was armed but the pistol wasn't loaded). After this the father of Dean's character promises his son that he'll be "strong," like his son always wanted; his mother, until then aggressive and domineering, takes on a more gentle tone; and Dean makes his relationship with the heroine official by telling his parents, without giving them a chance to respond: "This is Judy, she's my girlfriend." The entire society has been reminded of its values by the adolescents, who impose their own rules: affection, respect, independence, and the right to "go steady."

The regenerative task is entrusted to young males, backed up by devoted female characters who are equally significant, though fewer in number and, especially, less central to the story. When they appear, everything that is different about the image of the adolescent forged by 1950s American culture becomes immediately apparent. In *Picnic* (1955) by Joshua Logan, a frustrated and irritable mother pins all her hopes on her eldest daughter (Kim Novak), who is nineteen years old and brimming with youth and beauty in the measurable sense of the time (waist, hips, breasts), but not with intelligence or personality. The mother places great stock in her daughter's being voted beauty queen during their town's festival, but especially in a possible marriage with the son of the local magnate. The questions she asks her daughter are heavy with hope: "Does he ever want to go beyond kissing?" But all her hopes will be dashed by her daughter's choice: a pleasant but unemployed young man (William Holden), who embodies the old American ideal of the drifter with a big heart. The young heroine, provocative but bland,[117] who may have represented the dream of more than one teenager, rejects the social promotion through marriage that her mother wanted and prefers to go off with the drifter. Her decision, in the climate of the time, certainly marked a very strong break.

Far more subtle is the sexuality of *Baby Doll* (1956), by Elia Kazan, an adaptation of a work by Tennessee Williams. Baby Doll (Caroll Baker) is seventeen (the number of charms on her bracelet), but she is already married to a not-very-attractive man (played by Karl Malden), who promised his father-in-law that he would wait until she turned eighteen to consummate the marriage. The situation is already spicy in and of itself when a neighbor of Sicilian origin (Eli Wallach) enters the picture, with whom Baby Doll begins playing games; they chase each other, laughing, throughout the big dilapidated house, from which most of the furniture has been seized by creditors. We are in the South, amid real fires provoked by jealousy, and the symbolic conflagration of meaning. Baby Doll wears the practical yet sexy type of pajama that would later bear her name. The triumphant eroticism of the film is made up of allusions, malice, little complicitous games—it's an eroticism connected to laughter, an eroticism of "expectation and ellipsis."[118] The openly childish heroine (her husband secretly watches her suck her thumb in an old crib) represents both innocence and sin; she expresses so well the adult fascination with adolescents that the film provoked a scandal equal to that of Nabokov's *Lolita* and the indignation of Cardinal Spellman upon his return from a trip to Korea. *Baby Doll* took the other side of the virtuous debate on the "immaturity" of girls and portrayed a typical figure of the male erotic imagination in all its ambiguity. Once again the adolescent girl appears as a grave threat to the social and psychic order. The roles attributed to girls in these films are therefore always centered around sexuality; the characters are not accorded full awareness of this but rather a kind of secret capacity to forge their path amid many dangers. No prospect for autonomous action is proposed for the heroines other than a conjugal relationship with the opposite sex.

These films were still addressed to a multigenerational public, even if the heroes were young rebels and the films contained messages laden with meaning for teenagers and those who dealt with them. In addition to these films, there existed another very important genre destined exclusively for adolescents, and which many adults considered both horrifying and incomprehensible. The first of the major successes that excluded adults was *Rock around the Clock;* it was deliberately conceived solely for the adolescent market, and caused a great deal of agitation, even in England. The screenings of such a film in downtown theaters lent a kind of legitimacy to adolescent culture, and they were occasions for young audiences to publicly show their existence, their identity, and their solidarity.[119]

Record and movie combinations also favored the success of films based on famous songs, such as those by Pat Boone and Elvis Presley. From the perspective of imagery, Presley was the more important of the two (Boone was such a perfect personification of the "good boy" that he refused to kiss on screen), though the great variety of symbolic figures proposed to youth was significant, insofar as the same audiences could love personalities as different as James Dean, Pat Boone, and Elvis Presley. The type of rebellion incarnated by Elvis was less complex than that of James Dean but was deeply rooted in the American imagination nonetheless, as demonstrated by the persistence of the Elvis cult. A troubled gaze through often half-shut eyelids, sensual, disdainful lips, swaying pelvis: the symbolism was sexual, but combined with an attitude of defiance toward the established order and the world of culture, at least until 1958. In *Jailhouse Rock* (1957) Presley gets out of prison, where he discovered his talent for singing, and is amusing himself by scandalizing the parents of the girl who helps him make his first record (and who loves him). Not only does he start off by informing them of his ex-con status, but he also reacts violently to their comments about Dave Brubeck, Lennie Tristano, and other jazz figures. When courteously asked for his opinion, Elvis responds curtly:

"Lady, I don't know that the hell you talkin' about," refusing all "culture," anything outside of what is sanctioned by the market. Beginning in 1958, Presley would become mainly a performer, but before then, he carried a message of autonomy that went something like: "I am what I am and I only bend to the laws of the market, because they serve me."

Metaphysics of Youth

"Youth is in the central position from which novelty is born," wrote Walter Benjamin in 1914, adding "we have recently witnessed the arrival of a generation that claims to find itself at the crossroads, but this intersection doesn't exist."[120] Today we might add that one of the phases of the metaphysics of youth, in which Benjamin was immersed, is now over. "The teenager is dead," declared the expert Dick Hebdige, because the image of the teenager had lost its weight both in the imagination and on the consumer market; other more seductive images have replaced it, such as that of the child between the ages of six and nine.[121] There is no youth at the crossroads, nor, for that matter, is there a crossroads, as Benjamin had guessed, and the central position of which he spoke has also grown volatile. Novelty seems to be heading off into a distant future, or sinking into unknown aspects of society, or dispersing in a diaspora of immigrants and cultures.

We can thus rightfully attempt to write a history of the metaphysics of youth, and after having relieved youth of its baggage, write a history of the condition of youth. It would in fact be more correct to speak of the conditions of youth, in the plural; its multiplicity must be taken into account, along with its polymorphism, as recent studies on American adolescents have clearly emphasized. To undertake such a study is perhaps also to partake of a broader process by which society, reclaiming the images it initially projected onto youth, succeeds in developing a self-reflective image of itself, or at least in critiquing its overly facile illusions of regeneration and its desires for and fears of apocalypse.

It would also be interesting to analyze the continuities and ruptures in the history of the metaphysics of youth. While this essay has not reached the appropriate stage, some directions for research can nonetheless be indicated. One would be the exploration of the historical antecedents of the two debates analyzed here; another would look at the relationship of continuity and rupture between the theme of youth culture in the fifties and the political development of the student movements in the second half of the sixties;[122] a third might be a comparative analysis of the value of the various debates according to their sociocultural context, in various countries and at various periods.

NOTES

CONTRIBUTORS

INDEX

NOTES

2 THE MILITARY EXPERIENCE

1. Gabriele d'Annunzio, *Per la più grande Italia: Orazioni e messagi* (Milan, 1915), p. 68; Giovanni Pascoli, *La grande proletaria si è mossa*, November 21, 1911; F. Tomaso Marinetti, "Guerra sola igiene del mondo," in L. De Maria, ed., *Teoria e invenzione futurista* (Milan, 1968), pp. 269–289. On bellicist discourse, see Mario Isnenghi, *Le guerre delgi Italiani: Parole, imagini, ricordi, 1858–1945* (Milan, 1989), pp. 32, 205, 220.

2. Ezra Pound, "Hugh Selwin Mauberley" [1920].

3. See Antonio Gibelli, *L'officina della guerra: La Grande Guerra e le trasformazioni del mondo mentale* (Turin, 1991), chapter 2.

4. See Alessandro D'Ancona, "Poesia e musica populare italiana del nostro secolo," in *L'illustrazione italiana* (1882), nos. 12–13; Roberto Leydi, *Canti sociali italiani*, pp. 399–401, 404–407, quoted in Gianni Oliva, *Esercito, paese e movimento operaio: Militarismo e antimilitarismo in Italia dal 1861 all'età giolittiana* (Milan, 1986), p. 54.

5. See Geoffrey Parker, "Il soldato," in Rosario Villari, ed., *L'uomo barocco* (Bari, 1991).

6. See André Corvisier, "Problèmes de recrutement des armées du XIVe au XVIIe siècle," in *Gli aspetti economici della guerra in Europa (sec. XVI–XVIII)* (Prato: Fondazione Datini, 1984).

7. See Michael Howard, *War in European History* (Oxford, 1976).

8. See John Childs, *Armies and Warfare in Europe* (New York, 1982); A. Corvisier, *Armées et sociétés en Europe de 1949 à 1789* (Paris, 1976).

9. See Corvisier, *Armées et sociétés;* N. Brancaccio, *L'esercito del vecchio Piemonte: Gli ordinamenti* (Rome, 1923); Gordon A. Craig, *The Politics of the Prussian Army, 1640–1945* (Oxford, 1955).

10. See Jean-Paul Bertaud and Daniel Reichel, eds., *Atlas de la Révolution française: L'armée et la guerre* (Paris, 1989); Alan Forrest, "La formation des attitudes

villageoises envers le service militaire: 1792–1814," in Paul Viallaneix and Jean Ehrard, eds., *La bataille, l'armée, la gloire, 1745–1781* vol. 1 (Clermont-Ferrand, 1985).

11. See Richard B. Challener, *The French Theory of the Nation in Arms, 1866–1939* (New York, 1965).

12. See Jules Mauri, "Les progrès vers l'égalité des citoyens devant le service militaire dans le loi de recrutement (1871–1914)," in *L'armée et la société de 1610 à nos jours*, Acts of the 103rd Congrès national des sociétés savantes (Nancy and Metz, 1978).

13. See Gooch, *Armies in Europe* (London, 1980).

14. Quoted in Gaetano Bonetta, *Corpo e nazione: L'educazione ginnastica, igienica e sessuale nell'Italia liberale* (Milan, 1990), p. 84.

15. See Howard, *War in European History*, chapter 6.

16. See Yves Charbit and André Béjin, "La pensée démographique," in Jacques Dupâquier, ed., *Histoire de la population française*, vol. 3 (Paris, 1988).

17. Charbit and Béjin, "La pensée démographique."

18. Geoffrey Parker, *The Army of Flanders and the Spanish Road, 1567–1659* (Cambridge, 1972), pp. 36–37; A. Corvisier, *L'armée française de la fin du dix-septième siècle au ministère de Choiseul: Le soldat* (Paris, 1964), pp. 615–637; S. Loriga, *Soldati: L'istituzione militare nel Piemonte del Settecento* (Venice, 1992), chapter 5; Fred Anderson, *A People's Army: Massachusetts Soldiers and Society in the Seven Years War* (Chapel Hill, 1984), p. 231.

19. A. Corvisier, "La société militaire et l'enfant," in *Annales de démographie historique* 1973: 327–343. For the medieval period, see Philippe Contamine, *Guerre, armée et société à la fin du Moyen-Age* (Paris, 1972), p. 27.

20. See Loriga, *Soldati*, chapter 2.

21. See, notably, Michael Mitterauer, *Sozialgeschichte der Jugend* (Frankfurt am Main, 1986), who considers that at the time, biological maturity was reached at a later age: growth in height continued until the age of twenty-six and that of the musculature until twenty-eight.

22. See Loriga, *Soldati*, chapter 5.

23. Marquis de Sade, *Oeuvres complètes*, vol. 4 (Paris, 1973), p. 283, quoted G. Festa, "Sade et la guerre," in Viallaneix and Ehrard, eds., *La bataille, l'armée*.

24. Keith Thomas, *Age and Authority in Early Modern England*, Raleigh Lecture on History, Proceedings of the British Academy, vol. 62 (London, 1976), pp. 19–25.

25. See Corvisier, "La société militaire et l'enfant."

26. The introduction of obligatory conscription was accompanied by the fixing of a maximum age limit (in general, twenty-five).

27. Still today, the enlistment of children is practiced by the armies of certain countries, such as Nicaragua, Iraq and Romania, where, after the fall of Ceauşescu, the army adopted hundreds of children ages six to thirteen, pre-

viously recruited by the dictator's secret police, which had taken them from orphanages. See Claudio Fava, "In divisa a sette anni: E' questa la nuova Romania," *L'Europeo,* May 3, 1991; Covisier, "La société militaire et l'enfant," pp. 333–337.

28. See Corvisier, "La société militaire et l'enfant."

29. See Barton C. Hacker, "Women and Military Institutions in Early Modern Europe: A Reconnaissance," *Signs* 4 (1981); Parker, *The Army of Flanders,* pp. 81–93; Corvisier, *L'armée française,* p. 760.

30. This drama by Mercier, published in 1770 and presented at the court and at the Théâtre-Italien (on June 25, 1782), tells the story of a soldier, Durimel, who explains his desertion as follows: "I had fallen under a colonel, the hardest, most inflexible of men, whose pleasure was to crush all his subordinates with his authority"; he is condemned to death, "for there were twenty-seven desertions in three days." The story was so distressing that Marie-Antoinette asked for the ending to be changed. On Mercier, see Anne Boës, "Les militaires dans le théâtre français, 1746–1789," in Vaillaneix and Ehrard, eds., *La bataille, l'armée,* vol. 1. Regarding women disguised as soldiers, see R. M. Dekker, *The Tradition of Female Transvestitism in Early Modern Europe* (New York, 1989); one may also refer to Léon Hennet, *Une femme, soldat: Rose Barreau, de Semalens (Tarn), volontaire de la République en 1793* (Albi, 1908).

31. Corvisier, *L'armée française. . . ,* pp. 757–772.

32. Ibid., p. 761.

33. See Robert Laulan, "Un philanthrope militaire, le brigadier-général Merlet et la création des écoles d'enfants de troupe," *83ᵉ Congrès des Sociétés Savantes* (Aix and Marseille, 1958), pp. 171–180; Loriga, *Soldati,* chapter two. The idea of militarizing the institutions for orphans and abandoned children would be revived under Napoleon. See Franco Della Peruta, *Esercito e società nell'Italia napoleonica* (Milan, 1988), pp. 147–150.

34. See Corvisier, *L'armée française,* p. 761.

35. Stendhal, *The Life of Henry Boulard,* chapter 12.

36. Ugo Foscolo, *Prose politiche e apologetiche, 1817–1827* (Florence, 1964), part 2, p. 111.

37. S. Begué, "Le régiment des pupilles de la Garde, 1812–1814," *97ᵉ Congrès des Sociétés Savantes* (Nantes, 1972); G. Merlier, "Les bataillons scolaires en Haute-Normandie et dans l'académie de Rennes, 1882–1890," *97ᵉ Congrès des Sociétés Savantes* (Nantes, 1972). In 1885, there were 12,000 children in the battalions of the department of the Seine, 6,165 in that of the North, 2,288 in Charente-Inférieure, and 1685 in Seine-Inférieure; see Y. Joselau, *Le rôle de l'armée dans l'évolution de l'enseignement des activités physiques en France (de 1850 à 1914)* (Mémoire ENSEPS, 1972), p. 25, quoted in Maurice Crubellier, *L'enfance et la jeunesse dans la société française, 1800–1950* (Paris, 1979), chapter 9.

38. "With an outmoded concept, incompetent personnel, and an ignorance of the mentality of children, the battalions made many mistakes; their failure would favor the development of a liberal reaction rejecting all exercises that resembled military exercises" commented René Meunier in 1892. See Crubellier, *L'enfance et la jeunesse,* chapter 9.

39. Bonetta, *Corpo e nazione,* p. 189.

40. See Hacker, *Women and Military Institutions.* But during the course of the Second World War, the U.S. Army included 140,000 women (including 4,000 black women); see Charity Adams Early, *One Woman's Army: A Black Officer Remembers the WAC* (College Station, Texas, 1989). On the presence of women in the U.S. Army after Vietnam (where there were volunteers only), see the commentary of Furio Colombo, "Povero è il soldato," *La Stampa,* December 12, 1990.

41. See J.-P. Bertrand's contribution to the International Colloquium of Clermont-Ferrand, the acts of which are published in Viallaneix and Ehrard, eds., *La bataille, l'armée;* Jean Waquet, "La société civile devant l'insoumission et la désertion à l'époque de la conscription militaire," in *Bibliothèque de l'Ecole des Chartres* 126 (1968): 191.

42. See Loriga, *Soldati,* chapter 5.

43. See Alan Forrest, *Déserteurs et insoumis sous la Révolution et l'Empire* (Paris, 1988), chapter 3.

44. See Isser Woloch, "Le barreau devant la conscription napoléonienne," in Viallaneix and Ehrard, eds., *La bataille, l'armée.*

45. See Forrest, *Déserteurs et insoumis,* chapter 3.

46. See Jean Vidalenc, "Les conséquences sociales de la conscription en France, 1798–1848," in *Cahiers internationaux d'histoire économique et sociale* 5 (1975).

47. See Bernard Schnapper, *Le remplacement militaire en France* (Paris, 1968); Forest, *Déserteurs et insoumis,* chapter 3.

48. See Della Peruta, *Esercito e società,* pp. 88–91.

49. See Forrest, *Déserteurs et insoumis,* chapter 3.

50. See Oliva, *Esercito, paese,* pp. 41–43.

51. See Della Peruta, *Esercito e società,* pp. 88–91.

52. See I. Woloch, "Napoleonic Conscription: State Power and Civil Society," *Past and Present* 1986: 11.

53. See Forrest, *Déserteurs et insoumis,* chapter 5.

54. E. J. Hobsbawm, *Bandits* (London, 1969), pp. 27–28, has observed that after 1860, many bandit leaders in southern Italy were deserters or former soldiers in the army of the Bourbon king.

55. See Piero Del Nego, *Esercito, stato, società* (Bologna, 1979), p. 174 ff. Oliva, *Esercito, paese,* p. 18 ff.

56. In Naples, the rate was 57.2 percent; in Catania 45.6 percent; in Palermo 44.4

percent; in Trapani 41.3 percent; in Urbino 40.5 percent. At the same time, the phenomenon was far less pronounced in the provinces, where obligatory conscription had already been in practice for some time, such as in Sardinia, where it dated from 1848, and where the rate of those who failed to join was only 3.4 percent. See Oliva, *Esercito, paese*, p. 18.

57. See Aldo De Jaco, ed., *Il brigantaggio meridionale: Cronaca inedita dell'Unità d'Italia* (Rome, 1969), pp. 50–51.

58. See G. Rochat and G. Massobrio, *Breve storia dell'esercito italiano dal 1861 al 1943* (Turin, 1978), pp. 51–52.

59. This occurred in conjunction with the sharp increase in immigration from the south: thus Turin, which in 1863 had a fairly low rate of absenteeism (that of Piedmont was 1.1 percent) saw dodging increase to 10 percent.

60. See Corvisier, *L'armée française*, p. 449 ff.; Jean Ruwet, *Soldats des régiments nationaux au XVIIIe siècle* (Brussels, 1962); Loriga, *Soldati*, chapter 5.

61. See Anderson, *A People's Army*, p. 53.

62. See John R. Gillis, *Youth and History: Tradition and Change in European Age Relations 1770–Present* (London, 1974), p. 5; Alan Macfarlane, *The Family Life of Ralph Josselin* (Cambridge, 1970), p. 209.

63. See, for example, R. S. Schofield, "Age-Specific Mobility in an Eighteenth-Century Rural English Parish," *Annales de démographie historique* 1970: 261–274; Paul A. Slack, "Vagrants and Vagrancy in England, 1598–1664," *Economic Historical Review* 27 (1974): 365–366; A. L. Beier, "Vagrants and the Social Order in Elizabethan England," *Past and Present* 64 (1974): 9–10; Olwen Hufton, *The Poor of Eighteenth-Century France, 1750–1789* (Oxford, 1974); Douglas Lamar Jones, "The Strolling Poor: Transiency in Eighteenth-Century Massachusetts," *Journal of Social History* 7 (1974): 28.

64. See K. Thomas, *Age and Authority*, pp. 14–15; on the disparity between work and emancipation, see also Michael Anderson, *Family Structure in Nineteenth-Century Lancashire* (Cambridge, 1972), pp. 35–36.

65. See Natalie Zemon Davis, *The Return of Martin Guerre* (Cambridge: Harvard University Press, 1983), chapter 2.

66. See Jules Maurin, *Armée-guerre-société: Soldats languedociens (1889–1919)* (Paris, 1982), pp. 224–35.

67. See Crubellier, *L'enfance et la jeunesse*, p. 131.

68. See Gillis, *Youth and History*, pp. 55–57, 125; on the patriarchal nature of the work relationships in factories, see M. Anderson, *Family Structure*, pp. 115–119.

69. See Gillis, *Youth and History*, p. 118.

70. John Springhall, *Coming of Age: Adolescence in Britain 1860–1960* (Dublin, 1986), noted sixty books and ninety-three articles on the question of children and adolescents at work.

71. See Bonetta, *Corpo e nazione*, pp. 175–176, 116. In Italy, between 1862 and 1865,

the percentage of rejections for health reasons fluctuated between 23 and 28 percent of the conscripts, which represented more than 40 percent of those who underwent a medical examination. The rate of exemption for health reasons may also have been very high in France: according to Gustave Vallée *(Compte générale de la conscription de A.-A. Hargenvilliers* [Paris, 1936], chapters 3 and 6), the rate was 35 percent between 1801 and 1806.

72. F. Cortese, *Malattie ed imperfezioni che incagliano al conscrizione militare nel regno d'Italia: Mezzi e provevedimenti atti a prevenirle* (Milan, 1866), quoted in Bonetta, *Corpo e nazione,* p. 246. On the physical condition of recruits, see J.-P. Aron, P. Dumont, and E. Le Roy Ladurie, *Anthropologie du conscrit d'après les comptes numériques et sommaires du recrutement de l'armée, 1819–1926* (Paris, 1972); R. Livi, *Antropemetria militare* (Rome, 1896).

73. See François Furet and Jacques Ozouf, *Lire et écrire: L'alphabétisation des Français de Calvin à Jules Ferry,* vol. 1 (Paris, 1977), pp. 81, 205–302; see also Alain Corbin, "Pour une étude sociologique de la croissance de l'alphabétisation au XIXe siècle: L'instruction des conscrits du Cher et de l'Eure-et-Loir (1833–1883)," *Revue d'histoire économique et sociale* 1975: 99–120.

74. According to Camillo Corradini ("Il compito dell'esercito nella lotta contro l'analfabetismo," *Nuova antologia* 212 [March 1897]: 305 ff.), this reduction was due to the abolition of certain sanctions (such as that of delaying the release of conscripts who failed the reading exam) and to the decree of May 3, 1892, that delegated the task of organizing the literacy courses to the local commanders, which in practice rendered the course optional.

75. See G. Oliva, *Esercito, paese,* pp. 63–66.

76. D. Porch, "The French Army and the Spirit of the Offensive, 1900–1914," in B. Bond and I. Roy, eds., *War and Society* (London, 1975); see also W. Serman, *Les officiers français dans la nation, 1848–1914* (Paris, 1982).

77. See N. Marselli, *Gli avvenimenti del 1870–1871* (Turin, 1873), p. 142, quoted in Filippo Mazzonis, "L'esercito italiano al tempo di Garibaldi," in Filippo Mazzonis, ed., *Garibaldi condottiero: Storia, teoria, prassi* (Milan, 1984), pp. 187–251.

78. Andrea Borella, *Gazetta del popolo,* December 11, 1860, quoted in Oliva, *Esercito, paese,* p. 15.

79. Recruitment was regional in Prussia, and, beginning in 1873, in France. According to Jules Maurin *(op. cit.,* pp. 207–215, 307–308, 316–318), almost 10 percent of soldiers (mainly those who had been lacking in discipline) were sent outside of the mother county, most often to Africa, but also, in 1900, to China (against the Boxers) and in 1898–1899 to Crete to protect the Christian populations revolting against the Ottomans.

80. See Tullio de Mauro, *Storia linguistica dell'Italia unita* (Bari, 1991), chapter 3.

81. See Oliva, *Esercito, paese,* p. 32.

82. John R. Gillis (*Youth and History,* pp. 98, 101) insists on the limited autonomy of middle-class boys between fourteen and eighteen.

83. See E. J. Leeds, *No Man's Land: Combat and Identity in World War I* (Cambridge, 1979), chapter 1.

84. See O. Reshef, *Guerre, mythe et caricature: Au berceau d'une mentalité française* (Paris, 1984), chapter 6. On the patriotism of schoolbooks, see also Mona Ozouf, "Le thème du patriotisme dans les manuels primaires," *Le mouvements social* 49 (1964), and A. Prost, *Histoire de l'enseignement en France (1800–1967)* (Paris, 1968), pp. 335–340.

85. See Christian Amalvi, *Les héros de l'histoire de France, recherche iconographique sur le Panthéon scolaire de la Troisième République* (Paris, 1979).

86. See Bonetta, *Corpo e nazione,* p. 77. On physical exercise, see Stefano Jacomuzzi, "Gli sport," *Storia d'Italia,* vol. 5, *I documenti* (Turin, 1973), pp. 911–935; M. Spivak, "Contribution à l'histoire du nationalisme français: Gymnastique, exercices militaires et sports, de 1870 à 1914," *Bulletin de la société d'histoire moderne* 3 (1978): 24–31; S. Giuntini, *Sport scuola caserma dal Risorgimento al primo conflitto mondiale* (Padua, 1988); Eugen Weber, "Gymnastics and Sports in Fin-de-Siècle France: Opium of the Classes," *American Historical Review,* February 1971: 70–98; Jacques Thibault, *Les aventures du corps dans la pédagogie française* (Paris, 1977).

87. John R. Gillis (*Youth and History,* p. 95 ff.), recalls the extraordinary savagery with which "Mafeking night" was celebrated in London on May 18, 1900, and the attacks against the pacifist demonstrations in favor of the Boers.

88. Geoffrey Best, "Militarism and the Victorian Public School," in B. Simon and I. Bradley, eds., *The Victorian Public School* (London, 1975); John Springhall, *Youth, Empire and Society: British Youth Movements, 1883–1939* (London, 1977), p. 40; J. H. Grainger, *Patriotism: Britain 1900–1939* (London, 1986); Marie-Louise Christadler, "Kriegserziehung in Jugendbuch: Literarische Mobilmachung in Frankreich und Deutschland vor 1914," diss., Frankfurt am Main, 1977. In Christadler's study of books prior to 1914, she observes that in the vast majority of cases, the volunteers came from the more educated classes of the population. See also Alberto M. Ghisalberti, *Ricordi di uno storico allora studente in grigioverde (guerra 1915–1918)* (Rome, 1981); Rémi Fabre, "Un groupe d'étudiants protestants en 1914–1918," *Movement social* 122 (1983): 75–101.

89. See George L. Mosse, *Sessualità et nazionalismo: Mentalità borghese e rispettabilità* (Bari, 1982).

90. Gaetano Filangieri, *La scienza della legislazione* (Milan, 1786), book 4, part 1, p. 51.

91. Mosse, *Sessualità et nazionalismo.*

92. Reshef, *Guerre, mythe et caricature,* chapter 6.

93. Bonetta, *Corpo e nazione*, p. 91.

94. G. L. Mosse, "Introduction," in *Sessualità e nazionalismo*.

95. Bonetta, *Corpo e nazione*, p. 91.

96. Crubellier, *L'enfance et la jeunnesse*, chapter 9.

97. Bonetta, *Corpo e nazione*, p. 84.

98. Quoted in Reshef, *Guerre, mythe et caricature*.

99. Quoted in Mosse, *Sessualità e nazionalismo*, chapters 2 and 5.

100. The first monuments to the dead were erected at the end of the seventeenth century (the Hessendenkmal, erected by the Prussians in Frankfurt in 1793) but the custom did not spread until the second half of the nineteenth century. See June Hargrove, "Les monuments au tribut de la gloire," in Viallaneix and Ehrard, eds., *La bataille, l'armée*.

101. See Reshef, *Guerre, mythe et caricature*, chapter 6.

102. See David Cannadine, "War and Death, Grief and Mourning in Modern Britain," in Joachim Whaley, ed., *Mirrors of Mortality: Studies in the Social History of Death* (London, 1981).

103. R. Keastenbaum, "Time and Death in Adolescence," in H. Feifel, ed., *The Meaning of Death* (London, 1959), pp. 104–109.

104. Quoted in Cannadine, "War and Death"; see also Jean-Jacques Becker, "1914, la guerre inattendue?" in Viallaneix and Erhard, eds., *La bataille, l'armée*.

105. Harold Macmillan, *Winds of Change, 1914–1939* (London, 1966), p. 59.

106. See Keith Robbins, *The First World War* (Oxford, 1984), chapter 6.

107. See Robert Wohl, *The Generation of 1914* (London, 1980).

108. See, for example, Michel Bozon, *Les conscrits* (Paris, 1981), p. 119; Louis Pinto, "L'armée, le contingent et les classes sociales," *Actes de la recherche en sciences sociales* 3 (May 1975).

3 "DOING YOUTH" IN THE VILLAGE

1. On youth as a group, the best study is by Nicole Pellegrin, *Les bachelleries. Organisations et fêtes dans le Centre-Ouest, XVᵉ–XVIIIᵉ siècles*, Mémoires de la Société des Antiquaires de l'Ouest, 4th series, vol. 16 [1979–1982], (Poitiers, 1982). John R. Gillis, *Youth and History* (New York: Academic Press), 1974, provides an overview of the forms of the institution in preindustrial Europe (chapter 1); the same is true of Michael Mitterauer, *Sozialgeschichte der Jugend*, (Frankfurt am Main: Suhrkamp Verlag, 1986). The fact remains that despite the absence of a recognized organization and of a clear hierarchy, youth is a distinct, socially active age group; this problem was raised by Maurice Agulhon in *Pénitents et Francs-maçons de l'ancienne Provence* (Paris: Fayard, 1968), chapter 2. In the case we are taking as our point of departure, the hierarchy, with an

abbé or *capitaine de jeunesse*, attested in southern France in some places until the twentieth century (mainly in Provence), has disappeared; what remains are the terms *Junessa*, and *Jovent*, which designate an age, a sphere of intervention, and a style of behavior. On youth from the point of view of young girls, see Yvonne Verdier, *Façons de dire, façons de faire* (Paris: Gallimard, 1979), part 2, "La couturière."

2. The map was compiled by Gilliéron and Edmont in *L'Atlas linguistique de la France*. It is reprinted by Albert Dauzat in *Le Village et le Paysan de France* (Paris: Gallimard, 1943), p. 153, and by Henri Mendras in *Sociétés paysannes* (Paris: Armand Colin), 1976.

3. The *reinage* is a form of organization that has been analyzed in Robert-Henri Bautier, *Une institution religieuse du centre de la France: Les reinages* (Guéret, 1945); in L. Lamarche, "Reinages dromois," *Bulletin de la société d'archéologie et de statistique de la Drôme* 74, no. 330 (1958): 105–118; by J. P. Gutton, "Reinages, abbayes de jeunesse et confréries dans les villages de l'Ancienne France," *Cahiers d'histoire* 1975, no. 1. Emmanuel Le Roy Ladurie demonstrated their role in a particular case: *Le carnaval de Romans* (Paris: Gallimard, 1979), see in particular chapter 11.

4. *Les Propos rustiques* by Noël du Fail (1st ed., Lyons: Jean de Tournes, 1547) evokes in detail the *"jours festés"*; with *Contes et discours d'Eutrapel*, the same author (1st ed., Rennes, 1585) offers us a very lively picture of the behavior of young people in the early sixteenth century in the region of Rennes.

5. On the rites of youth becoming rites of obedience to the local lord, see Pellegrin, *Les bachelleries*, pp. 121–140. In the hamlets of the Montagne Noire—such as Revel—in the eighteenth century, youth was divided into three ranks, according to social standing.

6. This sampling of the forests was emphasized and commented on by Yvonne Verdier, "La forêt des contes," in *Coutume et destin* (Paris, 1995), pp. 209–222.

7. A kind of *"bal"* even more laden with greenery existed until the 1950s on the border of Languedoc and Catalonia; see Daniel Fabre, "Le sauvage en personne," *Terrain*, no. 6, "Les hommes et le milieu naturel," pp. 6–18.

8. *Tustet* comes from the *langue d'oc* word *tustat*, to hit, to strike; we are also familiar with the term *carillon*, which is very common in the legal documents of the eighteenth century, and the term *martelet*, which is more Mediterranean (see Catherine Robert and Michel Valière, "'Lo martelet,' un charivari occitan à Lespignan (Hérault)," in Jacques Le Goff and Jean-Claude Schmitt, eds., *Le charivari* (Paris: Editions de l'Ecole des Hautes Etudes en Sciences Sociales–Mouton, 1981), pp. 55–64.

9. The term *ostal* (from the Latin *hospitalis*) designates in Languedoc the "home" in the physical and sociological sense.

10. The Académie celtique, in its *Mémoires . . .* (Paris, 1807–1813), included several

studies of the ritual of marriage, which placed the accent on this accompaniment of songs and, implicitly, on the importance of the song as a language of sentimental education. The passage from the traditional song to the modern song, performed by a singer, has not significantly modified this function. On the place of the song as a mirror of youthful amorous emotions, one should closely reread the autobiography of Louis Simon; see Anne Fillon, "Louis Simon étaminier, 1741–1820, dans son village du haut Maine au siècle des Lumières, thesis, Le Mans, 1982, 2 vols., and, by the same author, *Les trois bagues au doigt, amours villageoises au XVIIIe siècle* (Paris: Robert Laffont, 1989), in particular chapter 6.

11. In 1959 Louis Girard, exploring *Le choix du conjoint en France* [The choice of a spouse in France], 2nd ed. (Paris: Cahiers de l'INED, 1974), confirmed that the dance was the primary meeting place for couples (22.3%). The role of dancing—for which the occasions and sites have evolved—remains important; see Michel Bozon and François Héran, "La découverte du conjoint: Evolution et morphologie des scènes de rencontre," *Population* [Nov.–Dec. 1987): 943–973, which notes a peak in rural areas in 1969–1975 (34.8%).

12. The passage from the *branle* "en chaine, en ronde . . ." to the contredanse in the eighteenth century, then to dancing in couples in the nineteenth century, is subtly highlighted in the work of Jean-Michel Guilcher. See, for example, *Le contredanse et les renouvellements de la danse français* (Paris: Mouton, 1970). On modern dances, see Rémi Hess, *La valse, révolution du couple en Europe* (Paris: Métaillié, 1989), and idem., *Le tango* (Toulouse: Université de Toulouse–Le Mirail, 1985). For a critique of the dance custom, see Paul Gerbod, "Un espace de sociabilité, le bal en France au XXe siècle," *Ethnologie Française* 19, no. 4 (1989): 362–370.

13. For a general presentation of the formative effects of conscription, see Michel Bozon, *Les conscrits* (Paris: Berger-Levrault, 1981), and, for a comparative point of view, Théodore Buhler, "Les conscrits," *Folklore suisse* 48, no. 3 (1958): 33–42; a thorough ethnography of the current hierarchy of a particular group of youth (as subconscript, conscript, military man, bachelor, and fiancé) is presented in Christian Hongrois, *Faire sa jeunesse en Vendée* (Maulévrier: Hérault-Editions, 1988).

14. On these seasonal migrations, read Abel Poitrineau, *Remues d'hommes,* Paris, Aubier, 1980.

15. This constant self-propelled refounding and exhibiting of the "village community" is analyzed in Daniel Fabre, "Une culture paysanne," in A. Burgière and J. Revel, eds., *Histoire de France,* vol. 4, *Les formes de la culture* (Paris: Seuil, 1993); see in particular chapter 2, "Un horizon social, le pagus."

16. The classic analysis of intermarriage and of village endogamy has long left out the fact that men and women who married outside their village, in the eighteenth and nineteenth centuries, were often more closely related to their spouses than

those who married within their village (see, for example, Jacqueline Vu Tien and André Sevin, *Choix du conjoint et patrimoine génétique: Etude de quatre villages du Pays de Sault oriental* (Toulouse and Paris: Editions du CNRS, 1978), which confirms the role of family as a network for matrimonial encounters. On the anthropological consequences of this phenomenon, see Françoise Zonabend, "Le très proche et le pas trop loin: Refléxion sur l'organisation du champ matrimonial," *Ethnologie française* 11, no. 4 (1981): 311–318, and Martine Segalen, *Quinze générations de bas-Bretons* (Paris: P.U.F., 1985).

17. On intervillage fights, *battestas* in Languedoc, see Yves Castan's finely tuned observations in "Mentalités rurale et urbaine à la fin de l'Ancien Régime dans le ressort du Parlement de Toulouse," in *Crime et criminalité en France, 17ᵉ–18ᵉ siècles* (Paris: Armand Colin, 1971), pp. 109–186 (in particular pp. 161–162). Other examples are found in Louis Mazoyer, "La jeunesse villageoise du Bas-Languedoc et des Cévennes en 1830," *Cahiers d'histoire et d'archéologie* 1948: 502–507 and Christian Durand, "Sociétés de jeunesse et communautés rurales en Quercy au XIXᵉ siècle," in *Cahors et le Quercy, actes du XXXIIᵉ congrès des sociétés savantes*, Languedoc-Pyrénées-Gascogne (Cahors, 1978), pp. 75–88.

18. The sixteenth-century word *estrangement*, often cited by Lucien Fébvre, is used in a very precise sense—the exhibiting within oneself of the strangeness which defines the other; see Fabre, "Une culture paysanne."

19. It must indeed be admitted that the night brings about a redefinition of roles and places; the circadian aspect of time—the cycle from light to dark—has been little studied, if only from the point of view of its disappearance, at the moment that public lighting was installed in the village—a project late in coming and incomplete; see, with respect to the history of artificial lighting, Wolfgang Schivelbusch, *La nuit désenchantée* (Paris: Le Promeneur, 1993).

20. The censoring of youth's activities was a secondary effect of the rigors of the Reformation and became, in the eighteenth and nineteenth centuries, a matter for the communal police. On this theme, see D. Fabre, "La fête éclatée," *L'arc* 65 (1976): 62–75.

21. This tension became acute in urban settings in the eighteenth century and therefore brought an end to the noisy disruptions; see D. Fabre, "Familles: Le privé contre la coutume," in *Histoire de la vie privée*, vol. 3, *De la Renaissance aux Lumières*, ed. Philippe Ariès and Roger Chartier (Paris: Seuil, 1986), pp. 543–579.

22. On this point, see Le Goff and Schmitt, eds., *Le charivari*, in particular the contributions by D. Fabre and B. Traimond, N. Castan, E. P. Thompson, I. Farr, and E. Hinrichs.

23. This theme is outlined in D. Fabre, "Passeuse aux gués du destin," *Critique* 402 (November 1980): 1075–1099 (in particular, 1088–1091); certain aspects are developed in "Le garçon enceint," *Cahiers de littérature orale* 20 (1986), "La

facétie," pp. 15–38; "L'ours, la vierge et le taureau," *Ethnologie française* 23, no. 1 (1993), "Textures mythiques," pp. 9–19.

24. Noël du Fail was the first to describe, for the modern world, the farce of boys disguised as ghosts (in J. Assézat, ed., *Contes et discours d'Eutrapel,* vol. 2 [Paris, 1874], p. 9 ff); on this theme, see D. Fabre, "Juvéniles revenants," *Etudes rurales* 105–106 (1987), "Le retour des morts," pp. 147–164.

25. This mimicking of death is ceremonialized in "L'enterrement de la vie de garçon," a ritual which Arnold Van Gennep initially considered to be of bourgeois origin and relatively recent—early nineteenth century (see *Manuel de folklore français contemporain,* vol. 1 (Paris: Picard, 1943), p. 318). In fact the ritual is very much alive, for example in Vendée (Hongrois, *Faire sa jeunesse en Vendée*), and its connection to the ritual intoxication of youth is illustrated by highly diverse ceremonial systems; see Christian Hongrois, "Des caves et des hommes en Vendée," *Terrain* 13 (October 1989): 29–41; Christiane Amiel, "Traverses d'un pèlerinage: Les jeunes, le vin et les morts," in ibid., pp. 15–28.

26. On this tension, see the articles of Henri Forestier, including "Le 'droit des garçons' dans la communauté villageoise aux XVIIᵉ and XVIIIᵉ siècles," *Annales de Bourgogne* 13 (1941): 100–114, which uses the scattered data in the work of Restif de la Bretonne. The necessary changes having been made, the emergence of the young rural delinquent could benefit from the analysis of Jean-Claude Chamboredon, "La délinquance juvénile: Essai de construction d'objet," *Revue française de sociologie* 12 (1971): 335–377.

27. Historians, in line with the new curiosities of historical demography, have been fascinated by the theme of prenuptial relations in the system of late marriages and by the erotic practices studied, for Northern Europe, in an ethnological classic: K. Rob. Wikman, *Die Einleitung der Ehe* (Turku: Acta Academiae Aboensis, 1937); see, for example, Jean-Louis Flandrin, *Les amours paysannes* (Paris: Gallimard-Julliard, 1975). In *Façons de dire, façons de faire,* Verdier examines the courtly preparation of girls; see also Nicole Belmont, "Rituels de courtoisie dans la société française traditionelle," *Ethnologie française* 8, no. 4 (1978): 279–286. A study of the whole of these gallant youthful exchanges is offered by Matti Sarmela, *Reciprocity Systems of the Rural Society in the Finnish-Karelian Culture Area (with Special Reference to Social Intercourse of the Youth)* (Helsinki: Suomalainen Tiedeakatemia, 1969). Claude Macherel's anthropological monograph, "La traversé du champ matrimonial: Un example alpin," *Etudes rurales* 73 (January–March 1979): 9–40 is important. For a precise analysis of the convergence of the languages of each sex, see D. Fabre, "La voie des oiseaux, sur quelques récits d'apprentissage," *L'Homme* 99 (1986): 7–40.

28. On one of these forms of male madness, implying a failure of the youthful

apprenticeship of virility, see D. Fabre, "La folie de Pierre Rivière," *La Débat* 1991 (September): 107–122.

29. A. Van Gennep was the first to insist on the importance these delaying rituals: *Manuel de folklore*, book 1, vol. 2, pp. 437–450; a very detailed monograph is offered in Paul Fortier-Beaulieu, *Mariages et noces campagnardes dans les pays ayant formé le département de la Loire* (Paris: Maisonneuve, 1945), pp. 237–244 in particular. The possibility of understanding certain enigmatic aspects of the marriage ritual, such as the "glance backward," in terms of the formation of sexual identity is illustrated in D. Fabre, *L'âge libertin* (Paris: Seuil, forthcoming).

30. On the farandole, see the thesis by Francine Lancelot, *La farandole en Provence et Languedoc*, Paris, Ecole practique des Hautes Etudes, 6th section, 1973, and the observation of a simple farandole in a festive framework very close to the one that served as the point of departure for this chapter, in "La danse à la fête votive du Caylar (Hérault)," *Arts et traditions populaires* 1968 (January–March): 63–66.

31. My choice of a seemingly ordinary festival was deliberate. It can be compared with more spectacular ceremonies, based on rare ethnographic descriptions: see F. Pomerol, "La fête patronale de Gerzat (Auvergne)," *Revue des traditions populaires* 15 (1900): 415–418; Jean Guilaine, "Les fêtes locales dans la région de Saint-Hilaire (Aude)," *Folklore*, no. 82 (1958): 3–7; Jacques Guigou, "Les jeunes ruraux dans le Languedoc méditerranéen," *Etudes rurales*, no. 19 (October–December, 1965): 32–66. A historical perspective is proposed by Abel Poitrineau, "La fête traditionelle," in *Les fêtes de la Révolution*, Clermont-Ferrand Colloqium (Paris, 1977), pp. 11–26, and Michel Vovelle, *Les métamorphoses de la fête en Provence* (Paris: Flammarion, 1976). The local festival as a "history trap" and an idealizing mirror for the collective is described for the current period in Patrick Champagne, "La fête au village," *Actes de la recherche en sciences sociales* no. 17–18 (1977): 73–84.

32. This photograph is the point of departure for the novel by Richard Powers, *Three Farmers on Their Way to a Dance* (New York, 1985).

4 WORKER YOUTH

1. Jean-Jacques Rousseau, *Emile*, book IV Paris: Gallimard, Editions de la Pléiade, 1969), p. 489.

2. Michel Foucault, *La volonté de savoir* (Paris: Gallimard), 1976, p. 40.

3. Catherine Duprat, "Le temps des philanthropes: La philanthropie parisienne, des lumières à la monarchie de Juillet: Pensée et action," State doctoral thesis, under the direction of Maurice Agulhon, University of Paris I, 1991; see vol. 5, "Action sociale: Contrôle social," notably chapter 1, "La famille menacée,"

pp. 1217–1315, and chapter 2, "Patronage," pp. 1315–1429 (a wealth of information).

4. Jules Simon, *L'ouvrier de huit ans* (Paris: Librairie Internationale, 1867).

5. Edouard Ducpétiaux, *De la condition physique et morale des jeunes ouvriers et des moyens de l'améliorer*, vol. 1 (Brussels: Méline Cans et Compagnie, 1843) p. 36.

6. Quoted in Duprat, *Le temps des philanthropes*, vol. 5, p. 1334.

7. Quoted by Michel Foucault in *Surveiller et punir: Naissance de la prison* (Paris: Gallimard, 1975), p. 297, taken from the *Gazette des Tribunaux*, August 1840.

8. Michelle Perrot, "Dans le Paris de la Belle Epoque: Les Apaches, première bandes de jeunes," *Cahiers Jussieu* 5 (Spring 1979), "Les marginaux et les exclus de l'histoire." This work was based in part on the master's thesis of L. Cousin, "Les Apaches," Paris VII, 1976. D. Kalifa returned to and amplified this research in a remarkable thesis, *L'Encre et le Sang. Récits de crimes dans la France de la Belle Epoque*, Paris VII, 1994, ed. Paris, 1995. See in particular the chapter entitled "L'invention de l'apache."

9. Joëlle Guillais-Maury, "Images de la grisette," in Arlette Farge and Christiane Klapisch-Zuber, eds., *Madame ou Mademoiselle? Itinéraires de la solitude féminine, XVIIIᵉ–XIXᵉ siècles* (Paris: Montalba, 1984).

10. Jean-Jacques Yvorel, "Drogues et drogués au XIXᵉ siècle," thesis, University of Paris VII, 1991, published under the title *Les poisons de l'esprit* (Paris, 1992).

11. Jacques Rancière, *Courts voyages au pays du peuple* (Paris: Seuil, 1990), p. 116.

12. Marina Bethlenfalvay, *Les visages de l'enfant dans la littérature française du XIXᵉ siècle: Esquisse d'une typologie* (Geneva: Droz, 1979).

13. Jean-Paul Aron, Paul Dumon, and Emmanuel Le Roy Ladurie, *Anthropologie du conscrit français* (Paris: Colin, 1972).

14. William Coleman, *Death Is a Social Disease* (Madison: Wisconsin University Press, 1982); Colin Heywood, *Childhood in Nineteenth-Century France: Work, Health and Education among the "Classes Populaires"* (Cambridge: Cambridge University Press, 1988), notably pp. 84, 151–164.

15. Louis-René Villermé, *Tableau de l'etat physique et moral des ouvriers employés dans les manufactures de coton, de laine et de soie* (Paris: J. Renouard, 1840, 2 vols.; unabridged reprint, Paris: EDIS, 1991).

16. Ducpétiaux, *De la condition physique.*

17. On these autobiographical aspects, see Michelle Perrot, "Vie ouvrières," in Pierre Nora, ed., *Lieux de Mémoire*, vol. 3, *Les France* (Paris: Gallimard, 1993).

18. Norbert Truquin, *Mémoires et aventures d'un prolétaire à travers la révolution: L'Algérie, la République argentine et le Paraguay* (Paris: Librairie des deux-mondes, 1888). See Michelle Perrot, "A Nineteenth-Century Work Experience as Related in a Worker's Autobiography: Norbert Truquin," in S. L. Kaplan and C. J. Koepp, eds., *Work in France* (Ithaca, N.Y.: Cornell University Press, 1986), pp. 297–317.

19. René Michaud, *J'avais vingt ans: Un jeune ouvrier au début du siècle* (Paris: Editions Syndicalistes, 1967), p. 39.

20. Pierre Pierrard, *Enfants et jeunes ouvriers en France (XIXe–XXe century)* (Paris: Editions Ouvrières, 1987), p. 183 ff.; Jean Delumeau, *La Première Communion: Quatre siècles d'histoire* (Paris: Desclée de Brouwer, 1987).

21. Jacques Carous-Destray, *Un couple ouvrier traditionnel: La vieille garde autoges-tionnaire* (Paris: Anthropos, 1974), p. 48.

22. Pierrard, *Enfants et jeunes ouvriers en France*, p. 184.

23. In 1880, ibid., p. 184.

24. Lise Vanderwielen, *Lise du Plat Pays* (Lille: Presses Universitaires, 1983), p. 38.

25. Heywood, *Childhood in Nineteenth-Century France*, p. 138.

26. Instituted in 1866 by Victor Duruy, minister of Public Education, the *certificat d'études* was organized by Octave Gréard in the department, or district, of the Seine in 1866; in 1878 it was awarded in eighty-three departments, and it was made official by Jules Ferry on March 28, 1882.

27. Vincent Viet, "Aux origines de l'inspection du travail au XXe siècle: L'inspection de 1892 à 1914," doctoral thesis, Institute d'Etudes Politiques de Paris, 1992; offers bountiful information on this subject and on the situation of young workers in general.

28. Alfred Goblot, *La Barrière et le Niveau* (1925; reprint, Paris: P.U.F., 1967).

29. Viet, *Aux origines de l'inspection du travail*, p. 226.

30. Ducpétiaux, *De la condition physique*, vol. 2, p. 45.

31. Ibid., p. 19: an administrative study to prepare the government bill on the work of children (1841); in question four of the study, the matter of "adolescents" is explicitly addressed.

32. *Les ouvriers des deux mondes*, vol. 4, monograph no. 36, published in 1862; recall that Frédéric Le Play initiated these family studies, which were published in several series—*Les ouvriers européens, Les ouvriers des deux mondes*—based on a unified questionnaire revolving principally around the makeup of the household budget, which was considered to reveal a family's habits. These monographs were full of information, notably concerning our subject, as the school of Le Play attached great importance to the types of family relationships.

33. Jean-Baptiste Dumay, *Mémoires d'un militant ouvrier du Creusot (1841–1905)* (Paris: Maspéro, 1976), pp. 84–85; this is the first unabridged edition of these memoirs.

34. Agricol Perdiguier, *Mémoires d'un compagnon* [1855], 2nd ed. (Moulins: Cahiers du Centre, 1914), p. 94. Note also the third unabridged edition, introduced by Maurice Agulhon (Paris: Imprimerie Nationale, 1992), in the series Acteurs de l'Histoire.

35. Ibid., p. 263.

36. Ibid., p. 332.

37. Heywood, *Childhood in Nineteenth-Century France,* p. 148 ff.

38. Marie-Véronique Gautier, *Chanson, sociabilité et grivoiserie au XIXe siècle* (Paris: Aubier, 1992).

39. A. Van Gennep, *Manuel de folklore français contemporain,* 9 vols. (Paris: Picard, 1943–1958), notably vol. 1; Michel Bozon, *Les conscrits* (Paris, 1981).

40. Yolande Cohen, *Les jeunes, le socialisme et la guerre: Histoire des mouvements de jeunesse en France,* foreword by Madeleine Rebérioux (Paris: L'Harmattan, 1989), p. 33; see the whole of her study regarding antimilitarism and youth.

41. Yvonne Verdier, *Façons de dire, façons de faire: La laveuse, la couturière, la cuisinière* (Paris: Gallimard, 1979).

42. Anne Monjaret, "La Sainte-Catherine à Paris de la fin du XIXe siècle à nos jours: Ethnographie d'une fête urbaine et professionelle," thesis, University of Paris X, Nanterre, 1992.

43. Martine Segalen, *Sociologie de la famille* (Paris: Colin, 1981), p. 109 (these average figures for the whole of France do not apply specifically to workers).

44. André Burgière et al., eds., *Histoire de la famille,* vol. 2, *Le choc des modernités* (Paris: Armand Colin, 1986); Philippe Ariès and Georges Duby, eds., *Histoire de la vie privée,* vol. 4, *Le XIXe siècle,* ed. Michelle Perrot (Paris: Le Seuil, 1987); English edition, *History of Private Life,* trans. by Arthur Goldhammer (Cambridge: Harvard University Press, Belknap Press, 1987).

45. See, for example, Hans Medick, "The Proto-Industrial Family Economy," *Social History* 3 (1976).

46. Serge Grafteaux, *Mémé Santerre: Une vie* (Paris: Marabout, 1975).

47. Serge Kropotkine, *Champs, usines et ateliers* (Paris, 1910).

48. See Mathilde Dubesset et Michelle Zancarini-Fournel, "Parcours de femmes: Réalités et représentations, Saint-Etienne (1880–1950)," thesis, University of Lyons II–Lumière, 1988, notably the second part, "Le fil du métier: Les rapports entre les sexes dans la rubannerie stéphanoise."

49. See Jacques Vallerant, "Savoir-faire et identité sociale," *Ethnologie française* 12 (April–June 1982), for an example of endogamous techniques in the southeast of France.

50. William H. Sewell, *Work and Revolution in France* (Cambridge: Cambridge University Press, 1980).

51. Michel Pigenet, *Les ouvriers du Cher (fin XVIIIe–1914): Travail, espace et conscience sociale* (Paris: Institute CGT d'histoire sociale, 1990), p. 80.

52. Ibid., p. 89.

53. Ibid., p. 43.

54. Michel Chabot, *L'Escarbille: Histoire d'Eugène Saulnier, ouvrier verrier,* afterword by Madeleine Rebérioux (Paris: Presses de la Renaissance, 1978).

55. Archives nationales (AN), F12, 4831, "Enquête du ministère de l'Agriculture et du Commerce auprès des conseils des Prudhommes sur l'apprentissage,

novembre 1877." This was a study peformed at the request of the German ambassador to France, at the end of 1876; it contains a great deal of unpublished information.

56. Yves Lequin, *Les ouvriers de la région lyonnaise (1848–1914)*, vol. 1 (Lyons: Press Universitaires de Lyon, 1977), p. 89. On the totality of these problems, see chapter 5, "La naissance et le métier," pp. 205–238.

57. Aside from the previously cited work of Yves Lequin, see Joan Scott, *The Glassworkers of Carmaux: Craftsmen and Political Action in the Nineteenth-Century City* (Cambridge: Harvard University Press, 1974).

58. Heywood, *Childhood in Nineteenth-Century France*, p. 137.

59. AN F12 4831, "Enquête."

60. Bruno Mattéi, *Rebelle, rebelle! Révoltes et mythes du mineur (1930–1946)* (Seyssel: Champ Vallon, 1987).

61. Rolande Trempé, *Les mineurs de Carmaux, 1848–1914*, (Paris: Editions Ouvrières, 1971); L. Murard and Patrick Zylberman, *Le petit travailleur infatigable ou le prolétaire régénéré* (Paris: Recherches, 1976).

62. Joël Michel, "Le movement ouvrier chez les mineurs d'Europe Occidentale (Great Britain, Belgium, France, Germany): Etude comparative des années 1880–1914," doctoral thesis, University of Lyons II, 1987. Note the first part, "Un monde se crée."

63. See Heywood, *Childhood in Nineteen-Century France*, and Yves Tyl, "Le travail des enfants au XIXe siècle: Une région: L'Alsace; Un métier: La verrerie," thesis, University of Paris VII, 1987, notably the fourth section, "Régression du travail des enfants," pp. 632–795.

64. Jean Allemane, quoted by Sian France Reynolds in "Biographie de Jean Allemane," thesis, University of Paris VII, 1978.

65. Heywood, *Childhood in Nineteenth-Century France*, p. 186, note 5.

66. Burgière et al., eds., *Histoire de la Famille*, vol. 2, p. 42 ff.

67. Characters in Marcel Proust's *Remembrance of Things Past*.

68. Ducpétiaux, *De la condition physique*, vol. 2, chapter 6, "De l'organisation de l'apprentissage."

69. Jules Simon, *L'ouvrier de huit ans* (Paris, 1867), gives the text of the law of March 4, 1851; on Simon's sharp critiques of Jules Simon, see p. 222 ff.

70. AN F12 4831, "Enquête."

71. Gilland, "Les aventures surprenantes du petit Guillaume du Mont-Cel," in *Les conteurs ouvriers* (Paris, 1849), p. 229.

72. Ibid., p. 230.

73. Pierre Pierrard, *Entants et jeunes ouvriers*, p. 72 (according to the *Gazette des tribunaux* of June 29, 1841).

74. Simon, *L'ouvrier de huit ans*, p. 249; see also Anthime Corbon, *De l'enseignement professionnel* (Paris: Imprimerie de Dubuisson, 1859).

75. Leonard R. Berlanstein, "Vagrants, Beggars and Thieves: Delinquent Boys in Mid-Nineteenth Century Paris," *Journal of Social History* 12 (1979): 531–552.

76. Lequin, *Les ouvriers de la région Lyonnais*, vol. 2, p. 69.

77. Michel Cordillot, *Eugène Varlin: Chronique d'un espoir assassiné* (Paris: Editions Ouvrières, 1992).

78. René Michaud, *J'avais vingt ans*, p. 94.

79. AN F12 4831, "Enquête."

80. Georges Duveau, *La pensée ouvrière sur l'éducation pendant la Seconde République et le Second Empire* (Paris: Domat-Montchestien, 1948).

81. *Compte rendu du Congrès de Marseille*, 1879, p. 431.

82. See Maurice Crubellier, *L'enfance et la jeunesse dans la société française, 1800–1950* (Paris: Colin, 1979); Jean-Pierre Guinot, *Formation professionnelle et travailleurs qualifiés depuis 1789* (Paris: Domat-Montchrestien, 1946).

83. Alain Cottereau, "Travail, école, famille: Aspects de la vie des enfants d'ouvriers à Paris au XIXe siècle," manuscript, Centre d'étude des mouvements sociaux, June 1977, p. 32; part of this study was published as "Méconnue, la vie des enfants d'ouvriers au XIXe siècle," *Autrement*, August 1977.

84. Chabot, *L'Escarbille*, p. 25.

85. Dumay, *Mémoires*, p. 82.

86. Chabot, *L'Escarbille*, p. 40.

87. Dumay, *Mémoires*, p. 86–87.

88. Perrot, *Les ouvriers en grève*, vol. 1, p. 315.

89. Chabot, *L'Escarbille;* on the inspectors, see p. 37.

90. Truquin, *Mémoires et aventures*, p. 70.

91. Perrot, *Les ouvriers en grève*, vol. 1, pp. 313–318, "Grèves de jeunes"; vol. 2, pp. 458–460.

92. Pigenet, *Les ouvriers du Cher*, p. 112.

93. Tyl, *Le travail des enfants*, p. 602.

94. Michel, *Le mouvement ouvrier*, vol. 2, pp. 428–430 and 634–635 (hauler strikes).

95. Perrot, *Les ouvriers en grève*, vol. 1, p. 316.

96. Dumay, *Mémoires*, p. 84.

97. On these professional journeys, which were very common, notably among glass- and metalworkers, see the outline established in Lequin, *Les ouvriers de la région lyonnaise*, vol. 1, pp. 531–541.

98. Dumay, *Mémoires*, pp. 95–110.

99. Chabot, *L'Escarbille*, pp. 68–69.

100. Ibid., p. 114.

101. André Rauch, *Boxe, violence du XXe siècle* (Paris: Aubier, 1992).

102. On their diverse leisure activities, see A. Corbin, ed., *L'avènement des loisirs, 1850–1860* (Paris, 1992).

103. Marin Nadaud, *Mémoires de Léonard, ancien garçon maçon* (Bourganeuf, 1895), pp. 149 and 134; one may also refer to the edition edited by Maurice Agulhon (Paris: Hachette, 1976). On worker violence in the nineteenth century, see Louis Chevalier, *Classes laborieuses et classes dangereuses à Paris pendant la première moitié du XIXe siècle* (Paris: Plon, 1958; Frédéric Chauvaud, *De Pierre Rivière à Landru: La violence apprivoisée au XIXe siècle* (Brussels: Brepol, 1991); Paul Willis, "L'école des ouvriers," *Actes de la recherche en sciences sociales* 24 (November 1978).

104. Pierre Caspard, "Aspects de la lutte des classes en 1848," *Revue historique,* July–September 1974.

105. Nadaud, *Mémoires de Léonard*, p. 198.

106. Maurice Agulhon, "Les chambrées en basse Provence: Histoire et ethnologie," *Revue historique* 498 (April–June 1971): 337–368, reprinted in *Histoire vagabonde* (Paris: Gallimard, 1988), pp. 17–59.

107. Cohen, *Les jeunes, le socialisme et la guerre,* is a very rich source for all these aspects, on which we are only touching here.

108. Chabot, *L'Escarbille,* p. 108: "In the courtyards of poor neighborhoods, the children had replaced the game of *manille* [a card game] with the 'Bonnot gang' game, in which, somehow, the police always lost."

109. Allain Cottereau, "Destins masculins et destins féminins dans les cultures ouvrières en France au XIXe siècle," *Mouvement social,* July–September 1983; Colin Heywood, "On Learning Gender Roles during Childhood in Nineteenth Century France," *French History* 5 (4): 451–466.

110. Agnès Fine, "A propos du trousseau: Une culture féminine?" in Michelle Perrot, ed., *Une histoire des femmes est-elle possible?* (Marseille: Rivages, 1984), pp. 55–89.

111. Dubesset and Zancarini-Fournel, *Parcours des femmes;* Helen Harden-Chenut, "Formation d'une culture ouvrière féminine: Les bonnetières troyennes, 1880–1039," doctoral thesis, University of Paris VII, 1988, notably the second section, "Une culture féminine du travail."

112. AN F12 4831, "Enquête."

113. Maurice Garden, *Lyon et les lyonnais au XVIIIe siècle* (Lille, 1970).

114. AN F12 4831, "Enquête."

115. Jeanne Bouvier, *Mes mémoires ou cinquante-neuf années d'activité industrielle, sociale et intellectuelle d'une ouvrière (1876–1935)* [1936], 2nd ed. expanded, presented, and commented on by Daniel Armogathe and Maïté Albistur (Paris: La Découverte, 1983); Karen Paul, "Les midinettes à Paris (1885–1914)," master's thesis, University of Paris VII, 1975.

116. Anne-Martin Fugier, *La place des bonnes: La domesticité féminine à Paris en 1900* (Paris: Grasset, 1979).

117. Ducpétiaux, *De la condition physique,* p. 326.

118. Marie-Victoire Louis, *Le droit de cuissage: Chair à travail, chair à plaisir, France, 1860–1930* (Paris: Le Seuil, 1993).

119. Heywood, *Childhood in Nineteenth-Century France,* pp. 102–103.

120. Tamara Hareven and Randolph Langenback, *Amoskeag: Life and Work in an American Factory City in New England* (Methuen, Mass., 1978).

121. Ducpétiaux, *De la condition physique,* vol. 2, p. 286.

122. Louis Reybaud, *Etudes sur le régime des manufactures: Condition des ouvriers en soie* (Paris: Michel Lévy, 1859); *Les ouvriers des deux Mondes,* vol. 4, monograph no. 26, on the weavers of Sainte-Marie aux Mines, (Vosges), p. 392 ff; Paul Leroy-Beaulieu, *Le travail des femmes au XIXe siècle* (Paris: Charpentier, 1888), p. 414 ff. Among the recent studies, aside from Lequin, *Les ouvriers de la region lyonnaise,* see Dominique Vanoli, "Les ouvrières en soie du sud-est de la France, 1890–1914," master's thesis, University of Paris VII, 1975; Claire Auzias and Annick Houel, *La grève des ovalistes, June–July 1869* (Paris: Payot, 1982).

123. Viet, *Les voltigeurs de la République,* passim.

124. Auzias and Houel, *La grève des ovalistes.*

125. Cottereau, "Travail, écoles, famille," pp. 41–42.

126. Dumay, *Mémoires,* pp. 91–92.

127. David Riesman, *La foule solitaire* (Paris: Arthaud, 1964).

128. Perdiguier, *Mémoires d'un compagnon,* p. 216.

129. Alain Corbin, *Filles de noce: Misère sexuelle et prostitution au XIXe siècle* (Paris: Aubier, 1978).

130. Jean-Louis Flandrin, *Les amours paysannes: Amour et sexualité dans les campagnes de l'ancienne France (XVI–XIXe siècle)* (Paris: Aubier, 1978).

131. Ducpétiaux, *De la condition physique,* vol. 1, p. 337.

132. Cordillot, *Eugène Varlin,* p. 120.

133. Bouvier, *Mes mémoires,* p. 83–85.

134. Emile Zola, *L'Assomoir,* in *Oeuvres* (Paris, 1961), pp. 137–138.

135. Michel Frey published on this point two complementary articles on this subject: "Du mariage et du concubinage dans les classes populaires à Paris en 1846–1847," *Annales ESC* 4, July–August 1978; "Les comportements concubins au sein des classes populaires à Paris en 1846–1847: Le rôle des prostitutées et des femmes logeant en garnis," in Paul Viallaneix and Jean Ehrard, eds., *Aimer en France, 1760–1860,* University of Clermont-Ferrand, Acts of the International Colloquia, 2 vols. (Clermont-Ferrand, 1980), vol. 2, pp. 565–587.

136. Perrot, *Les ouvriers en grève,* vol. 1, p. 314, according to AN C3018–3021, inquiry of 1872.

137. Lequin, *Les ouvriers de la région lyonnaise,* vol. 1, p. 209; Duprat, "Le temps des philanthropes," p. 1229. While criticizing Frey, Duprat emphasizes that one out of five couples were not legally married and that the highest rate of cohabitation

was found in the younger arrondissements, where a high percentage of the population was twenty to twenty-nine years old.

138. Ibid.

139. Ducpétiaux, *De la condition physique*, p. 234.

140. See note 135, notably "Du mariage et du concubinage," for the statistical study.

141. Chevalier, *Classes laborieuses;* Edward Shorter, "Illegitimacy, Sexual Revolution and Social Change in Modern Europe," *Journal of Interdisciplinary History II,* Autumn 1971.

142. Frey, "Les comportements concubins," p. 568.

143. Throughout the nineteenth century, feminists demanded the right to file paternity suits, which they obtained only at the start of the twentieth century and with certain restrictive conditions.

144. Rachel G. Fuchs, *Poor and Pregnant in Paris: Strategies for Survival in the Nineteenth Century* (New Brunswick, N.J.: Rutgers University Press, 1992), p. 11; this book offers a great deal of information about the sexual condition of poor Parisian women in the nineteenth century).

145. Caroux-Destray, *Un couple ouvrier traditionnel*, p. 70.

146. Joëlle Guillais-Maury, *La chair de l'autre: Le crime passionnel à Paris au XIXe siècle* (Paris: Orban, 1986).

147. On all these points, which we are not developing here, see Cohen, *Les jeunes, le socialisme et la guerre.* The assimilation of youth into charitable societies constitutes a considerable chapter; for the first half of the nineteenth century, it was studied by C. Duprat, but mostly concerning children. On the correction houses, see Henri Gaillac, *Les maisons de correction, 1830–1945,* 2nd ed. (Paris: Cujas, 1991), which also addresses the camps for young delinquents, who could be placed there until the age of twenty-one.

4 WORKER YOUTH

Bibliography

Yolande Cohen, *Les jeunes, le socialisme et la guerre: Histoire des mouvements de jeunesse en France,* foreword by Madeleine Rebérioux (Paris: L'Harmattan, 1989).

Maurice Crubellier, *L'enfance et la jeunesse dans la société français, 1800–1950* (Paris: Armand Colin, 1979).

Edouard Ducpétiaux, *De la condition physique et morale des jeunes ouvriers et des moyens de l'améliorer,* two volumes (Brussels: Méline Cans et Compagnie, 1843).

John R. Gillis, *Youth and History: Tradition and Change in European Age Relations, 1770–Present* (New York: Academic Press, 1974).

Colin Heywood, *Childhood in Nineteenth-Century France: World, Health and Education among the "Classes Populaires"* (Cambridge: Cambridge University Press, 1988).

Pierre Pierrard, *Enfants et jeunes ouvriers en France (XIXe–XXe siècle)* (Paris: Editions Ouvrières, 1987).

Louise A. Tilly and Joan W. Scott, *Women, Work and Family* (New York: Holt, Rinehart and Winston, 1978).

4 WORKER YOUTH

Principal Autobiographies Used

Jeanne Bouvier, *Mes mémoires ou cinquante-neuf années d'activité industrielle, sociale et intellectuelle d'une ouvrière (1876–1935)*, 1st ed., (Paris, 1936); 2nd ed. augmented, presented, and commented on by Daniel Armogathe and Maïté Albistur (Paris: La Découverte, 1983).

Michel Chabot, *L'Escarbille, histoire d'Eugène Saulnier, ouvrier verrier*, afterword by Madeleine Rebérioux (Paris: Presses de la Renaissance, 1978).

Jean-Baptiste Dumay, *Mémoire d'un militant ouvrier du Creusot (1841–1905)*, preface by Ernest Labrousse, text established and commented on by Pierre Ponsot (Paris: Maspéro, 1976).

René Michaud, *J'avais vingt ans: Un jeune ouvrier au début du siècle* (Paris: Editions Syndicalistes, 1967).

Martin Nadaud, *Mémoires de Léonard, ancien garçon maçon* (Bourganeuf: Duboueix, 1895); new edition presented by Maurice Agulhon (Paris: Hachette, 1976).

Agricol Perdiguier, *Mémoires d'un compagnon* [1855], 2nd ed., (Moulin: Cahiers du Centre, 1914); 3rd unabridged edition presented by Maurice Agulhon, in the series Les Acteurs de l'Histoire (Paris: Imprimerie Nationale, 1992).

Norbert Truquin, *Mémoires et aventures d'un prolétaire à travers la révolution: L'Algérie, la République argentine et le Paraguay*, ed. F. Bouriand (Paris: Librairie des deux-mondes, 1888; abridged ed., Paris: Tautin, 1974).

5 YOUNG PEOPLE IN SCHOOL

1. Christian Nique, *Comment l'école devint une affaire d'état* (Paris: Nathan, 1990).

2. Quoted in L. H. Parias, ed., *Histoire générale de l'enseignement et de l'éducation en France*, vol. 2 (Paris: Nouvelle Librairie de France, 1981), pp. 135 ff.

3. See *Les Lumières en Hongrie, en Europe centrale et en Europe orientale*. Acts of the Fifth Colloquium of Matrafured (Budapest: Akademiai Kiado and CNRS), 1984, 412 pages.

4. G. Mialaret and J. Vial, *Histoire mondiale de l'éducation*, vol. 1 (Paris: PUF, 1981), pp. 213–232.

5. Louis-Sébastien Mercier, in *Le tableau de Paris*, quoted by Maurice Gontard, *L'enseignement secondaire en France de la fin de l'ancien régime à la loi Falloux, 1750–1850* (Aix-en-Provence: Edisud, 1984), p. 10 ff.

6. Valentin Jamerey-Duval, *Mémoires: Enfance et éducation d'un paysan au XVIIIe siècle*, ed. J.-M. Goulemot (Paris, 1981). In France, the expression "société d'ordres" refers to the existence, before the Revolution of 1789, of a division of society into three large categories or orders, classified hierarchically: the clergy (first order), the nobility (second order) and the third estate (third order), the first two receiving special privileges. This organization was abolished by the French Revolution. (Trans. note)

7. Louis Trénard, "L'entre-deux-siècles," in Mialaret and Vial, eds., *Histoire mondiale de l'éducation*, vol. 2, pp. 359–393.

8. Bernardino Ferrari, *Le politica-scolastica del Cavour* [1857] (Milan: Vita e pensiero, 1982).

9. Chateaubriand, *Mémoires d'outre-tombe*, vol. 1 (Paris: Le Livre de Poche, 1973), pp. 76–77.

10. Kropotkin, *Autour d'une vie: Mémoires* (Paris: Stock, 1971), pp. 48–49.

11. Quoted in Michel Soëtard, *Pestalozzi* (Lucerne-Lausanne: Editions René Coeckelberghs, 1987), p. 142.

12. Antoine Prost, *Histoire de l'enseignement de France, 1800–1967* (Paris: A. Colin, 1968), p. 63.

13. Marie-Madeleine Compère, *Du collège au lycée (1500–1850)* (Paris: Gallimard, 1985).

14. Parias, *Histoire générale de l'enseignement*, vol. 3, p. 487.

15. *Lettres du Révérend Père Lacordaire à des jeunes gens* (Paris: C. Douniol, 1865), pp. 324–325.

16. Maurice Crubellier, *L'enfance et la jeunesse dans la société française, 1800–1850* (Paris: Armand Colin, 1979), p. 154 ff.

17. George Weill, *Histoire de l'enseignement secondaire en France, 1802–1920* (Paris: Payot, 1921), p. 115.

18. Jules Michelet, *Nos fils* [1869] (Geneva: Slatkine, 1980), p. 287.

19. For the figures, see Weill, *Histoire de l'enseignement secondaire;* Prost, *Histoire de l'enseignement;* Compère, *Du collège au lycée.*

20. Antonio Vinso Frago, *Politica y educación en los origines de la España contemporanea* (Madrid: Siglo XXI de España editores, 1982), p. 410 ff.

21. Alain Besançon, *Education et société en Russie dans le second tiers du XIXe siècle* (Paris: Mouton, 1974), pp. 45–47.

22. Compère, *Du collège au lycée*, p. 160.

23. W. Frijhoff and D. Julia, *Ecole et société dans la France d'ancien régime. Quatre examples: Auch, Avallon, Condom et Gisors* (Paris: A. Colin, 1975), p. 93; see also Compère, *Du collège au lycée;* R. Chartier, D. Julia, and M.-M. Compère, *L'éducation en France du XVIe au XVIIIe siècle* (Paris: SEDES, 1976).

24. Figures are from W. Frijhoff and D. Julia, quoted by Louis Trénard in, "Uni-

versités, collèges et écoles en France au Siècle des Lumières," in *Les Lumières en Hongrie*, pp. 263–288.

25. Patrick Harrigan with Victor Neglia, *Lycéens et collégiens sous le Second Empire: Etude statistique sur les fonctions sociales de l'enseignement secondaire public d'après l'enquête de Victor Duruy* (Lille: Editions de la Maison des Sciences de l'Homme, Publications of the University of Lille III, 1979), see table 2.

26. Robert Gildea, *Education in Provincial France, 1800–1914: A Study of Three Departments* (Oxford: Clarendon Press, 1983), p. 201. We are looking at the years 1863 to 1870.

27. F. Guizot, *Essai sur l'histoire et sur l'état actuel de l'instruction publique en France* (Paris, 1816), pp. 2–3.

28. Gontard, *L'enseignement secondaire en France*, p. 141.

29. Ibid., p. 33.

30. Honoré de Balzac, *Z. Marcas*, in *Oeuvres complètes* (Paris: Louis Conard, 1914), p. 425.

31. See Colin Shrosbee, *Public Schools and Private Education: The Clarendon Commission 1861–1865 and the Public Schools Acts* (Manchester: Manchester University Press, 1988).

32. Gildea, *Education in Provincial France*, p. 188. The years addressed are 1840 to 1851.

33. Report quoted in Paul Gerbod, *La vie quotidienne dans les lycées et collèges au XIXe siècle* (Paris: Hachette, 1979).

34. Ibid., p. 14.

35. Charles Jourdain, *Histoire de l'Université de Paris au XVIIe et au XVIIIe siècles* (Paris: Hachette, 1862–1866), pp. 238–252, title XI.

36. Louis Rajon, *La Garuche: Mémoires d'un collégien de 1900* (Paris: La Pensée universelle, 1990), p. 35 ff.

37. Honoré de Balzac, *Louis Lambert* (Paris: France-Loisirs, 1987), p. 34.

38. Alain Corbin, *Archaïsme et modernité en Limousin, 1845–1880*, 2 vols. (Paris: Marcel Rivière, 1975); see vol. 1, p. 374.

39. Michelet, *Nos fils*, p. 285.

40. Quoted by Gontarde, *L'enseignement secondaire en France*, p. 92.

41. Roger Merle, *Armand Barbès, un révolutionnaire romantique* (Toulouse: Privat, 1977), pp. 14–15.

42. See Vinão Frago, *Politica y educación*.

43. Comte d'Haussonville, *Ma jeunesse 1814–1830: Souvenirs* (Paris: Calmann-Lévy, 1885), p. 155 ff.

44. J. Vallès, "Chers parents!" in *Les enfants du peuple* (Tusson: Du Lérot, 1987), p. 125.

45. Compère, *Du collège au lycée*, p. 191.

46. Alphonse Daudet, *La petit chose* (Paris: Le livre de poche, 1983), p. 83.

47. Jean-Michel Gaillard, *Jules Ferry* (Paris: Fayard, 1989), p. 23.

48. *Hommage à Léon Gambetta,* catalogue from exposition organized by the Luxembourg Museum, November 18, 1982, to January 3, 1983, p. 14.

49. Besançon, *Education et société en Russie,* pp. 30–33.

50. Jourdain, *Histoire de l'Université de Paris,* pp. 238–252.

51. G. Dupont-Ferrier, *Du collège de Clermont au lycée Louis-le-Grand,* vol. 2, *1800–1920* (Paris, 1922), pp. 467–482.

52. Françoise Mayeur, in Parias, *Histoire générale de l'enseignement,* vol. 3, p. 497.

53. Olivier Devaux, "Les lycées impériaux, des casernes: Mythe ou réalité? L'example du lycée de Toulouse," in *Sources: Travaux historiques* 2 (1986): 67–71.

54. Maurice Gontard, ed., *Histoire des lycées de Marseille* (Aix-en-Provence, 1982), p. 55 ff.

55. Compère, *Du collège au lycée,* pp. 249–250.

56. Gontard, *Histoire des lycées de Marseille,* pp. 52–53.

57. Gontard, *L'enseignement secondaire en France,* p. 139.

58. See Gérard Cholvy, ed., *Mouvements de jeunesse: Chrétiens et juifs: Sociabilité juvénile dans un cadre européen, 1799–1968* (Cerf, 1985).

59. Marc Lanfranchi, *Mémoires de P.-A. Lanfranchi, instituteur à Guitera (1835–1875), suivies de la correspondance d'un lycéen corse à son père,* Corte, Le Signet, 1990, p. 143.

60. D'Alton-Shée, *Mes mémoires (1826–1848)* (Paris: Lacroix-Verboeckhoven, 1869), "Part One: 1826–1839," pp. 23–24.

61. Alfred de Musset, *La confession d'un enfant du siècle* (Paris: Gallimard-Folio, 1973), pp. 20–23.

62. Henri Dabot, *Lettres d'un lycéen et d'un étudiant de 1847–1854* (Peronne and Paris, n.d.), p. 20 (letter dated April 10, 1848).

63. Cf. Jourdain, *Histoire de l'Université de Paris.*

64. Mialaret and Vial, *Histoire Mondiale de l'éducation,* vol. 1, p. 99.

65. Alphonse de Lamartine, *Mémoires de jeunesse, 1790–1815* (Paris: Tallandier, 1990), pp. 54–55.

66. Gustave Flaubert, *Correspondance,* vol. 1 (Paris: La Pléiade, 1979), pp. 56–57, November 1839.

67. *La vie quotidienne dans les lycées,* Gerbod, p. 105.

68. Rajon, *La garuche,* p. 132 ff.

69. Besançon, *Educatión et société en Russie,* p. 30 ff., and Kropotkin, *Autour d'une vie,* p. 49 ff.

70. Alexandre Dumas, *Mes Mémoires,* vol. I, 1802–1830, R. Laffont, 1989, pp. 200–201.

71. See J. Michelet, *Ecrits de jeunesse* (Paris, 1959), p. 202, and *Lettres du R. P. Lacordaire à des jeunes gens,* pp. 444–445.

72. Crubellier, *L'enfance et la jeunesse,* pp. 150–151.

73. Lanfranchi, *Mémoires de P.-A. Lanfranchi*, p. 162.

74. Rajon, *La garuche*, pp. 132–33.

75. Balzac, *Louis Lambert*, p. 22.

76. The scene takes place in 1915. See Elias Canetti, *Histoire d'une jeunesse: La langue sauvée* (Paris: Albin Michel, 1980), pp. 142–144.

77. Michelet, *Ecrits de jeunesse*, p. 208.

78. Antoine Sylvère, *Toinou: Le cri d'un enfant auvergnat*, Plon, 1980, p. 269.

79. Affair cited by F. Mayeur in Parias, *Histoire générale de l'enseignement*, vol. 3, pp. 498–499.

80. Jourdain, *Histoire de l'Université de Paris*, pp. 238–252.

81. Balzac, *Louis Lambert*, p. 43.

82. Arthur Schnitzler, *Une jeunesse viennoise 1862–1889* (Paris: Le Livre de Poche, 1987), p. 105.

83. Alain Corbin, *Les filles de noce: Misère sexuelle et prostitution aux 19ᵉ et 20ᵉ siècles* (Paris: Aubier, 1978), p. 294 ff.

84. See Jean-Claude Caron, *Générations romantiques: Les étudiants de Paris et le Quartier latin, 1814–1851* (Paris: A. Colin, 1991), chapter 7: "L'étudiant dans la cité: Le 'mariage au XIIIᵉ.'"

85. Schnitzler, *Une jeunesse viennoise*, p. 120.

86. G. Milalaret and J. Vial, *op. cit.*, vol. 1, p. 183.

87. Robert Viala, *L'enseignement secondaire de jeunes filles 1880–1940, par ceux qui l'ont créé et celles qui l'ont fait vivre* (Sèvres: CIEP de Sèvres, s.d.), p. 43.

88. On secondary education for women, see Françoise Mayeur, *L'enseignement secondaire des jeunes filles sous la Troisième République* (Paris: Presses de la FNSP, 1977), and *L'education des filles en France au XIXᵉ siècle* (Paris: Hachette, 1979).

89. Crubellier, *L'entance et la jeunesse*, p. 274.

90. Willy Rudy, *The University of Europe 1100–1914: A History* (Rutherford, N.J.: Fairleigh Dickinson University Press, 1984), p. 122.

91. For Germany, see the book by James C. Albisetti, *Schooling German Girls and Women: Secondary and Higher Education in the Nineteenth Century* (Princeton, N.J.: Princeton University Press, 1988), from which most of the information concerning Germany was drawn.

92. Mialaret and Vial, *Histoire mondiale de l'éducation*, vol. 2, p. 167 ff.

93. See Linda L. Clark, *Schooling the Daughters of Marianne: Textbooks and the Socialization of Girls in Modern French Primary Schools* (Albany: State University of New York Press, 1984), p. 120; these numbers do not take into account the advanced primary schools.

94. Suzanne Voilquin, *Souvenir d'une fille du peuple* (Paris: F. Maspéro, 1978), p. 65.

95. Lanfranchi, *Memoires de P.-A. Lanfranchi*, p. 165.

96. Daniel Stern, *Mes souvenirs* (Paris: Calman-Lévy, 1877), pp. 37–38.

97. Ibid., p. 98 ff.
98. George Sand, *Histoire de ma vie,* vol. 1 (Paris: Gallimard, La Pléiade, 1978), p. 868.
99. Stern, *Mes souvenirs,* p. 159 ff.
100. J. Vallès, "Les lycées," an article that appeared in *La France,* August 4, 1882; reproduced in *Le tableau de Paris* (Paris: Messidor, 1989), pp. 149–153.

5 YOUNG PEOPLE IN SCHOOL

Bibliography

James C. Albisetti, *Schooling German Girls and Women: Secondary and Higher Education in the Nineteenth Century* (Princeton, N.J.: Princeton University Press, 1988).

Alain Besançon, *Education et société en Russie dans le second tiers du XIXe siècle* (Paris, 1974).

James Bowen, *A History of Western Education,* vol. 3, *The Modern West: Europe and the New World* (New York: Methuen and Co., 1981).

Jean-Claude Caron, *Générations romantiques: Les étudiants de Paris et le Quartier latin 1814–1851* (Paris: Armand Colin, 1991).

Thérèse Charmasson, Anne-Maris Lelorrain, and Yannick Ripa, *L'enseignement technique de la Révolution à nos jours,* vol. 1, *1789–1926,* INP (Service d'histoire de l'éducation) (Paris, 1987).

Roger Chartier, Marie-Madeleine Compère, and Dominique Julia, *L'education en France du XVIe au XVIIIe siècle* (Paris: SEDES, 1976).

Linda C. Clark, *Schooling the Daughters of Marianne: Textbooks and the Socialization of Girls in Modern French Primary Schools* (Albany: State University of New York Press, 1984).

Marie-Madeleine Compère, *Du collège au lycée, 1500–1850* (Paris: Gallimard, 1985).

Maurice Crubellier, *L'enfance et la jeunesse dans la société française, 1800–1950* (Paris: Armand Colin, 1979).

Bernardino Ferrari, *La politica scolastica del Cavour: Dalle esperienze prequarantottesche alle responsabilita di governo* (Milan: Vita e pensiero, 1982).

Wilhem Frijhoff and Dominique Julia, *Ecole et société sous l'Ancien Régime, Quatre exemples: Auch, Avallon, Condom et Gisors* (Paris: Armand Colin, 1975).

Paul Gerbod, *La vie quotidienne dans les lycées et le collèges au XIXe siècle* (Paris: Hachette, 1968).

Robert Gildea, *Education in Provincial France, 1800–1914: A Study of Three Departments* (Oxford: Clarendon Press, 1983).

Maurice Gontard, *L'enseignement secondaire en France de la fin de l'ancien régime à la loi Falloux, 1750–1850* (Aix-en-Provence: Edisud, 1984).

Patrick Harrigan, with Victor Neglia, *Lycéens et collégiens du Second Empire: Etude statistique sur les fonctions sociales de l'enseignement secondaire public d'après l'en-*

quête de Victor Duruy (1864–65) (Lille: Editions de la Maison des Sciences de l'Homme, 1979), a publication of the University of Lille III.

Antoine Léon, *Histoire de l'enseignement en France,* in the series, Que sais-je? (Paris: PUF, 1990).

Les Lumières en Hongrie, en Europe centrale et en Europe orientale, Actes du 5ᵉ colloque de Matafured, 1981 (Budapest: Akademiai Kiado and CNRS, 1984).

François Mayeur, *De la Révolution à l'école républicaine,* vol. 3 of *L'histoire générale de l'enseignement et de l'éducation en France,* ed. L. H. Parias (Paris: Nouvelle Librairie de France, 1981).

————, *L'education des filles en France au XIXᵉ siècle* (Paris: Hachette, 1979).

————, *L'enseignement secondaire des jeunes filles sons la Troisième République* (Paris, 1977).

Gaaston Mialaret and Jean Vial, eds., *Histoire mondiale de l'éducation,* vol. 2, *De 1515 à 1815;* vol. 3, *De 1815 à 1945* (Paris: PUF, 1981).

Antoine Prost, *Histoire de l'enseignement en France, 1800–1967* (Paris: Armand Colin, 1968).

Colin Shrosbee, *Public Schools and Private Education: The Clarendon Commission 1861–1864 and the Public Schools Acts* (Manchester: Manchester University Press, 1988).

Antonio Vinão Frago, *Politica y educación en los origines de la España contemporanea: Examen especial de sus relaciones en la enseñanza secundaria* (Madrid: Siglo XXI de España editores, 1982).

Georges Weill, *Histoire de l'enseignement secondaire en France, 1802–1920* (Paris: Payot, 1921).

6 YOUNG REBELS AND REVOLUTIONARIES, 1789–1917

1. See I. Woloch, *The New Regime: The Transformations of the French Civic Order, 1789–1820* (New York, 1994).

2. According to the famous book by Philippe Ariès, *L'enfant et la vie familiale sous l'ancien régime* (Paris, 1960 and 1973).

3. See J. R. Gillis, *Youth and History: Tradition and Change in European Age Relations, 1770–Present* (New York, 1974). pp. 76–82.

4. I am referring here to the now classic interpretation of E. H. Erikson, *Childhood and Society* (New York, 1963), and, by the same author, *Identity: The Youth Crisis* (New York, 1968).

5. See F. Moretti, *Il romanzo di formazione* (Milan, 1986); R. Terdimann, "Structure of Initiation: On Semiotic Education and Its Contradictions in Balzac," *Yale French Studies* 1982: 198–226; J. Siegel, *Bohemian Paris: Culture, Politics and the Boundaries of Bourgeois Life, 1830–1930* (New York, 1986).

6. L. Börne, *Gesammelte Schriften* (Hamburg, 1862), p. 63.

7. I refer the reader to J. C. Schmitt, "Generazioni," in *Enciclopedia Einaudi*, vol. 15, *Sistematica*, (Turin, 1982), pp. 266–275; and, for France, to M. Crubellier, *L'enfance et la jeunesse dans la société française, 1800–1950* (Paris, 1979).

8. K. Gutzkow, *Briefe aus Paris* (Leipzig, 1842), pp. 227–228.

9. Such as F. D. Wasserman, quoted in L. B. Namier, *La rivoluzione delgi intellecttuali e altri saggi sull'Ottocento europeo* (Turin, 1972), p. 212.

10. See W. Benjamin, "Paris, Capital of the Nineteenth Century," in *Reflections* (New York: Schocken, 1986).

11. R. Jakobson, "On a Generation that Squandered Its Poets," in *Language in Literature* (Cambridge: Harvard University Press, 1987), p. 299.

12. Such as D. Milo, *Trahir le temps* (Paris, 1981), p. 182.

13. Quoted in A. Chuquet, *L'Ecole de Mars* (Paris, 1899), p. 6 (the italics are my own); the quotations that follow are also taken from this wonderful book by Chuquet.

14. One should refer here to the book by M. Ozouf, *La fête révolutionnaire, 1789–1799* (Paris, 1986).

15. See J. F. Lyotard, "Futilité en révolution" [1974], in *Rudiments païens: Genre dissertatif* (Paris, 1977), pp. 147–212 (especially p. 198 ff.); L. Hunt, "The Unstable Boundaries of the French Revolution," in P. Ariès and G. Duby, eds., *History of Private Life*, trans. A. Goldhammer, vol. 4 (Cambridge, Mass., 1996), pp. 13–45; P. Viola, *Il trono vuoto: La transizione della sovranità nella Rivoluzione francese* (Turin, 1989), p. 76 ff.

16. C. Lacretelle, *Dix années d'épreuves pendant la révolution* (Paris, 1842), p. 202.

17. See R. Cobb, *Reazioni all Rivoluzione francese* [1972] (Milan, 1989).

18. Quoted in F. Gendron, *La "jeunesse dorée": Episodes de la Révolution* (Quebec, 1979), p. 164.

19. See J. P. Gutton, *Naissance du vieillard: Essai sur l'histoire des rapports entre les vieillards et la société en Europe* (Paris, 1988); and M. Ozouf, "Symboles et fonctions des âges dans les fêtes de l'Europe révolutionnaire," *Annales historiques de la Révolution française* 1970: 569–593 (notably p. 579 ff.).

20. Archives nationales, Assemblées législatives, C 226–232.

21. Moscow, Archives of the Institute of Marxism-Leninism, file on Jullien. Also on Jullien, see S. Luzzatto, *L'autumno della Rivoluzione: Lotta e cultura politica nella Francia del Termidore* (Turin, 1994).

22. M.-A. Jullien, *Entretien politique . . . sur la France* (Paris, year VIII [1799]), pp. 62–65.

23. See L. Guerci, *Libertà degli antichi et libertà dei moderni: Sparta, atene e i "philosophes" nella Francia di '700* (Naples, 1979).

24. I am referring here, of course, to A. de Musset, "La confession d'un enfant du siècle" [1836], in *Oeuvres complètes*, vol. 3 (Paris, 1866).

25. See J.-C. Caron, *Générations romantiques: Les étudiants de Paris et le Quartier Latin (1814–1851)* (Paris, 1991), p. 225 ff.

26. For a particularly rich and nuanced study of student circles during the Empire, see H. Gouhier, *La jeunesse d'Auguste Comte et la formation du positivisme*, vol. 1 (Paris, 1933); see also C. H. Pouthas, *Guizot pendant la Restauration: Préparation de l'homme d'État (1814–1830)* (Paris, 1923), pp. 5–27.

27. M.-A. Jullien, *Essai général d'éducation physique, morale et intellectuelle; suivi d'un plan d'éducation pratique pour l'enfance, l'adolescence et la jeunesse* (Paris, 1808), but the quote comes from the 1810 edition; the author, for his part, said that the work was ready in 1805 (p. 126).

28. A. Corbin, "Backstage," in Ariès and Duby, eds., *History of Private Life*, vol. 4, pp. 498–499. On this question, the seminal work is that of R. Sennett, *La tyrannie de l'intimité* [1976] (Paris: Seuil, 1979).

29. See P. de Vargas, "L'éducation du 'petit Jullien,' agent du Comité de salut public," in *L'enfant, la famille et la Révolution française* (Paris, 1990), pp. 219–239, which announces a study on Jullien as publisher of Saint-Just under the Directoire.

30. J. Michelet, *Histoire de la Révolution française* [1847–1853], vol. 2 (Paris, 1952), p. 1089.

31. I will refer here only to the never-surpassed study by L. Mazoyer, "Catégories d'âge et groupes sociaux: Les jeunes générations françaises de 1830," *Annales d'histoire économique et sociale* 1938: 385–423; to Y. Knibilher, *Naissance des sciences humanines: Mignet et l'histoire philosophique au XIXe siècle* (Paris, 1973); and to several interesting ideas in P. Rosanvallon, *Le moment Guizot* (Paris, 1985), p. 202 ff.

32. See S. Luzzatto, *Il Terrore ricordato: Memoria et tradizione dell'esperienza rivoluzionaria* (Genoa, 1988), p. 55 ff.

33. A. F. Carrion-Nisas, *De la jeunesse française* (Paris, 1820), p. 7.

34. See P. Sichorsky, *Naître coupable, naître victime* (Paris, 1988 and 1991).

35. On the echoes of the 1989 polemic over the "Jenninger affair," see M. Pirano, *Il fascino del nazismo* (Bologna, 1989).

36. Carrion-Nisas, *De la jeunesse*, p. 8.

37. The main reference work is that by A. B. Spitzer, *The French Generation of 1820* (Princeton, 1987).

38. See S. Charléty, *La Restauration* (Paris, 1921), p. 197.

39. A good reconstruction of the facts can be found in F. A. Isambert, *De la charbonnerie au saint-simonisme: Etude sur la jeunesse de Buchez* (Paris, 1966).

40. Ballanche was the author, among other things, of *Le vieillard et les jeunes* [1819], which was the most original theoretical attempt, during the Restoration, to reconcile old and new legitimists on the one hand, and old and new republicans on the other.

41. A. Galante Garrone, *Filippo Buonarroti e i rivoluzionari dell'Ottocento (1828–1837)*, new ed., (Turin, 1972), pp. 40–47.

42. I will merely point out, among the "sympathetic" historians, the classic work by S. Charléty, *Histoire du saint-simonisme* (Paris, 1931); among the "detractors," see L. Valiani, *Questioni di storia del socialismo* (Turin, 1958), p. 325 ff.; and especially G. G. Iggers, *The Cult of Authority: The Political Philosophy of the Saint-Simonians, a Chapter in the Intellectual History of Totalitarianism* (The Hague, 1958). For the definition of Saint-Simoniansm as the salvation of the bourgeoisie, see Benjamin, "Paris, Capital of the Nineteenth Century."

43. Uranbelt de Leuze [Laurent de l'Ardèche], *Réfutation de l'"Histoire de France" de l'abbé de Montgaillard* (Paris, 1828), p. 33.

44. See A. Galante Garrone, "I sansimoniani et la storia della Rivoluzione francese," *Rivista Storica Italiana* 1949: 251–278; and R. Pozzi, "La nascita di un mito: Robespierismo et giacobinismo nella Francia della rivoluzione di luglio," in M. Salvatori and N. Tranfaglia, eds., *Il modello politico giacobino e le rivoluzioni* (Florence, 1984), pp. 197–222.

45. [Laurent de l'Ardèche], *Réfutation*, pp. 283, 383, 435–437, 442.

46. According to the book by his son, H. Fazy, *James Fazy: Sa vie, son oeuvre* (Geneva and Basel, 1887), p. 40 ff.

47. See F. Ruchon, "Une famille genevoise: Les Fazy, d'Antoine Fazy, fabricant d'indiennes à James Fazy, homme d'état et tribun," *Bulletin de l'Institut national genevois* 1939: 1 ff.; and M. Vuilleumier, "Buonarroti et ses sociétés secrètes à Genève: Quelques documents inédits (1815–1824)," *Annales historiques de la Révolution française* 1970: 473–505.

48. As J. H. Billington highlighted in *Con il fuoco nella mente: Le origini della fede rivoluzionaria* [1980], (Bologna, 1986).

49. Geneva, Bibliothèque publique et universitaire, Fondation Fazy, cart. 5.

50. The term *gerontocracy* (which Fazy bragged of having invented) would soon be adopted by Béranger, the national bard and youth idol, in the title of a poem. See J. Touchard, *La gloire de Béranger* vol. 1 (Paris, 1968), pp. 525–529.

51. J. Fazy, *De la gérontocratie, ou abus de la sagesse des vieillards dans le gouvernement de la France* (Paris, 1828), pp. 5, 23.

52. See J. Fazy, *Principes d'organisation industrielle pour le dévelopement des richesses en France, explication du malaise des classes productrices, et des moyens d'y porter remède* (Paris, 1830).

53. *La Révolution de 1830*, December 21, 1830.

54. I will refer here only to the article by M. Agulhon, "1830 dans l'histoire du XIXe siècle français" [1980], in his book *Histoire vagabonde*, vol. 2, *Idéologie et politique dans la France du XIXe siècle* (Paris, 1988), pp. 31–47; and the classic synthesis of D. H. Pinkney, *The French Revolution of 1830* (Princeton, 1972).

55. For an overview, see A. Esler, "Youth in Revolt: The French Generation of

1830," in R. J. Bezucha, ed., *Modern European Social History* (Lexington, Mass., 1972), pp. 301–334.

56. E. Quinet, *Avertissement à la monarchie de 1830* (Paris, 1831), p. 5.

57. See Seigel, *Bohemian Paris,* pp. 25 ff.; and P. Bénichou, "Jeune-France et Bousingot," in *Revue d'Histoire littéraire de la France* 1971: 439–462.

58. Quoted in B. Guyon, *La pensée politique et sociale de Balzac* (Paris, 1947), p. 384 ff.

59. See Moretti, *Il romanzo di formazioni,* p. 211 ff.

60. This anecdote is found in R. Caillois, "Paris mythe moderne," *Nouvelle Revue Française* 1937: 698.

61. In *Notti fiorentine,* quoted by S. Kracauer, *Jacques Offenbach e la Parigi del suo tempo* [1937] (Casale Monferrato, 1984), p. 12.

62. See R. Treves, *La dottrina sansimoniana nel pensiero italiano del Risorgimento* (Turin, 1933), p. 17.

63. See S. Venturi, *Il populismo russo,* vol. 1, *Herzen, Bakunin, Cernysevskij* (Turin, 1972), p. 19.

64. The most up-to-date study on this question is that of L. Calvié, *Le renard et les raisins: La Révolution française et les intellectuels allemands, 1789–1845* (Paris, 1989); but the works of J. Dresch, *Karl Kutzkow et la jeune Allemagne* (Paris, 1904), and E. M. Butler, *The Saint-Simonian Religion in Germany: A Study of the Young German Movement* (Cambridge, England 1926), remain useful.

65. Quoted by F. Della Peruta, *Mazzini e i rivoluzionari italiani: Il "artito d'azione" (1830–1845)* (Milan, 1974), p. 60.

66. G. Mazzini, "D'alcune cause che impedirono finora lo sviluppo della libertè in Italia" [1832], in his *Scritti e inediti,* nat. ed., vol. 2 (Imola, 1907), p. 210.

67. Quoted by Della Peruta, *Mazzini,* pp. 204–217.

68. See Galante Garrone, *Buonarroti,* p. 340 ff.

69. See Della Peruta, *Mazzini,* pp. 204–217.

70. I will refer here only to the never-surpassed treatise of E. P. Thomson, *Rivoluzione industriale e classe operaia in Inghilterra* [1963] (Milan, 1969).

71. W. Lovett, *Life and Struggles . . . in Pursuit of Bread, Knowledge and Freedom* (London, 1981), p. 185.

72. See D. Vincent, *Bread, Knowledge and Freedom: A Study of Nineteenth Century Working Class Autobiography* (London, 1981), p. 185.

73. See Gillis, *Youth and History,* p. 37.

74. See D. H. Pinkney, *Decisive Years in France, 1840–1847* (Princeton, 1986), p. 93.

75. I will refer the reader at least to J. Grandjonc, *Marx et les communistes allemands à Paris, 1844: Contribution à l'étude du marxisme* (Paris, 1974).

76. See Calvié, *Le renard et les raisins,* p. 119.

77. The most recent study is that of L. S. Kramer, *Threshold of a New World: Intellectuals and the Exile Experience in Paris, 1830–1848* (Ithaca, N.Y., 1988). See

also N. Reeves, "Heine and the Young Marx," *Oxford German Studies* 1972: 44–97.

78. On these matters, see J. Seigel, *Marx's Fate: The Shape of a Life* (Princeton, 1978), pp. 154–169.

79. See Luzzato, *Il Terrore ricordato*, pp. 108–135.

80. In 1846 the son of George Couthon, the fearsome Jacobin who fell with Robespierre in Thermidor, compared the founders of the First Republic to antique statues: magnificent, silent figures like those of certain groups found in Herculaneum. Quoted in F. Mège, *Correspondance inédite de Georges Couthon, 1791–1794* (Paris, 1872), pp. 336–340.

81. J. Améry, *Rivolta e Rassegnazione: Sull'invecchiare* [1968] (Turin, 1988), p. 77 ff.

82. Benjamin, "Paris, Capital of the Nineteenth Century."

83. See M. Dommanget, *Auguste Blanqui: des origines à la révolution de 1848: Premiers combats et premières prisons* (Paris and The Hague, 1969), p. 8 ff.

84. *La Réformer,* August 18, 1846. On this whole question, see J. Granjonc, "A propos des relations des frères Blanqui entre eux et avec P. J. Proudhon: Quelques documents oubliés ou inédits," in *Blanqui et les blanquistes* (Paris, 1986), pp. 13–27 (which reprints the text by Blanqui).

85. J. Michelet, *Le peuple* [1846] (Paris, 1979), p. 139.

86. See R. Pozzi, *Gli intelletuali e il potere: Aspetti della cultura francese dell'Ottocento* (Bari, 1979), pp. 127–169.

87. See C. Durandin, *Révolution à la française ou à la russe: Polonais, Roumains and Russes au XIXe siècle en France* (Paris, 1989), p. 98.

88. Quoted in N. P. Smochina, "Sur les émigrés romains à Paris de 1850 à 1856," *Mélanges de l'école roumaine en France* 1933: 173.

89. The leaders of the German democratic movement, for their part, used still more disturbing reasoning: in the Frankfurt parliament, presented with a demand for freedom on the part of Czech youth, the leader of the extreme left, Arnold Ruge, spoke of the *Raum* (space) necessary for Germany if it wanted to complete its world mission. On this question, see Namier, *La rivoluzione dei intellectuali,* p. 160 ff.

90. According to the interpretation proposed by A. De Francesco, "Democratici e socialisti in Francia dal 1830 al 1851," *Il pensiero: Rivista italiana di scienze politiche* 1986: 459–494.

91. Quoted by P. Leroux, *La grève de Samarez, poème philosophique,* vol. 1 (Paris, 1863), p. 332. Godefroy Cavaignac died in 1845.

92. The average age of the insurgents, or at least of those who were brought before the court martial, was thirty-four. On this questions, see P. Caspard, "Aspects de la lutte de classes en 48: Le recrutement de la Garde Nationale Mobile," *Revue historique* 1974: 81–106.

93. See the studies, which are not always in agreement with Caspard's, of

M. Traugot, "The Mobile Guard in the French Revolution of 1848," *Theory and Society* 1980: 683–720, and R. Bezucha, "The French Revolution of 1848 and the Social History of Work," *Theory and Society* 1983: 447–482; other suggestions can be found in the old but fascinating work by J. Cassou, *Quarante-huit* (Paris, 1939), p. 247 ff.

94. I am referring here to the classic work by L. Chevalier, *Classes laborieuses et classes dangereuses à Paris dans la première moitié du XIXe siècle* (Paris, 1958), and in particular to the following pages from the Italian translation (Classi lavoratrici e classi pericolose [Rome and Bari, 1976]): pp. 240 ff., 314 ff.; 560.

95. Reported in A. Herzen, *Passé et médiations* [1876], vol. 2 (Lausanne, 1979), p. 113.

96. M. Du Camp, *Souvenirs de l'année 1848* [1876] (Paris, 1979), p. 91.

97. A. Delvau, *Histoire de la révolution de février* (Paris, 1850), p. 3.

98. Ibid., p. 316.

99. On the "political" Baudelaire, we find fascinating pages in A. Rey, *"Révolution," histoire d'un mot* (Paris, 1989), and naturally in Benjamin, "Paris, Capital of the Nineteenth Century."

100. A. Delvau, *H. Murger et la Bohème* (Paris, 1866), p. 48.

101. On this topic, nothing equals the book by G. La Ferla, *Renan politico* (Turin, 1953).

102. Péguy wrote in 1904: "[*The Future of Science*] remains for me Renan's most important work, and the one that truly gives the foundation and origin of his entire thought, if it is true that a great life is unfortunately almost always but a persevering, full-blown maturity, suddenly revealed in a flash of youth." C. Péguy, "Zangwill," in *Oeuvres en prose complètes*, new ed. (Paris, 1987), p. 1420.

103. E. Renan, "L'avenir de la science: Pensées de 48," in *Oeuvres complètes* (Paris, 1949), p. 995. The preceeding quotes are found, respectively, on pp. 756, 884, 750, 1064, 991, 990.

104. See I. Berlin, "Herzen, Bakunin e la libertà individuale [1955], in Berlin, *Il riccio e la volpe e altri saggi* (Milan, 1986); the quote by Herzen is on p. 175.

105. See Venturi, *Il populismo russo*, pp. 49 ff. and 177 ff.; the quote is on p. 177.

106. On the Second Empire's offensive against the novel in order to "defend" youth, see J. J. Darmon, *Le colportage de libraire sous le Second Empire* (Paris, 1972).

107. E. Quinet, *Lettres d'exil à Michelet et à divers amis*, vol. 1 (Paris, 1885), p. 70 (letter to Michelet, from Brussels, October 25, 1853).

108. Ibid., p. 28 (letter to Souvestre, from Brussels, February 17, 1853).

109. According to Durandin's keen analysis, *Révolution à la française*, p. 153.

110. Quoted in V. Strada, *Tradizione e rivoluzione nella literatura russa* (Turin, 1969), pp. 13–15. On the relations between Quinet and Herzen, see M. Mervaud, *Amitié et politique: Herzen critique de Quinet* (Paris and The Hague, 1976).

111. See Venturi, *Il populismo russo,* vol. 2, *Dalla liberazione dei servi al nichilismo,* p. 148 ff.; and T. Kondratieva, *Bolcheviks et jacobins: Itinéraires des analogies* (Paris, 1989), p. 46 ff. (for the quotes); see also A. Gleason, *Young Russia: The Genesis of Russian Radicalism in the 1860s* (New York, 1960).

112. On Serno-Solovievitch and the entire context, and for the quotes, see Venturi, *Il popoulismo Russo,* vol. 2, p. 128 ff.

113. Quoted in Strada, *Tradizione e rivoluzione,* p. 23.

114. Letter of June 23, 1867, quoted in V. Strada, "Introduzione," in A. Herzen, *Lettere a un vecchio compagno* [1870] (Turin, 1977), pp. xlvii–xlviii; italics are mine.

115. Republished in ibid., pp. 67–75; see also M. Confino, *Il catechismo del revoluzionario: Bakunin e l'affare Necaev* [1973] (Milan, 1976).

116. H. Heine, *Rendiconto Parigino* [1832] (Rome and Bari, 1972), pp. 57–58 (correspondence for the *Ausburger Allgemeine Zeitung,* February 10, 1832).

117. See Strada, "Introduzione," p. lv.

118. See P. H. Hutton, *The Cult of Revolutionary Tradition: The Blanquists in the French Politics, 1864–1893* (Berkeley, 1981), which is in contrast to M. Dommanget, *Blanqui et l'opposition révolutionnaire à la fin du Second Empire* (Paris, 1960).

119. Quoted in M. Paz, *Auguste Blanqui, un révolutionnaire professionnel* (Paris, 1974), from letters dated April 25, 1866, and January 8, 1868.

120. For an interpretation of the Commune from this point of view (and for Vallès's quote), see Seigel, *Bohemian Paris,* p. 170 ff.

121. See Benjamin, "Paris, Capital of the Nineteenth Century"; and A. Blanqui, *Instructions pour une prise d'armes: L'éternité par les astres* [1872] (Paris, 1972), p. 155.

122. I will refer readers, naturally, to C. Digeon, *La crise allemande de la pensée française (1870–1914)* (Paris, 1959).

123. On this question, the work by R. Girardet, *La société militaire en France, 1814–1939* (Paris, 1953), remains unequaled.

124. See Z. Sternhell, *La droite révolutionnaire: Les origines françaises du fascisme* (Paris, 1978), p. 45 ff.

125. See Venturi, *Il populismo russo,* p. 245 ff.

126. On Herr and the encounter with Lavrov, see D. Lindenberg and P. A. Meyer, *Lucien Herr: Le socialisme et sa destin* (Paris, 1977), p. 69 ff.

127. Here, of course, I am referring to the famous thesis by E. Weber, *La fin des terroirs: La modernisation de la France, 1870–1914* [1976] (Paris: Fayard, 1983).

128. L. Herr, *Choix d'écrits,* vol. 1 (Paris, 1932), p. 27 (published posthumously); for the reference to Renan, see E. Renan, *La réforme morale et intellectuelle de la France* (Paris, 1871), p. 68.

129. See Péguy, "Zangwil," p. 1420.

130. As V. Isambert-Jamati emphasized in *Crise de la société, crise de l'enseignement* (Paris, 1970).

131. See Sternhell, *La droite révolutionnaire:* and, by the same author, *Ni droite ni gauche: L'idéologie fasciste en France* (Paris, 1953).

132. A. Mathiez, *Jeunesse: Hier, aujourd'hui, demain,* (Montauban, 1889); republished in *Annales historiques de la Révolution française* 1977: 43–48.

133. See C. Charle, *Naissance des intellectuels, 1880–1900* (Paris, 1990), p. 92 ff.

134. See S. Luzzatto, *La "Marsigliese" stonata: La sinistra francese e il problema storico della guerra giusta (1848–1948)* (Bari, 1992).

135. As F. Venturi revealed in his time in *Jean Jaurès e altri storici della Rivoluzione francese* (Turin, 1948), pp. 95–96.

136. See P. Viola, "La storiografia francese sulla Rivoluzione da Albert Mathiez a Georges Lefebvre," in A. Saitta, ed., *La storia della storiografia europea sulla Rivoluzione francese* vol. 2 (Rome, 1990), pp. 143–159.

137. For all that follows on Lenin, see C. S. Ingerflom, *Le citoyen impossible: Les racines russes du léninisme* (Paris, 1988).

138. For this development, I am referring to P. Dogliani, *La "scuola delle reclute": L'Internazionale giovanile socialista dalla fine dell'Ottocento alla prima guerra mondiale* (Turin, 1983), as well as for the quote that follows by Max Adler, p. 20; for the French context, see Y. Cohen, *Les jeunes, le socialisme et la guerre: Histoire des mouvements de jeunesse en France* (Paris, 1989).

139. One cannot help but refer here to the remarkable work by C. E. Shorske, "Generational Tensions and Cultural Change: Reflections on the Case of Vienna," *Daedalus* 1978: 11–122, and, by the same author, *Vienne fin-de-siècle: Politique et culture* (Paris: Seuil, 1983).

140. My reference here is to F. Moretti, *"Un'inutile nostalgia de me stess": La crisi del romanzo di formazione europeo, 1898–1914,* forthcoming.

141. See R. Wohl, *1914: Storia di una generazione* [1979] (Milan, 1984), pp. 270–279.

142. E. Psichari, "Lettres du centurion," in *Oeuvres complètes,* vol. 1 (Paris, 1948), p. 265, letter dated May 1, 1913.

143. For the quotes, see, in order, C. Péguy, "Victor-Marie, comte Hugo" [1910], in *Oeuvres en prose,* vol. 2 (Paris, 1957), p. 768; idem., "Deuxième élégie" [1908], in *Oeuvres en prose complètes,* p. 1073; idem., "De la situation faite au parti intellectuel dans le monde moderne" [1906], in ibid., p. 539. On Péguy and aging, see P. Duployé, *La religion de Péguy* (Paris, 1965), p. 560 ff; on Péguy and Psichari, see Girardet, *La société militaire,* pp. 242–243; on Péguy and Renan, see S. Fraise, "Péguy et Renan," *Revue d'histoire littéraire de la France* 1973: 264–280.

144. Wordsworth, *Prelude II.*

145. See Luzzatto, *La "Marsigliese" stonata.*

146. J. de Saint-Prix, *Lettres* (Paris, 1924), letters to Romain Rolland dated November 4, 1917, and November 27, 1917, respectively, pp. 34 and 46.

147. See R. Rolland, "Préface," in ibid., p. 12.

148. Saint-Prix, *Lettres,* letter dated May 9, 1918.

7 THE MYTH OF YOUTH IN IMAGES

1. Pietro Maria Bardi, "Giovani," in *Gioventù Fascista* 1 (January 20, 1933): 7.

2. "La giovinezza è un simbolo," *Gioventù Fascista* 4 (February 10, 1932): 4.

3. M. Morgagni, "La leva fascista 'certezza di futuro,'" *Rivista Illustrata del Popolo d'Italia* (April 1927): 5.

4. "Fioritura nuova," *Giovinezza! Organo settimanale del fascismo giovane d'Italia* 1, no. 2 (January 1924).

5. Nino D'Aroma, "La voce della razza," *Giovinezza,* February 9, 1924.

6. "Il Duce ai giovani," *Gioventù Fascista* 1 (January 10, 1933): 1.

7. Ernst Hans Gombrich, *Symbolic Images: Studies in the Art of the Renaissance* (London, 1972), p. 5.

8. On the politics of imagery under fascism, see Laura Malvano, *Fascismo e politica dell'immagine* (Turin: Bollati Boringhieri, 1988).

9. Morgani, "La leva fascista."

10. D. Scifoni, "L'italiano nuovo," *Gioventù Fascista* 3 (February 1, 1934).

11. Margherita Sarfatti, "La seconda mostra del novecento a Milano," *Rivista Illustrata del Popolo d'Italia* 4 (April 1929): 42.

12. Alessandro Pavolini, *Il fascismo e le arti*, report to the First Assembly of the Fascist Corporation of Professionals and Artists of the Province of Ravenna, 1935, p. 19.

13. *Gioventù Fascista* 12 (June 7, 1931): 1.

14. *Buon senso e tricolore* (Florence: National Propaganda Institute, n.d. [May 1926]), a general catalogue of propaganda illustrations.

15. The *arditi* were elite troops in the Great War and were distinguished by their black uniforms. Fascism's first combat troops, before they were properly mobilized, were known as the *squadristi;* they acted in small, intimidating groups, and the *manganello* ("Saint Manganello," as it was known in a popular song of the time) was a wooden truncheon or stick, their chief weapon (Trans. note).

16. Dino Alfieri and Luigi Freddi, *Mostra della Rivoluzione Fascista* (Bergamo: Instituto Italiano Arti Grafiche, Rome: Partito nazionale fascista, 1933), p. 45.

17. Giorgio Nicodemi, "La Piazza della Vittoria a Brescia," *Emporium* 471 (March 1934): 143–151.

18. *Rivista Illustrata del Popolo d'Italia* 11 (November 1932): 63. On the major public sculptures of the regime, see Flavio Fergonzi and Maria Teresa Roberto, *La*

scultura monumentale negli anni del fascismo: Arturo Martini e il monumento al Duca d'Aosta (Turin: Allemandi, 1992).

19. Giuseppe Bottai, "Esposizione del '42," *Critica Fascista,* December 1938, p. 3, cited in G. Bottai, *Politica fascista delle arti* (Rome: Signorelli, 1940), p. 75.

20. On the use of the symbol as a form of self-representation in Europe (and the United States) in the 1930s, see Gian Piero Brunetta and Maurizio Vaudagna, *L'estetica della politica: Europa a America negli anni Trenta* (Rome: Laterza, 1989). The essays of George L. Mosse, Bruno Cartosio, Gian Piero Brunetta, and Antonio Faeta deal with the use of symbolic images by Nazism and fascism. On the debate surrounding this subject, see the review article by Laura Malvano, "La politica per simboli," *L'indice dei libri* 3 (March 1990): 20–21.

21. A huge exhibition on E 42 was held in Rome in 1987, sponsored by the Central State Archives; see *E 42: Utopia e scenario del regime* (Venice: Marsilia, 1987), 2 vols.

22. Ibid., vol. 2, p. 315.

23. The same subject is addressed in a sculpture from 1930 *(Balilla e Atleta),* included in the Toscana regional exhibition. On Griselli's E 42 figure, see Bruno Fattori in *Il Meridiano di Roma,* February 14, 1943. (*Lictorial* refers to the lictors of ancient Rome, officers who bore the faces as their insignia. Trans. note.)

24. *Il Lavoro—Le opere e i giorni,* painted by Sironi for the Fifth Triennial, was intended to symbolize "work in time," from the mythological era to the present. The painting, destroyed in 1934, was part of the theme of the Triennial, which was focused on the great murals. For Sironi, see the catalogue from the recent exhibition at the Gallery of Modern Art in Rome, *Sironi 1885–1961* (Milan: Electa, 1993).

25. Maraini had been appointed president of the Biennial in 1927. Starting in 1930, he introduced a cultural policy that sought a closer relationship between the Biennial and exhibitions tied to the structures of the regime (regional, national, syndicalist exhibitions). In 1932 he succeeded Oppo as national commissioner of the Syndicate of Fine Arts. On Maraini, see Pasqualina Spadini, "Antonio Maraini: Le gestione della Biennale di Venezia e del Sindacato Nazionale Fascista di Belle Arti: Primi risultati di une ricerca d'archivio," in *E 42,* vol. 1, pp. 261–265.

26. Augusto Turati, "Il partito per l'arte," *Critica Fascista,* February 15, 1929, p. 68.

27. Antonio Maraini, "Il ritorno dell'arte alla vita," *Rivista Illustrata del Popolo d'Italia* 2 (February 1936): 31.

28. On the Foro Italico, see Marcello Piacentini, "Il Foro Mussolini in Roma," *Architettura* 12 (February 1933): 31.

29. *Il Balilla* 8 (February 28, 1929).

30. Carlo de Leva, "Formare nei giovani il carattere fascista," *Gioventù Fascista* 34 (December 20, 1933).

31. Both quotations are from "Sfilare di corsa," *Gioventù Fascista* 4 (February 10, 1933).

32. Ugo Cuesta, "La gioventù fascista al servizio dello stato," *Gioventù Fascista* 1 (January 1, 1934).

33. *Rivista Illustrato del Popolo d'Italia* 1 (January 1935): 13.

34. G. Ruberti, "Lo sport nell'arte dei giorni nostri alla II Quadriennale romana," *Rivista Illustrata del Popolo d'Italia* 4 (April 1935): 36. Ruberti points out that only some seventy of the thousands of works exhibited actually dealt with the subject.

35. Ibid., p. 40.

36. Sarfatti, "La seconda mostra."

37. The two preceding quotations in this paragraph are from O. I. Taddeini and L. Mercante, *Arte fascista, arte per la massa* (Rome, 1935), p. 33.

38. Ruberti, "Lo sport," p. 37.

39. *Il Balilla* 29 (July 25, 1929).

40. On the use of this image in France, see Maurice Agulhon, *Marianne au Combat: L'imagerie et la symbolique républicaine de 1789 à 1880* (Paris: Flammarion, 1979); English ed., *Marianne into Battle: Republican Imagery and Symbolism in France, 1789–1880* (Cambridge: Cambridge University Press, 1981).

41. *Rivista Illustrata del Popolo d'Italia* 12 (December 1936): 25.

42. The winged Victory carved by Libero Andreotti in 1928 on the Roman-style pediment of Piacentini's monument sought to emphasize the presence of fascist Italy at the national borders.

43. This huge statue was eighteen meters high. It was unveiled in 1928. For a picture of its plaster model, see *Il lauro e il bronzo* (Turin: Circolo Ufficiali, 1990), p. 120, the catalogue of an exhibition of celebratory statuary from the nineteenth and twentieth centuries.

44. Alfieri and Freddi, *Mostra della Rivoluzione Fascista*, p. 96.

45. Ibid., pp. 216–218. This huge statue, "a creation of Roman boldness and greatness," was executed by Maiocchi and Ruggeri after a model by Sironi.

46. Ibid., p. 96.

47. *Rivista Illustrata del Popolo d'Italia* 11 (November 1936): 28.

48. The alert viewer will probably want to note, too, that her fasces, or hatchet, arm seems to subjugate a grossly inferior, stunted man. This, too, has its Roman overtones, for Roman victories featured the losers in chains (Trans. note).

49. This large decorative tableau was executed in 1935. Recently restored, it became the theme of an exhibition on the mural painting of the regime: *Gli artisti dell'Università e la questione della pittura murale* (Rome: Università degli studi "La Sapienza," 1985).

50. Ugo Cuesta, "Il destino delle nazioni è legato alla loro potenza demografica," *Gioventù Fascista*, June 15, 1934.

51. "Popolo in camicia nera," *Gioventù Fascista,* February 1, 1934.

52. *Mamma e Bimbi,* March 1, 1938.

53. D. Baldi, "Le confidenze di una mamma di dieci figli," *Mamma e Bimbi,* January 1939, p. 10. The Avant-gardists, Balilla, Young Italian Girls, and Sons of the Wolf were all official organizations within the fascist youth movement.

54. Manlio Pompei, *Son contadino e me ne vanto* (Rome, 1940), p. 68.

55. *Il Balilla* 15 (April 18, 1929).

56. The Cremona Prize was created in 1939 at the suggestion of Farinacci, federal governor of Cremona and a leader of the hard-line, antimodernist faction of the regime. The rules of the annual competition called for anonymity; artists used either a pseudonym or a "militant" slogan. The themes of the competition were closely linked to those of fascist "historical reality." The first competition had two sections: "Listening to the Duce on the Radio" (Prize A), and "States of Mind Induced by Fascism" (Prize B). In 1940, the theme was "The Battle for Grain," and in 1941 it was the GIL (The Lictorial Youth). The last competition, planned for 1943 but abandoned, was to have had as its theme "A New Europe Rises from Blood" and was to have been open to German artists.

57. Guido Piovene, "La mostra del III Premio Cremona," *Primato,* July 1, 1941, p. 20.

58. E. Gaifas, Jr., "Il III Premio Cremona," *Emporium* 506 (August 1941): 90.

59. Ibid., p. 92.

60. Sarfatti, "La seconda mostra," p. 45.

61. It would be more accurate to say from 1926 onward, by which time Mussolini's leadership of the party had been effectively consolidated. As Emilio Gentile points out in *The Sacralization of Politics in Fascist Italy,* trans. Keith Botsford (Cambridge: Harvard University Press, 1996), Mussolini's personality cult, in part due to the nature of the man, differed significantly from similar cults that formed around Hitler and Stalin (Trans. note).

62. On the creation of the myth of the Duce, see Luisa Passerini, *Mussolini immaginario: Storia di una biografia 1915–1939* (Rome: Laterza, 1991). On the image as a constituent part of the myth, see Laura Malvano, "L'immagine di massa: Il culto del Duce," in *Fascismo e politica dell'immagine,* pp. 62–70. See also, for both the myth and other interpretations, Gentile, *Sacralization.*

63. Alfieri and Freddi, *Mostra della Rivoluzione Fascista,* p. 178.

64. Ottavio Dinale, "La Mostra della Rivoluzione," *Gioventù Fascista,* March 1, 1934.

65. "La giovinezza è un simbolo," *Gioventi fascista* 4 (February 10, 1932).

66. Mario Carli, "Benito Mussolini," *Stile futurista* 1 (July 1934): 36.

67. "Le seminagione," *Il Balilla* 15 (April 18, 1929).

68. *Rivista Illustrata del popolo d'Italia* 7 (July 1939): p. 45.

69. It offered a formal typology that was to enjoy great success among the futurists. Besides the well-known *Plastic Synthesis of the Duce* by Enrico Prampolini (1925), other works include Mino Rossi's sculpture exhibited at the Exhibition of Mural Art in Genoa (1934); equally celebrated was another work with the same title as Prampolini's, by E. Michaelles (Thayath), which was reproduced on a full page of the *Rivista Illustrata del Popolo d'Italia* in the issue dedicated to the Exhibition of the Fascist Revolution, October 1932, p. 14. Shown at the Futurist Exhibition in Berlin in 1934, where it was installed in the entrance hall, it stood against Nazism's formal rigor as a guarantor of the "modernist" line of futurism. See Giovanni Lista, "Futurisme at cubofuturisme," *Cahiers des Musees Nationaux* 5 (September 1980): 487.

70. Morgagni, "La leva," p. 6.

71. G. Orioli, "Il partito e i bimbi," *Gioventù Fascista*, July 15, 1935.

72. O. Gregorio, in *La Famiglia Fascista* 6 (June 1939): 24. (The fascist "colonies" were primarily summer camps, though creches, orphanages, kindergartens, and special outings were every bit as organized. *Trans. note.*)

73. Morgagni, "La leva," p. 5.

74. For the quotations, see *Giovineʒʒa*, the organ of the provincial committee of the ONB, Messina, February 1, 1929. According to the legend of the "heroic kid," Giovanni Battista Perasso, known as Balilla, started the revolt against the Austrians in Genoa in 1746.

75. Morgagni, "La leva," p. 5.

76. A. Malatino, "Avanguardisti e Balilla, a noi!" *Giovineʒʒa*, February 1, 1929.

77. *Il Balilla* 25 (July 16, 1931).

78. D. Calcagno, "Avanguardopoli," *Il Balilla* 37 (September 17, 1931).

79. "Sane, forti e belle," *La Giovane Italiana* 1 (October 28, 1927): 7.

80. Ibid., p. 1.

81. *Il Balilla* 28 (July 16, 1931).

82. *Il Balilla* 51 (December 29, 1929). (The advertisement appeared after Christmas because Italians exchange gifts on January 6. Trans. note.)

83. "Il congresso della Massaie," *La Giovane Italiana* 1 (October 28, 1927): 2.

84. V. Parisi, "Donne e madri," *La Massaia: Rivista femminile illustrata per le moderne donne di casa* 1 (January 15, 1934).

85. M. Morgagni, "Gioventù Italiana del Littorio," *Rivista Illustrata del Popolo d'Italia* 7 (July 1937): 5.

86. Morgagni, "La leva," 5.

87. Ibid.

88. M. Pompei, "Tua madre donna fascista," *Gioventù Fascista* 17 (June 20, 1932): 5.

89. Massimo Scaligero, "La madre fascista," *Gioventù Fascista* 8–9 (March 23–30, 1932): p. 10.

90. Pompei, "Tua madre." On the role of women under fascism, see Victoria De Grazia, *Le donne nel regime fascista* (Venice, 1953): English ed., *How Fascism Ruled Women: Italy, 1922–1945* (Berkeley: University of California Press, 1992).

8 SOLDIERS OF AN IDEA

1. Gregor Strasser, *Kampf um Deutschland* (Munich, 1932), p. 171.
2. Baldur von Schirach, *Die Hitler-Jugend: Idee und Gestalt* (Berlin, 1934), pp. 18–19.
3. Ibid., p. 130.
4. Adolf Hitler, *Mein Kampf*, trans. Ralph Manheim (Boston: Houghton Mifflin, 1943, 1971), p. 328.
5. Hitler, Mein Kampf, pp. 427–428.
6. Alfred Rosenberg, quoted in Hermann Rauschning, *Die Revolution des Nihilismus: Kulisse und Wirklichkeit im dritten Reich* (Zurich, 1938), p. 88.
7. Alfred Bäumler, *Männerbund und Wissenschaft* (Berlin, 1934), pp. 159–165.
8. Friedrich Flieder, in *Nationalsozialistisches Bildungswesen*, April 1937, quoted in Erika Mann, *Zehn Millionen Kinden: Die Erziehung der Jugend im Dritten Reich* (Amsterdam, 1938).
9. Philipp Lenard, professor of physics at the University of Heidelberg, quoted in William Shirer, *Le Troisième Reich: Des origines à la chute*, vol. 1, (Paris, 1963), p. 260.
10. Quoted in Mann, *Zehn Millionen Kinden*, p. 166, taken from *Deutschlands Niedergang und Aufstieg: Bilder aus der Oberstufe der neuen Volksschule* (Leipzig, 1936).
11. For example, *Der Hungerpastor*, by Wilhelm Raabe (Berlin, 1863), p. 72: "Moses stood there, with his tangled black hair, constantly occupied with dissecting the colorful diversity of life and compressing it into the framework of a strict logic. The more he accumulated knowledge, the more his heart turned cold . . ." Quoted in S. Friedländer, *L'antisémitisme nazi* (Paris, 1971), p. 83.
12. Jakob Graf, *Familienkunde und Rassenbiologie für Schüler* (Munich, 1935), pp. 114–115; quoted in George L. Mosse, *Nazi Culture: Intellectual, Cultural and Social Life in the Third Reich* (New York, 1981), p. 80.
13. Mann, *Zehn Millionen Kinder*, p. 130.
14. Ibid., pp. 31–33.
15. Ian Kershaw, *Hitler* (London and New York, 1991), pp. 35 and 98–99. Before lunch, children in Cologne were asked to recite this prayer: "Führer, my Führer, bequeathed to me by the Lord / Protect and preserve me as long as I live! / Thou hast rescued Germany from deepest distress . . ."; quoted in John Toland, *Adolf Hitler* (Garden City, N.Y.: Doubleday, 1976), p. 404
16. "Die Schule der Nation," *Völkischer Beobachter*, September 14, 1935.

17. Norman H. Baynes, *The Speeches of Adolf Hitler*, vol. 1 (London, New York, and Toronto, 1942), pp. 542–543 (my italics).

18. Speech given in Reichenberg on December 4, 1938, quoted in Arno Klönne, *Jugend im Dritten Reich: Die Hitler-Jugend und ihre Gegner* (Cologne, 1982), p. 30.

19. Schhirach, *Die Hiitler-Jugend*, p. 18.

20. At the end of the Weimar Republic, the distribution of youths among the main leagues was as follows: 2 million in sports clubs, 1 million in Catholic clubs, 600,000 in Protestant clubs, 400,000 in young union groups, 90,000 in socialist clubs, and 45,000 in communist clubs (according to A. Klönne, "Jugend im Dritten Reich," in K. D. Bracher, M. Funke, and H.-A. Jacobsen, *Deutschland 1933–1945: Neue Studien zur nationalsozialistischen Herrschaft* (Düsseldorf, 1992), p. 223.

21. Joseph Rovan, "Le 1er décembre 1936,' in Alfred Grosser, *Dix leçons sur le nazisme* [1976] (Brussels, 1984), p. 102.

22. Ibid., p. 117.

23. Schirach, *Die Hitler-Jugend*, p. 34.

24. Bracher, Funke, and Jacobson, *Deutschland 1933–1945*, p. 226.

25. H. C. Brandenburg, *Die Geschichte der H.J.* (Cologne, 1968), p. 311, and Rovan, "Le 1er décembre 1936," p. 104–105.

26. Quoted in Joachim Fest, *Les maîtres du Troisième Reich* (Paris, 1966), p. 93.

27. Quoted in Shirer, *Le Troisième Reich*, vol. 1, p. 279, and Hannah Arendt, *Eichmann in Jerusalem: A Report on the Banality of Evil* (New York: Viking Press, 1963).

28. Quoted in Shirer, *Le Troisième Reich*, vol. 1, p. 262.

29. Adolf Hitler, in Klönne, *Jugend im Dritten Reich*, p. 30.

30. Adolf Hitler, in Baynes, *The Speeches of Adolf Hitler*, p. 542.

31. Rauschning, *Die Revolution des Nihilismus*, p. 77.

32. A. Klönne, *op. cit.*, p. 61.

33. *"Wir sind geboren, für Deutschland zu sterben";* quoted in Peter D. Stachura, "Das Dritte Reich und die Jugenderziehung: Die Rolle der Hitlerjugend 1933–1939," in K. D. Bracher, M. Funke, and H.-A. Jacobsen, *Nationalsozialistische Diktatur 1933–1945: Eine Bilanz* (Düsseldorf, 1986), p. 234, n. 46.

34. Hitler, *Mein Kampf*, p. 414.

35. *Der Kongress zu Nürnberg, vom 5. bis 10. September 1934*, (Munich, 1934), p. 170.

36. David Schoenbaum, *Hitler's Social Revolution: Class and Status in Nazi Germany, 1933–1939* (New York: Doubleday, 1966), p. 246.

37. With the war, these speeches became more constricting. Thus in 1940 the director of a secondary school addressed his students in the Reich-annexed Alsace: "You must now become aware that you are true Germans, and that the main duty of the German woman is to give the maximum number of children

to the führer, one a year if he orders it. For this there is no need to be married, as you have been told by the decadent peoples. Thus, do not reject the advances of young men; starting now, engage in intimate relations with them, and do so as often as possible. This is your strictest duty." Quoted in Marc Hillel, *Au nom de la race* (Paris, 1975), p. 38.

38. Rita R. Thalmann, "Zwischer Mutterkreuz und Rüstungsbetrieb: Zur Rolle der Frau im Dritten Reich," in Bracher, Funke, Jacobsen, *Deutschland 1933–1945*, p. 205.

39. Max Rumpf and Hans Behringer, *Bauerndorf am Grossstadtrand* (Stuttgart and Berlin, 1940), p. 398, quoted in Schoenbaum, *Hitler's Social Revolution*, p. 175, who adds (p. 197) that according to the HJ chief in charge of the study, "this testified only to the appeal 'cinemas, fashionable clothes and the other attractions of the big city.'"

40. Shirer, *Le Troisième Reich*, vol. 1, p. 264.

41. Quoted in Schoenbaum, *Hitler's Social Revolution*, p. 67.

42. Schirach, *Die Hitler-Jugend*, p. 76.

43. Klönne, *Jugend im Dritten Reich*, p. 88–93.

44. Mann, *Zehn Millionen Kinder*, pp. 268–272.

45. Hitler, *Mein Kampf*, op. cit. p. 408.

46. The final political training of this elite fell to various institutions: the Adolf-Hitler-Schulen, the Napola (National-politische Erziehungs-Anstalten), and finally the Ordensburgen, which was to train SS officers. On these schools, see Horst Ueberhorst, *Elite für di Diktatur: Die nationalpolitischen Erziehungsanstalten 1933–1945* (Königstein, 1980).

47. Melita Maschmann, *Fazit: Mein Weg in der Hitler-Jugend* (Munich, 1979), p. 153.

48. Schoenbaum, *Hitler's Social Revolution*, p. 101.

49. Robert Ley, *Soldaten der Arbeit* (Munich, 1938), p. 64.

50. Inge Scholl, *Die Weisse Rose* (Frankfurt, 1953).

51. Richard Wagner, *Die Kunst und die Revolution*.

52. Quoted in Peter Viereck, *Metapolitics: From the Romantics to Hitler* (New York, 1941), p. 132.

53. Heinrich Himmler, *Geheimreden 1933–1945 und anders Ansprachen* ed. Compiled by B. F. Smith and A. F. Peterson, (Frankfort: Propylaen Verlag, 1974). Himmler added: "The Führer is always right, whether it comes to evening attire, a bunker, or an autoroute for the Reich," p. 46.

54. Charles Baudelaire, *Curiosités esthétiques: L'art Romantique*, ed. H. Lemaitre (Paris, 1963), pp. 454–455.

55. In Baynes, *The Speeches of Adolf Hitler*, vol. 1, p. 568.

56. F. Schleiermacher, *Discours sur la religion à ceux de ses contempteurs qui sont des esprits cultivés* [1799], trans. I. J. Rougé (Paris, 1944), p. 232 (end of the third discourse).

57. Letter from J. Goebbels to W. Furtwängler, printed in *Lokal-Anzeiger*, April 11, 1933, quoted in H. Brenner, *La politique artistique du national-socialisme*, trans. L. Steinberg (Paris, 1980), pp. 273–274.

58. See Erwin Panofsky, *Idea: A Concept in Art Theory*, trans. Joseph J. S. Peake (Columbia: University of South Carolina Press, 1968).

59. Speech of May 1, 1936, in Berlin, in Baynes, *The Speeches of Adolf Hitler*, vol. 1, p. 548.

60. Jan Patočka, *L'art et le temps*, trans. E. Abrams (Paris, 1990), p. 359. He adds: "At first glance, nothing seems more desirable, more exultant than such a prospect. All the chains under which traditional humanity has suffered seem broken or in the process of being so. If one looks at it more carefully, however, the beneficiary of this liberation is not man as such, but production."

61. Adolf Hitler speaking at the party congress September 5, 1934, in *Der Kongress zu Nürnberg*, p. 28.

62. In April 1943 there were complaints that images of Hitler had become too rare in the news: "an image of the Führer that would have reassured you that his hair had not, as rumor had it, turned white, would have had a better effect on the behavior of our countrymen than all the words calling them to combat"; quoted in Eberhard Jäckel, "Hitler und die Deutschen," in Bracher, Funke, and Jacobsen, *Nationalsozialistische Diktatur 1933–1945*, p. 711.

63. Alfred Rosenberg, *Der Mythus des XX. Jahrhunderts* [1930] (Munich, 1941), pp. 234, 273, 394.

64. Quoted in Léon Poliakov, *Le mythe aryan* (Paris, 1987), p. 357.

65. Ferdinand Hoffmann, *Sittliche Entartung und Geburtenschwund* [1938], 5th ed. (Munich and Berlin, 1939), pp. 78–79 ("Politische Biologie," issue 4).

66. In *Uns geht die Sonne nicht unter: Lieder der Hitler-Jugend—zusammengestellt zum Gebrauch für Schulen und Hitler-Jugend vom Obergebiet West der Hitler-Jugend* (Leipzig, 1934), pp. 4–5.

67. Quoted in Arno Klönne, *Jugend im Dritten Reich*, p. 160.

68. See M. Burleigh and W. Wippermann, *The Racial State: Germany 1933–1945* (Cambridge, New York, and Melbourne, 1991), pp. 238–239.

69. Klönne, "Jugend im Dritten reich," in *Jugend im Dritten Reich*, p. 237.

70. See, especially, Detlev Peukert, *Die Edelweisspiraten: Protestbewegung jugendlicher Arbeiter im Dritten Reich, Ein Dokumentation* (Cologne, 1980).

71. In February 1943, the gauleiter of Bavaria, Paul Giesler, gave a speech to the students of the medical school in Munich in which he suggested that "they should stop wasting their time at the universities; it would be better," he added, "to 'give a child to the führer.'" These words, which clashed with a Catholic morality that was deeply rooted in many of the students, resulted in groups writing on walls in Munich "Down with Hitler!" or "Long live freedom!" and distributing tracts hostile to Nazism. Some of these students, who had already

belonged to a clandestine group of "passive resistance" called the White Rose, were arrested and were executed days later. See Scholl, *Die Weiss Rose*, p. 58 ff.

9 YOUTH AS A METAPHOR FOR SOCIAL CHANGE

I would like to thank Mario Isnenghi for having kindly provided a critical reading of this text.

1. George L. Mosse, *Le origini culturali del Terzo Reich* (Milan: Mondadori, 1968), pp. 253–281; see also, by the same author, *Sessualità e nazionalismo: Mentalità borghese e rispettabilità* (Rome and Bari: Laterza, 1984), p. 68 ff; Eric J. Leed, *Terra di nessuno: esperienza bellica e identità personale nella prima guerra mondiale* (Bologna: Il Mulino, 1985), p. 80 ff.

2. See Maria Cristina Giuntella, "I gruppi universitari fascisti nel primo decennio del regime," *Il movimento di liberazione in Italia* 24, no. 107 (April–June 1972); Felicita De Negri, "Agitazioni e movimenti studenteschi nel primo dopoguerra in Italia," *Studi storici* 16, no. 3 (July–September 1975).

3. Paolo Nello, *L'avanguardismo giovanile alle origini del fascismo* (Rome and Bari: Laterza, 1978), p. 23 ff; Maria Addis Saba, *Gioventù Italiana del Littorio: La stampa dei giovani nella guerra fascista* (Milan: Feltrinelli, 1973), chapter 1. [The Fasci combattimento (Combat Units) were part of the nationalist, antiparliamentarian movement created in 1919 by Mussolini, at the heart of which the Blackshirts would be the shock troops of the nascent fascism. (Trans. note)]

4. See Rino Gentili, *Giuseppi Bottai e la riforma fascista della scuola* (Florence: La Nuova Italia, 1979).

5. Quoted in Renato Treves, "Il fascismo e il problema della generazioni," *Quaderni di sociologia* 13 (April–June 1964).

6. See Paolo Nello, "Mussolini e Bottai: Due modi diversi di concepire l'educazione fascista della gioventù," *Storia contemporanea* 8 (June 2, 1977).

7. See Luigi Russo, "I giovani nel venticinquennio fascista (1919–1944)," *Belfagor*, 1, no. 1 (January 15, 1946).

8. Giovanni Papini, *Maschilità* (Florence: Vallechni, 1932). On the link between glorification of virility and fascism, see Luisa Passerini, *Mussolini imaginario* (Rome and Bari: Laterza, 1991), p. 99 ff.

9. *Il Paradosso* 5, no. 22 (1960).

10. Grildrig, *Le generazioni del fascismo* (Turin: Gobetti, 1924). Cappa emphasized a key problem for fascism—that of the very young, who had not participated in the war and had thus thrown themselves into the civil war, but who nonetheless constituted a threat for the future as they were not satisfied with the results.

11. At the end of the 1950s and in the early 1960s, the debate was translated into publications, conferences, and memoirs. See *Dall'antifascismo all resistenza:*

Trent'anni di storia italiana (1915–1945): Lezioni contestimonianze presentate da Franco Antonicelli (Turin: Einaudi, 1961), and *Lezioni e testimonianze* (Milan: Feltrinelli, 1962). I should point out the particular importance of the debate following the publication of the book by Ruggero Zangrandi, *Il lungo viaggio attraverso il fascismo: Contributo all astoria di una generazione* (Milan: Garzanti, 1962). On the crisis resulting from the war among young committed fascists, an exceptional document was published recently, the correspondence of Giovanni Pirelli, *Un mondo che crolla: Lettere 1938–1943*, ed. Nicola Tranfaglia (Milan: Archinto, 1990).

12. Alberto Folin and Mario Quaranta, eds., *Le riviste giovanili del periodo fascista* (Treviso: Canova, 1977).

13. Gino Germani, "Mobilitazione dall'alto: la socializzazione dei giovani nei regimi fascisti (Italia e Spagna), in *Autoritarismo, fascismo e classi sociali* (Bologna: Il Mulino, 1975); Tracy H. Koon, *Believe Obey Fight: Political Socialization of Youth in Fascist Italy, 1922–1943* (Chapel Hill: University of North Carolina Press, 1985).

14. The first such ceremony took place in 1932, as Fidia Gambetti has recounted; having reached the age of twenty-one, he was admitted into the party on that day. See *Gli anni che scottano* (Milan: Musia, 1978), pp. 179–180.

15. Arnaldo Mussolini, *Amonimentio ai giovani e al popolo,* (Rome: Libreria del Littorio, 1931), p. 40.

16. Luigi Collino, "Le organizzazioni giovanili," in Giuseppe Luigi Pomba, ed., *La civiltà fascista illustrata nella dottrina e nelle opere* (Turin, UTET, 1928). On women during fascism, see Maria Antonietta Macciochi, *La donna "nera"* (Milan: Feltrinelli, 1976); Piero Meldini, *Spoa e madre esemplare* (Rimini and Florence: Guaraldi, 1975); Nello, "Mussolini e Bottai," p. 360 ff.; Victoria De Grazia, *How Fascists Ruled: Italy, 1920–1945* (Berkeley: University of California Press, 1991).

17. Aldo Capitani, *Antifascismo tra i giovani* (Trapani: Edizioni Célèbes, 1966), p. 38.

18. Gastone Silvano Spinetti, *Difesa di una generazioni* (Rome: Edizioni Polilibraie, 1948), p. 121.

19. Ugoberto Alfassio Grimaldi, "La generazione sedotta e abbandonata," *Tempo presente* 8, no. 1 (June 1963); Tuggero Zangrandi, "I giovani e il fascismo," in *Fascismo e antifascismo: Lezioni e testimonianze*, vol. 1 (Milan: Feltrinelli, 1962).

20. "Young, Younger, Youngest" is the title of an article published in *Critica Fascista*, December 1, 1930. It alludes to the three generations that had contributed to the birth of fascism and that were facing off in the early thirties.

21. "Un regime di giovani," *Critica Fascista*, June 1, 1928.

22. Giordano Bruno Guerri, *Giuseppe Bottai, un fascista critico* (Milan: Feltrinelli, 1976).

23. Quoted in Treves, "Il fascismo e il problema delle generazioni."

24. Gian Paolo Callegari, "Cariche ai giovani ovvero giovani alla carica," *Critica Fascista*, October 1, 1930.

25. "Ancora sui giovani e il regime," *Bibliografia Fascista* 7, 1929.

26. Germano Secreti, "I giovani e il partito," *Critica Fascista*, August 1, 1928.

27. Giuseppe Bottai, "Il regno della noia," *Critica Fascista*, August 15, 1928.

28. Bottai, "Un regime di giovani."

29. Reprinted in ibid.

30. Camille Pelizzi, "Aprire le finestre," *Critica Fascista*, September 1, 1929, and the "Editor's Note" in the same issue; Gian Paolo Gallegari, "Elogio del vecchio," *Critica Fascista*, November 15, 1930.

31. Domenico Montalto, "La libertà e i giovani," *Critica Fascista*, August 15, 1929, critiqued in turn in Stefano Mario Cutelli, "Selezione, autorità e libertà," *Critica Fascista*, September 1, 1929.

32. Giuseppe Bottai, "Giovani e più giovani," *Critica Fascista*, November 15, 1930.

33. Callegari, "Elogio del vecchio."

34. Germano Secreti, "I giovani e il partito," *Critica Fascista*, August 1, 1928.

35. Germano Secreti, "I giovani," *Critica Fascista*, February 1, 1929.

36. *Il Resto del Carlino*, December 14, 1928.

37. "Il fascismo e i giovani," *Bibliografia Fascista* 5–6 (1929); Alessandro Pavolini, "Viva i giovani," *Critica Fascista*, March 1, 1929; "Ancora sui giovani e il regime," *Bibliografia fascista* 7 (1929).

38. Handwritten text reproduced by *Critica Fascista*, February 1, 1930. On the relationship between youths and Mussolini in the area of the imagination, see Passerini, *Mussolini immaginario*, pp. 184–208.

39. Paolo Nello, "Mussolini e Bottai: due modi diversi di concepire l'educazione fascista della gioventù," *Storia contemporanea* 8, no. 2 (June 1977): 341.

40. "Avviamento alle responsabilità," *Critica Fascista*, February 1, 1930.

41. From February 15, 1930; the "Editor's Note" followed the article by Domenico Montalto, "L'avvenire, contributo al problema dei giovani."

42. Cornelio Di Marzio, "Giovani e più giovani: Comando e moralità," *Critica Fascista*, January 15, 1930.

43. Luigi Russo, "Io dico seguitando . . . ," *La Nuova Italia* 1 (January 20, 1930), republished in *Elogio della polemica: Testimonianze di vita e di cultura (1918–1932)* (Bari: Laterza, 1933), p. 194 ff.

44. Alexander De Grand, *Bottai e la cultura fascista* (Rome and Bari: Laterza, 1978); see also "Giuseppe Bottai e il fallimento del fascismo revisionista, *Storia contemporanea* 6, no. 4 (December 1975), on Bottai during the period of opposition, 1922 to 1926.

45. Luisa Mangoni, *L'interventismo della cultura: Intellectuali e riviste del fascismo* (Rome and Bari: Laterza, 1974), pp. 197–206; Renzo De Felice, *Mussolini il duce*, vol. 1, *Gli anni del consenso 1929–1936* (Turin: Einaudi, 1974), pp. 232–244.

46. Mario Carli, *L'italiano di Mussolini: Romanzo dell'era fascista* (Milan: Mondadori, 1930).

47. "Gerarchia o burocrazia," *Critica Fascista*, February 15, 1931.

48. Letters and commentaries published in *Il Selvaggio*, October 30, 1931; December 30, 1931; March 31, 1932; May 1, 1932. [*Il Selvaggio* was an organ of the "Strapaese" literary movement (uniting writers such as Malaparte, Bilenchi, and Alvaro), created in 1926 to defend the peasant tradition within the culture. This earned it the mockery of *Critica Fascita*, which was always quick to denounce the obsequiousness and conservatism of the "egotistical, fearful, and boastful lower middle classes." (Ed. note.)]

49. Mangoni, *L'interventismo della cultura*, p. 202.

50. *Il Saggiatore* 3 (January 1933): 439.

51. "Il binomio fascio-sindacato," *Critica Fascista*, May 15, 1933.

52. Guerri, *Giuseppe Bottai*, pp. 136–137.

53. Nello, "Mussolini e Bottai," p. 366.

54. Giuseppe Bottai, "Funzione della gioventù," *Critica Fascista*, March 1, 1933; Giulio Santangelo, "Storia di una polverosa polemica," *Bibliografia Fascista* 4 (1933).

55. Agostino Nasti, August 1, 1933.

56. Giuseppe Lombrassa, "Prima studiare, poi discutere," *Critica Fascista*, February 15, 1931.

57. The two first quotes are taken from an editorial in *Critica Fascista*, "Compiti di ieri e di oggi," December 15, 1931, and from an article by Rodolfo de Mattei, "Discorso sul metodo," February 15, 1931; the rest are from Romano Bilenchi, "Indifferenza dei giovani," *Critica Fascita*, April 14, 1933.

58. Ugoberto Alfassio Grimaldi and Marina Addis Saba, *Cultura a passo romano: Storie e strategie dei littoriali della cultura e dell'arte* (Milan: Feltrinelli, 1983); Giovanni Lazzari, *I littoriali della cultura e dell'arte: Intellettuali e potere durante il fascismo* (Naples: Liguori, 1979); Roi Rossi, "Come si formo nei littoriali una opposizione giovanile al regime," *Incontri* 2 (February 1, 1954). We should also recall that the Lictorial Youth, created in 1934, admitted women only in 1939, in Trieste; the first volume quoted above in this note gives that organization's themes and classification (p. 230 ff.), but the feminine competitions were a caricature of the mens', for they included only written exercises and not oral ones, debate being considered unseemly for women.

59. Giaime Pintor, *Doppio diario 1936–1943* (Turin: Einaudi, 1978), p. 121.

60. The Italian cinema had gotten over the depression of the twenties, but just barely, thanks to the direct intervention of the fascist government. See Gian Piero Brinetta, *Cent'anni di cinema italiano* (Rome and Bari: Laterza, 1991), p. 166 ff.

61. I would like to thank Paolo Olivetti of the Archivio Nazionale Cinematografico

of Turin for having allowed me to consult the film documents and for giving me his advice; also Angelo Galli, from the University of Turin, for his collaboration at these viewings.

62. Brinetta, *Cent'anni di cinema italiano*, p. 161.

63. Giuseppe Lombrassa, "L'indifferenza male edi moda," *Critica Fascista*, January 1, 1930: "Scepticism is serious, but the worst state of abjection is indifference, the most modern spiritual attitude . . . it is a matter of foreign odes, the spiritual poses of the early part of the century, the blemishes of a civilization in decomposition: this entire world of importation, tainted and slimy, is creating a kind of tired and wrung out man, to which a recent, very successful novel gave the name Michele . . . Michele can only be born and live in a big city."

64. *Critica fascista*, November 15, 1931.

65. *Camicia nera*, which won the competition organized by the Instituto Luce for the best film devoted to a decade of "fascist revolution," strove to be a "cinematographic synthesis of the history of Italy from 1914 to 1932." At its debut, on March 23, 1933, it was shown simultaneously in all the big cities of Italy, as well as in Paris, London, and Berlin. As for knowing to what extent and in what way Italian cinema was fascist, one should refer to the interesting debate at the end of the 1970s, in particular the collection of work edited by R. Redi, *Cinema italiano sotto il fascismo* (Venice: Marsilio, 1979).

66. See Alfredo Baldi in Di Giamatteo, ed., *Dizionario universale del cinema* (Rome, 1984); see also the chart compiled by Paolo Olivetti and Franco Prono, *Archivio nazionale cinematografico della Resistenza*, 1987.

67. See E. Capizzi in Di Giammateo, ed., *Dizionario*, vol. 1, p. 6.

68. See Francesco Savio, "*Ma l'amore no*": *Realismo, formalismo propaganda e telefoni bianchi nel cinema italiano di regime (1930–1943)* (Milan: Sonzogno, 1975).

69. Filippo Sacchi, in *Corriere della sera*, August 12, 1932, pointed out that Camerini avoided the documentary pitfalls that reduced these types of films to a series of postcards on famous monuments. This was certainly the case of *Treno popolare*, which first showed the masses tourists, in all their naïveté, lingering in front of the cathedral of Orvieto and other city monuments, from the amphitheater to San Patrizio's well.

70. Savio, "*Ma l'amore no*," p. 378.

71. See G. P. Brunetta, *Cinema italiano tra le due guerre: Fascismo e politica cinematografica* (Milan: Mursia, 1975), p. 53.

72. Roi Rossi, "Come si formo," and *Il Popolo d'Italia*, April 18, 1934.

73. *Italia Letteraria*, April 30, 1933.

74. See Savio, "*Ma l'amore no*," p. 346.

75. See Peppino Ortoleva, *Cinema e storia: Scene del passato* (Turin: Loescher, 1991), pp. 101–102. The film particularly lends itself to the study of the relationship between reality and the imagination with respect to women's work; in fact, the

same critics emphasized that the automatic telephone rendered anachronistic the mediation between callers and switchboard operators, which was an element central to the story.

76. *Quaderni di Giustizia e Libertà,* June 3, 1932, pp. 92–93.

77. Kenneth Keniston, *Giovani all'opposizione* (Turin: Einaudi, 1972).

78. On the traditions and customs particular to youth, see John R. Gillis, *Youth and History: Tradition and Change in European Age Relations, 1770–Present* (New York: Academic Press, 1974).

79. Germani, "Mobilitazione dall'alto," p. 255.

80. Michel Mitterauer, *A History of Youth* trans. Graeme Dunphy (Oxford: Blackwell, 1993).

81. With respect to this theme, there was no lack of contradictions within fascism. When, at the end of 1931, Achile Starace replaced Giovanni Giurati in the post of secretary general of the Fascist Party, *Critica Fascista* felt obliged to specify: "We want a youth that knows how to use a rifle, to march in step, and that fills our ranks with joy, with luminous freshness, with songs and sermons, but also a youth that knows how to bend its agile back over a book, to listen in silence and meditate" ("Compiti di ieri e di oggi," December 15, 1931).

82. Franco Rositi, "La cultura giovanile," in *Informazione e complessità sociale* (Bari: de Donato, 1978).

83. G. Stanley Hall, *Adolescence: Its Psychology and Its Relations to Anthropology, Sociology, Sex, Crime, Religion and Education,* 2 vol. (New York, 1904).

84. Joseph F. Kett, *Rites of Passage: Adolescence in America, 1790 to the Present* (New York: Basic Books, 1977), p. 252 ff.

85. George Paloczi-Horvath, *Youth Up in Arms: A Political and Social World Survey, 1955–1970* (London: Weidenfeld and Nicolson, 1971), p. 78.

86. Elliot E. Cohen, "A Teen-Age Bill of Rights," *New York Times Magazine,* January 7, 1954, quoted in Thomas Doherty, *Teenagers and Teenpics: The Juvenilization of American Movies in the 1950s* (London: Unwin Hyman, 1988), p. 67.

87. See "Chronology: Events Relating to the History of the Health, Education, and Welfare of Children and Youth, 1933–1973," in Robert H. Bremner, ed., *Children and Youth in America: A Documentary History,* vol. 3, *1933–1973,* (Cambridge: Harvard University Press, 1974), pp. 1991–1992.

88. See Kett, *Rites of Passage,* p. 255.

89. James Gilbert, *A Cycle of Outrage: America's Reaction to the Juvenile Delinquency in the 1950s* (Oxford: Oxford University Press, 1986), p. 18. While in the 1950s only 50 percent of working-class children attended high school, in the early 1960s the figure reached 90 percent.

90. James S. Coleman, *The Adolescent Society: The Social Life of the Teenager and Its Impact on Education* (Glencoe, Ill.: Free Press, 1961), pp. 11 and 3.

91. Edgar Z. Friedenberg, *The Vanishing Adolescent* (Boston: Beacon Press, 1959), p. 115 (2nd ed., with Introduction by David Riesman, 1964). In another study, *Coming of Age in America: Growth and Acquiescence* (New York: Random House, 1963), Friedenberg compares adolescent society and the manner in which it was treated to nineteenth-century colonies and colonialism, p. 4 ff. On the concept of subculture applied to youth, see Mike Brake, *The Sociology of Youth Culture and Youth Subcultures: Sex and Drugs and Rock'n'Roll?* (London: Routledge and Kegan Paul, 1980), in particular p. 7: "The subcultures contain elements of class cultures, but are at the same time distinct. The subcultures have a relationship with the dominant culture as a whole, rendered inevitable because this culture penetrates everywhere, notably through the mass media. For example the sub-culture of the hippies, while having a relationship with progressive middle-class culture, is distinguished from it by its deviant nature." Another important work regarding this concept, even though it refers mainly to Great Britain, is that of Dick Hebdige, *Subculture: The Meaning of Style* (London: Methuen, 1979).

92. David Riesman, *The Lonely Crowd* (New Haven: Yale University Press, 1950); I should also cite the role played in the debate by the works of William H. Whyte, *The Organization Man* (New York: Simon and Schuster, 1956), on the ethic of large bureaucratized companies and the group identities they favored, and Talcott Parsons, *Essays in Sociological Theory* (New York: Free Press, 1954), which includes analyses on age and sex in American society of the period.

93. Erik H. Erikson, *Childhood and Society* (New York: Norton, 1950); his assessment of the debate is found in his preface to Erik H. Erikson, ed., *The Challenge of Youth* (Garden City, N.Y.: Anchor Books, 1965), first published in *Daedalus* in 1961. The reference to the relationship between psychologists and parents is found in Daniel R. Miller and Guy E. Swanson, *The Changing American Parent: A Study in the Detroit Area* (New York: John Wiley, 1958).

94. Grace and Fred Hechinger, *Teen-Age Tyranny* (New York: William Morrow, 1962), pp. x, 17, 18, 57.

95. See Coleman, *The Adolescent Society,* especially chapters 3 and 4.

96. David Riesman, "Introduction," in *The Vanishing Adolescent,* 2nd ed., p. xxii.

97. Bruno Cartosio, *Anni inquieti: Società media ideologie negli Stati Uniti da Truman a Kennedy* (Rome: Editori Riuniti, 1992), pp. 277–278.

98. On the fifties in the United States, see Paul A. Carter, *Another Part of the Fifties* (New York: Columbia University Press, 1983), and William H. Chafe, *The Unfinished Journey: America since World War II* (New York: Oxford University Press, 1986).

99. See Kett, *Rites of Passage,* p. 256.

100. Albert K. Cohen, *Delinquent Boys: The Culture of the Gang* (Glencoe, Ill.: Free Press, 1955); Paul Goodman, *Growing Up Absurd: Problems of Youth in the Organized System* (New York: Random House, 1960).

101. Frederic Wertham, *Seduction of the Innocent* (New York, 1954).

102. Nelson George, *The Death of Rhythm and Blues*, quoted by Wini Breines, *Young, White and Miserable: Growing Up Female in the Fifties* (Boston: Beacon Press, 1992), p. 158.

103. See Breines, *Young, White and Miserable*, pp. 125–126. On the formation of identity among adolescents, see Elizabeth Douvan and Joseph Adelson, *The Adolescent Experience* (New York: John Wiley, 1966), based on two national studies in 1955 and 1956, pp. 229–261. On conceptualization, see Angela McRobbie and Mica Nava, eds., *Gender and Generation* (London: Macmillan, 1984), notably the essay by Barbara Hudson, "Femininity and Adolescence."

104. See Doherty, *Teenagers and Teenpics*, p. 196; Goodman, *Growing Up Absurd*, p. 13; Friedenberg, *The Vanishing Adolescent*, p. 5.

105. William Graebner, *Coming of Age in Buffalo: Youth and Authority in the Postwar Era* (Philadelphia: Temple University Press, 1990), p. 69 ff.

106. Cartosio, *Anni inquieti*, p. 279; Kett, *Rites of Passage*, p. 6.

107. See Coleman, *Growing Up Absurd*, notably chapter 6, "Beauty and Brains as Paths to Success."

108. See Ellen K. Rothman, *Hands and Hearts: A History of Courtship in America* (New York: Basic Books, 1984), p. 301 ff.

109. Gilbert, *A Cycle of Outrage*, p. 21 ff.; Breines, *Young, White and Miserable*, chapter 3.

110. Graebner, *Coming of Age*, p. 52.

111. Breines, *Young, White and Miserable*, p. 125.

112. Ibid., p. 158; Doherty, *Teenagers and Teenpics*, p. 89.

113. Kett, *Rites of Passage*, p. 4.

114. Audre Lorde, *Zami: A New Spelling of My Name: A Biomythography* (Freedom, Calif.: The Crossing Press, 1982), p. 225.

115. See especially the study by Doherty, *Teenagers and Teenpics*, p. 89.

116. Reviews of the films cited can be found in Di Giamatteo, *Dizionario*.

117. Ibid., p. 784.

118. Ibid., p. 76.

119. Doherty, *Teenagers and Teenpics*, p. 98.

120. Walter Benjamin, *Metafisica della gioventu: Scritti 1910–1918* (Turin: Einaudi, 1982), p. 108.

121. Robert Gatii, "Morte del 'teenager': Incontro con Dick Hebdige," *Linea d'ombra* 53 (October 1990): 57.

122. Different analysts have mentioned these connections in various ways: see Kett, *Rites of Passage* p. 267; Graebner, *Coming of Age*, p. 127; Breines, *Young, White and Miserable*, pp. xii and 201–202. These are highly problematic connections, such as those that may exist between the agitation of fifties gangs and the revolt in the black ghetto of Watts in the sixties, or between the rebellion of girls in

the fifties and feminism, on which the existing studies give interesting but not yet sufficiently supported assessments. To convincingly establish the continuities and ruptures between phenomena of two decades, I believe one must proceed via new historical research or through a reexamination of the socioanthropological analyses of social movements.

CONTRIBUTORS

Jean-Claude Caron is Lecturer in Modern History at the University of Franche-Comté (Besançon). He is the author of *La Nation, l'Etat et la démocratie en France de 1789 à 1914* (1995) and the coauthor of *L'Europe au XIXe siècle: Des nations aux nationalismes* (1996).

Daniel Fabre is the author of many works, including *Carnaval, ou la fête à l'envers* (1992) and *La fête en Languedoc: Regards sur le carnaval aujourd'hui* (1977), and coauthor of *La vie quotidienne des paysans du Languedoc au XIXe siècle* (1973).

Giovanni Levi is Professor of Economic History at the University of Venice. He is the author of *Centro e periferia di uno stato assoluto* (1985).

Sabina Loriga is Professor of History at the Ecole Supérieure de Cadres pour l'Economie et l'Administration (Switzerland). She is the author of *Soldati: L'istituzione militare nel Piemonte del Settecento* (1992) and *La biographie comme problème* (1996).

Sergio Luzzatto is Assistant Professor of Modern History at the University of Genoa. He is the author of *L'autunno della Rivoluzione: Lotta e cultura politica nella Francia del Termidoro* (1994) and *L'impôt du sang: La gauche française à l'épreuve de la guerre mondiale, 1900–1945* (1996).

Laura Malvano is Professor of Art History at the University of Paris VIII (Vincennes). She is the author of *Fascismo e politica dell'immagine* (1988).

Eric Michaud teaches art history at the Université des Sciences Humaines in Strasbourg. He is the author of *La fin du salut par l'image* (1992) and *Un art de l'éternité: L'image et le temps du national-socialisme* (1996).

Luisa Passerini is Professor of Twentieth-Century History at the European University in Florence. She is the author of *Mussolini immaginario: Storia di una biografia, 1915–1949* (1991), and *Autobiography of a Generation: Italy, 1968* (1996).

MICHELLE PERROT is Professor of Modern French History at the University of Paris VII (Diderot). She is the author of *L'impossible prison* (1980) and coeditor of the five-volume *History of Women in the West* (Harvard, 1992–1994).

GIOVANNI ROMANO is Professor of the History of Medieval Art at the University of Turin. He is the author of *Studi sul pasesaggio* (1978, 1991) and the editor of *Gotico in Piemonte* (1992).

JEAN-CLAUDE SCHMITT is Director of Studies at the Ecole des Hautes Etudes en Sciences Sociales. He is the author of *La raison des gestes dans l'Occident médiéval* (1990) and *Les revenants: Les vivants et les morts dans la société médiévale* (1994).

INDEX